See No Evil

Also by Erik Banks:

DARK POOLS
DICTIONARY OF FINANCE, INVESTMENT AND BANKING
RISK AND FINANCIAL CATASTROPHE
THE CREDIT RISK OF COMPLEX DERIVATIVES, 3rd edition
FINANCIAL LEXICON
LIQUIDITY RISK
THE FAILURE OF WALL STREET
ASIA PACIFIC DERIVATIVE MARKETS
EMERGING ASIAN FIXED INCOME MARKETS
THE CREDIT RISK OF FINANCIAL INSTRUMENTS
CORPORATE GOVERNANCE

See No Evil
Uncovering the Truth Behind the Financial Crisis

Erik Banks

© Erik Banks 2011

Softcover reprint of the hardcover 1st edition 2011 978-0-230-27893-6

All rights reserved. No reproduction, copy or transmission of this publication may be made without written permission.

No portion of this publication may be reproduced, copied or transmitted save with written permission or in accordance with the provisions of the Copyright, Designs and Patents Act 1988, or under the terms of any licence permitting limited copying issued by the Copyright Licensing Agency, Saffron House, 6-10 Kirby Street, London EC1N 8TS.

Any person who does any unauthorized act in relation to this publication may be liable to criminal prosecution and civil claims for damages.

The author has asserted his right to be identified as the author of this work in accordance with the Copyright, Designs and Patents Act 1988.

First published 2011 by
PALGRAVE MACMILLAN

Palgrave Macmillan in the UK is an imprint of Macmillan Publishers Limited, registered in England, company number 785998, of Houndmills, Basingstoke, Hampshire RG21 6XS.

Palgrave Macmillan in the US is a division of St Martin's Press LLC, 175 Fifth Avenue, New York, NY 10010.

Palgrave Macmillan is the global academic imprint of the above companies and has companies and representatives throughout the world.

Palgrave® and Macmillan® are registered trademarks in the United States, the United Kingdom, Europe and other countries.

ISBN 978-1-349-32668-6   ISBN 978-0-230-29917-7 (eBook)
DOI 10.1057/9780230299177

This book is printed on paper suitable for recycling and made from fully managed and sustained forest sources. Logging, pulping and manufacturing processes are expected to conform to the environmental regulations of the country of origin.

A catalogue record for this book is available from the British Library.

A catalog record for this book is available from the Library of Congress.

10 9 8 7 6 5 4 3 2 1
20 19 18 17 16 15 14 13 12 11

Transferred to Digital Printing in 2013

Contents

Acknowledgments	vi
Prologue: Crisis Redux	1
1 A Quick Recap	5
2 The US Banks Got It Wrong...	32
3 ...and So Did the European Banks	58
4 The Fannie and Freddie Sinkhole	78
5 Fuel to the Fire I: The Rating Agencies	93
6 Fuel to the Fire II: Regulators, Politicians, and Lobbyists	105
7 A Handful of Sages	130
8 The Blame Game: Fingerpointing and Apologies	147
9 Closing the Barn Door	162
10 Get Ready for the Next One...	186
Notes	199
Index	235

Acknowledgments

Great thanks to Lisa von Fircks at Palgrave Macmillan for all of her support and guidance on this project. Thanks also to Renée Takken and the editing, production, and marketing teams at Palgrave for their work in producing the book.

And to Milena, my biggest thanks of all...

EB

Prologue: Crisis Redux

I call it the "risk manager's moment": a point when you feel nervous tension, light-headedness, a sense of disbelief (and yet, somehow, not really), perhaps a tinge of nausea. And helplessness: complete inability to do anything to stop the train wreck. The risk manager's moment arrives, of course, when things are going pear-shaped: the deal is collapsing, the client has announced plans to file for bankruptcy, or the markets are in freefall. Nothing to do but watch the whole thing go absolutely wrong.

All of us who have worked in the banking industry have experienced this moment. Why? Because things go wrong – quite often. Deals collapse, companies go under, and markets plunge pretty regularly. And every so often they do so very spectacularly. As a 25-year veteran of risk management in investment banking, international banking, and hedge funds, I've been through the "risk manager's moment" more times than I care to remember: the emerging markets debt crisis in the late 1980s, the S&L crisis of the same time period, the October 1987 stock market crash, the 1990 junk bond crash, the 1992 ERM currency crisis, the 1994 Mexican Peso crisis, the 1994 derivatives scandals, the 1994 Orange County debacle, the 1995 Barings collapse, the 1997 Asian crisis, the 1998 Russian default and LTCM debacle, the 2001 Enron collapse, the 2001–2 dot-com bubble burst. Bad moments, indeed: lots of red ink, lots of sleepless nights, lots of wondering what should have, could have, been done better.

All in preparation, I guess, for the granddaddy of the "risk manager's moments": the 2007 Credit Crisis, with its tentacles stretching across time and geography to create extended periods of confusion, disbelief, panic. Though there were white-knuckle moments in late 2007 and again in early 2008 as JP Morgan rescued Bear Stearns, for most of us the crisis reached its apex during the weekend of September 15, 2008 when banks and regulators decided to walk away from Lehman Brothers, setting the stage for the world's largest bankruptcy. That was a very, very unpleasant time – wondering if the world would keep on turning or if we were, indeed, about ready to turn out the lights. By now we all know what followed: shotgun marriages, wholesale guarantees of national banking systems, de-facto nationalizations of many banks, and lots of money pumped into the markets. It worked.

But will it work next time?

As the dust from the Crisis begins to settle I, like many, have had a chance to reflect on the whole disaster. To try and understand what happened, and why, to try and make some sense of things. To try to figure out what could have been done better and to see if things can be changed so that these moments happen a little less frequently in the future.

As I sifted through lots of analysis, research, media coverage, and annual reports two things became clear to me. First, many got it wrong. Not just the bankers, but others: credit rating agencies, the housing agencies, regulators, central bankers, politicians, lobbyists, and even the man and woman on Main Street. Second, as awful as it has all been, it wasn't really that unusual. Bigger and more wrenching – yes. But unusual – no. Which led me to my next thought – that this will happen again, because it is the history of the financial markets and it is the nature of human behavior. It doesn't matter what regulators do to try and prevent the next crisis – it doesn't matter what kind of new rules are put in place. All of this is bound to happen again. Another set of "risk manager's moments" is around the corner.

In the mid-1990s I wrote a [slightly dry] financial history book called *The Rise and Fall of the Merchant Banks*, which traced the fall from grace of the large British merchant banks – the very institutions that once ruled the world through their financial influence. Writing about it taught me that all of the financial crises we were going through in the 1990s (like Mexico, and LTCM and Russia and Barings and, and, and...) were really nothing new – they had been going on for decades, throughout the Golden Age of merchant banking, when bankers and politicians and central bankers routinely got it wrong. Then, in 2004, I wrote another book called *The Failure of Wall Street*, outlining all the ways in which banks had screwed clients, shareholders, regulators, and one another with cooked books, false research, bad risk management, and fraud. Again, the bits of research that went into the book just showed that it was all more of the same, and that nothing had ever really changed. It's not terribly polite to quote oneself, but in that book, coming three years before the crisis, I observed that *"[i]f the Street is unwilling to change its stripes (or doesn't believe that it has to, to any significant degree) the status quo remains. That means we shouldn't be surprised to see more of the same mistakes and misbehavior... [i]nternal and external stakeholders will continue to be hurt."*[1]

And here we are again.

So, am I surprised that another financial crisis has occurred? Not really – it's just another sequel to the same movie. Of course, I readily confess that the toppling of the dominos after the Las Vegas-subprime-condo trade blew up was much more extensive than I would have expected, and the final tally had one or two extra zeroes on it. Yes, together with my executive committee colleagues I made some good decisions in the lead-up to the crisis to get rid of some toxic instruments that could have proven damaging, and yes we had certain risk standards that kept us away from lots of other damaging business. But I surely didn't get everything right! And I confess that I put all my chips on black in thinking Lehman Brothers would be rescued – wrong. But as far as the onset of another crisis...no surprise at all, the plot is quite familiar.

And am I surprised about the hubris and arrogance of some of the financial "wizards" who architected this piece of work? Nope. I've been a banker for nearly 25 years, and it's always been that way. To be sure, not all of my colleagues and ex-colleagues are arrogant SOBs that are in for the kill at any price. But I can surely tell you many stories of clever things that have been (and continue to be) cooked up in order to generate revenues, which generate bonuses.

And am I shocked by the political games of slick legislators, or the blindness of the regulators who aided and abetted? Nope. All of these folks are routinely a few steps behind what's going on...sometimes they even help make things worse.

And am I surprised that our 24/7 business news channels were touts on the way up, and holier-than-thou on the way down? Nope. Good for ratings (just remember the dot-com bubble).

And how about all those folks on the Main Street who overextended themselves by buying houses or second homes they couldn't afford, took out home equity loans to tart up their kitchens and bathrooms, or didn't read the fine print on their adjustable mortgages – surely they are just innocent victims? I don't think so.

So the question is not that any of this happened – it happened because we don't learn from history and are willing to overlook past indiscretions if we can make a bit of money, advance our political careers, look good on TV, or outdo the neighbors. If we see an opportunity to line our pockets, we forgive the sins and excesses of the past – whatever the future cost. If my colleagues cook up the next exotic instrument that pays 9 percent instead of the 2 percent on the savings account, I bet lots of us will line up to buy it...never mind the risks or that it might be tied into some systemic time bomb, or that we don't really know what we are buying, or that the bank offering it lost $20b during the crisis, or...memories are truly short when money is involved.

So, as I've thought about this crisis and surveyed all the evidence it is not too difficult to see how this colossal disaster occurred: how the mavens of banking (including the risk management fraternity) got it all wrong, how politicians and regulators overseeing the stuff spoke regularly with forked tongue so they could pander to their constituents and get re-elected, how the regulators continued their regular habit of stumbling in the dark, how the toothsome financial TV anchorettes told us that the market would keep rallying, and how homeowners and consumers thought that they could pile on debt without consequence. It is a reminder that we shouldn't believe everything we hear, because everyone always talks his or her own book. It is also a reminder that personal and professional responsibility is sorely lacking. And it is a reminder that the experts really aren't…experts. We don't really understand everything we think we do, and I surely place myself in that category.

We still need bankers, and politicians and regulators and the media, but in an era where responsibility is sometimes scarce, we ought to hold all of these people – and ourselves – to account. Will we get there? I don't think so, and I don't mean to be cynical – just realistic. Money is powerful, politics are malleable, and memories are short. Banks cannot and will not be regulated out of existence, so there will be another crisis. It will appear in another form, but it will appear – crisis redux. Meaning more "risk manager's moments." Judge for yourself.

1
A Quick Recap

Lots of red ink was spilled during the 2007 Crisis, and lots of black ink has been spilled writing about the events and the culprits ever since that time. And little wonder – with the quantity of money that was lost during a very short three-year period – between $2 and $3 trillion directly according to estimates from the International Monetary Fund (IMF), plus lots more indirectly – there are lots of questions out there: what, why, who? And, perhaps more importantly, will it happen again?

So I will add to the black ink, hopefully in a unique and useful way. I've decided not to go for a semi-nonfiction retelling of the unraveling of the financial system, or the "I-was-a-fly-on-the-wall-at-the-midnight-meetings-of-the-power-players" discussion regarding the inevitable fate of this bank or that banking system. There are several good accounts done in this "business thriller" voice. And I am avoiding the banker's techno-speak version of events, laced either with technical terms (you know, conduits, correlation, Alt-A, monoliners, superior senior, synthetic tranches, covenant lites, system repos, quantitative easing, and on and on) or an alphabet soup of acronyms (you know, SIVs, NINJAs, ABS, CDOs, CDO^2, TALF, TARP, RMBS, CP, CDSs, ABCP, CLOs, PPIP, CVRs, and on and on).

Instead, I've chosen to write about the crisis by reflecting on the words and comments of those who were involved, those who were responsible, and those who provided interesting insight before, during, and after the meltdown. Naturally, I risk oversimplifying what has obviously been a complex, multiyear sequence of forces, events, and decisions. Still, I'm sure that I can get you to the final destination in good shape: understanding what happened and why, and armed with some thoughts on what might happen in the future.

Setting the stage

Let me start my "jargon-free" journey by rewinding to the early part of the millennium, when Alan Greenspan, then head of the US Federal Reserve (or

Fed, the country's central bank) was in a battle to restart the US economy – an economy that had been badly hit by the bursting of the dot-com stock bubble and various corporate scandals, and which was sorely in need of a boost. So, what was Greenspan's main tool to get things going? Short-term interest rates. By lowering rates, he hoped to create an environment where individuals and companies would be enticed to use cheap credit to invest and spend – thereby kick-starting the economy. All of that investing and spending would increase the demand for goods, services, and assets, thereby pushing up prices – including, of course, the price of real estate.

And that's what he did: between 2001 and late 2003 the Fed lowered short-term rates from 6.5 percent to 1 percent, which meant cheap money for everyone: companies, to be sure, but also consumers that made active use of credit cards and took out home mortgages. Though the Fed gradually started to hike rates after that, the great real estate asset bubble had already started inflating. By the way, during these critical years, there was a strong belief from Greenspan (and others) that the financial system had reached a state of enlightened stability: *"Not only have individual financial institutions become less vulnerable to shocks from underlying risk factors, but also the financial system as a whole has become more resilient."*[1] Keep that thought in mind.

So, how big a role did cheap money play in creating the foundation of the crisis? Though Greenspan and his successor, Ben Bernanke, would later downplay (even refute) the claim that cheap credit was a driving factor, Professor John Taylor of Stanford University had rather a different take: *"[T]he classic explanation of financial crises is that they are caused by excesses – frequently monetary excesses – which lead to a boom and an inevitable bust. This crisis was no different: A housing boom followed by a bust led to defaults, the implosion of mortgages and mortgage-related securities at financial institutions, and resulting financial turmoil.*[2] So did Texas Congressman Ron Paul (a long-time critic of the Fed's monetary policies that I'll come back to in Chapter 7): *"[w]ith lots of cheap money available, businesses and individuals spend with less discipline and incur more debt."*[3] Furthermore, he said: *"Interest at 1 percent, overnight rates, loaning to banks, encouraging the banks and investors to do the wrong things causes all the malinvestment. These conditions were predictable."*[4] Jamie Dimon, CEO of JP Morgan, expressed a similar view, noting that all the cheap money helped *"fuel asset appreciation, excessive speculation, and far higher credit losses."*[5] And, from the UK's then-Chancellor of the Exchequer Alistair Darling: *"credit chased a limited amount of assets which put up their prices. I think there were many people who came to believe that somehow this could just go on and on."*[6] Morgan Stanley economist and senior executive Stephen Roach echoed something similar: *"central banks decided that easy money was the world's just reward. That set in motion a chain of events that has allowed one bubble to beget another – from equities to housing to credit.*"[7] And let me add one more observation, for good measure, from Lloyd Blankfein, CEO of Goldman Sachs, who stated that *"the roots of the damage to our financial system are broad and deep. They coalesced over many years to create a sustained period of cheap credit and excess liquidity."*[8] You get the point. Incidentally, the US was not alone in this cheap credit "bubble" process – the same was happening in various other countries around the world.

One of the key beneficiaries of this tidal wave of money was, of course, the US residential real estate market, which rose steadily, and in some cases sharply, in value: hot spots like Las Vegas, Southern California, Arizona, and Florida, among others, registered double digit gains in value as homeowners "traded up" or bought 2nd and 3rd homes as investment properties. Between 1995 and 2005 US housing prices rose by an average of 135 percent – a fantastic return. Not surprisingly, similar forces were at play in other countries: during the same period home prices increased more than 130 percent in Ireland, 120 percent in the UK and Spain, and over 100 percent in France. So, there you have the making of a bubble...a big one.

Let me now add bankers to the mix. Bankers are of, course, the middlemen who translate interest rate policies into action: they grant loans to companies and individuals that want to borrow. When rates are low, the demand for loans increases because borrowing is cheap, and bankers are all too happy to be part of the game – that's how they make money. Bankers work on an incentive basis, getting paid bonuses or commissions for bringing in the business. This generally works okay – banks have been doing this for centuries (though, it must be said, with some spectacular blowups every so often). But sometimes it doesn't matter if the business is good or not – as long as loans get on the books, bankers get paid. You can already see how a little problem might develop, especially in an overheated market where credit and asset demand are strong and the sun is still shining. By the middle of the decade this was particularly true in housing loans: as the real estate markets kept climbing, bankers started loosening their credit standards, thinking (1) the markets would keep going up, so the loans would be fine (even if some of the borrowers looked a little dodgy on paper) and (2) they would get some really nice bonuses.

While lots of these loans were sound, some of them were not. And here I introduce a term that has become part of the public's lexicon: "subprime," the name given by bankers to folks with a less-than-creditworthy financial situation. During this euphoric period, say 2003 into 2006, bankers loosened their lending standards, making subprime loans to a rather motley crew: those who couldn't put any money down (i.e., lending 100% or more against a property instead of the more usual 70% or 80%); those with bad or damaged credit history; those with very low income levels, who would have to strain and stretch to make their monthly payments; and, those without proof of job, income, or assets. In some cases the bankers made these loans look really appealing to would-be borrowers by tarting them up with artificially low rates for the first few years. But, with the end of the "teaser period" came bad news: a jump in rates to levels that, for many, created severe financial pressures, or worse – foreclosure. By the way, the idea of offering customers alternatives to the standard 30-year fixed mortgage was deemed to be a good thing, to wit Greenspan's comments in 2004: *"American consumers might benefit if lenders provided greater mortgage product alternatives to the traditional fixed rate mortgage. To the degree that households are driven by fears of payment shocks but are willing to manage their own interest rate risks, the traditional fixed-rate mortgage may be an expensive method of financing a home."*[9] Really? How many households know how to manage interest rate risk?

As it happens, some of these subprime loans were simply unwise – or worse, fraudulent. John Robbins, Chairman of the Mortgage Bankers Association (MBA, a key lobbying group), would know: *"bad loans were made. They were not made responsibly or with the best interest of consumers in mind."*[10] Bradley Rock, head of the American Bankers Association (ABA, another lobbying group), offered a similar perspective, though one focused more on nonbank lenders: *"With the frenzy that ensued, sound underwriting practices were often sacrificed – primarily by non-bank originators – for immediate gains...that have caused a lot of damage for consumers and for the industry."*[11] Even the bankers agreed. Dimon, for instance, said that *"you never saw losses in these new products, because home prices were going up, people were making money...I think there were some...unscrupulous mortgage salesmen and mortgage brokers. And you know, some people missold."*[12] Citigroup's CEO Vikram Pandit concurred: *"...so yes, I think Wall Street, financial institutions went a little bit further, went to a point where they started encouraging people to use those savings.... [s]ome of the practices did go a little far, and quite a lot far in terms of what and how they encouraged people to buy homes. And when the other side of things happened, they all sort of roll into a place where sometimes you create a bubble."*[13] Phil Angelides, in his capacity as head of the Congressional Financial Crisis Inquiry Commission, noted that *"[i]n September 2004, the FBI's head of the criminal division warned that mortgage fraud was so rampant in this country that it was a potential...'epidemic' and that, if unchecked, it would result in a crisis as big as the S&L crisis."*[14] Much bigger, as it happens. Incidentally, the same bad practices were happening in the UK's own subprime market. Peter Tutton, Senior Policy Officer at the UK Citizens Advice, testified that *"we argued very strongly but the problem that we were seeing in the market was about bad practices, bad selling practices, and the regulators out there need to do more about it."*[15]

Let me take a short, but important, detour here. Why would a banker lend money to what even on the surface seems like a potentially bad risk? Aren't bankers supposed to be boring and conservative and take smart risks? What's the story? Three points.

First, many banks suffered from weak internal oversight, and the risk controls surrounding some bank businesses were in poor shape. Risk managers, who are supposed to be "cops on the beat" and keep too much risk from coming through the doors, fell down on the job – for reasons that I'll discuss in the next few chapters. Furthermore, most of the banks that would eventually get caught up in the maelstrom had very sleepy board directors – the very individuals that are supposed to watch out for the interests of shareholders were not paying attention, were not up to the job – or both. With all of these weak internal controls, aggressive bankers were able to book all kinds of risky business.

Second, the real estate market was red hot: bankers felt that even under a worst case scenario, they would be able to get their money back. The game went something like this: if a bank lent Mr Subprime Smith $100,000 to buy a condo in Las Vegas that was worth $100,000 (100% financing!) and offered him a really low rate for the first two years – no principal payments, and a very low floating interest payment – Mr Smith would manage to scrape up the money to remain current. If the worst happened and Mr Smith couldn't make his mortgage payment after the end of the two-year teaser, no problem: the bank would just take the condo back and sell it to someone else. Remember, the condo would be worth $110,000 or $120,000 by then, because Vegas condos always went up – hot housing market. So, even in a worst case scenario, the bankers couldn't lose money and actually stood to make some – maybe not so unwise? And even if some of the defaults left the bank underwater, remember that they were doing so much high-margin lending business, that they could easily absorb some of the rotten apples. In the words of Ron Paul: *"when credit is cheap, why not loan money more recklessly to individuals who normally would not qualify? Even with higher default rates, lenders could make huge profits simply through volume. Subprime lending is a symptom of the housing bubble, not the cause of it."*[16]

Sidebar: Some of the loan documents had lots of fine print, sort of telling Mr Smith that the low interest rate he enjoyed for the first two years would ratchet up dramatically thereafter – so if Mr Smith could barely afford the monthly payment beforehand, he would surely not be able to afford it after that. A bit tricky on the part of the banks, but a little stupid on the part of Mr Smith, who probably decided that he had better things to do than read the fine print. Personal responsibility was sometimes a bit scarce during this go-go period, but more on this later in the chapter. Why not take a chance, especially when rates were low and housing prices were heading up?

Third, the bankers never really intended to keep all of these loans on the books. Rather, they used the mortgages (both prime and subprime) as "raw material" to create special mortgage-backed bonds that were supported by pools of these mortgages. The concept behind this bit of "financial engineering" (aka "securitization") was, and still is, simple: a bank puts the mortgages in to a big pool, and uses the principal and interest from the pool of mortgages to pay the investors; investors bear the risk of nonpayment by the homeowners, but that risk is really, really small in a big, diverse pool. This whole exercise takes the mortgages off of the bank's balance sheet, meaning it is free to go out and create more mortgages, which it can repackage and sell to investors, and so on, in a great, never-ending cycle. Everybody wins in the "originate and distribute" world.

The key to the whole thing is to create a good pool: one that is big and diverse and has enough of an extra cushion to cover the fact that some people will invariably default. Since the pool is a mix of mortgages from Las Vegas, Santa Fe, Chicago, New York City, Tampa, and other places, the assumption is that even if one of these local markets or economies weakens (putting some mortgages at risk) the rest will do okay and generate enough mortgage payments to satisfy the investors holding the mortgage bonds. To make totally sure the pool is created properly, the bank contracts with a credit rating agency, which puts the whole thing into an assumption-based black box model, which spits out the parameters needed to call something AAA (top quality), AA (slightly lesser quality) and so on. That agency imprimatur is vital and lets investors buy the bond they feel is most appropriate for them. Note that I have used the word "assumption" twice – assumption and reality are often different things, as I'll point out later.

The Financial Times' (FT) Gillian Tett (more on her in Chapter 7) put this in a form that all nonvegetarians might appreciate: *"So it's a bit like making sausages. You take lots of different pieces of meat from lots of different animals, chop it up, mix it up, put it into casings, and suddenly you end up with a bunch of shiny sausages which look great. The only problem is that no one really knows what quality the meat is inside of those sausages."*[17] In fact, some of the meat was of inferior quality and some of it had actually gone bad.

William Irving, portfolio manager at Fidelity observed that *"[w]ithout a doubt, securitization played a role in this crisis ... the 'originate-to-distribute' model of credit provision seemed to spiral out of control. Under this model, intermediaries found a way to lend money profitably without worrying if the loans were paid back."*[18] Former Royal Bank of Scotland (RBS) Chairman Sir Tom McKillop, commenting on the whole notion of mortgage-backed bonds, noted that *"[t]his was distributing risk. This was making the whole system more stable."*[19]

Of course, this financial wizardry (some might prefer alchemy) isn't anything new – it has been used, generally to good effect, since Salomon Brothers,

Merrill Lynch, Bear Stearns and a few other banks helped create the business in the 1970s. But mortgage-backed bonds really hit the mainstream through the efforts of Fannie Mae and Freddie Mac, two US government-sponsored enterprises that have been in the press a lot – for all the wrong reasons, as I'll discuss in Chapter 4. In fact, Fannie and Freddie have served as the linchpin of the US housing market for the past few decades, helping promote affordable housing goals by buying up mortgages from banks and savings and loans, putting them into pools of their own, and repackaging them as bonds – giving banks the ability to extend more mortgages (which they might either repackage themselves or sell to Fannie and Freddie). Even though Fannie and Freddie operated as shareholder-owned companies, they enjoyed an implicit government guarantee, which let them grow their balance sheets dramatically. And a significant part of the growth was based on the subprime category. Between 2004 and 2007, Fannie and Freddie became the largest purchasers of subprime mortgages from the banks. Unfortunately they, like the mortgage originating banks, loosened their standards over time. While former Fannie CEO Franklin Raines testified that both Fannie and Freddie *"employed strict credit standards for the mortgage assets they held"*[20] those standards ultimately proved to be wholly inadequate.

The Fannie/Freddie subprime effort got a big public boost when Massachusetts Representative Barney Frank, ranking Democrat on the influential House Banking Committee noted in 2003 that *"I want to roll the dice a little bit more in this situation towards subsidized housing."*[21] Subsidized housing is, of course, a politically correct euphemism for subprime. Nifty. I'll point out later in the book that when the government tried to clamp down on the two agencies and tighten standards, howls of anger and indignation came from the opposition party, which managed successfully to delay any attempts to strengthen controls. As Stanford's John Taylor noted, *"Fannie Mae and Freddie Mac were encouraged to expand and buy mortgage-backed securities, including those formed with the risky subprime mortgages."*[22] The two agencies would go on to become the single largest sinkhole of US taxpayer money.

So there are three reasons why banks played heavily in risky loans – the detour is finished, back to my story. For all of this cleverness, the banks (and Fannie and Freddie) weren't always willing or able to sell all of the mortgage-backed bonds they had put together. Clearly, if you won't or can't sell the bonds to investors, you aren't distributing risk, meaning risky concentrations start building up on balance sheets. The banks and housing agencies were sitting on a ticking time bomb. So why wouldn't they get rid of the risk? A couple of reasons: they liked having these "proprietary" positions because they considered them attractive from a return perspective, particularly since they were low risk (AAA); they felt no urgency to get rid of these bonds (or the "raw material" mortgages) because they had enough capital (and the property markets were going up); or their risk managers didn't force them too (i.e., they were weak or had completely underestimated the risks). As I'll point out later by the time the crisis arrived, "wouldn't sell" turned into "couldn't sell" and it was too late.

Of course, banks were also involved in lots of other activities that were unrelated to the housing market – that's what they do. So, they were extending huge loans to finance the acquisitions of companies, they were writing credit derivatives (basically insurance policies on the likelihood that individual companies would continue to pay on their own bonds), and they were cooking up new financial instruments with particularly bizarre and complicated dimensions of risk – some of them not easily understood by anybody but the rocket scientists building them – not their bosses, not the bank leadership, not the board directors, and not the regulators. Alexandre Lamfalussy, professor at University of Louvain and one-time head of the Bank for International Settlements (BIS), observed that *"[t]here was not an intermediate group of people who were sufficiently young and bright to understand what was happening but who had at the same time the capacity to explain it to top management."*[23] In a replay of Enron and Parmalat from earlier in the decade, banks also had a bunch of risky things sitting in special vehicles off their balance sheets which compounded their overall exposures even further. And the supposedly smart and independent bank risk managers went along for the ride.

It wasn't just banks doing all of this, of course: they were joined by others, like hedge funds, private equity funds, captive finance companies, and other non-bank financial institutions – the so-called "shadow banking system." In fact, these kinds of activities are pretty normal for the banking and shadow banking systems, but in the heady days of 2005 and 2006, individual institutions were doing everything in much bigger size. At some point the potential profit that could be earned for taking a particular risk started going down (read: becoming misbalanced) – so, in order to keep generating the same amount of revenues (and, by extension, bonuses) the players needed to do larger amounts of risky business – mostly by leveraging themselves, or borrowing money to put on more risk positions. There was an awful lot of leverage in the system going into 2007. It's a bit like the drunkard: while a shot or two of Jack Daniels may provide the desired results during the first trip to the local pub, several bottles may be needed to achieve the same results on the thirtieth outing.

Still, there was no hint of trouble from the world's leading lights. In Spring 2006 the IMF waxed poetic about the new era of financial stability created by Wall Street inventions like securitization and credit derivatives, to wit: *"[t]here is growing recognition that the dispersion of credit risk by banks to a broader and more diverse group of investors ... has helped to make the banking and overall financial system more resilient...new participants...help to mitigate and absorb shocks to the financial system.... The improved resilience may be seen in fewer bank failures and more consistent credit provision. Consequently, the commercial banks, a core segment of the financial system, may be less vulnerable today to credit or economic shocks."*[24] Well, not quite, as it happens. Furthermore, the IMF gurus noted, *"new instruments may also influence the dynamics of credit cycles...In this way, bank behavior may become less procyclical, and credit cycles less volatile."*[25] In fact, the opposite occurred. And in the Spring of 2007, the Group of 7 Finance Ministers and Central Bank governors provided no warning of the impending storm, noting confidently that *"... the global economy is having its strongest sustained expansion in more than 30 years and is becoming more balanced...recent developments in global financial markets, including hedge funds...along with the emergence of advanced financial techniques such as credit derivatives, have contributed significantly to the efficiency of the financial system."*[26] Efficiency of the financial system? Not a clue.

So, the world in early 2007 was characterized by frothy real estate markets, lots of leverage, tricky risk products, and a general sentiment among various regulators, board directors, executives, and risk managers that things were still generally okay.

The dominos fall

With the stage set for some real problems, let me now move into the first phase of the crisis. The Fed's slow ratcheting up of rates (starting in late 2003), meant that borrowing gradually became more expensive. By mid-decade this gave homebuyers more pause when buying, meaning that sellers could no longer get their prices – they had to be willing to negotiate, even in hot US marketplaces. So, the strong seller's market turned into a buyer's market: the upward trajectory in housing prices slowed and then reversed. In late 2006 and into early 2007 sharp downward corrections hit almost every market – but especially in the once-desirable markets of Arizona, Nevada, California, and Florida, which, in the span of 12 months, fell by 20 percent, 40 percent, and in some cases even more. Imagine that – Mr Smith bought a Vegas condo for $100,000 and two years later found that it was only worth $60,000 – and yet his mortgage might still be $100,000 (100% financing, remember?), meaning negative equity of $40,000. Couple this with a spiking monthly mortgage payment from the expiring teaser rate and perhaps throw in loss of job (a process that invariably accelerated as the crisis took hold) and you have the makings of a disaster. James Lockhart, head of the revamped Fannie/Freddie regulator, said that *"[Fannie/Freddie] management and the models they relied on failed to identify how badly the mortgage market was deteriorating...[u]nfortunately, the...hubris extended to the whole mortgage market."*[27]

Importantly, this is where assumptions underpinning the mortgage-backed bonds clashed with reality: not only did a few mortgages in some of the bond pools go under, lots of mortgages in lots of pools went under. Why? Because the housing crash affected virtually all markets, by an amount that was much, much larger than anything assumed either by banks or the rating agencies. So, the original assumptions for creating the mortgage pools backing bonds might have centered on a softening of the Miami and Chicago housing markets by 5 percent. They most assuredly did not call for a simultaneous 40 percent plunge in Miami, Chicago, Santa Fe, Las Vegas, Boston, Tucson, Little Rock, DC, and San Diego. That's not supposed to happen. It hasn't happened before, right? Indeed, Dimon revealed a flaw that was common to most banks: *"I would say that was probably one of the big misses. We stressed almost everything else, but we didn't see home prices going down 40 percent."*[28] Not surprisingly, pools with lots of subprime mortgages got hit the hardest. Once this happened, the value of the bonds plummeted, creating lots of red ink for those holding them – which happened to be banks, Fannie and Freddie, sophisticated investors, and a few others from the shadow system. But more on this below.

A whole series of financial dominos began to topple with the bursting of the US housing bubble. And this is where lots of us missed the plot – not so much that dominos could or would topple, as they do so from time to time – but that the toppling would be so deep and wide, and occur so rapidly. Many in the banking world (including me), were unable to connect the dots between all the dominos. It was difficult to understand, at this early stage, that the collapse of the Las Vegas condo market would ultimately cause the borrowing costs on AAA-rated corporate bonds to rise to unprecedented levels, that equity markets would crack, that banks would stop lending to one another, that fire sales of all types of assets would occur, that a bunch of state banks in Germany would be drowning in losses from speculative assets and have to be bailed out by the German taxpayers, that previously well-regarded institutions such as Bear Stearns, RBS, and Lehman Brothers would collapse or be taken over, that Iceland would all but sink into the ocean, that major governments would have to guarantee deposits of their national banks to protect customers....

Why such dramatic toppling? Because business was being conducted on the basis of assumptions that bankers thought would hold true (and that ultimately didn't), because risk-taking was large, leveraged, sometimes casino-like, and often imprudently managed, and because the global financial system is so unbelievably linked that what happens in Las Vegas doesn't stay in Las Vegas...it can affect Dusseldorf, Dublin, Newcastle, Milan, Charlotte, and lots of other places. Former Securities and Exchange Commission (SEC) Chairman Chris Cox observed that *"[b]ecause the current credit market crisis began with the deterioration of mortgage origination standards, it could have been contained to banking and real estate, were our markets not so interconnected. But the seamlessness which characterizes today's markets saw financial institutions in every regulated sector suffer significant damage.*"[29] There's no escape from the global web that ties everything together.

The crisis didn't follow a neat path – it was messy and it came in waves, hitting different markets, players, and products at different times, making it all the more difficult to grasp and manage. Still, it was very fast: in little more than 18 months the global financial system was on its head and collective losses to a whole universe of stakeholders were so colossal (trillions with a "t") that it still boggles the mind. Stephen Green, HSBC's Chairman said: *"The sheer speed with which it swept through country after country and company after company was, I think unprecedented."*[30] The first wave hit the banks directly during the last two quarters of 2007 and into early 2008 – impacting especially those sitting on the exploding time bombs, such as mortgage bonds (subprime or not), unsold leveraged loans, credit derivatives, and other risky deals. Remember the brilliance of the "originate and distribute" model? It didn't work too well. McKillop admitted that *"It has not turned out that way. It has turned out completely the opposite to expectations. Everyone has been surprised about that, the regulators, the companies and the banks involved in it."*[31]

Pretty much everyone lost billions in this wave, which is another way of saying that they all got it wrong: big US banks such as Bank of America, JP Morgan Chase, Citibank, Wachovia, and Wells Fargo; big US investment banks such as Goldman, Morgan Stanley, Merrill Lynch, Bear Stearns, and Lehman Brothers; multiline insurers such as AIG and monoline specialists such as MBIA, FGIC, and ACA; UK banks such as RBS, Barclays, HBOS, Bradford & Bingley, and HSBC; and Continental banks such as Deutsche Bank, Dresdner Bank, Commerzbank, UBS, Société Générale, Fortis, WestLB, and others. To some degree it even spilled into the Asian and Australian banks. There were fatalities at this early stage: UK mortgage lender Northern Rock ran out of cash in late 2007 and had to be taken over by HM Treasury in early 2008; two German regional banks, IKB and Sachsen Landesbank, were loaded to the gills with AAA-paper that wasn't really AAA at all, blew up in late 2007, and had to be rescued by their state governments; subprime specialist Countrywide had to be taken over by Bank of America in January 2008; and many smaller US subprime mortgage specialists didn't even make it to 2008.

As the banks started posting multibillion dollar losses (all unexpected), they stopped lending to one another, to individuals, and to companies; almost simultaneously the market for very short-term loans (so-called commercial paper, where investors provide funds to big companies) froze up. This was a critical problem, because when all forms of credit freeze, the economic engines can't run, and when engines can't run, production sputters and layoffs begin – precisely what started happening in late 2007, continuing on through 2008 and into 2009. Risk aversion had set in – with a vengeance. At the time, French President Sarkozy expressed concern about the knee-jerk reaction that caused banks to withhold lending: *"For banks, playing their part does not mean lending more to speculators than to companies and households. It does not mean tightening credit to the economy to compensate for the excessive risks they have taken on the financial markets."*[32]

Fears were palpable. Ed Balls, former chief economic advisor to HM Treasury, said at the time that *"[t]hese are seismic events that are going to change the political landscape. I think this is a financial crisis more extreme and more serious than that of the 1930s."*[33] Jochen Sanio, Head of the German financial regulator Bafin, observed that *"[t]he financial crisis has triggered a deep global recession which in turn may have repercussions for financial markets. One alarming scenario would be if banks still burdened with toxic assets were forced to carry out major value adjustments which could worsen the crisis again."*[34] In fact, that is precisely what happened, leading to a further toppling of dominos into 2008.

US (and global) housing prices continued to slide, and forced selling of exotic mortgage securities into an illiquid market led to lower asset valuations and more forced selling – a kind of self-fulfilling downward spiral that made a bad situation even worse. In fact, these forced sales of assets were very damaging. Lord Adair Turner, Chairman of the UK's Financial Services Authority (FSA) explained the fire sale problem this way: *"a greater proportion of credit assets were held by investors seeking reassurance from credit ratings, and thus increased the potential aggregate effects of forced selling by institutions using predefined investment rules based on ratings (e.g., only hold bonds with rating A or above)."*[35]

The tumult and uncertainty shook national economies: unemployment crept up, and many countries slipped into recession. Taro Aso, who went on to serve as Prime Minister of Japan for 12 months starting in September 2008, voiced a cautionary note at the time: *"America is facing a financial crisis...we must not allow that to bring us down as well."*[36] In the event, Japan remained somewhat insulated from the worst of the crisis, though its big banks and brokers posted billions in losses on the same mortgage securities. Aso later said he was *"proud that Japan was not involved in that money game."*[37] Reflecting on the Anglo-Saxon disaster, economist Akio Makabe noted that *"Japan learned its lesson in the 1990...It was wise when Wall Street was foolish."*[38]

The first half of 2008 was unsettling as some more big names dropped by the wayside, including US investment bank Bear Stearns (taken over by JP Morgan in March) and mortgage lender IndyMac (placed into receivership by the regulators in July). By mid-year, most major banks were still bleeding from all of their risky positions. Added to this were mounting problems at the monoline insurance companies that had guaranteed lots of the credit derivatives and mortgage bonds being traded in the market – suddenly they didn't have enough capital to run their businesses, and were on the ropes. Some large hedge funds started to feel the pain, and the global stock markets started posting new lows (even after appearing somewhat "bullet proof" in the first months of the crisis). Fannie and Freddie confessed to huge losses of their own, and mega-insurer AIG appeared to be a toxic dump.

Interestingly, senior officials didn't necessarily think, at this stage, that a second round of domino toppling was in the offing. In late 2007 Mario Draghi, Italy's central bank governor, downplayed the situation: *"You cannot call it a crisis, but turbulence."*[39] Bank of England head Mervyn King noted that *"...regulators around the world have said...and I think they're right, that for the major banks in the world, they have the ability to cope with this crisis – not without losing money, not without losing bonuses and in the case of some individuals not without losing their jobs – but nevertheless, it isn't a threat to the banking system as a whole."*[40] Furthermore, he said: *"It's quite possible that at some point we may get an odd quarter or two of negative growth, but recession is not the central projection at all."*[41] The then-Treasury Secretary Hank Paulson observed in May 2008 that *"[t]he worst is likely behind us,"*[42] and *"[i]n my judgment, we are closer to the end of the market turmoil than the beginning...I have great, great confidence in our capital markets and financial institutions."*[43] President George Bush sounded a similar theme : *"I think the system is basically sound, I truly do."*[44] Even Warren Buffett, the "Oracle of Omaha," didn't get it quite right, noting that *"I don't think the situation will get worse in financial markets. General conditions in the business world will get worse, but it will only last a while."*[45] In fact, they were all wrong.

More dominos fall

Then came September 2008, which set in motion the second, much larger, round of toppling. With losses rising at all of the major banks, the rumor mill was working overtime on who might follow Bear Stearns down the tubes – and the leading candidate was Lehman. In the span of just a few short weeks the storied bank suffered cancelled credit lines, strained liquidity, doomed capital-raising efforts, and short selling pressure. The failure by global regulators and bankers to cobble together a rescue package for Lehman's black hole balance sheet during a tense weekend in mid-September meant the game was up: Lehman became the largest casualty of the crisis, creating a real sense of panic almost everywhere. Commenting on the US financial system during the tense post-Lehman days, President Bush noted famously: *"This sucker could go down."*[46] Former UK Prime Minister Gordon Brown was equally forthright: *"The problems that started in America have now hurt every banking system in every continent of the world. The global financial market has ceased to function, putting in danger the necessary flow of money to businesses and families on which all of us depend in our daily lives."*[47] Sounds a bit alarmist – but it wasn't. It was all quite real.

In fact, the Lehman collapse forced every major country to step up and guarantee, in some form, the bank deposits of retail clients in order to prevent massive bank runs. And lots of other [very expensive] triage was needed, too: the US Government bailed out the teetering AIG, and then the rapidly sinking Fannie and Freddie (never mind ex-CEO Raines' statement in 2000 that *"[a] Fannie Mae bankruptcy is so far up in the realm of fantasy that it's hard to even imagine what the circumstances would be"*[48]). Goldman and Morgan Stanley became bank holding companies, and Merrill Lynch sold itself at a discount to Bank of America, marking the end of the US investment banking sector.

These emergency actions calmed the situation for a short while, but didn't remove the fundamental problem: insufficient capital in the banking system. Housing values were still sliding, mortgage securities were being downgraded and forced selling and deleveraging were causing asset prices to fall. The resultant losses for those revaluing their trading books every day created more red ink and more need for capital – but there was simply no private capital to be had. Critically, banks were still not lending to one another. Economist and Nobel laureate Joseph Stiglitz put it this way: *"So deceptive were the systems of creative accounting that the banks had employed that, as the crisis evolved, they didn't even know their own balance sheets, and so they knew that they couldn't know that of any other bank. No wonder then that no bank could trust another, and no one could trust our banks. No wonder then that our system of credit – the lifeblood on which the economy depends – froze."*[49]

More formal national measures followed in late September and into October. The Bush Administration, incurring the wrath of free-marketers, assembled a $700b banking bailout package – one originally designed to buy toxic assets from the banks, but used ultimately to recapitalize them through preferred stock purchases. Similar bailout mechanisms were created in other countries. The UK set up a £500b pool to buy up bank preference shares and provide bank guarantees and targeted liquidity injections, all of which Gordon Brown said were *"designed to put the British banking system on a sounder footing"*.[50] (Darling quickly added: *"[w]e are not seeking to take public control of these institutions, we are absolutely not doing that."*[51]) The Swiss, for their part, provided capital injections, soft loans backed by toxic assets, and asset guarantees, with the Finance Ministry saying that *"this package of measures will contribute to the lasting strengthening of the Swiss financial system...[and] is beneficial for overall economic development in Switzerland and is in the interests of the country as a whole.*"[52] In other words, this wasn't a bailout for the bankers, but a bailout for the citizens. The Germans set up a €500b domestic bailout fund including bank guarantees and additional capital for weakened banks, prompting Chancellor Angela Merkel to say *"[n]either I nor many others could have imagined the government would have to rescue banks overnight and at great expense...we have reacted appropriately to the unthinkable."*[53] The French created a €360b guarantee and capital pool, Sarkozy noting *"[t]his...was necessary to avoid the total collapse of the system – the only way to protect French savings and employment,"*[54] adding also that *"[t]hose who have done wrong will be punished."*[55] The Italians made available capital injections in exchange for nonvoting bank shares, the Spanish crafted a €100b plan of their own, and so forth. Only Iceland emerged as the odd man out, almost literally seeing its entire banking system slip into the ocean.

A central tenet of free markets, bankruptcy, was brushed aside by the bailout schemes and the support of those deemed to be "too-big-to-fail" – which caused great ire among the public in the US, Europe, and beyond. Former head of the New York Fed and Goldman partner Gerald Corrigan observed that *"I think the public at large understand very well the problem of too big to fail. By any standard, that is what really has the public so angry."*[56] California Congressman Brad Sherman was rather more explicit: *"The public is very angry at Wall Street... [b]ut they are constantly told by all the respected voices that if we don't protect and preserve the institutions on Wall Street, we'll be fighting for rat meat on the streets."*[57] But as David Wessel from the *Wall Street Journal* observed, *"The bailouts weren't designed to be fair. They were designed to prevent a financial virus from infecting the entire economy...[i]t's like watching the emergency room doctors save the life of the drunk driver who just plowed into the car your family was driving."*[58]

The government actions, coming some 18 months after the unofficial start of the crisis, brought the world's banks back from the brink. Unfortunately, that still wasn't the end of the story: 2009 was a rocky year as well, and governments had to dole out second and third helpings of capital to some big players. While a series of massive liquidity injections by the world's central banks, commencing in 2008 and carrying on through 2009, helped loosen credit conditions a bit, lending remained tight and recessionary conditions took greater hold almost everywhere: virtually every major economy contracted during this period. Naturally, unemployment rose in tandem (jumping in the US from pre-crisis levels of 5% up to 10%, whilst in Europe most countries surpassed 10% and in some cases 15% and even 20%). The other knock-on effects were obvious: weak consumer sentiment (and thus spending) and continued softness in housing prices (with a bottoming-out remaining on hold till 2010). John Dugan, Head of the Office of the Comptroller of the Currency, stated in October 2009 that *"[w]hile over-leverage and falling housing prices were the* initial drivers of delinquencies and loan losses, borrower strains resulting from rising unemployment and underemployment are an increasingly important factor."[59]

In fact, it wasn't till the banks started making money again in mid-2009 that things started feeling a bit better. And though capital coffers were replenished and credit loosened up, the damage had been done – trillions of dollars in wealth had been destroyed, economies had suffered major setbacks, and the rules of the free market had been rewritten. The reputation of banks rightly plummeted. Stiglitz echoed what many undoubtedly felt: *"If I gamble in Las Vegas and lose, only I (and my family) suffer. But in America's casino capitalism, when the banks gambled and lost, the entire nation paid the price."*[60] Jean Claude Trichet, head of the European Central Bank was critical of a global banking system that had focused on speculation, which he described as a *"system that had moved away from its traditional role of supporting trade and real investment...a financial system in which speculation and financial gambling had run rife...a system no longer managing genuine economic risks but one actually creating and assuming financial risks."*[61]

The crisis had reached almost every corner of the world. The IMF's Dominique Strauss-Kahn observed: *"You may call it the dark side if you want, but it is clearly a globalized crisis...[t]his is really a global crisis."*[62] Germany's Sanio: *"The suddenness and violence of the monster storm that roiled the financial markets and wreaked terrible havoc on the international financial system was almost beyond belief."*[63] French Finance Minister Christine Lagarde provided her own summary of the situation: *"I'd use one word – excess...[i]t was excess in all categories."*[64] Business Secretary and MP Vince Cable called it *"the economic equivalent of the Iraq war."*[65] And a puzzled Queen Elisabeth II, visiting the London School of Economics, asked a simple question: *"Why did nobody notice it?"*[66] Why, indeed? A battery of economists returned with this answer: *"your majesty, the failure to foresee the timing, extent and severity of the crisis...was principally a failure of the imagination of many bright people...to understand the risks to the system as a whole."*[67]

Who else?

So, cheap credit, a housing bubble, and banks with weak risk controls, a proclivity for risky things and a love of big bonuses, led to massive trading and credit losses, a freeze-up in credit and, ultimately, a global recession with very significant unemployment – a disaster of horrific proportions, and one that should be laid squarely at the feet of the bankers (as I shall describe further in the next few chapters). But was it just the banks? Were they the only ones doing damage? Or were there other bad actors? Who else needs to take some responsibility? Though one hates to disagree with Warren Buffett, his comments of May 2008 seem now not to be totally accurate: *"The banks exposed themselves too much, they took on too much risk ....It's their fault. There's no need* to blame anyone else."⁶⁸ Not quite: a couple of others had a hand in this mess. Charles Dallara, Head of the International Institute of Finance (a bank lobbying group, to be sure) noted that *"[w]e are beyond the point where we can allow the entire blame to be laid at our doorstep...[d]oes anyone really believe the crisis happened because a few bankers failed to manage their risks?"*⁶⁹ Goldman's Blankfein said that *"without trying to shed one bit of our industry's accountability, we would also further our collective interests by recognizing other contributing causes to the severity of the crisis. Factors from both Main Street and Wall Street contributed to today's circumstances. Neither part of our economy acted completely independently of the other."*⁷⁰

In spite of some protestations to the contrary, there were, in fact, other guilty parties, including the rating agencies, regulators, legislators, and lobbyists, and even some men and women on Main Street.

Rating agencies

Let me begin with the rating agencies – companies staffed with financial analysts that evaluate a country, company, or structured transaction and assign a "credit opinion." The three majors, Moody's, Fitch, and Standard and Poor's (S&P), hold a very powerful position in the financial markets, assigning ratings to every bond or public financing for a fee (paid by the issuers, mind you). Realistically no bond or public financing deal can come to market without a rating, as many investors can't or won't buy unrated paper. So, the agencies have the keys to the kingdom. Add to this a touch of oligopoly power, a propensity to use the "black box" approach when assigning ratings (meaning no one really knows what's going on), a tendency to mix structuring assignments with ratings advice, and a history of being sometimes late to the party when it comes to downgrades or defaults (e.g., Enron, WorldCom, Orange County, Delphi, GM, Pacific Gas, Mercury Finance, and many others), and you have the makings of a real problem.

This became abundantly clear during and after the crisis, when evidence surfaced that all three had, in many cases, overstated the ratings of the mortgage-backed bonds and other structured products that were held by banks and investors. Their black box models were flawed, mostly because they assumed housing markets wouldn't fall by as much as they did, and that subprime borrowers wouldn't default as frequently as they did – two very bad assumptions, as it happens. To give you a taste of how the agencies saw it, Deven Sharma, president of S&P, said: *"Put simply, our assumptions about the housing and mortgage markets in the second half of this decade did not account for the extraordinarily steep declines we have now seen...had we anticipated fully the speed and scope of the declines in these markets at the time we issued our original ratings, many of those ratings would have been different."*⁷¹ Greenspan noted that *"[t]he venerated credit* rating agencies bestowed ratings that implied AAA smooth-sailing for many a highly toxic derivative product."[72]

So a German state bank or a US pension fund that thought it had invested in a AAA-rated mortgage bond might have actually been holding a A or BBB-rated bond...which obviously had a lot less value, especially when things started falling apart. The mere fact that the agencies had rated literally tens of billions of dollars of such bonds meant that their role in the crisis was not insignificant. Senator Richard Shelby, ranking minority member on the US Senate Banking Committee, was one of many critical voices: *"I strongly believe that the credit rating agencies played a pivotal role in the collapse of our financial markets."*[73] I'll get back to the agencies in Chapter 5.

Regulators

Next in line are the regulators, government institutions that set policies that are meant to keep the financial markets on an even keel. They also establish the "rules of the game" to make sure that stakeholders are properly protected. George Soros, long-time hedge fund manager said: *"The authorities, the regulators – the Federal Reserve and the Treasury – really failed to see what was happening.... [A] number of people could see it coming. And somehow the authorities didn't want to see it coming. So it came as a surprise."*[74] The same, of course, happened in the UK, Germany, France, Italy, and other countries. Johan Norberg, fellow at Cato, provided another harsh assessment: *"Look no further than the US federal institutions in Washington, DC, and we find 12,113 individuals working full time to regulate the financial markets. What did they do with the powers they had? Made mistakes. American politicians, central banks and regulators were just as eager as speculators to expand the housing bubble. They just had a bigger pump."*[75]

Central banks are surely part of this story. Many implemented easy money policies during the first half of the decade, and these ultimately proved damaging. Roach had some choice words on the topic: *"For the second time in seven years, the bursting of a major-asset bubble has inflicted great damage on world financial markets. In both cases – the equity bubble in 2000 and the credit bubble in 2007 – central banks were asleep at the switch."*[76] Ron Paul was equally critical of the US central bank, noting presciently before the crisis that *"[w]hen the bubble finally bursts completely, millions of Americans will be looking for someone to blame. Look for Congress to hold hearings into subprime lending practices and 'predatory' mortgages. We'll hear a lot of grandstanding about how unscrupulous lenders took advantage of poor people, and how rampant speculation caused real estate markets around the country to overheat.... [b]ut capitalism is not to blame for the housing bubble, the Federal Reserve is...[i]magine a Brinks truck driving down a busy street with the doors wide open, and money flying out everywhere, and you'll have a pretty good analogy for Fed policies over the last two decades."*[77]

Then there's the actual financial authorities that set rules for banks, insurers, and others, so that they can't jeopardize financial standing of clients or other stakeholders. This group did very poorly indeed. Willem Buiter, formerly of the Bank of England and the London School of Economics (LSE) and latterly of Citigroup, provided a view that seems applicable globally: *"I do not think that regulators saw what was coming... the magnitude of what was going wrong was not seen by anybody, at least nobody that went on the record. There were warnings and they were not heeded."*[78] This was seconded by Ed Balls: *"People are quite right to say that financial regulation wasn't tough enough in Britain and around the world, that regulators misunderstood and did not see the nature of the risks of the dangers being run in our financial institutions – absolutely right."*[79] From King's perspective, *"No regulatory system in the world really dealt well with what happened."*[80] And he had some particularly unkind words for his cross-Atlantic counterparts: *"It is not numbers here. The Americans had tens of thousands of people involved in monitoring their financial sector but it did not help one jot."*[81] Mario Draghi gave a more technical explanation: *"We failed to recognise the extent to which savings-investment imbalances, the growth of complex securitised credit intermediation, changing patterns of maturity transformation, rising embedded leverage, a burgeoning shadow banking sector, and rapid credit-fuelled growth, had created large systemic vulnerabilities."*[82] Well... that's a lot of misses.

Dimon, for his part, noted that *"[t]he current regulatory system is poorly organized with overlapping responsibilities, and many regulators did not have the statutory resolution authority needed to address the failure of large, global financial companies."*[83] Economist and Nobel Laureate Paul Krugman, reflecting on off-balance sheet activities and nonbank institutions, said that *"[a]s the shadow banking system expanded to rival or even surpass conventional banking in importance, politicians and government officials should have realized that they were re-creating the kind of financial vulnerability that made the Great Depression possible – and they should have responded by extending regulations and the financial safety net to cover these new institutions."*[84] Sanio expanded on Krugman's view: *"In the end, non-consolidation created one of the biggest parts of the shadow banking system, a shaky structure, with no capital backing at all, that could come tumbling down in heavy weather. I think I am right in saying that these examples describe a case of serious regulatory failure."*[85]

Nouriel Roubini, an economist I shall reintroduce in Chapter 7, said that *"[i]t is clear that the Anglo-Saxon model of supervision and regulation of the financial system has failed. It relied on self-regulation that, in effect, meant no regulation; on market discipline that does not exist when there is euphoria and irrational exuberance; on internal risk management models that fail... rating agencies that had massive conflicts of interest and a supervisory system dependent on principles rather than rules. This light-touch regulation in effect became regulation of the softest-touch."*[86] In fact, it has become painfully evident that most of these public servants were absent: no single regulator seems to have spotted the asset bubble, or anticipated the unwinding of the housing market; no single regulator really knew the kinds of risks their charges were taking or what to do when the bubble burst; no single regulator had any idea of the level of leverage and systemic risk that had worked its way into the global markets; and, very few regulators seem to have operated in a coordinated fashion in the first crucial months of the crisis. More generally, the regulatory class was slow off the mark, and didn't necessarily fathom the depth of the crisis as it was unfolding. US Treasury Secretary Tim Geithner noted that *"[t]he government of the United States, along with governments around the world, did not move early enough...to address this crisis. It underestimated the strength of the recession, underestimated the damage it was going to do. And underestimated what it was going to take."*[87]

What happened, what went wrong, why did regulators fail? In fact, there were lots of problems: slow reaction time, bad communication, fractionalized structures, overlapping or underlapping responsibilities, turf battles, inadequate skills, overworked staff, ineffective (sometimes even contradictory) rules and regulations, and lack of scrutiny. And perhaps some complacency: a belief (or desire to believe) that financial wizardry and the structure of the financial system had created what has come to be known as the "great moderation" – a state of play where everything in the marketplace operates on an even keel, with no sharp peaks or dips.

To consider just how blind the regulators were, let me point you to some comments delivered by Geithner, when he was still head of the NY Fed, to an audience in late 2006: *"The resiliency we have observed over the past decade or so is not just good luck. It is the consequence of efforts by regulatory, supervisory and private financial institutions to address previous sources of systemic instability. Risk management has improved significantly, and the major firms have made substantial progress toward more sophisticated measurement and control of concentration to specific risk factors...."*[88] Less than a year later all of these comments would prove questionable at best, dead wrong at worst.

If the remit of financial regulators is to protect depositors or clients, to make sure that institutions don't take so much risk that they put themselves and others in financially jeopardy, then they failed miserably. Or, as Exchequer Darling has said: *"I think clearly mistakes were made at the supervisory and regulatory regime."*[89] Back to King: *"We have been through a period in which the UK had light-touch regulation, the Americans had pretty intrusive regulation, hundreds if not thousands of bank examiners sitting and working full time inside the banks, in Europe we have had governments deeply involved in the banking system and different systems in Asia. Every single one of them failed to spot the seriousness of the risk-taking that was going on."*[90]

To be sure, regulators don't get paid the same as bankers so they didn't (and don't) draw the same ire. It's easy to get upset at the Goldman trader that made $5m for himself while injecting lots of risk on to Goldman's books and into the system at large. But if the poor overworked case officer at the SEC that is supposed to watch over Goldman only makes $150,000, well...poor guy, he did the best he could against the greedy trader (and all of the trader's other colleagues). They both screwed up, but one earns more, so he is more responsible. In fact, the Goldman trader might be more responsible than the case officer – but because of the risk that was created, not the paycheck that was received. The two issues need to be separated. In the end, the case officers failed to keep pace with what was going on, so they must share in some of the responsibility. I'll get back to the regulators in Chapter 6.

Politicians

Next I come to the political and legislative class. As a group, politicians tend to be relatively unpopular amongst most of the citizenry, and when you consider some of what they said and did before and during the crisis, their profiles sink even further. In the main, politicians are meant to create the laws that govern all activities, including those that touch the financial system. In looking at previous crises, it becomes pretty clear that politicians have had a tendency to blow with the prevailing wind: when financial regulation appears too stifling, they pass laws to deregulate. When a financial crisis appears, the political pendulum swings the other way – they conduct their witch hunts and then impose strict, sometimes unwise, laws, some of which wind up crimping business – until lobbyists (and even constituents) make enough noise, and persuade them to change the laws. The cycle then starts anew. This means that politicians often add no particular value – and can arguably make things even worse. Unfortunately, their errors are compounded by their desire to promote unwise policies (e.g., subprime) and their failure to diligently oversee financial regulators.

Same thing in this crisis. For instance, politicians missed lots of opportunities during the decade to bring derivatives generally, and credit derivatives specifically, under tighter control. The growth in this market during the early 2000s was phenomenal, and unregulated, in part because politicians didn't know or care, or were otherwise charmed by the dulcet tones of the lobbyists. Another example: a whole group of US politicians stuck their heads in the sand when it came to the fiscal health of Fannie and Freddie – trying to pretend that everything was okay, even as the two firms were promoting subprime, cooking their books, and apparently not controlling their risks properly – helping set the stage for a much bigger disaster. Economist and commentator Larry Kudlow put the Congress in his crosshairs: *"Sub prime, sub standard loans were a creature of the US Congress in the 90's and the 2000's*"[91] – and the performance record of subprime is by now well known. Chris Whalen of Institutional Risk Analytics saw it this way: *"Spurred on to chase the 'policy outcome' of affordable housing, an entire range of deliberately opaque and highly leveraged financial instruments were born with the full support of Washington, the [government sponsored enterprises] and the Congress."*[92] Greenspan echoed a similar view: *"...Fannie Mae and Freddie Mac, pressed by the U.S. Department of Housing and Urban Development and the Congress to expand 'affordable housing commitments,' chose to meet them in a wholesale fashion by investing heavily in subprime mortgage-backed securities.... Fannie and Freddie paid whatever price was necessary to reach their affordable housing goals."*[93] Former Fannie CEO Daniel Mudd said that: *"...Congress and the executive branch...required the [agencies] to take increasingly larger roles in fostering homeownership and affordable housing for underserved populations...in the realm of public and political opinion, the companies were challenged to support a variety of initiatives to increase homeownership on a local basis...."*[94]

So politicians urged the expansion of homeownership, setting the tone and standards. Back in 1995, then-Housing and Urban Development Secretary Henry Cisneros spoke of the Clinton initiative to *"lift America's homeownership rate to an all-time high by the end of the century.... [L]ending institutions, secondary market investors [Fannie Mae and Freddie Mac], and other[s]...should work collaboratively to reduce homebuyer downpayment requirements."*[95] Let me be perfectly clear: this was a decade-long, government-sponsored effort to create access for those who couldn't really scrape up the needed downpayment. Blankfein observed that we follow *"the official policy of promoting, supporting and subsidizing homeownership"*[96] – sounds like trouble. In fact, some folks don't belong in purchased homes, they should remain in rentals. Numerous legislative proposals put forth in the first half of the decade to tighten controls on Fannie and Freddie were effectively shot down by the opposition – another shining moment in the history of the US Congress. Predictably, many of these politicians have since attempted to disavow any culpability. Sidebar: for all these political initiatives, Robert Wilmers, CEO of M&T Bank, observed that *"since the early 1970s...the percentage of American households owning homes has increased by merely four percentage points to 67%."*[97] Lots of thunder and lightning, but no real results.

Peter Wallison of the American Enterprise Institute had an accurate ex-post take: *"In typical Washington fashion, everyone has amnesia about how this disaster occurred...[p]oliticians in positions of authority today had an opportunity to prevent this fiasco but did nothing."*[98] Of course, similar forces were at work in the political systems of other countries. Buiter: *"Yes, I think the political classes were part of a wider climate of opinion that believed in the great moderation. The 'end of boom and bust' is just another word for the great moderation."*[99] There was, and is, no great moderation. Again, in the interest of getting the story straight, the politicians (and their lobbying friends) must accept their role in the fiasco – more on this group in Chapter 6.

Mom and pop

Finally, I come to the man and woman on Main Street. This one is a bit delicate, as no one wants to blame Mom and Pop – these are hard working salt-of-the-earth folks that just want to have a decent and comfortable life and provide for their families. And most are decent and hard working, and have acted responsibly and done the right thing. But some haven't, and it is instructive to see how they, too, contributed to the problem. As Mike Mayo, a well-regarded bank analyst at CLSA, has noted, *"consumers went along. There's some personal responsibility here."*[100]

It goes a bit like this: home ownership is a dream to which many aspire. Fulfilling that dream is predicated on some degree of prudent financial behavior and of living within one's means. Unfortunately, this concept isn't always well understood or regularly practiced – particularly in my country. Those of us in the US live in a society where debt-fuelled consumption is preferable to savings, where instant gratification is infinitely more fun than waiting till you can afford that gratification, and where keeping up with the neighbors is standard operating procedure that adds to financial pressures. While this is true for things like cars and plasma TVs and Playstations and Disney vacations and elective cosmetic surgery, it is also true for homes.

So, the bankers spotted an opening – a weakness they could take advantage of – and pounced. The Federal Deposit Insurance Corporation's (FDIC) head, Sheila Bair, testified that *"[t]he limited reach of prudential supervision allowed these [subprime] activities to grow unchecked. Laws that protected consumers from abusive lending practices were weak."*[101] Blame the bankers (and regulators and lawmakers), but don't forget that quite a number of families have to step up and take responsibility, too. As far as I can tell, the banker from Wachovia or Countrywide or Citi wasn't sitting in the office with the Smith family holding a loaded pistol to their heads, forcing them to sign the loan docs.

In testimony, Bair acknowledged that in the lead-up to the crisis even prime credit homeowners were becoming super-leveraged: *"[c]onsumers refinanced their mortgages, drawing ever more equity out of their homes as residential real estate prices grew beyond sustainable levels."*[102] Bradley Rock, Chairman of the ABA, also talked above overextension: *"[i]n many cases, individuals were purchasing homes with the intent of 'flipping' them – investing money into upgrades and then hoping to quickly sell at a significant profit. Others purchased houses as mere investment properties with the intent of renting them out to others and then selling once the property* had appreciated. *In other cases, loans were being made to first-time homebuyers who may not have fully appreciated or understood the terms of their loan agreement. Still others were simply cashing out their equity by re-financing.*"[103] Dimon concurred: *"...there was a lot of speculation, far too many people buying second and third homes using these things, as opposed to the place you're going to live."*[104] In fact, several million families in the US took on far more mortgage debt than they could comfortably afford, bought into a booming market, and then paid the ultimate financial price when the market collapsed. Turner noted that *"[i]n the years running up to the crisis in the US housing market and to a lesser degree in the UK it was clear that significant numbers of people who took on mortgage commitments really could not afford to pay it back in the hope that three years later the value of their homes would have gone up and they would then be able to remortgage."*[105] A pretty risky strategy. A quick note on the UK market: by 2007, about 1/3 of all mortgages were used for primary home purchases – the 2/3 balance was used either for investment properties (i.e., buy-to-let) or to take out existing equity (i.e., increase personal leverage). Dangerous in a market about ready to fall.

Subprime borrowers made things even worse. Lower income families or those with a checkered financial past, who couldn't really afford a home at all, were persuaded by the government and various activist groups that they could, indeed, afford one: in fact, the mantra from some of these activists was that owning a home must be considered a right, not a privilege. This belief is particularly insidious, as it sets such families up for even greater financial hardships if things don't turn out precisely as planned – if a job is lost or an adjustable rate causes the monthly payment to become unaffordable, the trip from home to sidewalk is short indeed. So, the system is set up for failure. Bank of America's CEO Brian Moynihan observed that *"[l]oans were made to people with poorer credit histories in greater amounts on the expectation that home values and economic fortunes would be stable or continue to rise – an expectation drawn from recent history."*[106] Unfortunately, the trend of ever-rising housing prices didn't play out. In some cases prospective borrowers lied on their applications in order to get mortgages, basically committing fraud. As Dimon noted *"it's apparent that excess speculation and dishonesty on the part of both brokers and consumers further contributed to the problem."*[107] Former Freddie Mac CEO Richard Syron put it concisely: *"The problems in the subprime market remind us of a longstanding truth that was nearly obscured during the last years of the long housing boom: not every family that wants to own a home is financially ready for homeownership. We need to face the fact that, as a matter of both policy and attitude, our nation did not sufficiently question whether homeownership is the right thing for every household in America at every point in time."*[108] Similar comments came from Robert Shiller, professor at Princeton and co-creator of the Case–Shiller real estate index (the price index many have come to dread), who wrote that *"...the subprime housing dilemma in the United States points up the problems with over-promoting homeownership.*

Homeownership, for all its advantages, is not the ideal housing arrangement for all people in all circumstances."[109] Per Kudlow, a harsh reality: "*...not everyone can afford a home...[s]ome people have to rent.*"[110] And yet, anyone proposing this would be treading on politically incorrect ground.

The subprime problem was not confined to the US, but became evident in other countries such as the UK, which has for years operated an active alternative mortgage market (low income, low documentation, high leverage – basically subprime). The possibility of fraud being perpetrated by both lenders/brokers and borrowers has always existed, but became more prevalent as property prices continued to rise. In testimony, Richard Pym, then-Chairman of troubled UK building society Bradford & Bingley, noted that *"[o]ne of the emerging issues for the mortgage market as a whole is mortgage fraud, and certainly the Financial Services Authority [FSA] thematic review does point out that in some areas of the buy-to-let market there is high fraud...this is also a market that has attracted people with less than honest motivations."*[111] This was affirmed by Turner: *"It is obviously the case that at the end of the boom period...that a set of frauds which had been covered up have been revealed."*[112]

The bottom line is that if the first line of defense – the potential home buyer – is weak, then you may be sure that the voracious real estate agents and greedy bankers will jump in and take full advantage of the situation. If the first line of defense is strong, then the likelihood of mischief declines. Personal responsibility and financial prudence – when lacking – were clearly contributing factors in the saga.

No one saw any evil

And so there is a very brief recap of the disaster – devastating by any measure and, as Greenspan has said *"much broader than anything I could have imagined."*[113] Housing was obviously the nexus of the crisis, to wit former Treasury Secretary Snow's neat summary: *"Throughout the housing finance value chain, many participants contributed to the creation of bad mortgages and the selling of bad securities, apparently feeling secure that they would not be held accountable for their actions. A lender could sell exotic mortgages to homeowners...a trader could sell toxic securities to investors...[a]nd so it was for brokers, realtors, individuals in rating agencies, and other market participants, each maximizing his or her own gain and passing problems on down the line until the system itself collapsed."*[114] Of course, in the end it went well beyond housing, to engulf all manner of assets, institutions, and marketplaces.

Naturally, there are lots of other technical intricacies involved in the whole process, like the effect of fair value accounting rules and the pro-cyclicality of capital buffers, the amount of leverage in the system, and stuff like that.

But getting into the weeds doesn't change the picture described above. And it doesn't change the fact that, apart from a small handful of folks that I'll introduce in Chapter 7, everyone got it wrong: the central bankers, the bankers, the rating agencies, the lobbyists, the politicians, the regulators, and even the man and woman on the street. Snow indicated that "...*what we have witnessed is a breathtaking breakdown in traditional risk management activities in the financial sector, from lax lending practices...to the spread of highly complex and opaque financial products the risks of which weren't properly evaluated by issuers, investors, or rating agencies, all of which combined to create immense risks the scale of which wasn't readily apparent to anyone.*"[115] Christian Noyer, Governor of the Banque de France, summarized it this way: "*That unsustainable process has abruptly come to an end with the burst of the credit bubble. During that period, rating agencies, accounting rules, unregulated and off balance sheet entities as well as very poor risk management all contributed, willingly or unwillingly, to weaken our financial systems. Those weaknesses are at the origin of the crisis. Had they been addressed in due time, most of the problems we are now dealing with could have been avoided.*"[116]

Lamfalussy noted that "*[t]he top management of the banks did not understand what was happening in the banks, and that fact was not understood or not even investigated by the regulators and the supervisors.*"[117] Sanio captured it this way: "*We did not know about the dangerous goings-on that were happening across the Atlantic over the past years. Specifically, this involved US mortgage financers, who were more or less unsupervised, granting more and more loans to individuals unworthy of credit. The extremely great risk resulting from that situation was then mostly passed on, using complex securitisation transactions, to other financial actors who, when purchasing the securities, relied on the ratings given by the rating agencies.*"[118]

Mayo, for his part, was very clear: "*Excesses were condoned. Yes, they were conducted by bankers, but they were also conducted by accountants, regulators, government and consumers....we ignored the long-term risks. And I say we collectively.*"[119] Turner echoed a similar thought: "*a lot of very, very clever people in regulators, in central banks, in banks, in the IMF, did not see this thing coming,*"[120] while German Finance Minister Steinbrueck observed that "*[t]he cause of the crisis was the irresponsible exaggeration of the principle of a free, unrestrained market. This system, which in many ways is inadequately regulated, is now collapsing.... Wall Street and the world will never again be the way they were before the crisis.*"[121] Charlie Munger, Vice Chairman of Berkshire Hathaway and Warren Buffett's right-hand man, was critical of the banking system: "*[it] is a very defective system.... When systems are defective, very good people will start doing things...that are counterproductive.*"[122] But he was also critical of regulators, noting through a charming analogy that "*[w]hen the tiger gets out and starts creating damage, it's insane to blame the tiger, it's the idiot tiger keeper.*"[123]

And so I can assign varying degrees of blame – a sort of rank ordering, with the bankers occupying the seat of (dis)honor. Barclays CEO John Varley noted: *"There are a number of players in this drama. They include governments, central banks and they certainly include banks. If you ask me as I sit here today, 'Is it understandable that the public sentiment is that the banks have the majority of blame?' – in other words, if you think about blame attributable to any particular sector, is the largest particular sector the banks? – I think that is a perfectly understandable and reasonable conclusion."*[124] More broadly, he noted that *"[i]t would be true to say that the financial system did not properly understand the risks."*[125] James Grant, market analyst, said: *"The substitution of collective responsibility for individual responsibility is the fatal story line of modern American finance."*[126] Probably the story line of global finance.

Goldman's Corrigan, for his part, said *"The fact of the matter is that, whether it is Goldman Sachs or the industry as a whole, I think it is perfectly understandable that people are angry."*[127] Andrew Newington, managing partner of a private equity firm, observed that *"[w]hether you're an investment bank, whether you're [RBS's] Fred Goodwin, whether you're a private equity firm or hedge fund, it doesn't matter...[y]ou appear on a placard...with a noose around your neck."*[128] Peter Sands, CEO of Standard Chartered: *"I think the banks have not helped themselves at all. We have been tone deaf and shot ourselves in the foot. We all need a little humility."*[129] And MP John Thurso commented, rather colorfully, what many have probably felt: *"I have to say, 99% of my constituents feel that if a great black hole opened up and every merchant banker in the world and arbitrage trader and credit derivative inventor disappeared down it the world would be a better place and could we get back to Captain Mainwaring running a bank we could trust!"*[130]

So, yes, the bankers were at the heart of this. But make no mistake: no one saw any evil.

2
The US Banks Got It Wrong...

It is easy to be a pundit sifting through the wreckage of the banking system with all the evidence at hand. All the warnings seem so obvious, all the mistakes seem so astounding, and all the motivations seem so wrong. Reality, experienced in the heat of the moment, was rather different. To be sure, warning signals surrounding the housing and financial markets were there, but they weren't necessarily easy to interpret or act on. In the interest of full disclosure, I count myself amongst the group of bankers that got some of it right, but missed a whole lot of things – I certainly didn't expect the crisis to play out with such fury, and I didn't think that the safest, most mundane, nonmortgage assets would suffer. I think Goldman's Blankfein is correct in stating that *"[a]fter the fact, it is easy to be convinced that the signs were visible and compelling."*[1]

That said, as I've embarked on my archaeology expedition I've been a bit surprised about the amount of overconfidence and arrogance that characterized the US bankers in the lead-up to the crisis, and their reactions as events unfolded. It all seems somehow unnecessary and misplaced, and is certainly fair game for discussion and criticism. I've also been surprised at how many mistakes were made – including repeats of the very same ones that led to problems in the 1980s and 1990s: too many "me too" business strategies, too much leverage, too much concentrated risk, too much reliance on faulty risk models, too much disregard for balanced risk/return. Of course, it's okay to make mistakes; everyone screws up. But when those mistakes are pretty much the same ones that caused past crises – when nothing has been strengthened, nothing improved, nothing learned – then that's another story. Shame on the bankers.

Good banking?

Good banking is a combination of strong leadership and a sound, clear, disciplined business strategy built atop undoubted controls – particularly risk management controls, which keep risk exposures prudent and in check. It also depends on robust governance – directors that protect investors, and investors that are vigilant to what's happening with their capital (to wit Richard Lambert of the CBI (the UK Business Lobby): *"supervision is very important, and that means the supervision exercised by boards of directors, by investors, by others who have an interest in the good performance of the system."*)[2]

As it happens, very few banks seem to have exhibited any of these essentials in the lead-up to the explosion – despite some declarations to the contrary. Most seem to have been unaware that anything at all was brewing, meaning they were marching headlong like lemmings toward – and then over – the credit cliff. Executives sanctioned the pursuit of all manner of business, some of it particularly leveraged, particularly risky. Board directors failed to provide any rigorous review of strategies or risks – emerging as rather useless representatives of their shareholders.

And of course compensation was heavily geared, as it always has been on Wall Street and in the City, toward short-term profitability – meaning bankers had every reason to push into complicated and risky areas where the margins are fatter and easy to disguise. Some of these products were ill-conceived and sometimes badly marketed, to wit Goldman's Fabrice Tourre, one of the masterminds behind some very complicated and toxic bonds sold to a range of institutional investors: *"the type of thing which you invent telling yourself: Well, what if we created a 'thing,' which has no purpose, which is absolutely conceptual and highly theoretical and which nobody knows how to price?"*[3] Well, I guess there's some chance you'll get caught out – though not before bagging a big bonus. A further e-mail of his noted that *"I've managed to sell a few Abacus bonds to widows and orphans that I ran into at the airport, apparently these Belgians adore synthetic ABS CDO^2"*[4] – where a synthetic ABS CDO^2 is not something you really want to know about. Pesky e-mails. That deal became the basis of an SEC fraud suit against Goldman.

The bankers also had every incentive to "arbitrage" rules and regulations to create some seemingly low-risk profits. Bafin's Sanio saw it this way: *"Clever financial engineers used the gaps in national and international supervisory regulations, they circumvented Basel I, the body of rules and regulations for banks, and they staged a widescale regulation arbitrage ... [b]anks were able to load up with risks unchecked since they did not have to back this with equity."*[5]

Of course as more banks started chasing the same business, profit margins compressed. So they turned to their age-old standby: leverage. Injecting borrowed funds into any equation boosts profits (and bonuses) but, alas, boosts the chances of a very negative result if things go pear-shaped. Unfortunately, banks weren't the only ones levering up: finance companies, hedge funds, private equity funds, sovereign wealth funds injected their share, meaning the entire financial structure became increasingly fragile after the first half of the decade.

But none of the bankers ultimately had much to lose – most enjoyed (and still enjoy) a free option: heads I win, tails you lose. As Nassim Taleb (writer, hedge fund manager, and "black swan" proponent I shall reintroduce in Chapter 7) has noted, *"When a bank or banker trades, it's not his neck on the line... and like [former Merrill Lynch CEO] Stanley O'Neal, if you follow the strategy you're going to make $160 million, and keep it, even if you blow up. And you'll do it again."*[6]

Naturally, there's nothing wrong with taking risks – as long as a bank is getting properly paid to take those risks, and it doesn't take too much of any particular kind of risk. As you might guess, most failed across both dimensions. Perhaps even more important, however, is the fact that bankers were often not prevented by their risk-management teams from taking stupid risks – a spectacular failure in governance and control. Banking is all about risk-taking, and if it isn't managed properly then problems arise. And problems certainly arose during this crisis.

So why did risk management fail? From my colleagues, former colleagues, and acquaintances in the risk community I hear different stories about why their specific practices failed: in some cases warning signals raised by risk managers to senior managers or executives were ignored or criticized, in other cases risk managers didn't even see the warning signals. In some instances the products being created and traded were just too complicated for everyone to figure out. Back in 2004, writing about Wall Street's various failures, I asked somewhat rhetorically *"[w]hy is risk taking so dangerous? Because it's hard to manage all of the moving parts properly, meaning there are lots of ways to screw up. More, in fact, than the person on Main street knows."*[7] And so it was in the latest crisis: some of the instruments, and their attendant risk factors, were too difficult to figure out. And yet at least some risk managers imagined they could...

And in many cases risk managers blindly followed their risk models, forgetting to inject common sense into the process, and forgetting to measure the extreme tail events properly – blind faith in models came, in part, because regulators had blessed those models. Unfortunately, models are always flawed or limited in some way, so the seeds of destruction were being sown within any bank that subverted common sense in favor of model output, or which refused to consider the possibility of the "black swan" – the rare and devastating event. To his credit, Geithner said in 2006 that *"[w]e should focus more attention on parts of the risk-management process where uncertainty is greatest and materiality of the risks that we can't readily quantify is highest. ... [i]t means more attention on assessing potential exposure in extreme events that lie outside past experience, not just those outside of the recent past."*[8] Unfortunately, very few did. Greenspan proffered a view as well: *"The whole intellectual edifice...collapsed in the summer of last year because the data inputted into the risk management models generally covered only the past two decades, a period of euphoria."*[9] Furthermore, he said: *"The risk management paradigm...harbored a fatal flaw. In the growing state of euphoria, managers at financial institutions, along with regulators...failed to fully comprehend the underlying size, length, and potential impact of the so-called negative tail of the distribution of risk outcomes ..."*[10]

In other words, banks were managing aspects of their risk using very questionable tools. Christopher Whalen of Institutional Risk Analytics noted that *"Whereas financial models were once merely arithmetic expressions of expected cash flows, today in the world of financial economics, models have become vehicles for rampant speculation and outright fraud.... The use of [value-at-risk] type models, including the version imbedded in the Basel II agreement, involves a number of assumptions about risk and outcomes that are speculative."*[11] Charlie McCreevy, UK's Commissioner of Single Markets, put it quite succinctly: *"As to value-at-risk models, suffice to say that we now have inconvertible evidence they are very useful when they don't matter and totally useless when they do matter."*[12] Back to Taleb: *"Banks are now more vulnerable to the Black Swan than ever before with 'scientists' among their staff taking care of exposures."*[13] Tuner: *"This technique, developed in the early 1990s, was not only accepted as standard across the industry, but adopted by regulators as the basis for calculating trading risk and required capital."*[14]

And where was the common sense? Missing in action, apparently. Richard Bookstaber, a long-time risk manager at various hedge funds and investment banks: *"Whatever the limitations of...models, they were not the key culprits in the case of the multi-billion dollar writedowns during the crisis. The large bank inventories were there to be seen; no models or detective work were needed.... [I]t is hard to understand how this elephant in the room was missed, how a risk manager could see inventory grow from a few billion dollars to ten billion dollars and then to thirty or forty billion dollars and not react by forcing that inventory to be brought down ..."*[15]

Regardless of the specific risk-management deficiencies, let me state the obvious: there is no point in having a risk-management function if it doesn't serve to properly control risk. Risk managers are basically goal keepers in suits, and executives, loan officers, and traders are constantly taking shots on goal – they do whatever they can to slip one through. Take enough shots on goal and you are bound to get things in the net. Short seller Jim Chanos (who I'll return to in Chapter 7) summarized the banking community thus: *"Theirs is a record of lax risk management, flawed models, reckless lending, and excessively leveraged investment strategies. In the worst instances, they acted with moral indifference, knowing that what they were doing was flawed, but still willing to pocket the fees and accompanying bonuses.*"[16] Scathing, but unfortunately true. Ken Griffin, head of hedge fund Citadel Investment, had a similar take: "*we have all seen the consequences of taking* imprudent *risk. Failures to understand and manage risk can be severe....*"[17] And, from Stiglitz: "*There is an ongoing dispute: was it poor models (which predicted that events such as those that occurred in 2007–2008 would occur less often than once in the lifetime of the universe), poor risk management, or the off-balance-sheet shenanigans that nearly brought down our banking system and with it the global economy? None of these possibilities puts a positive light on our bankers.*"[18]

So, the tenets of good banking were missing in the lead-up to the crisis. Mind you, all of these shortcomings were evident in the European banks I discuss in the next chapter – the failure was quite universal. With this background in mind, let me now turn to some of the players that helped create and fuel the problems – bearing in mind that this is just a small sampling.

The banks and securities firms

I have to start with Merrill Lynch – as an alumnus it seems like a logical choice. Merrill, once a powerhouse in both investment banking and retail investing, missed the plot entirely. Consider, for instance, that a year and a half before his ouster, Merrill's CEO Stan O'Neal said that "*we have the right people in place, as well as good risk management and controls.*"[19] Well, actually, no. I had the good fortune of working at the bank for nearly 15 years during its heyday in the late 1980s and 1990s, when we spent time and money overhauling the bank's risk processes – many of which were dismantled in the early part of the millennium with a change in executive leadership. Furthermore, a number of the real business experts – those that knew the ins and outs of the most complicated stuff and were voices of sanity – were summarily dismissed by the leadership team as a result of internal politics. This meant the bank entered the pre-2007 crisis period without the full complement of skills and controls it needed.

Still, in early 2007 O'Neal made it seem like controls were robust. He reported that "*[w]e reorganized our institutional fixed income division to better manage risks.*"[20] Wow – lucky for the shareholders – I guess that means if they hadn't reorganized the division to better manage risks, they would have lost not $25b, but $40b? $50b? He went on to say that "*[g]rowth, consistency of returns and capital could be jeopardized if we do not effectively manage risk.... [W]e continually strive to strengthen our global market and credit risk controls and avoid undue concentrations.*"[21] Well, that didn't work too well, did it?

Merrill also blundered strategically, buying First Franklin's (heavily subprime) mortgage business at the top of the market (November 2006) because "*there* is tremendous upside, because the environment for the intermediate and long term should continue to be very constructive,"[22] and to *"provide an additional source of origination for our…securitization and trading platform, enhancing revenue velocity relative to assets and thereby increasing our returns."*[23] More like increasing the velocity of losses and chewing up shareholder's capital.

As the crisis deepened, the bank became a disaster zone, losing billions in 2007 (and many, many, many billions in 2008). Even as Merrill took an $8b loss on its mortgage bond portfolio in October 2007, O'Neal tried to do a soft-shoe shuffle: *"We have tried to capture everything that we can capture at this point, in the market…I cannot tell you what the market trajectory might be from here, but as of the date that we took these markdowns, and even looking at it as we sit here today and observing the general environment, we are comfortable that we have marked these positions conservatively."*[24] The same line from Jeff Edwards, CFO: *"…we took substantial markdowns here. We think that reflects conservative assumptions, again."*[25] In fact, these initial write-downs were just the beginning.

In spite of the losses, O'Neal remained aloof: *"I'm not going to talk around the fact that there were some mistakes that were made."*[26] Analyst Mayo observed: *"O'Neal increased risk and got paid based on the good times, but losses related to his decisions didn't become apparent until this year…. [I]n a period of just three weeks, Merrill disclosed $3 billion in additional write-downs."*[27] That speaks poorly of both management and risk control.

Merrill's old guard drew out the long knives as O'Neal's stumbled. While the bank had long been an organization that took care of its own (for better or worse, though in retrospect it sure seems like for better), O'Neal fundamentally changed that during his tenure as CEO, noting that *"the Mother Merrill, cradle-to-grave thing isn't possible to do. It's not even smart to do."*[28] And, later, *"To the extent that it is paternalistic and materialistic, I don't think that is healthy…. I guess there is something instinctive in me that rebels against that."*[29] As I noted above, O'Neal jettisoned hundreds of very senior executives and thousands of junior staffers as part of Merrill's "makeover." Win Smith, one-time head of international operations, noted that O'Neal *"got rid of people with hundreds and hundreds of years of experience. When you get rid of people who have gone through problems in the past, you increase the probability that a mistake is going to happen again."*[30] In fact, Smith was right.

The game was up for O'Neal in late 2007: years of piling on risk in a mad search for profits and market share had boomeranged. But, unlike mere mortals that get fired when they screw up, the board let him "retire" so he could keep all his stock and options – valued at $160m+ at the time (though considerably less as the crisis dragged on). Even as he walked out the door O'Neal insisted that all of his *"efforts have enabled us to make Merrill Lynch a much more competitive and international company capable of realizing the full potential of a brand that is synonymous with excellence and client service."*[31] I don't think so. He also added that *"[t]he company has provided me with opportunities that I never could have imagined growing up, culminating with my leadership of the company over the past five years."*[32] Lucky for the shareholders, right? In the end, it is unfortunate that O'Neal's declaration from 2004 didn't come to pass: *"No big mistakes. We cannot afford lapses in judgment…in decision making. We cannot let our clients or shareholders down."*[33] On that score, he failed miserably.

Exit Stan, enter ex-Goldman and New York Stock Exchange boss John Thain, who swung into action: *"we have moved quickly to strengthen our balance sheet, capital position and risk management"*[34] even as the firm announced a full year 2007 net loss of $8.7b from its mortgage businesses and its unsold leveraged loans. He stressed that *"[o]ver the last few weeks we have substantially strengthened the firm's liquidity and balance sheet."*[35] Not quite! Another early observation was that *"credit risk management was separate from market risk management, and that doesn't make sense.…We are combining market and credit risk."*[36] Also, "Merrill had a risk committee. It just didn't function."[37] His conclusion: *"[this] must never happen again. Since my arrival, we have moved to restructure risk management.…I have also bolstered our risk management process to include a committee of senior executives, combining credit and risk management functions, which now reports directly to me every week."*[38] Sidebar: since all of this brings back vivid memories of my own days let me say that Merrill reorganized its risk function before the turn of the millennium by – you guessed it, combining credit and market risk, creating risk governance committees, and having the chief risk manager report to the CEO. In other words, Thain was simply going back to the organizational model that O'Neal had sought to dismantle a few years earlier. What a waste.

And what about Merrill's board? What was their view of the bank's mortgage-related risk? According to Ann Reese, head of the board's audit committee, the *"board initially didn't realize that prices of [collateralized debt obligations] were linked to the U.S. housing market…. [F]or reasons that we have subsequently explored, there was not a sense that these triple-A securities should be included in the overall exposure to residential real estate."*[39] Minimum qualifications for board directors?

Curiously there seemed to be little recognition within the bank as to the real extent of the problems – either that, or someone in investor relations opted for platitudes. Why else start the 2008 Annual Report with the declaration that *"[w]e enter 2008 from a position of strength and optimism"*[40]? Why would Thain say in January that *"I don't think we are struggling"*[41] or in April that *"[w]e have plenty of capital going forward"*[42]? Did the executive team really not have a grip on how bad things were? Things remained rocky during the second quarter– the bank continued to post more losses and was forced to raise capital several times, management credibility suffering with each new capital call. The end was near.

On the same weekend of Lehman's demise (below), Merrill's board agreed to a quick-fire sale to Bank of America – a deal that later became the subject of lots of fingerpointing between Thain and Bank of America's CEO Ken Lewis, and the subject of regulatory scrutiny. Ex-post, Thain insisted the sale was the right thing to do: "*[n]o one knows for sure if Merrill would have survived the week that followed, but the risk was too high not to do something.*"[43] He also noted that the full buyout by Bank of America he recommended to the board was ultimately preferable to a minority sale to Goldman, which was also being contemplated: "*When Bank of America offered $29 a share on Sunday afternoon, it was clear to me that was the best thing for our shareholders…now, for me personally, it might have been better. But my job was to protect the shareholders.*"[44] Well, at least he took one for the little guys. All of this was short lived, of course, because following a heated row over bonuses, expensive office redecoration, and questions regarding the massive write-downs Merrill took post-acquisition, Thain was shown the exit and Lewis tightened his grip – for awhile. Once in Bank of America's arms, Merrill reported fourth quarter losses of nearly $16b – including a massive $28b in the markets and trading areas. So much for O'Neal's "reorganization" of the fixed income areas to "better manage risks" and Thain's attempts to "bolster risk management processes."

While I'm on the subject, let me turn to Bank of America (B of A). During the crisis period the mighty retail bank sought to capitalize on both the Merrill opportunity as well as the Countrywide acquisition (more of which below), despite the fact that its own books were chock-full of risk. But one wouldn't necessarily know that from reading the 2006 annual report, which noted that "*[w]e believe we are in a good position to weather any credit issues we currently see on the horizon…and as our risk managers analyze information…in ever more sophisticated ways, we can grow our portfolio without significantly increasing our risk.*"[45] Well that sounds like a neat trick, but in my experience mostly smoke and mirrors. Though B of A managed to keep its overall losses to "only" several billion during the 2007–8 season, CEO Ken Lewis was unable to weather the storm – difficult to say what eventually forced him to step down, but a good guess would be the whole affair surrounding the Merrill acquisition: sloppy at best, something more nefarious at worst. In the aftermath it became clear that the bank had performed no in-depth due diligence (only 25 hours worth), had no real understanding of just how toxic Merrill's books were (as noted, Merrill revealed $16b of losses in December 2008, far more than Lewis or the bank's board had expected), and apparently had no understanding of an agreement to pay billions in bonuses to Merrill employees, even as that bank was blowing a hole in B of A's own bottom line.

Lewis tried to back out of the Merrill deal in December 2008, but was "encouraged" not to by the US government. In congressional testimony held in June 2009 Lewis noted that *"in mid-December...I became aware of significant, accelerating losses at Merrill Lynch and we contacted officials at the Treasury and Federal Reserve to inform them...we considered declaring a 'material adverse change' [MAC]...which...can allow an acquirer to avoid consummating a deal. Treasury and Federal Reserve representatives asked us to delay any such action and expressed significant concerns about the systemic consequences and risk to Bank of America of pursuing such a course."*[46] Sounds a bit like a threat. Hank Paulson commented that *"all public officials involved, including Mr. Bernanke and me, believed that the failure to consummate the merger would likely create immediate financial market instability, would threaten the viability of both firms, and would call into serious question the judgment of Bank of America's leadership."*[47] Bernanke, for his part, indicated that *"[t]hese actions were taken under highly unusual circumstances in the face of grave threats to our financial system and our economy."*[48] In the event, Treasury and the Fed won the day, persuading Lewis not to scuttle the acquisition – in exchange for additional financial support. Bair of the FDIC: *"The FDIC's Board ultimately was persuaded that BOA's condition presented a systemic risk, and that the ring fence transaction would mitigate that risk – and the risk to the Deposit Insurance Fund – in a cost effective manner."*[49]

Messy times, indeed, which would only get messier for Lewis. Despite his hesitation in December, Lewis went on to say *"[t]he failure of Merrill Lynch, particularly on the heels of Lehman's failure, could have caused systemic havoc...I am proud that Bank of America had the strength to step forward."*[50] Then why the hesitation? Why force the Fed and Treasury to backstop? And why didn't B of A execs know more about what was going on at Merrill in October or November? Representative Dennis Kucinich, member of the House Oversight Committee, was troubled: *"Due to the secretive and unaccountable conduct of the Fed throughout its interventions addressing the current financial crisis, many questions about the Bank of America–Merrill Lynch deal and bailout have, until today, remained unanswered."*[51] Furthermore, he said, *"we discovered that top officials at the Federal Reserve had come to the conclusion that Bank of America knew or should have known in mid-November about the mounting losses that ultimately led them to appeal to the U.S. Government for a rescue."*[52] In the aftermath of the deal Allfriend, a senior executive of the Federal Reserve Bank, noted that Lewis *"is worried about stockholder lawsuits; knows they did not do a good job of due diligence and the issues facing the company are finally hitting home and he is worried about his own job after cutting loose lots of very good people."*[53] Well, Lewis finally retired in September 2009 about 2 months before the SEC filed civil fraud charges against him over the Merrill affair.

B of A veteran Brian Moynihan took over for the embattled Lewis, providing additional color on the inside scene: *"[a]t Bank of America Securities...trading* *account losses were $5.9 billion in 2008...[t]hese losses were significant, but not debilitating, and we never experienced a liquidity crisis."* Like others, he admitted, *"we didn't do the kind of testing you actually do in a trading book saying what if housing goes down 40 percent and test what your thought would be irrespective of the probability of just how you protect your firm."*[54] More importantly, *"the greatest risk came from our acquisition of Merrill Lynch...suffice it to say that as losses at Merrill Lynch accelerated in mid-December 2008 due to an unexpected downturn in market conditions, Bank of America grew concerned and considered abandoning the transaction and not proceeding to close."*[55] Yet another big bank that got it wrong – on multiple fronts.

Next up is Citigroup, the financial supermarket that emerged as one of the most striking examples of poor controls, weak leadership, and questionable strategy. Buiter, formerly at LSE and eventually an economist at Citigroup, said of his future employer that it was *"a conglomeration of worst-practice from across the financial spectrum."*[56] Let me step back to 2004, when Chuck Prince, newly minted CEO, observed that *"clients want to be with a bank that's been here for 200 years, I know we'll be here the next 200 years."*[57] Perhaps...but only through the grace of US taxpayers (who collectively took a big stake in Citi in 2009). In the 2006 annual report, Prince was saying that *"I feel good about the progress we are making."*[58] And, *"as we look to 2007, we believe the credit environment around the world, with some exceptions, is good".*[59] Oops. In fact, lots of these comments were just a veneer covering all manner of problems.

Of course, Prince will really be remembered for his colorful, and very badly timed, statement that reflected the fact that the bank seemed to have no clue: *"When the music stops, in terms of liquidity, things will be complicated. But as long as the music is playing, you've got to get up and dance. We're still dancing."*[60] Unfortunately, the music stopped playing just a few weeks later, by which time Citi was fully loaded with all kinds of leveraged risk that it could no longer get rid of. As the first leg of the crisis deepened Prince reflected some bravado – he remained the picture of calm and cool, noting that *"[w]e see a lot of people on the Street who are scared. We are not scared. We are not panicked. We are not rattled. Our team has been through this before."*[61] In fact, Citi should have been scared – very scared – as they had every conceivable type of adverse risk exposure, in size: the bank had a $2 trillion balance sheet, plus loads of additional things off balance sheet.

Even though the bank had already accumulated lots of toxic assets through the middle of the decade, it continued to buy residential mortgages, including many that were apparently substandard. Richard Bowen, a senior underwriter at Citi, testified that *"[i]n mid-2006 I discovered that over 60% of these mortgages purchased and sold were defective. Because Citi had given reps and warrants to the investors that the mortgages were not defective, the investors could force Citi to repurchase many billions of dollars of these defective assets. This situation represented a large potential risk to the shareholders of Citigroup.*"[62] These concerns were e-mailed to executive board member Robert Rubin, CFO Gary Crittenden and others in 2007: *"The reason for this urgent email concerns breakdowns of internal controls and resulting significant but possibly unrecognized financial losses existing within our organization."*[63] Management later claimed to have acted on that e-mail, though by then it was obviously way too late.

By the third quarter of 2007 Citi was on the ropes, but Prince was apparently unable to gauge the bank's true risk and P&L position. And yet, he was sticking with Citi's strategy: *"... no one can be happy with the results in our fixed-income business or with the results that relate to that. But I think if you are able to look at the other parts of our business, if you look at the strategic plan that we are executing on, I think any fair-minded person would say that strategic plan is working."*[64] What about US home lending? What about its hedge fund and asset management operations? What about the Japanese joint venture? In fact, the strategy was collapsing.

After pre-announcing a third quarter loss of around $3b, Prince had to amend his estimates just weeks later by reporting red ink equal to four times that amount. That was it for Chuck, who turned in his resignation. Prince Alwaleed, the Saudi billionaire and Citi's largest shareholder, was understandably furious: *"You can't go publicly and say that our losses are around $3 billion post-tax and then all of the sudden add another $11 billion loss."*[65] He was understandably irate: *"This is unacceptable....[m]y backing was withdrawn immediately. You should never commit to something that you can't deliver. Never."*[66] And, of course, he was quite justified in saying that *"I am extremely disappointed with Chuck Prince and I believe that Chuck Prince let down the shareholders completely. Citibank did not conduct itself in the right way. The risk-management situation was very wrong at Citibank."*[67] But on one point Alwaleed was mistaken: *"Citibank will withstand everything. Frankly speaking, you can imagine the strength of this company... this company can withstand a lot of pressure and a lot of stress because its equity is so big."*[68] In fact, Citi's equity was razor-thin and the bank was teetering on the edge.

Prince later expounded on the whole disaster: *"What I can tell you, with the luxury and benefit of hindsight, is that we, like many other experienced members of the industry, failed to recognize that there was a real possibility of the kind of catastrophic residential real estate crash that our country has experienced.... I regret that I and my colleagues did not see that coming, but we did not."*[69] One of the main black holes was Citi's $43b portfolio of super senior mortgage bonds – which eventually led to a staggering $30b of losses. Prince said: *"it is hard for me to fault the traders who made the decisions to retain these positions on Citi's books. After all, having $40 billion of AAA+-rated paper on the balance sheet of a $2 trillion company would* *typically not raise a concern."*[70] Furthermore, he said, *"[s]itting here today, that belief looks pretty unwise. But I think at the time, people believed that the structuring process had gotten to a point where that top level would be immune from the problems that were being seen at the lower levels."*[71] Never mind, said Phil Angelides in his 2010 questioning of Prince: *"You were either pulling the levers or asleep at the switch."*[72]

Rubin expressed a similar view from his vantage point as executive board director and "special advisor" within the bank: *"while the Board required and received extensive financial and risk reporting I do not recall knowing before September 2007 that these super senior positions had been retained...ultimately Citi took nearly $30b of losses on its...positions."*[73] And what did the bank's then-head of risk, David Bushnell, say? *"Clearly, Citi and virtually all other market participants failed to anticipate the dramatic and unprecedented decline in the housing market that occurred in 2007 and 2008. Risk models, which primarily use history as their guide, assumed that any annual decline in real estate values would not exceed the worst case historical precedent. At the most basic level, Citi did not contemplate the possibility of an unprecedented, across-the-board, nation-wide collapse in real estate prices."*[74] True enough...but why hold $43b of complex mortgage securities (along with lots of other stuff)? Maybe $43b of Treasuries or gilts or other government bonds, but $43b of complex mortgage securities?

Enter new CEO Vikram Pandit, formerly of Morgan Stanley and his own hedge fund (which he had sold to Citi for a pile). In his inaugural statements as CEO, Pandit indicated that he was *"aggressively building a new risk culture at Citi. My goal is to have the best risk management in the business."*[75] Admirable, of course, but that didn't do much for all of the legacy businesses and risk positions: its investment bank swung from a $3b profit to a $7b loss – just the beginning of the bank's net losses, which reached a whopping $28b in 2008. In a slight tip o' the hat to Prince, Rubin and some of the other Citibankers, Pandit made note of all the garbage he found when he took over: *"we inherited many high risks that were not essential to our core business...resources...that did not create enough value for our clients...or shareholders...and an outsized cost structure and inefficient technology systems."*[76] And, later: *"What went wrong? What went wrong is we had tremendous concentration in the sense we put a lot of our money to work against U.S. real estate...in a size that was probably larger than what we ought to have done."*[77] Sounds like a recipe for disaster. Pandit also observed in retrospect: *"Given Citi's size and global reach, and its exposure to subprime-related asset classes, the systemic factors at the root of the financial crisis, and their confluence, combined to impact Citi's financial performance dramatically."*[78]

Like his colleagues on the Street, Pandit made clear in 2008 that the bank hadn't done a good job in looking at the real downside: *"...then say, okay, the U.S. real estate has almost always gone up and frankly since the Depression, it really* hasn't gone down much. *So if you're risk managing, and think about real estate saying, oh, it could really go down. How much do you think would be a prudent amount for a risk manager to think about how much it could go down, 5 percent maybe? Ten percent ? Fifteen percent?...How should I stress them? Well, let's assume housing prices are down 15%. Let's even – let's suppose if they had done that, you'd still have had a problem, because housing prices are down a lot more than that..."*[79] Yes, like 40%+.

In the event, Citi's losses had become so large that it was forced to take an initial helping of $25b from the US Government capital buffet in November 2008, another $20b at the end of the year, and then came back for a $300b government guarantee in early 2009. When all was said and done US taxpayers wound up owning a 1/3 stake in Citi so that it wouldn't go down the tubes and create more seismic waves. Death of the financial supermarket concept? Probably. At least for the next five years, when the "strategic diversification" cycle will begin anew. In the aftermath, King had some observations: *"Who were the people running Citibank? Some of the cleverest and brightest people you can imagine, with a wealth of experience in Wall Street, in government, in investment banking, in academia and in emerging market debt crises. They knew a lot about what had happened in the past. It was not in their interests to take risks that would turn catastrophic later on. They did not set out to destroy Citibank but they were as aware as any regulator of what they were doing and what the risks were, yet the outcome was a disaster for the bank."*[80]

Let me now move on to Morgan Stanley, where CEO John Mack and his team were busy, in the middle of the decade, ramping up risk-taking, perhaps in a bid to emulate the boys downtown – Goldman Sachs. In fact, Stanley's 2005 annual report proclaimed that *"[w]e are masters of complexity,"*[81] and *"[w]e are experienced risk managers."*[82] Well...maybe not. A year later the firm was crowing that *"[w]e have enhanced our risk profile...[through] proactive, measured risk-taking"*[83] which in my mind is risk-speak for "we're taking lots more risk and crossing our fingers."

As it happens, Stanley was no different from any of the other big banks: in late 2007 it suffered $9.4b of losses from its mortgage bonds and other credit positions (including $7.8b from a pure proprietary, rather than client-driven, position). Mack later noted that *"[t]hese early losses were a powerful wake-up call for Morgan Stanley, and we began moving aggressively in late 2007 and early 2008 to adapt our business to the rapidly changing environment – reducing leverage, trimming the balance sheet, raising private capital, and further strengthening risk management."*[84] Nice, but again rather late.

Further losses came in 2008 but the bank dodged the proverbial bullet just as Lehman was collapsing by converting to a bank holding company, which allowed it to tap the Federal Reserve for more money as needed. Mack eventually conceded that *"[w]hile the Firm's residential mortgage related business was not as large as some of our peers, Morgan Stanley participated in the markets for residential mortgage-backed securities and collateralized debt obligations, and suffered losses as a result."*[85] In a rather colorful description of the bank's risk situation, he observed that *"[w]e did eat our own cooking, and we choked on it, so – we – we kept positions, and it did not work out."*[86] In the cold light of dawn Mack would realize that *"[t]here is no question that we did not put enough resources into our risk management system"*[87] and admitted during a grilling by a special congressional panel inquiring as to the work done in stress-testing for a drop in the housing market that *"that was one we missed."*[88] So much for "experienced risk managers" and "masters of complexity."

Over at Bear Stearns, once upon a time Wall Street's premier mortgage bond house, the scene was no different: the bank had lots of risk on its books which it really wasn't managing too well. In fact, in mid-2007 two Bear hedge funds lost $1.7b, providing a good clue that all was not well in the mortgage market. While the bank bailed them out, it eventually had to wind them down at a big loss. This stumble was significant, as Bear was widely regarded as the best mortgage trader on the Street – if they couldn't get it right, could anyone? Unfortunately, the bank suffered within its core operations as well. During the third quarter the bank reported net losses of $700m, and followed with another $1.9b loss in the fourth quarter – which really unsettled the market. Clearly, there were problems with risk management. Still Jimmy Cayne, Bear's long-time CEO, defended his risk team: *"Bear Stearns had a strong culture of risk management."*[89] So did Warren Spector, Bear's president at the time: *"In my opinion, Bear Stearns' risk management practices were robust and effective."*[90] But Alan Schwartz, Cayne's eventual successor as CEO, was more guarded: *"I believe that we did not foresee the extent to which housing prices had been driven to unsustainable levels. We…relied on the belief that the market for highly rated tranches of structured securities, including those supported by Fannie Mae and Freddie Mac mortgages, would remain liquid."*[91]

While Cayne was considered a strong leader during much of his 14-year tenure in the top spot, he was also criticized for being a bit too wrapped up in bridge tournaments and golf outings even as the markets were collapsing and Bear was riding the hot rails to hell. Schwartz defended his boss, noting that *"[a]nyone who thinks that Jimmy Cayne isn't fired up every day and ready to get to work hasn't been living in my world."*[92] Still, that didn't really alter the sense that leadership was lacking. Of course, it didn't help that Bear's previous CEO, Alan Greenberg, was critical of his former underling: *"Jimmy was not interested in my point of view. He was a one-man show – he didn't listen to anybody."*[93] In the event, after the hedge fund fiasco and large losses from continuing operations, Cayne saw the writing on the wall and retired at the end of 2007 – leaving Schwartz in charge of a sinking ship.

Unfortunately, Schwartz's observation in early 2008 that *"people realize that we have righted our ship and our businesses are off to a strong year,"*[94] was way off the mark. In fact, I'm not sure that anyone realized that. Liquidity pressures mounted during the first quarter, and got so bad that Schwartz had to go on CNBC in early March to defend the firm's cash position: *"[p]art of the problem is that when speculation starts in a market that has a lot of emotion in it, and people are concerned about the volatility, then people will sell first and ask questions later, and that creates its own momentum."*[95] Indeed, liquidity proved to be Bear's Achilles heel and by mid-March the situation had become critical.

Cayne described the liquidity pressures this way: *"In view of Bear Stearns' leading role in the mortgage industry, these developments gave rise to market uncertainty about the firm. We believed that this concern was unjustified and that the firm had ample capital and liquidity."*[96] But once the market felt uneasy, the risk of liquidity being withdrawn rapidly became very real. Jim Chanos, head of short-selling fund Kynikos (who I'll come back to in Chapter 7) observed that *"[w]hat everyone missed in Bear Stearns was [that] the run preceded the rumors ... money was leaving cash and margin accounts."*[97] Cayne went on: *"brokerage customers withdrew assets and counterparties refused to roll over repo facilities. These events resulted in a dramatic loss of liquidity. The market's loss of confidence, even though it was unjustified and irrational, became a self-fulfilling prophecy."*[98]

Then-CFO Sam Molinaro saw it this way: *"The life blood of an investment bank is liquidity ... we worked to develop a liquidity strategy that would ensure the continuity of our funding during periods of market stress."*[99] That was obviously a flawed strategy, because it didn't allow Bear to avoid the liquidity squeeze. And what of the final days? Molinaro: *"By Thursday evening, these rumors, which were magnified by press reports, had escalated into a panic. In this panic, an increasing number of prime brokerage clients began to request that their available cash and securities be moved to other brokers. Moreover ... a significant proportion of our repo counterparties informed us that they would no longer lend to us ...."*[100] Schwartz: *"... there was, simply put, a run on the bank."*[101] Since Bear was an investment bank, it had no access to the Fed as lender of last resort. Curtains.

Enter JP Morgan, which bought the bank for $10 a share – a bargain considering that the US Government provided a backstop guarantee on part of the firm's toxic balance sheet. Cayne called the deal *"a marriage of convenience that was supported by the Fed ... The outcome was the best that could be anticipated when the world ended."*[102] Dimon, for his part, said: *"We were not buying a house, we were buying a house on fire."*[103] The deal allowed Bear to avoid bankruptcy, meaning there was no additional blow to the system from creditor losses. But it destroyed the wealth of stockholders, many of them employees. Cayne ultimately admitted that *"[t]he efforts we made to strengthen the firm were reasonable and prudent, although in hindsight they proved inadequate."*[104] And, further: *"I was shocked beyond belief that we failed."*[105] Schwartz observed that *"I just never frankly understood or dreamed it could happen as rapidly as it did."*[106] A Wall Street nameplate gone.

Goldman Sachs has been, and remains, the powerhouse of Wall Street – a dominant force that has navigated previous crises rather adroitly, taking advantage of dislocations to enrich employees (and, since going public in 2000, investors). Its success has also historically been a magnet for those who can't stand the billions it makes and pays out to its employees and investors. Corrigan: *"...I think the public is pretty damned angry at financial institutions generally, pretty much around the world. I do not think it is unique to Goldman Sachs. Goldman Sachs probably have been disproportionately singled out. Part of that is because it has been quite successful in both managing the crisis and in its performance after the crisis."*[107] Of course, the public was also kind of angry when it started reading internal e-mails related to Goldman's selling of some risky mortgage products.

Still, everyone is fallible, and in the lead-up to the crisis, even the gurus got it wrong. In its 2006 annual report the firm noted that *"we have been committing increasing amounts of capital in many of our businesses and generally maintain large trading and investing positions."*[108] Same thing in 2007. By the time the crisis hit there was a tacit acknowledgement that they missed it, with CEO Blankfein noting that *"[i]n the day-to-day management of our business, identifying a bubble and calling its exact end is difficult."*[109] So, even mighty Goldman stumbled during this crisis – proving it was as vulnerable as the rest of the pack. Blankfein admitted: *"[W]hen conditions deteriorate, losses are unavoidable. And in the course of the year, we were not immune to them."*[110] Furthermore, he said, *"we were going to bed every night with more risk than any responsible manager should want to have, either for our business or for the system as a whole – risk, not certainty."*[111] Blankfein noted in the aftermath that *"[I]n late 2006, we began to experience losses in our daily residential mortgage-related products P&L as we marked down the value of our inventory...[w]e certainly did not know the future of the residential housing market in the first half of 2007 any more than we can predict the future of markets today."*[112] He also noted that *"...we didn't dodge the mortgage mess. We lost money, then made more than we lost because of shorts. Also, it's not over, so who knows how it will turn out ultimately."*[113] When called to testify, Blankfein insisted that *"[w]e didn't have massive short against the housing market and we certainly did not bet against our clients."*[114]

As if to defend the losses, there was a bit of a feeble attempt to pin it all on client business: *"Because we are in the business of assuming risk on behalf of our clients, we know we will have losses from time to time."*[115] Mark me down as skeptical on that one. Just a guess, but I'm thinking that just a little bit of that risk-taking (and the attendant losses) came not from client flows, but from pure prop plays? Nothing wrong with that, but why not say it like it is? In the event, more severe losses emerged during 2008, with Blankfein noting that *"[r]isk management will come to define the events of 2008 and beyond. Our firm certainly didn't get everything right and there are some decision we would prefer to take back."*[116] – probably those that caused record losses of $3b in corporate bonds and equities, $4b in principal investments and equity stakes, and $3b in commercial and residential mortgages. Sorry, Lloyd, no mulligans.

Goldman, like Morgan Stanley, converted to a bank holding company just as Lehman was sinking; Corrigan explained the hasty decision this way: *"...there was a joint decision by the Treasury and the Federal Reserve that they concluded that it was in the interest of the cause of greater financial stability that Goldman Sachs and Morgan Stanley were given the opportunity to become bank holding companies, which did bring with it at the time the potential...to draw on Fed discount window facilities...."*[117] As former Fed chief Paul Volcker noted, *"Goldman Sachs is a wonderful investment bank, has a very proud history. They're very proud of their risk management techniques. They're proud of their trading prowess...they lived for decades and decades very nicely until 2008 when they suddenly got a banking license in extremis...."*[118]

But perhaps even more important than the losses the bank suffered was the reputational blow it took at the hands of politicians and the public: Goldman is, to Main Street, the personification of all that is wrong with banking and bankers, and this became particularly true once the bank resumed its bonus payment scheme in 2009. All fair in the eyes of Blankfein, who claimed to the chagrin of many that he was *"doing God's work."*[119] And, unfortunately for Goldman, just as some of the anger was subsiding, the SEC slapped the bank with a fraud suit for mishandling the sale of the mortgage-related bond deal I mentioned at the beginning of the chapter – which reopened all the wounds and set the stage for another round of back and forth.

Jamie Dimon, ex-Citi executive, guided JP Morgan Chase through the early part of the storm in reasonably good shape. But in the end even his bank was tripped up by the same problems, posting billions in losses from various portfolios. In fact, the timing of some of the bank's strategic moves was rather unfortunate, as a successful partnership between the home lending and investment banking divisions led to the creation of even more mortgage-related "stuff." The 2006 Annual Report reflects a top-ticking of the market: *"our Investment Bank moved up several places in league-table rankings for mortgages... [w]e now believe we have the opportunity to be one of America's best mortgage companies."*[120] How unfortunate. With regard to risk management, Dimon apparently had no particularly worries, saying *"[w]e think we did a fairly good job overall."*[121] The bank may have done a good job in a calm environment, but what about in a nasty one? Had it been tested? As it happens – no. To the bank's credit, they were already hinting at things to come: *"We do not know exactly what will occur or when, but bad things do happen."*[122] But knowing this, shouldn't the bank have taken some preemptive action?

Fast forward 12 months: with the crisis now in its first stages, Dimon declared in the 2007 letter to shareholders that *"subprime mortgages...were more dangerous than we thought"*[123] ($1.4b of losses in 2007 alone), and threw in the usual *"we will redouble our efforts to ensure this doesn't happen again."*[124] Leveraged loans, which weren't even highlighted in previous management letters as an area of concern, caused another $1.3b of losses, *"which makes us very unhappy."*[125] Dimon and company would be really, really unhappy in 2008 when the investment bank's leveraged loan and mortgage books generated another $10b in write-downs and its consumer lending operation dropped a further $2b. All of this red ink was flowing while the bank was trying to digest Bear as well as Washington Mutual (WaMu, a large West Coast subprime lender that JP bought for $1.9b after the FDIC forced it into receivership – a point which then-CEO Kerry Killinger decried: *"[F]or those that were part of the inner circle and were 'too clubby to fail' the benefits were obvious. For those outside the club, the penalty was severe."*[126]). Despite running a large mortgage operation, Dimon eventually had to admit that his risk-management team had failed to do the mega-stress tests that might have revealed problem areas: *"[W]e didn't stress test housing prices going down by 40%."*[127] Oh well, no one else did either. Further: *"We missed the ferocity and magnitude that was lurking underneath."*[128] In fact, just another bank that got it wrong.

Let me now turn briefly to Countrywide Financial, a West Coast-based subprime mortgage specialist (#1 market share in loan originations) that was run by Angelo Mozilo, an individual whose name would become synonymous with political influence-peddling (i.e., "Friends of Angelo" loans for politicians, more of which in Chapter 6). Since Countrywide specialized in lending to individuals with weak credit standing it should have been aware of the leading edge of problems as the real estate market peaked in 2006 and then started to slide. Unfortunately, it wasn't, meaning it was highly exposed to the downturn. Still, Mozilo attempted to defend the bank's subprime business: *"...here's the reality of it. It's our money. We're lending the money....We never make a loan where we think that we're creating a situation where we couldn't be paid back. We try to underwrite these loans prudently.... there's no advantage to Countrywide or to any mortgage company to foreclose on people. We lose on those."*[129] Unless home values have gone up – which they did, for years. Though Countrywide was a major subprime player, Mozilo indicated he was uncomfortable with some of the products being offered to consumers: *"In all my years in the business I have never seen a more toxic prduct [sic]. It's not only subordinated to the first, but the first is subprime. In addition, the [credit scores] are below 600, below 500 and some below 400."*[130] That said, he was a strong advocate of "no downpayment" loans, commenting in 2003 that downpayments were *"nonsense,"*[131] *"credit score requirements still much too high"*[132] and suggesting that *"[t]he only way we can have a better society is to make sure those who don't have a house have the opportunity to get one."*[133] Lovely.

But Countrywide's heavily subprime business model couldn't withstand credit losses from a plunging real estate market. As a prelude to an eventual acquisition by B of A that saved it from bankruptcy, Countrywide was forced to accept a $2b infusion in August 2007, which Mozilo spun as a positive: *"[I] think it's a win-win situation for us. Bank of America, world class firm...to come into Countrywide, do extensive due diligence...[and] want to invest $2 billion is great endorsement for what we believe we have at Countrywide....gives us [a] vote of confidence in this environment when everybody was in a panic, things being said about Countrywide which were not true. So from our viewpoint that is priceless endorsement for us."*[134] Actually, the nasty untruths to which Mozilo alluded turned out to be quite true, and B of A kind of blew it, getting saddled with an investment that would become a bigger headache. Mozilo noted at the same time *"I can tell you there is no more chance for bankruptcy today for Countrywide than six months ago, two years ago, when the stock was $45 a share. We are a very solid company."*[135] Actually, no – 5 months later the bank would be on the brink. As Countrywide's performance continued to deteriorate (to wit, its mortgage delinquency rose 900% between 2007 and 2008), B of A had to save the company in January 2008 in a $4b deal, if only to preserve its original (seemingly unwise) $2b investment. It then had to add $8.7b to its legal provisions to settle fraud charges filed by 11 state attorneys general. So, B of A added significantly to its mortgage operations, but at what price? Mozilo, for his part, was ultimately charged by the SEC with fraud.

Mega-disasters

While all of the institutions I mentioned above missed the crisis and suffered very heavy losses as a result, let me now turn to the two that were the real disasters – the two that almost brought the global financial system to its knees. I refer, of course, to Lehman Brothers and AIG.

Lehman has the unfortunate distinction of being the one major investment bank that paid the ultimate price during the crisis. As I pointed out in Chapter 1, the bank was allowed to fail (unlike others before and after, which received some form of assistance), becoming the catalyst that forced governments the world over to move rapidly into crisis mode to save the global financial system. In fact, Lehman's collapse focused everyone's attention on just how close we really were to the precipice.

Since being spun off from the American Express combine in the 1990s Lehman had become a bond powerhouse, expanding swiftly and profitably under the leadership of CEO Dick Fuld and competing successfully in fixed income with the likes of Goldman, Merrill, and Stanley. Unfortunately, in the years leading up to the crisis Lehman had also started delving more deeply into commercial mortgages and real estate – things that were both riskier and far less liquid. Still, Fuld noted mid-decade that *"we don't warehouse this stuff, we sell."*[136] But somewhere along the line Lehman's salesmen obviously forgot to sell, as the bank was fully loaded with unsold mortgages and mortgage bonds as the crisis loomed. In fact, Fuld changed his tune a bit in 2007: *"Do we have some stuff on the books that would be tough to get rid of? Yes…Am I worried about it? No. If you have some repricing of these things will we lose some money? Yes. Is it going to kill us? Of course not."*[137] Hmmm.

Though 2007 was challenging for Lehman, the turning point for the bank came during the second quarter of 2008, when the bank looked particularly inept: new CFO Erin Callan (once touted by the *Wall Street Journal* as *"a galvanizing force…a finance chief who topples much of the conventional wisdom about CFOs"*)[138] was unable to properly or adequately address concerns about the bank's enormous mortgage portfolio, which had curiously suffered only modest write-downs. This stumbling caused short-sellers to criticize Fuld, Callan, and the rest of the management team. David Einhorn of Greenlight Capital, who at the time held short positions in Lehman, stated in an April 2008 speech: *"There is good reason to question Lehman's fair value calculations.…Lehman could have taken many billions more in write-downs than it did.…I suspect that greater transparency on these valuations would not inspire market confidence."*[139] The bank reported net losses of $2.8b in the second quarter – bad, to be sure, but not horrific, leading some to wonder whether the bank was taking a full measure of write-downs. During this vital period Fuld observed *"the SEC and Fed actively conducted regular, and at times, daily oversight of both our business and balance sheet….[T]hey saw what we saw in real time as they reviewed our liquidity, funding, capital, risk management and mark-to-market process."*[140] It sounds a bit like crew and passengers sitting on the deck of an ocean liner watching the approaching iceberg.

In fact, an ex-post postmortem revealed all manner of sleight-of-hand being perpetrated in the critical months before the bank's demise – including an ill-conceived attempt to make Lehman's balance sheet look better than it actually was. For instance, Lehman's Global Financial Controller Martin Kelly confirmed that *"the only purpose or motive for [Repo 105] transactions was reduction in the balance sheet…there was* no *substance to the transactions."*[141] Lehman controller Matthew Lee testified that *"I think the public were misled as to the true leverage of Lehman Brothers."*[142] Furthermore, he said: *"I identified several accounting and corporate governance issues that caused me considerable concern…I attempted to bring these issues to the attention of executive management...within days of first raising issues...I was terminated."*[143] Fuld, for his part, disavowed knowledge of the deals: *"I have absolutely no recollection whatsoever of hearing anything about Repo 105 transactions while I was CEO of Lehman."*[144] He then went on to dispute the findings of the bankruptcy examiner, Anton Valukas: *"I believe that the Examiner's report distorted the relevant facts, and the press, in turn, distorted the Examiner's report. The result is that Lehman and its people have been unfairly vilified."*[145] Later on, in a bizarre replay of the Enron movie, it was revealed that Lehman operated an "alter ego" company, Hudson, which also helped it disguise the true picture of its balance sheet.

Risk management was undoubtedly the bank's weak point: Lehman was chock-full of risk, from real estate, to mortgages, to leveraged loans. Valukas reported that *"we found that Lehman was significantly and persistently in excess of its own risk limits. Lehman management decided to disregard the guidance provided by Lehman's risk management systems."*[146] Furthermore, he said: *"[I]n the face of exceeding its risk limits, Lehman did not take steps to reduce risk; rather, it simply raised the risk limits."*[147] Not much point in having a risk-management function, is there? Equally damning: *"We found that the SEC was aware of these excesses and simply acquiesced."*[148] How wonderfully useful. As one former risk manager, Vincent DiMassimo, said, *"whatever risk governance process we had in place was ultimately not effective in protecting the Firm.... The function lacked sufficient authority within the Firm. Decision-making was dominated by the business."*[149] That spells trouble. This view was seconded by others, including Lehman's head of commodities, Satu Parikh, who noted in an e-mail that *"I am shocked at the poor risk mgmt at the highest levels...It is all unbelievable and I think there needs to be an investigation into the broader issue of malfeasance. Mgmt gambled recklessly with thousands of jobs and shareholder wealth."*[150] Maybe part of the problem was that some heads were buried in the sand: Fuld insisted, nearly two years after the bank's collapse that *"[w]e were risk averse."*[151] Thank heavens they were risk-averse! Can you imagine how much they would've lost if they would've had a real taste for risk-taking?

Attempts to raise additional capital during the crucial summer of 2008 led nowhere as Fuld reportedly drove a hard bargain with would-be investors. It probably didn't help that Fuld had sharp words with then-Treasury Secretary Paulson during this period, noting that *"I've been in my seat a lot longer than you were ever in yours at Goldman. [D]on't tell me how to run my company."*[152] I suppose that it's never particularly wise to piss off someone that might actually be able to help you out of a tight squeeze. According to Valukas' testimony *"on June 13, 2008 – three months before Lehman's bankruptcy – Donald L. Kohn, Vice Chairman of the Federal Reserve, sent an e-mail to Chairman Bernanke stating that "the question is when and how [Lehman] go[es] out of business not whether."*[153] Too bad they didn't do a bit of advance planning.

In the event, reports of a nearly $4b third quarter loss seemed to be the icing on the cake, and the end was in sight: with counterparts pulling their lines and clients fleeing, hopes were placed on some type of government-orchestrated "arranged marriage" a la JP Morgan/Bear. A direct bailout by the US Government was not on the cards: both Paulson and Bernanke were under pressure after the de-facto bailout of Bear (yes, JP Morgan bought them, but the US Government provided a loss guarantee). Paulson said: *"I'm being called Mr. Bailout – I can't do it again."*[154] Same tune from Bernanke, who noted *"we got a lot of flak on Bear."*[155] Treasury Secretary Geithner, who was head of the NY Fed at the time, recalled that: *"We were looking at different options for solving Lehman but also how to put 'foam on the runway'... figuring out how to contain the damage if we failed to find a solution."*[156]

Even though a few banks, including Barclays, had a look at acquiring Lehman over the weekend of September 15, there were ultimately no takers. Indeed, Chancellor Darling reportedly told Paulson in response to a potential bid by Barclays that *"we don't want to import your cancer"*[157] (never mind that cancer was already on the march in the UK via RBS, Northern Rock, HBOS, Bradford & Bingley, etc.). Paulson would go on to tell Darling that *"we were stunned to learn the FSA was refusing to approve the Barclays transaction,"*[158] and, ultimately, *"the British have screwed us."*[159]

Tense times, clearly. Fuld: *"by the end of that Sunday, it was obvious that the Federal Reserve had made a decision it would not provide support for a transaction involving Lehman Brothers. Had that decision been different, further dislocations in the markets might have been avoided."*[160] Though Fuld was obviously wrong about many things, he's probably right on that point. Supporters and detractors of the "non-bailout" lined up – conventional wisdom seems to point to the fact that some sort of rescue should've taken place, if only to avoid spending a lot of money on stabilizing the financial system. For instance, France's Finance Minister Lagarde said that *"[w]hat was dramatic, in a way, was Henry Paulson's decision to drop Lehman Brothers... [t]he bank must have had bad management and bad decisions were taken. From my viewpoint for the equilibrium of the world financial system, it was a true mistake."*[161] Why? *"You knock over a domino and the rest runs the risk of falling, as well."*[162] Ireland's Finance Minister, Brian Lenihan, had a similar view, saying that the US authorities *"were mistaken in permitting that bank to go to the wall because it has had very serious consequences for the world financial system."*[163]

According to Geithner, there was no intent to make an "example" out of Lehman: *"You can't solve the problem by teaching people a lesson. That's not a strategy for solving the crisis."*[164] Further: *"People got the impression that we were trying to make a point. There's zero truth in that. Understandably, there was a deep public antipathy to *putting public money at risk, to rewarding firms for taking too much risk. But that was not relevant. What was relevant in the end was that the government of the U.S. did not have the ability to help rescue Lehman in the absence of a willing buyer.*"[165]

So that was the end of storied Lehman and the start of a tense six-month period in the global markets. Somehow, Fuld's statement that *"the key to risk management is never putting yourself in a position where you can't live to fight another day"*[166] must've sounded a bit hollow to the creditors and investors that had collectively lost billions on the bank's misadventures. Weeks after the collapse, Fuld testified that *"[w]e did everything we could to protect the Firm."*[167] Again, there are more than a few stakeholders that might dispute that claim. Furthermore: *"at Lehman Brothers' annual shareholder meeting, I too said what I absolutely believed to be true at the time – that the worst of the impact to the financial markets was behind us. With the benefit of hindsight, I can now say that I and many others were wrong."*[168] Barclays, the subject of discussion in the next chapter, swooped in after the bankruptcy filing and managed to pick up major portions of Lehman's business for bargain basement prices. Barclays President Bob Diamond was thrilled: *"I still can't believe, and I never expected to have, the opportunity to buy a U.S. bulge-bracket firm...[it] gives us scale in the U.S....[t]his has been transformational."*[169] Japan's Nomura also got some choice bits of the fallen firm out in Asia.

And then there's AIG, the diversified insurance and financial conglomerate. The company, which commenced as an insurer in 1919, developed a broad and geographically diverse set of sound and rather boring business lines over the years, and enjoyed top credit ratings. Though AIG was, and is, known primarily as an insurer, it also owned several banks and at least one rather dangerous subsidiary run by former bankers. More specifically, in 1987, in an effort to further diversify revenues, then-CEO Hank Greenberg created a little laboratory called AIG Financial Products (FP, with hubs in Connecticut and London), staffed with a bunch of seemingly clever folks. Too clever, as it happens: they cooked up all manner of financial wizardry, playing in parts of the rates and commodities markets that even some of the big boys on Wall Street wouldn't touch. And when products on credit defaults started looking interesting, they jumped into that market, too, in a very big way.

But let me go back a bit. Commenting on 2005's operations CEO Martin Sullivan, who had replaced Greenberg (who had gotten caught up in the NY Attorney General Spitzer's buzzsaw on some financial statement irregularities, more of which below) indicated that *"we made major changes in our corporate governance and management practices"*[170] as a way of reinforcing controls. I guess the governance and management practice memo didn't make it over to Connecticut or London, where FP was busily printing trades that would ultimately sink the firm. Sullivan didn't realize just how wrong the standard corporate catch-all statement would be when the crisis hit: *"AIG is financially strong and well positioned for the future."*[171] The Financial Services/Capital Markets unit, including FP's business, boasted of the company's *"risk management acumen,"*[172] even as it became clear that no one had a clue. A touch of hubris, too: *"Capital Markets is well regarded in the industry for its intellectual capital...[i]t routinely combines high quality counterparty risk with market risk lower than its capital markets peers."*[173] In fact, then-head of FP Joe Cassano noted in August 2007: *"It is hard for us, without being flippant, to even see a scenario within any kind of realm of reason that would see us losing one dollar in any of those [credit derivative] transactions."*[174] Well, actually, Joe, try billions of dollars...

There was more of the same blather in a review of 2006's operations, with no hint that the markets were becoming nervous or that the company had some big exposures. FP, for its part, was proudly noting that it *"has created a specialized credit business... distinguishing itself... as a unique credit-oriented asset manager."*[175] Anything but, as would soon be revealed. Underneath the glossy exterior was a more troubling message: AIG was still having problems with its internal controls. According to Lynn Turner, the SEC's Chief Accountant, not only were AIG's reported financials *"grossly in error leading to a May 2005 restatement of its financial statements for each of the years 2000 through 2004"*,[176] but *"[in] 2006 and 2007, the company continued to report 'out of period adjustments' – another way of saying it continued to have errors in its financial statements."*[177] As if that wasn't enough, the firm's external auditors said in its 2007 annual report that *"controls over the AIGFP... swap portfolio... were not effective."*[178] So, in the lead-up to the crisis, the world's largest insurance company, and its little laboratory, had serious internal control problems. Is it any wonder that it stumbled so badly?

And then the bottom fell out. In 2007, AIG got blindsided by the crisis and its own risks, losing $11.5b on the valuation of that nasty FP credit portfolio – creating a $3.5b bottom line loss for the whole firm. So much for all that "risk management acumen" and "intellectual capital." No worries, though, because Sullivan and company were committed to *"addressing these weaknesses through operational and structural investments and improvements"*.[179] Unfortunately, all of this was too late. Still, the firm indicated that *"[w]e are confident that we have the right strategies and resources to succeed."*[180] It makes me wonder how clients receiving risk management advice from AIG were feeling even as AIG appeared incapable of managing its own risk.

That was Sullivan's last communiqué as chief: he was ousted in 2008 as the insurer continued its downward spiral. Enter Robert Willumstad, a non-executive board member and ex-Citibanker, who took over as AIG's new CEO (*"I was initially reluctant to do so"*[181]). In fact, more massive losses – including, get this, $62b in the third quarter alone and nearly $100b for the full year – plus a crisis of confidence led to a liquidity drain. But Willumstad was still hopeful at this point: *"[T]hrough the first week of September, we believed AIG could weather the difficulties in the financial markets, and we believed we would be able to announce and implement the new strategic plan on September 25."*[182]

That hope didn't last long, as Willumstad later noted: *"In the unprecedented market wide crisis of the week of September 8, fears of a further downgrade and the frozen credit markets fed into the crisis of confidence that led AIG to need the liquidity ultimately provided by the Federal Reserve plan. We and our advisors explored every avenue to protect AIG's shareholders. There was no private market solution to AIG's situation..."*[183] Warren Buffett was approached to invest in the firm, but from his perspective saying "no" was easy: *"It wasn't very tough...[t]hey needed more than we could supply by far. I didn't know the extent of it, but I knew that."*[184] In fact, just days after Lehman's collapse, Willumstad recalls that *"AIG was preparing for the unthinkable: bankruptcy."*[185] But the US Government decided it couldn't let AIG go down the tubes so soon after Lehman, as the shocks would have been seismic – AIG had written more than $400b of credit derivatives around the world, and default would have had an implication on all of those holding such contracts, plus all those holding regular, boring life and car insurance policies. So the insurer received an initial $85b loan in exchange for 80% of its equity, effectively becoming part of the US Government – staving off default but pulverizing shareholders in the process. A harsh deal for investors but, as Willumstad said, *"[t]he terms of the offer were non-negotiable."*[186]

Bernanke was not pleased: *"We did this very unhappily...If there's a single episode in this entire 18 months that has made me more angry I can't think of one, than AIG."*[187] Though he was upset at being forced to the wall, Bernanke admitted that *"it was well-known in the market that many major financial institutions had large exposures to AIG. Its failure would likely have led financial market participants to pull back even more from commercial and investment banks, and those institutions perceived as weaker would have faced escalating pressure."*[188] Hank Paulson, for his part, stated that *"[i]f, if, if, if AIG had failed, with the system as fragile as it was, I believe it would have taken down the whole financial system and the economy...this would have been an economic nightmare."*[189] This corresponds with Corrigan's view: *"there is virtually no doubt in my mind that a day or two after the failure of Lehman Brothers had AIG also gone into bankruptcy the consequences for financial markets in the real economy in the United States and around the world would have been calamitous."*[190] Geithner's opinion: *"[t]hat action was based on a judgment...that AIG's failure would have caused catastrophic damage – damage in the form of sharply lower equity prices and pension values, higher interest rates, and a broader loss of confidence in the world's major financial institutions."*[191] Importantly, *"we did not have the ability to contain that damage through other means...[a]nd we did not have the authority to unwind AIG."*[192]

Further cash injections followed in 2009, including $40b from the US Government. The reins were then handed to Ed Liddy, a brave caretaker who volunteered to guide the company transitionally for $1...and who became the focus of ire as the true depths of AIG's problems were revealed. Liddy began with the requisite confessions: *"[T]he implosion of the US housing market exposed AIG's concentrations in mortgage-backed securities"*[193] and, further, AIG had *"strayed into businesses outside of its core competencies"*[194] – for a whole decade, while management stuck its head in the sand and the board members dozed. But wait, I thought that these guys had lots of "risk acumen" and "intellectual capital"? No, I guess not.

In the end, AIG represents breathtakingly awful corporate governance, business leadership, and risk management. Though it's not polite to point fingers, Blankfein's not wrong in his ex-post analysis: *"AIG was bent on taking a lot of credit risk. They took that credit risk in the derivatives market. They took that business by writing insurance against credit events. They took it by holding securities. It was a failure of risk management of colossal proportion."*[195]

Of course, many other US financial institutions were caught up in the same problems: Wachovia (which was eventually acquired by Wells Fargo, which itself had problems), US Bancorp, SunTrust, and others. And it wasn't just the big household names that got it wrong. The bulk of the nonbank lending sector, basically mortgage companies that originated subprime loans, disappeared from the face of the earth. Consider a few facts: between the peak years of the US real estate bubble, 2005–7, the top 25 subprime lenders originated $1t in mortgages, about 72% of the total. Of those, 20 went under, stopped lending or sold themselves to bigger banks. While some are still in business, such as HSBC Finance, Wells/Wachovia, and Chase Home Finance, they no longer play in that part of the market. And big originators such as Ameriquest, New Century, First Franklin (formerly part of Merrill), Long Beach/WaMu, Option One, Fremont, WMC/GE, and others that helped build and define the market are totally gone. Clearly, none of them really understood what they were doing. The regional and community banks fared slightly better in the first round because they didn't hold the same amount of toxic assets. But they eventually got hit by regular old credit losses and suffered from lack of business. And the monoline insurance companies – those whose business it was (and is) to guarantee bonds and some of the default insurance contracts traded by banks – suffered as well: FGIC, Ambac, ACA, and other specialized firms all blew it.

So, the US financiers got it very wrong.

3
...and So Did the European Banks

Pre-crisis blindness was not confined to the US: there were plenty of heads-in-the-sand in the UK and on the Continent. In fact, some of the biggest European banks got it quite wrong, including household names like RBS, HSBC, HBOS, and Barclays of the UK, once-bulletproof Swiss behemoth UBS, Benelux giant Fortis, and even the leading light of German banking, Deutsche Bank. And a bunch of smaller, more specialized, banks like Northern Rock, Bradford & Bingley, Sachsen Landesbank, and IKB got it wrong, too.

But why did the European banks fare so poorly? Wasn't this, after all, mostly about a collapse in the US housing market, and its spillover into the weakest part of the business, subprime borrowers? Why should the Europeans suffer in the same way?

In fact, I can think of at least four reasons why Europe didn't escape the turmoil. First, some of the biggest European banks were (and still are) quite involved in the US markets, helping to originate or repackage the very mortgages that eventually went sour. Household names like Deutsche, Barclays, RBS, and HSBC had their hands on the same loans that eventually blew up. Second, many banks, including smaller regional players, wound up buying the supposed high-quality AAA-rated mortgage bonds for their investment portfolios – in some cases "outsourcing" their decisions to the rating agencies. And, so, when they thought they were buying AAA securities, they actually weren't, and suffered horrific consequences. In Greenspan's view, "*Foreign investors, largely European, were drawn to the above-average yield on these securities and the seemingly below-average risk reflected in a foreclosure rate on the underlying mortgages that had been in decline for two years. At the peak of demand in 2006...a significant part of subprime securities were sold abroad...a fact confirmed by the recent heavy losses on U.S. mortgages reported by European investors.*"[1] Third, some of the European property markets underwent a similar bubble and collapse cycle, just like the US. The UK, Irish, and Spanish housing markets, for instance, declined in value, leading to many of the same issues the US banks discovered on their own home turf. Of course, once the initial mortgage-related dominos started to topple into other credit areas, like leveraged loans and even more mundane assets like corporate bonds, the Europeans were wildly at risk because they owned plenty of these. And, fourth, the European banks suffered from the same governance, executive management, and risk-management lapses as their US counterparts...

The big players...

The European leg of the crisis didn't discriminate by size – bankers at large, internationally focused institutions got it quite wrong, as did those running smaller, regional, or national institutions. Let me start with the big guys.

HSBC, a truly global institution with major operations in the UK, Europe, Asia, and the Americas (built through years of acquisitions and growth), has historically been known as a conservative shop. Interestingly, in this particular crisis the bank actually provided one of the "early warning signals" for the entire world: its consumer lending and finance subsidiary in the US had the misfortune of posting attention-grabbing losses ahead of most others, suggesting that all was not going smoothly in the mortgage world. In fact, there was an indication that all was not well when Chairman Stephen Green said in 2006 that the bank managed to increase profits *"despite a major setback in part of our mortgage business in the United States"*[2] – which cost the bank what now seems like a pittance, $725m; much of that came from the Household Finance Corp (HFC) unit HSBC had acquired some years earlier. Furthermore, said Green, *"we have effected broad changes in management and strengthened risk controls and processes."*[3] I'm not terribly sure about that, as the red ink continued to flow for a few more years. Green also noted at this point that the financial markets were evincing signs of weakness and that *"[w]e will ensure our credit appetite reflects these risks."*[4] However, it's once again difficult to connect the thought behind the statement with the subsequent losses posted by the bank. By 2007 Green noted that *"the management team has taken vigorous action to address and mitigate the problem"*[5] caused by the Personal Finance Services unit, which recorded a remarkable $6.2b loss (most of which came from the aforementioned US mortgage unit). Remember, when this loss was reported during the second quarter of 2007, no other financial institution had reported anything of a similar magnitude, so it caught almost everyone off guard. Was this a harbinger of things to come, or was it more narrowly confined to HSBC's own operations? Not to be overlooked: the bank's investment banking unit lost a further $2b from leveraged loans and credit trading activities.

Things went from bad to worse in 2008, with Green noting that *"[w]e at HSBC were not immune from the crisis"*[6] and *"[v]irtually no one then foresaw the subsequent scale of the deterioration in the US economy and financial markets.*"[7] Indeed. The US operations went from bad to worse, recording a $15.5b loss, partly from further portfolio deterioration and partly from permanent closure of the mortgage business, Green confessing *"with the benefit of hindsight this is an acquisition [HFC] we wish we wouldn't have undertaken."*[8] That view was seconded by HSBC's CFO Douglas Flint: *"It was a mistake with hindsight but it was not a black swan.... [T]he buying of business dependent on the US consumer and the US housing market at the time did not look a great risk. With hindsight, it was, yes."*[9] HSBC also swallowed another $5b of losses from trading and leveraged loans. In early 2009 the bank had to replenish its capital coffers, doing so via a mammoth £12.5b rights issue. So, while HSBC is often portrayed, ex-post, as one of the banks that emerged relatively unscathed (perhaps because they weren't forced to accept any government help), it is pretty clear that they stumbled, costing their shareholders tens of billions. Green summarized it this way: *"The truth is we didn't get it all right, to put it mildly."*[10]

Next there's Royal Bank of Scotland (RBS) – the bank that, according to its marketing campaign, likes to "Make It Happen."™ Well the bank did, indeed, make it happen – just substitute "it," with "losses" and you'll get the picture. Let me rewind to 2006 when Sir Fred Goodwin, veteran CEO of RBS, was telling shareholders that *"we actively manage the trade-off between growth, risk and return...[and] we have retained our inherently cautious stance towards higher risk activities such as unsecured consumer lending and sub-prime credit markets generally. We face the future confidently."*[11] Furthermore, he noted, *"[s]ound control of our risks is fundamental to our business, and here our results are reassuring."*[12] I'm not sure about these statements – though the bank posted strong earnings for the year, the rot had already set in, and less than 12 months later RBS would be a different bank – caught up in the crisis, as well as an ill-advised, expensive, and complicated purchase of the Dutch bank ABN-Amro (complete with a record price tag of €71b – RBS footing the largest share, followed by its acquisition partners Santander and Fortis).

Move forward to late 2007, when the first wave of the crisis started to hit home. In addition to coping with the integration of ABN-Amro, Sir Fred admitted that RBS had a bit of garbage on its balance sheet: *"[R]esults have been held back by the second half credit market deterioration, which led our...Global Banking and Markets division to incur writedowns on its US mortgage-related and leveraged finance exposures."*[13] That cost £1.1b. It sounds a bit different than the "inherently cautious stance" of a year earlier – either they booked all the bad stuff in a 12 month span, or they didn't really realize what they had or what was coming. Curiously, there was no mention at all of the fact that 2008 might be challenging. Quite the contrary: *"[I]t is clear that we enter 2008 with real momentum behind our organic growth, and with our product range, distribution capabilities and customer franchises materially enhanced."*[14] Rose colored glasses?

Things unwound very quickly from that point on: during the first months of 2008 the bank was forced to take another £5.9b in write-downs from its mortgages, leveraged finance, and other credit activities – the resulting net bottom line loss was, according to Sir Fred, *"a chastening experience."*[15] Again, it's difficult to reconcile multibillion pound write-downs with "sound control of our risks." The bank then had to launch a monster £12b capital raising to plug the hole. A second £7b issue couldn't be placed, leaving the bank in a weakened state and as losses mounted throughout 2008 RBS looked hopelessly undercapitalized and increasingly vulnerable.

Post-Lehman the pressures become untenable and the UK government was obliged to step in and recapitalize the bank, taking a 70 percent ownership stake. And that was the last of Sir Fred, who departed in October 2008. While the massive losses and the botched capital-raising had taken their toll, the ill-advised ABN-Amro deal surely played a part. Goodwin alternated his view between *"I know the jury's out"*[16] and something more definitive: *"I think that, as we currently sit here today, I can only say that it was a bad decision. Who knows in years to come, but right here and right now it was certainly mistimed and I think that, if we knew then what we know now, we would not have taken the risk of finding out."*[17] Former RBS Chairman Sir Tom McKillop was more forthright, saying that *"[i]n retrospect we bought ABN Amro at the top of the market, so anything we paid was an error...we did in fact make a bad mistake in purchasing ABN Amro. At the time it did not look like that. It is easy in retrospect."*[18] FSA's Turner was critical of the deal: *"[T]he RBS bid for ABN Amro...[was a] risky mistake, and while several institutional shareholders expressed significant concerns that the time, they were not able or willing to force a change of strategy."*[19]

The media soon came to dub Goodwin as the "world's worst banker" – perhaps he's one of them, though I can think of several other candidates who might vie for the same title. In the aftermath Sir Fred tried to convey his inner conflict: *"I would find this easier to reconcile in my mind if there had been a siren call that had been overlooked or overturned. As we go back through...the siren call is not there."*[20] And, later, a little of the familiar we-weren't-the-only-ones refrain: *"I have gone over this time and time and time again in my own mind as to what was the point at which we should have seen this differently...It was not that our business was premised on everything continuing to go upwards forever but that things could turn as quickly as they did, I do not think anyone saw. I do not think, in fairness even to the Bank of England, that they really saw that it was going to turn this quickly."*[21] Sir Tom admitted: *"We had no idea of the speed and the interconnectedness and how quickly it could all have turned out."*[22] Nevertheless, Sir Fred still defended his bank's approach to risk: "*The traders were trading within limits that would have been set; there were not any rogue elements to it; they were conducting activities which they were authorised to conduct...[a]t the heart of this I think there was an issue not about risk recognition but about how the risk was calibrated.*"[23] In visions of Citi's Chuck Prince on the dance floor, Goodwin described RBS's mortgage business model: "*[W]e packaged them and distributed them, and that business can be conducted largely without incident and, when the music stopped...we had inventory.*"[24] Through a risk manager's lens all of this means that the bank didn't have a good grip on its total risk and the relative enormity of its exposures.

MP Thurso was distraught about the governance failures: "*I look at RBS, a once proud Scottish banking institution, British banking institution, brought to its knees. I look at those names on that nonexecutive board and say to myself, how come none of them said, 'No, this is nuts'?*"[25] MP McFall was equally critical: "*The business models have been admitted to be faulty, and when it comes to the decisions within the banks, for example the Royal Bank of Scotland, they have the brightest and the best on the board...but they were duped, they didn't look at the situation as it was...[t]hat signals a real failure of corporate governance.*"[26] MP Fallon was more blunt, telling Goodwin: "*You've destroyed a great British bank.*"[27] Even Gordon Brown weighed in: "*Yes, I'm angry about what happened at the Royal Bank of Scotland...[n]ow we know that so much was lost in sub-prime loans in the US and now we know that some of that was related to the purchase of ABN Amro, I think people have a right to be angry that these write-offs are happening.*"[28]

Enter new CEO Stephen Hester, who was tasked with trying to right the government-owned bank – a bank which posted a bottom line loss of £9b for full year 2008. Hester began the process of cleaning things up and availed himself of the government's Asset Protection Scheme to backstop some of the bank's bad assets. A complete overhaul of controls was also essential, according to Hester: "*The most important thing is some very big elements of control which I think we can improve.*"[29] He was realistic, though: "*I think, frankly, the risk management systems at RBS need a lot of change, and I cannot do it all in a couple of weeks, and so we need to keep upgrading and keep improving. We are putting in major changes as we speak, but it will take some time to get those absolutely right.*"[30] And, he added, "*we are making progress in recognizing excess risk and dealing with it*"[31] – all a bit late, of course. As part of the triage he observed that "*the epicentre of the restructuring of the bank, the area that needed the biggest surgery, was the investment bank. We have approximately halved the size of the investment bank...that notwithstanding, the investment bank is a very important and very profitable part of what we do but it is much smaller and, I believe, much safer than it was a year ago.*"[32] In the event, losses continued through 2009, though at a decreasing pace. In the end, Hester admitted that "*RBS became cruelly exposed to a downturn which has proven to be the greatest of modern times... [c]learly RBS's exposure was about decisions that RBS made.*"[33]

Though Barclays, another of Britain's global players, fared better than its rival RBS, it was not totally without problems. Back in 2006, Group CEO John Varley was telling shareholders that *"[w]e enter 2007 with strong income momentum in Barclays, driven by high levels of customer activity and good risk control. The global economic outlook continues to be positive and we are well positioned to capture further growth in the years ahead."*[34] Actually, risk control was lacking and the global economic outlook was dimming. Barclays went on to describe at length the degree to which it stress-tested its portfolios, noting *"[s]pecific stress test analysis is used across all risk types to gain a better understanding of the risk profile and the potential effects of changes in external factors. These stress tests are performed at a number of different levels."*[35] I do wonder what their global housing crash stress test looked like?

In the event, things started going pear-shaped during 2007, notwithstanding Varley's comment that the bank's investment banking division *"handled well the stress test of market turbulence in the second half of 2007"*[36] – which, for the record, included £782m of charges from subprime and related risks, along with net losses of £1.64b from other credit activities. Varley continued to state the obvious: *"In an environment such as this we will have to be disciplined in our risk management and rigorous in our approach to lending."*[37] Again, this came a little bit late, as the risk was already on the books and had no particular place to go.

Things got much worse in 2008 as Barclays posted credit-related losses of more than £8b. In his review of the year Varley indicated that *"the economic and business environment will remain very difficult, and the quality of our assets and risk management capability will again be tested. The scale of our market presence in the geographies where we do business means that we will not avoid the consequences of a severe downturn."*[38] He also noted that *"[a]lthough we have been careful over recent years to avoid inappropriate risk concentration in our major loan books in retail and commercial banking, our plans for 2009 assume that impairment will continue to be at a high level."*[39] I wonder whether Barclays shareholders were meant to be happy that, because of the bank's apparent "disciplined" risk management and "rigorous" lending standards it only dropped £8b, instead of £10b, £12b or some other double-digit billion? Difficult times, even for Barclays. To its credit the bank didn't take UK government funds like some of its peers, and rebounded from the crisis more rapidly than many others. It also remained strong enough to scoop up parts of fallen Lehman for a song. All of that gave Barclays President Diamond the opportunity to throw a jab at its competitors: *"The failures of Citi and UBS weren't about the model, they were about management."*[40] Maybe true, but somehow glass houses and stone-throwing come to mind...

Let me next touch on the case of HBOS (product of a one-time merger between Halifax and Bank of Scotland), which landed in the arms of Lloyds TSB with a bit of help from HM Treasury. Going back to 2006, then-CEO Andy Hornby declared that the *"[c]orporate credit experience continues to reflect the most benign credit environment for some 30 years...[i]n International, credit conditions remain resilient."*[41] Furthermore, he said, *"[w]hile we are not seeing any material signs of stress, we have maintained prudent exposure limits."* In fact, those prudent exposure limits would prove to be rather imprudent – so imprudent that the bank would eventually post fatal losses. Finally, Hornby noted, *"reputation risk is high on the alert list as we strive to ensure that in our policies and practices we, at all times, behave in an appropriate way, as a banker for our customers and an employer for our colleagues. The reputation of HBOS and its major brands is of paramount importance and we guard it jealously."*[42] Unfortunately, HBOS's reputation would be consigned to the rubbish bin within 18 months.

Just a year later then-Chairman Stevenson indicated that *"[w]e are, I believe, rightly proud as a Board that we have been altering the risk profile of our liquidity requirements over the last four years...without any external pressures from regulators or other shareholders but purely as part of being good custodians of your business. You may be quite sure that we will continue to bring to bear the same standards of rigour and financial conservatism as the business moves forward."*[43] Well, that obviously didn't work out too well, as liquidity problems were central to HBOS' downfall. Hornby, for his part, said *"we continue to concentrate on markets where we have real expertise and can generate superior returns...going forward, we expect some modest deterioration in certain sectors and markets."*[44]

And then came the collapse, with the bank posting huge losses from its corporate and real estate activities (amounting to £8.5b in 2008) and suffering from lack of funds (so much for "altering the liquidity risk profile") forcing the bank to accept an offer from Lloyds TSB. The last comments from HBOS as an independent bank: *"HBOS's 2008 trading has been further impacted by increasingly difficult market conditions, an acceleration in the deterioration of credit quality and falls in estimated asset values.... [T]he Board of HBOS sought to restore confidence and stability through an agreement to be acquired by Lloyds TSB."*[45]

By all accounts the bank was simply too concentrated in the real estate sector ("prudent exposure limits"?). Stevenson admitted in the aftermath that *"[t]he Bank of Scotland has always been a specialist in commercial property. The exposure as a percentage of the balance sheet to commercial property has not increased dramatically over time, that is not what has happened. Looking back, with the wisdom of hindsight, we did not foresee the deterioration in asset values that took place, it is as simple as that."*[46] But wait, there's more: *"We were already by then lowering our growth, as it turned out by not enough. I would say to you absolutely frankly it is quite clear, with the wisdom of hindsight, that we were over-exposed, that we lent too much at the wrong parts in the cycle. Simple as that."*[47] If everything seems so "simple", then what happened? Where were the directors, the executives, the risk managers?

In fact, Stevenson also had to confess that the bank's risk processes had not worked as expected: *"[W]e failed to consider some of the extreme scenarios that have actually happened"*[48] – meaning *"stress testing that did not stress adequately."*[49] Also, the bank didn't *"predict the wholesale collapse of wholesale markets."*[50] That's rather problematic for a bank so heavily reliant on wholesale funds. A rather telling ex-post revelation by a senior risk officer, Paul Moore, spoke volumes: *"When I was head of group regulatory risk at HBOS, I certainly knew that the bank was going too fast (and told them), had a cultural indisposition to challenge (and told them) and was a serious risk to financial stability (what the FSA call "maintaining market confidence") and consumer protection (and told them)...I told the board they ought to slow down but was prevented from having this properly minuted by the chief financial officer."*[51] Furthermore, he said, *"I strongly believe that the real underlying cause of all the problems was simply this – a total failure of all key aspects of governance....[i]n my view and from my personal experience at HBOS, all the other specific failures stem from this one primary cause."*[52] Wow.

So, an aggressive and concentrated business strategy coupled with heavy wholesale funding, and weak governance and risk controls created pools of red and loss of independence. Lloyds TSB CEO Eric Daniels, commenting on the wisdom of the government-assisted acquisition, said that *"I do not believe that anyone was hoodwinked. What we believe is this is a very good deal for our shareholders and will prove to be in the medium term – our shareholders including the taxpayer...[i]t would have been, I think, had HBOS gone down much more serious...than the current crisis that we are experiencing."*[53] The end result was, of course, another set of investors taking it on the chin. And taxpayers, too: after the big UK bailouts, how much of the retail banking market did the taxpayers actually own? According to Darling, *"we own quite a substantial amount of it at the moment. Lloyds is a third, from recollection, and RBS is about 40% in total, I am told."*[54]

On to the Continent. UBS, the stalwart of Swiss banking, had long been regarded as a safe pair of hands. Despite a few missteps in the late 1990s with the Russia/Long Term Capital Management debacle, the bank was believed to have had a risk culture strong enough to support its expansive businesses. In fact, UBS was courteous enough to warn clients and investors in its 2006 annual report that *"our risk management and control processes may not always protect us from losses."*[55] True enough, and it should have stopped right there. Unfortunately, the bank committed the cardinal sin of hubris a few pages later by noting that *"as the economic cycle matures, investors might become more sensitive to any disappointing political or economic development, so our top-class risk control remains paramount.*"[56] Well, I'm glad they think they had a "top class risk control" function – I can only imagine what would've happened had it operated with an "average" or "bad" risk control function.

In reality they didn't have a top-class risk control function at all. The bank spent the first half of the 2000s loading up its balance sheet with lots of stuff – including doubling up on its risk positions through an "internal hedge fund" (Dillon Read), which made matters particularly bad when the markets turned. Former Chairman Marcel Ospel would later comment: *"[C]learly, there was a problem when you build such a concentrated exposure and it doesn't appear on any of the appropriate radar screens."*[57] Yes, that can indeed be a problem. Dillon Read's difficulties, which included large losses in all manner of instruments and markets, came to light in early 2007, leading to a virtual revolving door in the executive suite, and hinting at much deeper institutional flaws. Turner observed that *"[i]f you look at the management report which the board of UBS developed...it was clearly a case of profits and funding made in the retail and commercial bank being used to fund a blow-up of a proprietary trading activity, so it is a very major issue."*[58] In fact, Dillon's losses sealed the fate of its leader, John Costas, the head of investment banking, Huw Jenkins, CFO Clive Standish and CEO Peter Wuffli – leaving former risk and private banking chief Marcel Rohner in charge.

And so Rohner delivered a CHF4.4b loss for the 2007 fiscal year, which included a shocking CHF20b+ hit on US real estate/mortgages. As the red ink flowed, Ospel tried to clarify the situation a bit: *"People think we gave subprime mortgages in the U.S. We did not."*[59] Who cares? They had billions of bonds backed by the same stuff, so what's the difference? Robert Wolf, head of the US investment banking unit, admitted that *"[w]e like to say we're in the moving business, not the storage business...[b]ut we got away from that philosophy."*[60] Ospel also commented on the reputational aspects of the disaster, which were very damaging: *"[u]ntil recently we had the reputation of being a cautious, even risk-averse bank...[w]e were therefore all the more disappointed that we had failed to recognize the signals from the U.S. housing market in time."*[61] However, he added, *"I would never thoughtlessly relinquish my responsibility, and I intend to ensure that UBS gets back on the road to success."*[62] Easier said than done.

Rohner did the best he could with the hand he had been dealt, raising some capital and trying to pare back on risk a bit. He later noted that *"[w]e are very happy that we undertook measures, at a very early point in the crisis, to deal with it, that we raised capital twice and severely reduced our risk exposure. These measures have armed us well to weather this extremely difficult market situation."*[63] As it happens, those measures were wholly insufficient, and the Swiss government had to intervene in the post-Lehman period with an illiquid asset purchase agreement that took some of the garbage off the bank's books: UBS availed itself of a government scheme that transferred the equivalent of $60b of its toxic assets and $6b in capital to a government entity that assumed ownership of the portfolio. After inking the deal, Rohner said: "*This transaction gives us comfort. The extremely difficult market environment led us to accelerate our risk reduction with a definite move. Our aim is to protect our clients from the impact of the crisis to the fullest extent possible and to provide our shareholders an opportunity to renew confidence in the bank.*"[64] That might take a while.

The 2008 accounts reflected total net losses of CHF21b (including CHF27b of red from its trading and investment banking businesses), spelling the end for Rohner, who remained a class act even as he left in April: "*[T]he last thing you want to do is manage a bank through difficult situations like these based on emotions such as pride or embarrassment.*"[65] Not to worry, he was joined on the way out by Ospel. Sergio Marchionne, UBS vice chairman and head of Fiat, stated the obvious as the two gents left the executive suite: "*The events since the summer of 2007 have affected the bank to an unexpected degree and have proved a great challenge for management and the board of directors.*"[66] Ossie Grubel, late of crosstown rival Credit Suisse, took over for Rohner, observing in the bank's annual report that "*[c]lients have, understandably, expressed their disappointment to us about our losses*".[67] I would think so, yes. So what happened? According to Grubel, "*[o]ur balance sheet was too large, and systems of risk management and risk control that should have limited our exposure failed. We placed too much emphasis on growth and not enough on controlling risks.*"[68] Don't forget, in 2007 they had a "top-class risk control" function. Maybe not. Ospel observed in the aftermath that "*[p]eople were proud that a Swiss firm had established such a significant footprint in the most competitive market on the globe ... [s]o the greater the disappointment with what they have had to digest.*"[69]

While I'm on the Continent, let me turn to Germany. German bankers were not able to escape damage: Commerzbank and Dresdner (who eventually merged), and Deutsche Bank, the domestic powerhouse that converted itself into a global investment bank during the 1990s, all lost heavily. The same happened at some of the state banks, as I'll note later.

Let me first take the case of Deutsche, long regarded as extremely sophisticated and an excellent manager of risk. In fact, it stumbled, just like its peers. Back in early 2007, CEO Josef Ackermann, reporting on the bank's strong 2006 results, noted that "*we invested significantly in the future ... our purchase of MortgageIT, an originator of residential mortgages, represents a significant step forward in the North American securitization market, by creating added scope for us as a leading issuer of residential mortgage backed securities.*"[70] The bank reinforced this later: "*[O]ur sustained expansion into residential mortgage-backed securities in the U.S. proved successful, with the business gaining both in earnings and in market share. We took major steps forward in building our U.S. franchise with our acquisitions of mortgage*

68   See No Evil

origination platforms, Chapel Funding and MortgageIT."[71] To me, this means two things: Deutsche had no idea that the market for US mortgages was ripe for a tumble and that it bought a specialist mortgage company at the top of the market – neither of which makes one feel like they had any clue.

Ackermann also spoke of the bank's intent to *"maintain the cost, risk and capital discipline which have served us well since 2002"*[72] – which again didn't work out too well. The bank was also busy touting *"[o]ur world-leading investment banking platform, and our outstanding franchise for high-value, 'intellectual capital' products,"*[73] both of which would create some big holes in the profit and loss accounts less than one year later. Sidebar: though a few data points don't make a trend, I have now given some examples of both US and European institutions who describe how their "intellectual" depth creates value. I would suggest the opposite: when these guys cite the size of their intellect, it means they are creating things that even they don't understand, which necessarily means there's going to be a bloodbath at some point. Keep this in mind, as I'll come back to it later in the book.

Even as the crisis unfolded during 2007, the bank steadfastly clung to the belief that things were okay, with Ackermann noting in early 2008 that *"[w]e were less impacted by the sub-prime crisis than some other major banks, having positioned ourselves defensively, at an early stage, in the areas most directly affected by the crisis. We also benefited from effective risk management and a well-diversified business model."*[74] Kudos to the bank? It posted increased profits and boosted its dividend, even as it noted *"some credit trading businesses, notably in areas related to sub-prime, were impacted by the turbulent markets."*[75] And, further on, *"our debt origination business was affected by difficult markets for leveraged finance and high-yield debt, which necessitated write-downs on our holdings of leveraged loans and loan commitments."*[76]

Unfortunately, 2008 was bad: Ackermann and co were forced to concede that *"these extraordinary conditions severely impacted the banking industry, and Deutsche Bank was no exception."*[77] Apparently the "effective risk management" wasn't enough to stop the bank from losing a rather formidable €8.5b in its investment banking operations. According to Ackermann *"[t]his result principally reflects the impact on our business model of the market conditions in the fourth quarter"*[78] – which is a fancy way of saying the bank had lots of risk on its book and the markets went against them. He clarified this point later, saying that *"these losses were in large part attributable to substantial proprietary trading activity, the absolute size of some positions, and the complexity of some highly-structured products."*[79] Oh well. In the event, the bank moved to shut the barn door: *"[W]e have closed proprietary trading desks and significantly reduced our overall exposure to proprietary activity...we have scaled back resources dedicated to highly illiquid businesses."*[80] A bit late, but there you go.

Benelux bancassurance giant Fortis was another Continental casualty, suffering from a portfolio of risky deals and investments, a fragile liquidity profile, and a hefty payment (€24b) for its share of the ABN-Amro acquisition I mentioned earlier (joining with RBS and Santander to take a share of the spoils at peak prices). In the afterglow of the acquisition, Chairman Maurice Lippens and CEO Jean-Paul Votron were pleased with their handiwork: *"We believe that our acquisition of selected activities of ABN Amro can be described as truly transformational.... This historic acquisition sets the stage for an exciting future for Fortis. We can look forward to solid long-term growth prospects in a number of selected businesses."*[81] Furthermore, the pair said: *"The compelling strategic logic of our acquisition of the selected ABN Amro businesses has become even more relevant during this period, increasing our retail funding capacity and...providing us with a large and very predictable earnings stream and lowering the overall risk profile of our company."*[82] In fact, none of those key aims came to pass.

Despite the fact that Votron insisted that Fortis wouldn't need to raise additional capital to finance the ABN deal, it was ultimately forced to do so through a €8.3b capital call that infuriated investors – leading ultimately to Votron's departure (Lippens wasn't far behind). Huybrechts, head of the Flemish Federation of Investment, said colorfully that *"[t]he former shareholders of ABN Amro are now taking a bath in champagne...Who makes such big mistakes, must bear the consequences and therefore resign."*[83] Enter new CEO Filip Dierckx, who admitted that *"I am...not going to deny that if you look at some of the decisions that were taken in the past then you can say that probably they were done at the wrong moment...[i]f you want me to say that there were some decisions that were not the best I will indeed confirm."*[84] Much like the executives at RBS, Dierckx confessed that *"indeed there was bad timing in the ABN Amro deal."*[85]

But the group's real problem was funding: in the aftermath of the Lehman failure Fortis became the subject of bankruptcy rumors, which created serious liquidity problems. The bank lost €20b in customer deposits in a single day, and the prospect of losing even more prompted emergency action: the governments of Belgium, Luxembourg, and the Netherlands partially nationalized the bank via an €11.2b capital injection – which helped stem the flood of deposit withdrawals. After the initial stabilization injection, different pieces of Fortis became the subject of a complex tripartite horse-trade: the Dutch government took over the Dutch banking and insurance businesses, whilst the Belgian and Luxembourgoise governments cut some side deals with BNP Paribas. A real dog's breakfast. All of these deals led to legal wrangling, which delayed the dismantling for a while.

Even as the complicated demerger details were being worked out the bank posted staggering losses of €28b for full year 2008, proving that it had gotten everything quite wrong: its acquisition plan, its liquidity management, and its risk management. Dierckx noted that *"[w]e're disappointed by these results"*[86] and *"[w]e are turning a black page in the history of the bank and as the management want to thank our customers, staff, the Belgian and Luxembourg states and BNP Paribas for their support and trust in these difficult times."*[87]

Lots of other big banks got caught in the grinder – losing billions and in some cases requiring capital calls or even government help: Société Générale, BNP Paribas, UniCredit, Santander, Calyon, and others were all on the wrong side of the trade. A few, like Credit Suisse, did relatively "less bad" (which is not to say "good"), but they were in the minority. Pretty much all of the European megabank universe had a poor showing.

...And the smaller ones...

And what of the smaller shops? Did they manage to get it right – or at least "less wrong"? Unfortunately, in many cases they did as poorly as their larger cousins.

Let me kick off with Northern Rock, the UK's first black eye in the crisis. The building society, formed through mergers of several small building societies in the 1970s and 1980s, floated itself on the London Stock Exchange in the 1990s and expanded its mortgage portfolio to become one of the top five mortgage lenders in the UK – offering buy-to-let loans (mortgages for investment properties) as well as a range of subprime equivalents, like no documentation/self-employed loans ("self-certs") and highly leveraged loans (125% loans), all of which were as treacherous as the products being offered in the States. In March 2005 then-CEO Adam Applegarth explained that *"we don't compete in the housing market, we compete in the home loan market, which also includes people refinancing, remortgaging; it's investment in residential property, it's older people stripping out equity to support lifestyle."*[88] In other words, the risky bits of the market. Critically, the bank entered into an arrangement with Lehman in 2006 where it lent its name to subprime mortgages underwritten by Lehman – enough said. In addition, the bank had a rather substantial portfolio of nasty mortgage-backed securities, which ultimately proved very costly.

But back in October 2006 Applegarth was optimistic, noting that *"[c]redit quality, in each of our loan books has remained good and shows no deterioration."*[89] Then-Chairman Ridley boasted of the bank's *"strategy of using growth, cost efficiency and credit quality to reward both shareholders and customers."* Furthermore, Ridley commented, the coast was clear: *"[W]e continue to see little prospect of a severe house price correction...support for the housing market remains strong."*[90] Wrong. And Applegarth noted, rather unfortunately: *"[T]he appetite for securitisation, particularly in the US and Europe, remains huge...we now have a total securitisation* book of £40.3b."⁹¹ In fact, the bank had a very aggressive, high-risk business model and was very dependent on other banks for its funding.

When the crisis hit, Northern Rock became one of its earliest casualties. In fact, the bank stumbled a year before Lehman's collapse, suggesting it already had big structural problems. Northern Rock's problems came to a head in September 2007 when the bank found itself short of cash – this, despite Applegarth's claim earlier in the year that funding had been expanded and diversified and *"[w]e see plenty of scope to increase our funding in these markets to support our growth."*⁹² Apparently not. In mid-September King warned that bank bailouts were not in the offing: *"The provision of such liquidity support undermines the efficient pricing of risk by providing ex-post insurance for risky behavior... [t]hat encourages excessive risk-taking and sows the seeds of a future financial crisis."*⁹³ Still, there was growing recognition that some sort of help would be needed for Northern Rock (and others).

Days after King's pronouncement the Northern Rock rumor mills were working overtime and liquidity was drying up. There were TV images of retail depositors lining up outside the bank's branches (prompting Ed Yingling, head of the ABA, to note *"[t]he importance of this public confidence should not be underestimated, nor should its existence be taken for granted: witness the lines in front of the British bank Northern Rock at the beginning of this crisis"*⁹⁴) – but the real liquidity crisis occurred in the wholesale markets, where interbank lenders and institutional investors had gradually stopped rolling over their deposits. And Northern Rock relied very, very heavily on such wholesale funding. A full-fledged bank run was nigh, prompting Chancellor Darling to state publicly that the government would guarantee all of the bank's deposits. Despite his earlier pronouncement King defended the bailout actions: *"It would have been deeply unfair on the retail depositors to allow them to suffer in that way, so again we need a system in this country in which we can prevent the retail depositors from being trapped. The United States has a system, Canada has a system, other countries have a system – that's why we could not allow Northern Rock just to fail."*⁹⁵ He also explained that *"there was always a hope...I think it was clear that Northern Rock was a bank that was running out of money, but there was always a hope that it might find it from somewhere, maybe it would be able to sell some of its mortgages, maybe it would be able to persuade someone to lend to it. There were a number of ideas that were floating around."*⁹⁶ Waiting for Godot.

Even after the deposit guarantee, Northern Rock's fate was in the balance: from September through February 2008 the bank received a number of takeover proposals – from Virgin, a private equity group, and others. One scheme called for Lloyds TSB to step in and absorb the bank, with £30b in assistance from the Bank of England. The FSA supported the deal, but King did not: *"[T]his is not something a central bank can do ... [t]hey don't normally finance takeovers by one company for another, let alone to the tune of £30 billion."*[97] By year's end Ridley and Applegarth were out, the dividend had been cut and things looked bleak.

With no other solution at hand, HM Treasury took over in February. New Chairman Sandler and new CEO Hoffmann took command of the operation even as the Treasury assumed "temporary public ownership" of the bank. There were mixed views about the bailout. Chris Wood, CLSA strategist, was critical: *"What the Bank of England has done doesn't really pass the smell test ... Northern Rock was just about the most extreme mortgage lending model you could find. It managed to run into trouble even before a housing market downturn in the UK, which is a truly astonishing feat."*[98] Further, *"[i]t is amazing that the Bank of England has felt it necessary to come to the rescue of an institution that had been run in such a reckless fashion."*[99] Lord Oakeshott, Liberal Democrat, said: *"Northern Rock was an accident waiting to happen. There's been a lot of loose lending in the UK and Gordon Brown's system [for regulating it] has been tested and fallen apart."*[100] MP Fallon was critical of the FSA's oversight: *"You are dealing with a bank whose lending has quadrupled from £25bn to £100bn – it was taking one in five mortgages – and you were not doing a full assessment for three years."*[101] Hector Sants, then-CEO of FSA said that *"[i]t is clear ... that our supervision of Northern Rock in the period leading up to the market instability of late last summer was not carried out to a standard that is acceptable."*[102] He also added that *"[i]n terms of the probability of this organisation getting into difficulty we had it as a low probability ... [w]hen events transpired, that proved to be incorrect."*[103] And, finally, *"[w]e were uncomfortable with their scenarios but regrettably it was late in the day."*[104] MP McFall wasn't happy: *"This isn't just a failure of the supervisors of Northern Rock; it's a failure of the management of the FSA."*[105] Vince Cable, for his part, went on record to say that *"[t]he Government dithered for far too long before concluding that Northern Rock had to be nationalized."*[106] He also let it be known that the FSA had disregarded his warnings: *"Sir Callum [FSA] said I was scaremongering, that there was no problem with the bank, it had a good loan book and any problems were due to international markets beyond its control .... I told him it was obvious the bank had acted recklessly."*[107]

Sandler's introductory statement to newly screwed shareholders was that *"2007 was a difficult and challenging year for Northern Rock, with the effects of the severe reductions in the levels of global liquidity having a significant impact on the Company."*[108] Rather. The bank had a rough go of things even after the nationalization, with Hoffman commenting that *"we expect that the company will continue to be significantly loss-making through 2009 ... [t]he consequence of house price deflation on Northern Rock has meant a substantial increase in arrears over the last few months. I think there is also a risk that we are knocked off track generally by all the noise that is round Northern Rock."*[109] And, of course, that portfolio of toxic mortgage securities continued to be a millstone: *"We took some substantial write-*

downs in our first-half results, and some in the third quarter as well. Clearly, there is risk in there and continuing risk as we look forward."[110] Sandler also noted renewed efforts to recast risk management, which had obviously failed under the Ridley/Applegarth regime: *"The principal conclusions have been to create a much more independent and much stronger risk function within the business, and to embed principles of risk management much more deeply in the business than was hitherto the case."*[111] Unfortunately for the UK taxpayer, all of this came a bit too late.

Whilst in the UK, let me also talk about Bradford and Bingley (B&B), once one of the UK's largest independent building societies. B&B, active in home mortgages, was enjoying the heady years of property appreciation and low rates during the early part of the millennium. In reviewing 2006's results, then-Chairman Rod Kent noted that *"[t]he credit performance of all our portfolios has been very good. The Group's experience in specialist lending and prudent approach to underwriting continues to preserve the quality of our lending book."*[112] And, according to Kent, the outlook was good: *"Our specialist markets continue to grow at a faster rate than the mainstream mortgage market. We expect this outperformance will continue for the foreseeable future."*[113] And yet, just 12 months later, Kent was announcing lower profits, noting that *"the disappointment of the year has been the writedowns and impairments caused by the manifesting of the liquidity crunch."*[114] Basically, they got tagged on their portfolio of mortgage exotica, which they didn't know how to assess or value. But Kent and co did explain that *"[b]efore 2007 no payment problems and no credit concerns had been encountered by these assets."*[115] So what? That's a bit like saying my car was shiny and new before I smashed it into the wall. Of course, but who cares?

In closing for the year, Kent added that *"[t]he Board believes Bradford and Bingley has the...expertise and policies to respond well to these conditions."*[116] In fact, they didn't: within months of the publication of the accounts, it was lights out for Kent and B&B. Enter Richard Pym, B&B's new Chairman, who joined in August 2008, a month before Lehman blew up, to oversee what would be *"a very disappointing year."*[117] Rather an understatement. In fact, Pym inherited a bank on the brink: one with a rapidly deteriorating loan portfolio (with delinquencies tripling in one year, despite the aforementioned "prudent approach to underwriting"), a devalued mortgage investment portfolio, very strained wholesale liquidity access, and a shrinking retail deposit base. In fact, it was too late for Pym to do anything at all, and in late September the regulators served notice that B&B no longer qualified as a deposit-taker.

That was the end of the line – the building society was effectively nationalized, with some portions of the bank transferred to Abbey (which would itself become wholly owned by Spanish bank Santander). For Pym, *"[t]his was a hugely disappointing outcome for the bank."*[118] During ex-post testimony he noted

74 See No Evil

the almost certain fate that awaited B&B during the turbulent September 2008 period: *"[P]oor little Bradford & Bingley, the last mortgage bank standing was always going to be the centre of media attention and, therefore, there was a loss of customer confidence. There is no denying that a mortgage bank with a large element of self-certified mortgages and a buy-to-let book is not going to be an attractive asset in these financial markets."*[119] Labour MP Jim Cousins noted with some disbelief that *"when Bradford & Bingley's buy-to-let mortgage book was nationalized, we have effectively got under public control something like 20% of the buy-to-let market in the whole of the United Kingdom."*[120] That's a lot of questionable mortgages resting on the shoulders of the British citizenry.

Back over to Germany for a quick look at the state banking sector (Landesbanken), which accounts for 40 percent of the national marketplace, and which has long been characterized by opacity and mismanagement, very high leverage, and more than a few "accidents" (some of these problems no doubt fueled by a 2001 ruling that granted Landesbanken unlimited state guarantees on all debt that they issued – meaning they could use funds backed by the taxpayer base to dabble in risky things). As Finance Minister Steinbrueck noted after the crisis, Germany has *"too many state banks and many lack a convincing business model."*[121]

Two of the earliest casualties of the crisis were Landesbank Sachsen Girozentrale (SachsenLB) and IKB Deutsche Industriekredit (IKB), who were very actively involved in all manner of exotic instruments – their portfolios were chock-full of things with very sharp edges (the German regulators and the state governments were apparently unaware). SachsenLB held a formidable €17b portfolio of mortgage paper on and off balance sheet as a means of boosting revenues, but which wound up generating losses of €1.7b in 2007 and a similar amount in later years. Bad luck! In the end, SachsenLB was rescued by the state of Saxony and Landesbank Baden-Wurtenburg through a special €17.3b credit line.

IKB, for its part, held an equally formidable €17.5b portfolio of subprime garbage through an off-balance sheet vehicle, which it had used to juice up its income. Even as the rumblings of the mortgage crisis were sounding IKB's CEO Ortseifen indicated that the *"uncertainties in the American mortgage market...[would have] practically no effect"* on the bank.[122] Well, not quite: during the first leg down in August 2007, the value of its portfolio plummeted and losses soared. In order to avoid a collapse, the German government orchestrated a €3.5b bank rescue; this was followed by a series of additional steps in November 2007 and February 2008, by which time the total rescue tab came in at €9.2b – or, as Nicolas Veron, financial analyst said: *"a staggering cost to the taxpayer, given IKB's size."*[123] State bank KfW became the major shareholder in IKB through the bailout. What of all this speculative activity? Did the bank know what it was doing? A Deutsche trader indicated that *"IKB was still buying strong in early 2007, but they were very specific about the collateral they wanted in the [bonds]. They had a big research team of 20 guys and would inspect the asset quality outside of what any rater was saying about the bond. They wanted subprime paper.*"[124] In fact, they were well known in the market as "yield chasers" – buying in whatever they could for a few extra basis points of yield. Oops.

Since IKB was one of the first large public bailouts, Steinbrueck felt compelled to provide some defense: "*IKB would have been the first European bank to go bankrupt as a direct consequence of the US subprime crisis...[w]e can ill-afford this as a symbol of the German banking market.*"[125] So, a point of national pride, rather than one of systemic national importance? No, said Steinbrueck: "*[t]he issue here is ultimately about choosing the lesser evil, and about what is less damaging to the economy...[o]therwise, we could have seen massive effects on the banking sector, with corresponding effects on the real economy.*"[126] In the aftermath, the bank's management decided to reinvent itself a bit: "*Innovative financing solutions will remain an integral part of the business model, while investments in international securities portfolios will not. IKB's new business model creates a suitable platform for generating stable future returns, although at a significantly lower level compared to the previous financial years.*"[127] Indeed: you can't generate the same returns if you can't lever up and buy risky securities. In the aftermath, Wolfgang Gerke, head of the Bavarian Finance Center, echoed the view of many: "*I would have never thought that IKB or SachsenLB would get into so much trouble.*"[128] Indeed, who would have suspected that these taxpayer-funded banks would have had more leverage and more toxicity than most hedge funds. It sounds a little bit like Fannie and Freddie (as you'll see in the next chapter).

And then there's Westdeutsche Landesbank (WestLB), which at one time aspired to the big international league, a la Deutsche, even though it had experienced past stumbles. Back in 2006, then-Chairman Thomas Fischer declared that "*[t]he legacies of the past have largely been eliminated. We are now looking forward with optimism. It is our wish and our aim to grow – self-confidently, while at the same time maintaining a consistently moderate risk profile.*"[129] In fact, it didn't have a "moderate risk profile" at all, but a very aggressive one. In the event, Fischer was ousted in 2007 over some proprietary trading screwups, and was replaced by Alex Stuhlmann. Stuhlmann sought to distance his bank from other high-profile disasters, noting that we "*won't be the next SachsenLB or IKB because [the bank] has high liquidity and minimal subprime exposure.*"[130] Actually it wasn't different at all. The bank had a €23b portfolio of risky bonds sitting off balance sheet, which would eventually be written down to approximately €7b – not a brilliant investment. Why did a German state bank have such a huge portfolio of subprime and other mortgage bonds? What of Fischer's "moderate risk profile"?

In early 2008 Stuhlmann and the board noted that "*[a]s a consequence of the persistently difficult market developments, which have deteriorated further in recent* weeks, the managing board no longer believes that a positive group result can be achieved in 2007."[131] Meaning, it had to write down the value of its mortgage bonds. The bank reported a full year loss of €1.7b, with Stuhlmann saying that WestLB was *"faced with probably the most challenging situation in its history, not least because it additionally had to shoulder substantial losses in its proprietary trading activities."*[132] Moderate risk profile? He also noted that *"[w]e must immediately begin to shape the future of WestLB and to make the remaining jobs as safe as possible."*[133] The bank ring-fenced its toxic portfolio in a special "wind down" vehicle and obtained a €5b loss guarantee from the state, causing Stuhlmann to say that *"WestLB is today freed from most of the burdens of the capital markets' crisis."*[134] Shortly thereafter Stuhlmann was out and new CEO Heinz Hilgert was in.

Hilgert and his team continued to work on a further restructuring of the bank, but at least some remained skeptical. Simon Adamson, analyst at CreditSight, noted in 2009 that *"WestLB is living on borrowed time…If it hadn't been for the support from the state and owners, WestLB wouldn't still exist. You always expect the worst from WestLB."*[135] Hardly a ringing endorsement, but not an uncommon view: Dieter Hein, analyst at Fairesearch, said *"WestLB was the most powerful state-owned bank in Germany about 10 years ago…[n]ow it's been hit by trading problems and sub-prime and is seeking a merger from a weakened position."*[136] Hilgert eventually lost the support of the state owners and departed in May 2009. Enter interim management and regulators, who put together a broader restructuring plan, creating a good bank and a bad bank (the latter holding €85b of garbage). It is fair to say that WestLB represents a lesson in international capital markets dealing and speculative investing gone horribly wrong.

Commenting on all of these failures, Steinbrueck noted acidly that the banks *"did not apparently have the know-how"*[137] to engage in such business lines. Adam Posten, Peterson Institute of Economics saw it this way: *"The Landesbanken, and IKB of a similar ilk, suffer from much the same tension, yielding much the same results. With expectation of their ultimate government guarantee, as demonstrated in recent months, the managers of these German financial hybrids could recklessly pursue profits in instruments they did not understand."*[138] Naturally, the German tax payer got taken in all of this, footing the bill for the misadventures of the state banks (as well as a few others, like Hypo Real Estate, Bayersiche Landesbank, Dresdner, et al.).

EU Commissioner Günter Verheugen held the German banks to the fire, noting that they had been *"world champions in risky banking transactions."*[139] In fact, the political-regulatory establishment also received some blame. An op-ed in Süddeutsche Zeitung asked: *"Who is responsible when something goes wrong in a state-run bank? A range of politicians sit at the head of KfW's supervisory board…of course these bank managers can't personally follow every securities transaction. But it must have been clear to these political leaders that something had gone wrong with the bank's risk-management capability... The IKB debacle cost the KfW – and, in the end, German taxpayers – billions. Handlers around Steinbrück... should have done everything in their power to prevent another collapse. Instead, Steinbrück has used every opportunity to wag his finger (at private banks) and talk down the damage this financial crisis will cause the German economy. Anyone who calls for better risk management in private banking has to first make sure that his own house is in order."*[140]

And then, of course, there's Iceland's disaster, which saw its three largest banks – Glitnir, Kaupthing, and Landsbanki Islands – fail in the weeks after Lehman as a result of illiquidity, bad (corrupt?) lending, intercompany shenanigans, cross equity holdings, and bad investments. The collapse of the country's banking system had a devastating impact on the local economy and the public at large, and led to a change in government. In the aftermath of the national disaster, a 2300 page postmortem (ominously titled the "Black Report") singled out mismanagement by seven senior government officials as well as a bunch of bank executives. Newly elected Prime Minister Johanna Sigurdardottir said: *"[T]he private banks failed, the supervisory system failed, the politics failed, the administration failed, the media failed, the ideology of an unregulated free market utterly failed."*[141] Sounds like a good piece of the island nation fell down on the job. Special criticism was directed at former PM Haarde and central bank head Odsson; Pall Hreinsson, Chairman of the investigative committee put it this way: *"They had the necessary information but did not act accordingly, each point the finger at the next person."*[142]

In literally all of the cases I've described in this chapter, board directors were again asleep at the wheel, providing no especial critique of what was going on. McFall: *"These are pretty distinguished people. What happened? Were they scrutinising the chief executives or do the chief executives just run amok?"*[143] Turner indicated: *"There is an issue, I think, about simply the total amount of time the non-execs spend on businesses as complicated as banks and insurance companies.... you really do have to put a hell of a lot of time into it."*[144] It seems few of them did.

To be sure, a small number of European banks fared better than others. But why? Thurston, head of HSBC's UK businesses, captured the essence: *"[N]ot all European banks fared as poorly... [t]hose with less exposure to the nastiest areas escaped relatively unscathed in the first wave, though virtually all of them stumbled in the second wave as the dominoes kept toppling in directions that no one really expected. So, while they may look a bit better on paper because they posted less red ink, many of them did so on the basis of luck rather than foresight or risk management skill. Does that make anyone feel any better?"*[145] In the end, the European bankers were just as wrong as their US colleagues.

4
The Fannie and Freddie Sinkhole

Let me now shift my focus from the seemingly incompetent bankers to those operating outside the world's financial capitals. I'll start in this chapter with Fannie and Freddie, the powerful government-sponsored (and now government-owned) entities at the heart of the housing crisis, and move on to the rating agencies in the next and the regulators, politicians, and lobbyists in the following one.

Fannie and Freddie have been at the center of the US mortgage industry for decades and, given the sheer size of the marketplace, their activities have historically had a direct and indirect effect on homeowners in the US and investors around the world. Little wonder, then, that the two agencies featured so prominently in the crisis.

Setting the stage

Before I explore how Fannie and Freddie fared during the crisis, it's helpful to look at some of the particulars characterizing the two – this gives a flavor as to why things went so terribly wrong.

Schizophrenic business model
I'll begin with the Fannie/Freddie business model. The two agencies have always seemed somewhat schizophrenic in trying to serve two very different stakeholders – shareholders and politicians – which is perhaps why they lie on life support in the hands of US government. Perhaps that is just as well, as their mission is more political than commercial, and they've always had to dance to the tune played by their handlers on Capitol Hill.

In fact, the Fannie/Freddie business model seemed contradictory even before the crisis: on one hand, they had to maximize earnings for their shareholders, while on the other hand they had to fulfill increasingly risky government-mandated housing goals. And, they had to achieve both goals whilst keeping risks under control. How could they do all of that, successfully? Well, the answer is that they couldn't. Leaders of the two institutions realized that at the turn of the millennium, and began taking more risk and manipulating their earnings. Of course, when the earnings debacle was uncovered politicians and regulators should've realized that the firms were out of control – and that it would just be a question of time before the excessive leverage and increasingly risky portfolios would create bigger problems. But virtually no one did, and certainly no one did anything to change course.

And what of this schizophrenia? Back in 2005, Congressman Ron Paul noted that *"[t]he connection between the [enterprises] and the government helps isolate the [enterprises'] managements from market discipline."*[1] Peter Wallison of the American Enterprise Institute noted that *"[t]he S&L analogue at Fannie and Freddie is that no financial institution can serve two masters. Government-sponsored enterprises – to the extent that they are owned by shareholders but also have a government 'mission' – are living contradictions."*[2] James Lockhart, one-time head of Office of Federal Housing Enterprise Oversight (OFHEO), and then head of its more powerful successor Federal Housing Finance Authority (FHFA), testified that *"[b]oth CEO's told me that one of their worst fears was missing their affordable housing goals, which they ended up doing in 2008...Probably worse from the CEO's standpoint it would have incurred the wrath of their Congressional supporters."*[3] If your worst fear as a shareholder-owned corporation is missing government goals rather than failing to deliver returns to shareholders, then there's a problem.

Former Freddie CEO Richard Syron noted a year before the company blew up that Freddie *"has to answer to shareholders, to our regulator and to Congress, and those groups often demand completely contradictory things."*[4] Former Fannie CEO Dan Mudd conceded the same: *"Maintaining the delicate balance between profitability as a private company and service to a public mission became impossible."*[5] More tellingly, he said, *"in 2008 the [agency] model became, in hindsight, the 'Pit and the Pendulum'."*[6] So, in the end the shareholders got screwed, the US taxpayers got screwed, investors in Fannie and Freddie bonds got screwed. And the regulators and politicians just whistled in the wind.

Big, leveraged and risky

Recapping a bit from Chapter 1, the collective Fannie/Freddie mission is simple: facilitate the origination of home mortgages in the US by buying mortgages from banks and then repackaging them into mortgage bonds (to be sold to lots of institutional investors around the world) or by actually purchasing such mortgage bonds directly from other banks and holding them on their own books. The pair have also historically acted as a de-facto liquidity backstop, buying up mortgage bonds to keep bond prices well supported. The confluence of these activities has created efficiencies that have led to lower mortgage rates for homeowners, creating something of a virtuous cycle. But also some very, very big and leveraged balance sheets. Indeed, as early as 2001 the Bush Administration noted that *"[t]he size of the two GSEs is a potential problem [because] financial trouble of a large GSE could cause strong repercussions in financial markets, affecting Federally insured entities and economic activity."*[7] Rather prescient – coming seven years before the twins blew up.

To put their might and clout into perspective, Fannie and Freddie directly or indirectly touch 9 of 10 mortgages originated in the US. And they've historically been able to do so because of their ability to raise really cheap funds. Why so cheap? Because people have long believed that even though Fan and Fred were shareholder corporations, they benefited from an implicit US Government guarantee. Apparently one of the few people who didn't realize that was Representative Barney "Roll the Dice" Frank, who noted a few years ago that *"[n]obody should be under any illusions that there is any guarantee, implicit, explicit, whatever-plicit. It just ain't there."*[8] And then a few years later he said it again: *"Let me say right now, if you are listening, if you are buying Fannie or Freddie's paper because you think I am going to vote to bail you out, sell it, and cash it in, I am not going to do that. I do not think there is a Federal guarantee."* Well, Barney, that's not quite true: in September 2008 the implicit Federal guarantee became very explicit – to the tune of trillions of dollars.

And what does that kind of market dominance mean? That the agencies were, and still are, very, very big and influential. As the crisis was erupting Fannie had securitized or guaranteed $2.8t of mortgages, Freddie another $1.9t; they also had "purchased" as investments a collective $1.4t of bonds. That's a total of $6.1t – meaning lots of room for error. Back in 2005 Wallison put it all into perspective: *"[O]nly two companies – both of which are GSEs and implicitly backed by the U.S. government – account for more default risk than all other U.S. corporations combined."*[9] A bit scary. JP Morgan's Dimon: *"you know, I've always looked at Fannie Mae and Freddie Mac as being part of the issue in how they grew over time…. I do think they were part of the problem for the industry as a whole."*[10]

Unfortunately, they supported all of this mortgage activity on the thinnest sliver of capital. Leverage was excessive, a by-product of political maneuvering that allowed Congress, rather than the regulator, to set capital levels. And Congress set really low capital levels. Why? Apparently they were persuaded that the mission was worthy and the assets were low risk. During testimony before the crisis, Fannie's former CEO Raines said that *"[t]hese assets are so riskless that their capital for holding them should be under 2%."*[11] Furthermore, he said that *"banks are in a far more risky business than we are."*[12] Wrong. Armando Falcon, one-time head of OFHEO, noted that *"[t]he lack of flexibility on setting capital requirements was especially troubling. By statute, the enterprises' minimum capital requirement was set at 2.5%, which permitted them to operate at a highly leveraged level with very little margin for error. We never received the regulatory discretion to raise this standard."*[13] That view was seconded by the FDIC's Bair: *"[C]apital requirements for holding residential mortgage risk were lower than the regulatory capital requirements that applied to banks and thrifts."*[14] And despite protestations from Lockhart that *"I was...making it clear that the law was inadequate as it allowed the Enterprises to be too highly leveraged"*[15] Congress, in its wisdom, thought it knew best: Fannie and Freddie had very "low risk" portfolios, therefore didn't need much capital. Wrong again. I'll come back to this point in Chapter 6.

So Fannie and Freddie were (and still are) big, important and, of course, a perfect vehicle for all manner of political nonsense. In fact, it is worth going on a slight detour to understand how Fan/Fred wound up with portfolios that had a certain amount of bad stuff. The catalyst can be traced to the 1977 Community Reinvestment Act, which legislators drafted to promote lending to hard hit areas: banks had to fill certain loan quotas if they wanted regulatory approval to open new branches – a little quid pro quo. Fan and Fred would buy up these mortgages and everyone was happy. This worked okay for some years, as the quotas were pretty reasonable and the really dangerous subprime products didn't yet exist. In fact, during the 1980s and 1990s the two companies were quite profitable, enjoying the benefit of an implicit government guarantee to borrow at cheap rates, and of course enjoying a virtual duopoly on major portions of US conforming home mortgages.

In 1995 the government took another step, letting the agencies use subprime mortgage bonds as credit toward their low income housing quotas. Instead of buying loans, they bought mortgage bonds. Meaning? That instead of scrutinizing individual loans, they outsourced the underwriting to banks assembling the bonds, losing control of detailed risk evaluation – you can see where this one was headed. And then they really lost their way: in 1999 the Clinton administration, under Housing and Urban Development (HUD) secretary Andrew Cuomo, demanded an increase in the percentage of loans banks made to lower-income folks – basically using legislative and regulatory tools to reshape bank risk portfolios. Specifically, according to HUD, *"Secretary Cuomo established new Affordable Housing Goals requiring Fannie Mae and Freddie Mac to buy $2.4t in mortgages in the next 10 years...new affordable housing for 28.1 million low- and moderate income families."*[16] In effect, the rules required Fan and Fred to increase by more than 20 percent their purchases of low and moderate income stuff. And, though the intent was to use the Fan/Fred underwriting standards to guide subprime loan origination, banks ignored this approach, originated with all manner of gimmicks (teasers, negative amortization, no money down, low/no documentation, etc.) and persuaded Fan and Fred to ease their standards; despite some initial resistance, the two eventually gave way, opening the floodgates for the next four years.

Sanda Fostek, a former HUD regulator, said that the two firms *"made no progress in civilizing the market."*[17] Indeed, in a speech to the Mortgage Bankers Association in 2004, Raines said that he and his rivals at Freddie *"made no bones about their interest in buying loans made to borrowers formerly considered the province of nonprime and other niche lenders,"*[18] and were happy to *"push products and opportunities to people who have lesser credit quality."*[19] When the Bush administration increased quotas even further in 2004, the two started buying even more subprime loans and securities. Christopher Caldwell, *Weekly Standard*: *"Bill Clinton's claim that minorities were excluded from housing markets turned into a self-congratulatory crusade (under Clinton himself, but much more so under George Bush) to push loan on un-creditworthy poor people."*[20] According to Freddie spokeswoman Sharon McHale: *"The market knew we needed those loans ... [the higher goals] forced us to go into that market to serve the targeted populations that HUD wanted us to serve."*[21] So, the balance sheets were chock-full of subprime stuff. William C. Apgar Jr., an assistant HUD secretary under Clinton, regretted allowing the companies to count subprime securities as affordable: *"It was a mistake ... [i]n hindsight, I would have done it differently."*[22] And, from Lockhart's perspective as regulator: *"I believe that high affordable housing goals and the resulting political pressure compounded by the Enterprises' drive for market share and short-term profitability were major reasons why they lowered their underwriting standards."*[23]

Daniel Mudd, speaking to a Congressional panel after the crisis hit, observed that *"Fannie Mae-quality, safe loans in the subprime market did not become the standard, and the lending market moved away from us."*[24] While Fannie (and Freddie) claimed to have turned away some of this business, it's clear that they didn't do enough goal-tending. The weak standards, when coupled with a sharply declining housing market and the absolute magnitude of the Fan/Fred balance sheets, were enough to create massive problems. Dr Susan Wachter, of the Wharton School, observed that *"[a]fter they started losing market share to PLS [private label securities] ... shareholder and other pressures led them to purchase PLS backed by non-standard mortgages for their portfolio. To be clear, they did not create the risky mortgage-backed securities that caused the crisis, but they did become a burden to the taxpayer because they were allowed to purchase them after private institutions had manufactured them."*[25] Wallison said, *"By the early 2000s, Fannie and Freddie were buying loans which involved no downpayment at all. The result is clear today. At the time Fannie and Freddie had to be taken over by the government, they held or had guaranteed 10 million subprime and Alt-A loans."*[26] Wow.

Another sign things weren't going too well: a 2004 memo prepared by one-time chief risk officer Andrukonis for Syron expressed concern about Freddie's increasing moves down the credit spectrum. In the memo he said these weak loans *"would likely pose an enormous financial and reputational risk to the company and the country."*[27] Furthermore, he said, *"[t]he push to do more affordable business and increase share means more borderline and unprofitable business will come in. The best credit enhancement is a profit margin and ours is likely to get squeezed as we respond to these market pressures."*[28] He was right, he was ignored, and he left, noting later that *"[e]verybody understood that at some level the company was putting taxpayers at risk."*[29]

Cooking the books

And then there was a damaging sideshow reflecting that the teams in charge were just as greedy as their Wall Street brethren, putting their own personal interests ahead of anything else. In the late 1990s the pressure for continued profits and rising stock prices caused both firms to start cooking their books. OFHEO discovered in 2004 widespread accounting irregularities covering a three-year period (2001–4). Fannie ultimately had to restate $6.3b of falsely inflated profits (spending another $1.6b to put the right fixes in place) and ousted Raines along with the CFO and controller. By the way, the trio had been paid over $115m in incentive comp for hitting their [falsely created] earnings. The government filed civil charges against them, recouping some of the comp in 2008 (Raines spun it this way: *"[the] process invoked against me by OFHEO was fundamentally unfair. While I long ago accepted managerial accountability for any errors committed by subordinates while I was CEO, it is a very different matter to suggest that I was legally culpable in any way. I was not."*[30]) Oh. Congressman Ron Paul had a different take: *"There has been much evidence of fraud at Fannie and Freddie, but when one man, Franklin Raines, defrauded the organization out of millions of dollars through illegal accounting tricks, and ends up agreeing to pay back just a fraction, one could argue that it was well worth it to him."*[31] And in Lockhart's view, *"The image of Fannie Mae as one of the lowest-risk and 'best in class' institutions was a façade. Senior management manipulated accounting; reaped maximum, undeserved bonuses; and prevented the rest of the world from knowing."*[32]

Sidebar: in an interesting bit of bravado, Raines reported in Congressional testimony that *"[a]s we expanded home ownership and our service to the market, Fannie Mae also met or exceeded the safety and soundness requirements of the 1992 Act. In 2000, we adopted six voluntary initiatives to enhance our liquidity, transparency and market discipline"*[33] – this, though his finance team was busy cooking the books. Let's see, I'm not a lawyer, but...if the testimony was given under oath, and financials were being gamed...I think that's perjury?

Same game over at Freddie: in 1999 it overstated its earnings by $1b, and between 2000 and 2002 it understated its earnings by approximately $5b, and had to go through the same drill as Fannie, firing top executives and spending a bundle to shore up its internal controls; new Chairman O'Mallley, commenting on the results of a seven-month investigation related to the disclosure problems, noted that *"[t]his is a painful day for Freddie Mac."*[34] Indeed. If only shareholders had abandoned ship at this point, they would have preserved at least some of their capital.

Returning to a familiar theme, I'm not entirely sure where the directors at Fannie and Freddie were whilst billions of dollars of profits were being manipulated, but perhaps that should've been a warning that they were not in control of the executive team or the business. In a tap dance before Congress, Freddie Director George Gould noted that *"[a]s frustrating as these accounting issues are, let me say a few encouraging words about safety and soundness. Freddie Mac's franchise is rock solid. Our exposure to both credit risk and interest rate risk remains extremely low."*[35] Wrong on every count. Again, the accounting misdeeds should have been an early warning signal: if the business can't be properly controlled during good times, how can it be controlled during bad times?

Still, some politicians didn't get it, to wit Barney Frank: *"I would also say that with all of the misdeeds of Fannie and Freddie, their safety and soundness has not been called into question. Yes, there were accounting misdeeds...but safety and soundness has not been called into question."*[36] Really? Really? Actually, Barney, their houses were already starting to rot. Others, happily, were a bit more critical, such as Texas Representative Jeb Hensarling, who pointed out what no one wanted to say – that because Fan and Fred financed lower-income housing, they were somehow special: *"[w]e have now seen in recent years the largest financial restatement in history, dwarfing the financial restatements that we saw at Enron and WorldCom...when we saw all of these accounting irregularities earlier on with the Enrons and WorldComs of the world, Congress was outraged....[b]ut all of a sudden, there seems to have been a deafening silence when we see Fannie and Freddie engaged in activities that with respect to the financial restatements rival those that I have described."*[37] A double standard? Where politics are involved – certainly.

Obstruction

During the first half of the decade warnings from OFHEO, the Fed, and the Treasury regarding the growing risks posted by the two were ignored by many politicians, and attempts to introduce new regulations came to naught (a point I will discuss in a bit more detail in Chapter 6). Politics reared its ugly head: any real attempts at reform were interpreted by Fannie-Freddie champions in the Congress as somehow threatening the social housing mission. Senator Chuck Schumer's comments in 2003 were typical of the DC-speak that prevented meaningful change: *"...my worry is that we're using the recent safety and soundness concerns, particularly with Freddie, and with a poor regulator, as a straw man to curtail Fannie and Freddie's mission. And I don't think there is any doubt that there are some in the administration who don't believe in Fannie and Freddie altogether, say let the private sector do it.*"[38]

Obstruction of reform was the order of the day. Karl Rove, then advisor to President Bush, observed that *"the GSEs fought back. They didn't want to see the Bush reforms enacted, because that would level the playing field for their competitors."*[39] Falcon testified that *"the Fannie and Freddie political machine resisted any meaningful regulation using highly improper tactics. OFHEO was constantly subjected to malicious political attacks and efforts of intimidation."*[40] Like what? Well, according to Falcon, on the eve of releasing a report on systemic risk that was critical of the agencies, *"Frank Raines, called me to protest about the release of the report and its conclusions. He urged me not to release it and when I reaffirmed my plans, he threatened to bring down me and the agency."*[41] Raines and co had to make their earnings targets, and could suffer no disturbance from a humble regulator. Remember, meet the earnings target, get more stock and options in the bonus package. Sounds like Wall Street.

Falcon wasn't alone in experiencing the pushback. Lockhart said that *"President Bush had been pushing for GSE reform for many years before I joined OFHEO. The need for legislation was obvious as OFHEO was regulating two of the largest and most systematically important US financial institutions and yet its powers were much weaker than bank or even state insurance regulators. Unfortunately, it took Congress, especially the Senate much too long to pass the legislation. It only happened 38 days before we had to place the Enterprises into conservatorship."*[42] In testimony Lockhart quoted from an e-mail from *"then Fannie Mae COO, Dan Mudd, to its CEO Frank Raines, in which he said that 'The old political reality was that we always won, we took no prisoners ... we used to ... be able to write, or have written rules that worked for us.'"*[43] Just a few well-placed roadblocks: that's how Washington works, to the ultimate detriment of the taxpayers.

Downward spiral

With that background in mind, let me turn to the crisis period. In the lead-up to the dislocation, the two agencies lurched forward with new management, obviously questionable controls, and risky balance sheets, still trying to give the appearance that everything was okay. In fact, the agencies were already a very, very highly leveraged bet on a single marketplace that had appreciated substantially in recent years – a recipe for disaster. Mudd insisted in 2005 that *"we have made fundamental changes to the Fannie Mae of old. While we initiated many changes to correct problems in accounting, controls, and structure, our overall ambition was to build an ever-stronger, more capable business."*[44] Well, that obviously didn't work out too well. In fact, Lockhart saw it quite differently: *"When*

86 *See No Evil*

I joined OFHEO in May of 2006, both Fannie Mae and Freddie Mac were very troubled as they were recovering from their accounting scandals. They were unable to produce timely financial statements and had serious deficiencies in systems, risk management and internal controls."[45] Falcon said: *"Fannie and Freddie executives worked hard to persuade investors that mortgage related assets were a riskless investment, while at the same time covering up the volatility and risks of their own mortgage portfolios and balance sheet."*[46] Yes, indeed. Of course, they were already undercapitalized at this juncture, holding far too little capital against their portfolios to protect them from the looming storm.

Still, Mudd insisted that *"as we worked through these transitional changes, we kept our business balanced in a tough market, delivering reasonable – but not stellar – results and maintaining a solid risk profile ... [w]e chose to stand back from the frenzy and avoid competing for mortgage assets and securitization business we thought too risky or unprofitable."*[47] Fundamentally, he believed, Fannie *"maintained a solid book of business with a relatively low-risk profile in an exceptionally high-risk market ... put[ting] Fannie Mae in a stronger position to deal with turmoil in our market today."*[48] Thank goodness they had a "solid risk profile," and stood back from the "frenzy" – or else they would have lost more tens of billions than the tens of billions they wound up losing.

The picture started changing in 2007, with the first market rumblings creating a $2b loss at Fannie. Never mind, said Mudd: *"in market crises, firms that husband capital, invest wisely where others retreat, and prudently manage their risks tend to thrive in the long run. That is our approach at Fannie Mae."*[49] That didn't work out as planned, leading one to wonder where the disconnect occurred? Risk management? Well, apparently not, because according to Mudd, *"[w]e have completed a three-year rebuilding of a new executive team and a Board with deep expertise in financial and credit risk management,"*[50] and, *"through our new Chief Risk Officer and his staff, as well as the risk managers in each business unit, we are managing our interest rate, credit, and operational exposures amid the turbulence in the markets."*[51] Mudd closed on an upbeat note, seemingly not capturing the essence of what was going on or what was coming: *"We believe Fannie Mae is in a solid position to continue weathering the market turmoil as it continues through 2008."*[52] How is it possible, at this point, that one of the key players in the US housing market could not understand the depth and breadth of the crisis and its potential impact on its own operations? How could it claim its risks were prudent? It stretches credulity. Of course, in the aftermath, Mudd changed his tune: *"in hindsight, though, less exposure to new homeowners, non-traditional products and regions of the country in economic downturn might have reduced losses."*[53] D'ya think?

An equally surreal situation was playing out at Freddie. In early 2006 Syron was trying to polish the company's image after its accounting mishap, focusing on how good it was in managing its housing market risks: *"We achieved...healthy growth by executing on our underlying franchise strengths of excellent credit and interest-rate risk management...Regarding our...risk management record, it remains a hallmark of the industry...we continue to manage risk prudently and consistently in a world of rapidly changing rate conditions."*[54] Words to remember: "a hallmark of the industry." When leaders speak of their capabilities in such glowing terms, look out. And, unfortunately, a bit of hubris: *"Freddie Mac's financial strength is beyond question. Abundant capital. Disciplined risk management. Strong customer relationships. An established franchise in a defined and growing market. These are Freddie Mac's continuing strengths."*[55] More words to remember: "financial strength is beyond question." Unfortunately nothing in this world is beyond question; when leaders speak of "beyond question" and "undoubted," a world of hurt is probably approaching very quickly. In fact, even as Syron was spinning all of this, Lockhart was getting nowhere with the board: *"At the Freddie Mac Board meeting I went through a long list of issues to convince the Board that it would be prudent to cap their portfolios. I mentioned growing credit risk. The pushback from the Board was quite intense as they and most Americans in the summer of 2006, despite the growing housing bubble, were in denial."*[56]

A year later Syron still sounded reasonably confident: *"[D]espite last year's many challenges...Freddie Mac made continued progress. We increased our earnings, served our vital public mission and strengthened our franchise."*[57] This was accompanied by a note of caution: *"[w]hile we are in better position than many, we have set aside increased loan loss reserves, as our credit portfolio remains vulnerable to significant declines in house prices."*[58] But also one that would fall far short of the mark: *"[A]s we complete our financial reporting and internal controls remediation, I hope we will be in a better position to return some of the capital in excess of our statutory minimum that we have accumulated over the past several years."* Not only would Freddie not return capital to investors, it would absorb piles of new capital from US taxpayers.

Not surprisingly, the world changed for Freddie during 2007, when *"weakening house prices and punishing deterioration of credit hurt Freddie Mac's results, along with those of other mortgage market participants"*[59] – to the tune of $3.1b. So much for "disciplined risk management." Then it was just a bit more of the requisite corporate banter, with some evidence that the company still didn't have a clue that it was about to get pulverized: *"[A]s a company that prides itself on our singular focus and expertise in managing mortgage risk, we can and must do better...we believe our sound credit standards and policies will stand us in good stead. The company remains safe and sound."*[60] Syron's last comments as CEO seem now a bit bizarre: *"I can say this with confidence: the housing finance companies that prosper most in the long term will be those that have built the strongest foundation for the future. And Freddie Mac, albeit with some difficulty, has built such a foundation in the last several years."*[61] Indeed, there was no foundation at all.

The continued slide in housing prices, the spike in delinquencies and foreclosures, and the sharp decrease in mortgage bond prices created tens of billions of losses for the beleaguered pair. The jig was up in early September 2008 when the extent of accelerating losses became untenable. Just days before Lehman's collapse the two were placed under conservatorship by the new regulator FHFA, becoming wards of the state. Fannie, now under leadership of ex-Merrill president Herb Allison, noted: *"This adverse market environment intensified in the second half of 2008 ... we and Freddie Mac were placed into conservatorship."*[62] It was all quite breathtaking: just months earlier Fannie was touting its risk management prowess and its solidity, and then it booked $58b in losses and was nationalized. And the same over at Freddie: despite the great foundation the company claimed to have built, it managed to lose $50b in 2008. According to new CEO David Moffett: *"[w]e absorbed heavy financial losses last year, driven primarily by mark-to-market items and credit-related expenses."*[63] Sidebar: within 6 months Moffett would discover that it "ain't no fun" working for the government – and quit.

Of course, there was really no choice but to nationalize the two: their portfolios were chock-full of bad stuff (some of which they picked up as they tried in vain to support the market) and they had way too little capital to support what they were doing (never mind that Mr Raines and the pack of ultrasharp legislators thought that they had too much capital and were sound enterprises). Lockhart indicated that *"[u]nfortunately, as house prices, earnings and capital have continued to deteriorate, their ability to fulfill their mission has deteriorated."*[64] How is it possible that the two entities, with their hands on the pulse of the US housing market, mortgage risk, got it so wrong? Lockhart's view: *"over the last three years OFHEO, and now FHFA, have worked hard to encourage the Enterprises to rectify their accounting, systems, controls and risk management issues.... Unfortunately, the antiquated capital requirements and the turmoil in housing markets over-whelmed all the good and hard work put in by the FHFA teams and the Enterprises' managers and employees."*[65] I would go a bit further: years of risk mismanagement, lax regulation and oversight, and partisan politics had come home to roost.

The size of the problem was considerable. Between the conservatorship announcement in September 2008 and the end of 2009 Fannie and Freddie sucked up a collective $127b in bailout money from US taxpayers, and on Christmas Eve Day the US Treasury said there would be no limit to the amount of taxpayer money that would be allocated to keep them alive – in other words, an infinite call on the pocketbook of the US taxpayer. Freddie's new CEO Charles Haldeman (the third in less than two years, in case you are counting) noted that *"we expect to request additional funds from Treasury as this prolonged deterioration of market conditions continues to negatively impact our financial results."*[66] In fact, the losses were so staggering that they are still difficult to understand. Kyle Bass of Hayman tried to put the red ink into perspective this way: *"Fannie Mae lost 20½ years of its profits in the last 18 months...Freddie Mac lost 11½ years of profits in a little bit more than a year."*[67]

With the two firms under direct government control, the Obama administration then sought to bail out homeowners (forget personal responsibility), implementing some "loan modification programs" within the banking sector and via Fan and Fred. In fact, Fan and Fred became great vehicles for social welfare handouts and targeted funding of priority areas – easy to do when you are part of the government rather than a commercial enterprise. Haldeman made the point very clearly in early 2010: *"We're making decisions on [loan modifications]...without being guided solely by profitability, that no purely private bank ever could."*[68] More precisely, as Mudd observed in 2010, the entities are run *"as an instrument of national economic policy, not as a business."*[69] Same over at Fannie, where new CEO Mike Williams said *"we are helping homeowners across the country, supporting affordable housing and providing financing to keep the residential markets functioning."*[70] That sounds like a political rat-hole. In fact, it cost US taxpayers $26.4b in 2009 alone to help Fannie restructuring bad mortgages, and a slightly smaller amount at Freddie. To add insult to injury, some 25 percent of those receiving modified loans defaulted again in the 2009–10 period. As Stanford economist Thomas Sowell so aptly stated: *"Bailing out people who made ill-advised mortgages makes no more sense than bailing out people who lost their life savings in Las Vegas casinos."*[71]

In the aftermath Senator Christopher Dodd (head of the Banking Committee and also a friend of Angelo Mozilo and his preferred mortgage program) summarized the situation this way: *"Let me just say: Fannie and Freddie were neither the villains that caused the crisis, as some claim, nor the victims of that crisis, as others would make them out to be. They didn't create the subprime and exotic loan market – but they did chase it to generate profits. And, like many of the supposedly private financial institutions that ended up becoming equivalent to GSEs, Fannie and Freddie enriched their shareholders and management, while the public took the losses."*[72]

Like Dodd, Raines believed that *"Fannie Mae did not cause the current crisis."*[73] He also added that *"Fannie Mae was certainly leveraged...and, over the last decade, regulators, commentators, and company executives paid an extraordinary amount of attention to Fannie Mae's leveraged investments held in its mortgage portfolio."*[74] Really? US taxpayers can be thankful for their collective diligence. More tellingly, he went, on: *[T]he credit risk profile of Fannie Mae changed after 2004 because Fannie Mae, like a lot of smart investors, changed its appetite for credit risk in response to the changing market...Fannie Mae initially resisted pressures to relax its credit standards until 2006 to 2007. This helps to explain why Fannie's losses, while large in absolute dollar amount, are relatively small compared to mortgage credit losses suffered by the market as a whole.*"[75] Help me, Franklin, I'm struggling with this: the agencies lost enormous quantities of money, but since it was just a fraction of the total market losses, me and my fellow taxpayers should feel okay? Because it could have been worse? It's little wonder the two got into trouble. But on one point Raines seems correct: *"[n]o regulation or law forced banks or the GSEs to acquire loans that were so risky they imperiled the safety and soundness of the institutions. The acquisition of such loans was a business judgment made by management and the boards of directors."*[76] And they screwed up.

It's very difficult to understand how all of this got to such an awful state. Falcon is surely correct when he said that *"[t]he failure of Fannie Mae and Freddie Mac will be a case study in business schools for decades. How do you operate a business with the most generous government subsidies possible, which confer very powerful market advantages, and run the business into the ground?"*[77] Reflecting on the disaster in late 2008, Mudd observed that *"[y]ou've got the worst housing crisis in U.S. recorded history, and we're the largest housing finance company in the country, so when one goes down, the other goes with it."*[78] Interesting thought – shouldn't have this occurred to Fannie (and Freddie) before the crisis? Shouldn't they have figured that one day things in the housing market would go south? Did they not have a contingency plan? Syron, for his part, noted in a rather bizarre manner that *"If I had better foresight, maybe I could have improved things a little bit. But frankly, if I had perfect foresight, I would never have taken this job in the first place."*[79] Really? For the record, for the five years Syron served in the awful job, he earned $38m.

How much and what's next?

So what's the tab on the fiasco? How big is this particular sinkhole? Hayman's Bass: *"when you look at Fannie and Freddie particularly, that's $5.5 trillion of liabilities, OK? To put that into perspective, the mortgage market, at the end of '07, was about $10 trillion prime, $1.2 trillion subprime, $1.5 trillion Alt-A... We've already given Fannie and Freddie $183 billion alone, and we've opened the spigots, as of Christmas Eve, for as much capital as they need. We at Hayman think they'll lose $375 billion or more in the crisis."*[80] Wallison's numbers were of the same magnitude: *"when it is all said and done, cleaning up the mess at Fannie and Freddie will probably cost the American taxpayers $200 to $400 billion."*[81] William Shear, of the US Government Accountability Office, confirmed that *"the total cost of Treasury financial assistance will be nearly $400 billion."*[82] A Wall Street Journal op-ed reminded us the figure is so big that *"[t]he Obama Administration won't even put the companies on budget for fear of the deficit impact."*[83] And Kenneth Rosen, head of real estate research at University of California, said that *"[e]veryone's trying to* *sweep it under the rug, but there's a very large embedded loss that hasn't been fully realized yet ... [s]omeone's going to have to write a check, and it's very large."*[84]

By the way, the total losses on the US S&L crisis of the 1980s, which covered thousands of institutions, was less than $150b. So Fannie and Freddie handily eclipsed that disaster ... on their own. And, unlike the money given to Citi, B of A, JP Morgan, et al. during the crisis (already repaid, with a profit to the taxpayer), the money given to Fannie and Freddie almost certainly will never be repaid. So, yes, blame the bankers, but please don't forget that Fannie and Freddie, and the entire political and regulatory constellation surrounding the two gets its share of the blame, too.

In the end CLSA analyst Mayo observed that *"government facilitated allocation of capital to the housing market, so government's involved here, too."*[85] Furthermore, *"[a] massive amount of capital ... was allocated to the housing sector, government-incurred with a government guarantee, and that encouraged a whole industry off these government- sponsored entities. And that was a mistake, easy to say in hindsight. Many of us in the industry saw it for a while."*[86] Reflecting on a time when the agencies were still profitable, Wallison provided a neat summary: *"It looks today as though the allocation of those profits was pretty much as one would expect – first to the management, then to the losses incurred in their affordable housing mission, then to the shareholders in the form of dividends, and finally 7 basis points of benefit to home buyers. Of course, the embedded losses were reserved for the taxpayers, who never had an opportunity to reject the honor."*[87] Falcon's assessment was that the collapse was *"a failure of management ... and a deep rooted culture of arrogance and greed."*[88] Sounds like Wall Street.

These organizations have been a colossal disaster – mismanaged, misregulated, and subject to all manner of political shenanigans. Even though Acting FHFA Director DeMarco stated that *"[t]he businesses are trying to mitigate the losses to remediate the problems that led to conservatorship"*[89] others in Washington say it's time to pull the plug and create a new US housing finance system. Senator Richard Shelby confirmed that *"[a]s we consider the future of the GSEs, we would be wise to remember the disastrous consequences that poorly regulated GSEs can have on our financial markets."*[90] Treasury Secretary Geithner, for his part, indicated that *"we are going to have to bring very substantial reform to Fannie and Freddie, absolutely. And we are completely committed to that ... we ... need to make sure that we take a cold, hard look at what the future of those institutions should be in our country."*[91] Because, as the *Wall Street Journal* editors noted, *"[r]eforming the financial system without fixing Fannie and Freddie is like declaring a war on terror and ignoring al Qaeda."*[92] Of course Barney Frank weighed in, too: *"The committee will be recommending abolishing Fannie Mae and Freddie Mac in their current form and coming up with a whole new system of housing finance."*[93] Yes, we shall see – you may imagine there will still be lots of political resistance. Robert Wilmers, Head of M&T Bank: *"I recall a personal conversation with a member of Congress, who despite saying he understood my concerns about the two GSEs, admitted he would never push for significant change because 'they've done so much for me, my colleagues and my staff.'"*[94] The big US financial reform bill of 2010 didn't deal with Fannie/Freddie. Wallison noted that *"the bill does nothing to address this issue, and that the losses of Fannie Mae and Freddie Mac – whose chief sponsor over many years was the same Barney Frank – will cost the payers far more than the [bank bailouts]."*[95] And when the Republicans introduced an amendment to the bill to convert Fannie/Freddie into a private company with no further government subsidies, it was voted down by the Democrats with Senator Dodd leading the "nays."

Politics lives on...

5
Fuel to the Fire I: The Rating Agencies

Let me switch gears slightly, away from the bankers and housing enterprises, toward the credit rating agencies. More specifically, in this chapter I want to explore the role of "big three" agencies in the crisis. Standard and Poor's (S&P), Moody's, and Fitch are responsible for analyzing all manner of liabilities (like commercial paper, notes, and bonds), providing "opinions" on the likelihood issuers will continue to perform. While the agencies have been late to the party a few times with downgrades of failing companies, their overall record has generally been pretty good – at least for corporate obligations.

Not necessarily so in the area of "structured finance," which centers on structuring and rating of the very mortgage bonds and exotic instruments at the heart of the crisis. Rating these instruments proved rather more difficult than even the experts expected. And, unfortunately structured finance ratings became a big revenue engine for the agencies, meaning they were keen to keep the show going – rating anything and everything. As Harold McGraw III, former CEO of McGraw-Hill, the parent of S&P, said in 2007, *"[w]hat we do is provide access to the capital market. If the markets want those kinds of products and the institutional investors want those products, then we move with the market and we're going to rate whatever."*[1] That sounds just a bit frightening...rating "whatever"? In fact, the "whatevers" became a problem for all of the major agencies, adding plenty of fuel to the fire.

Issuer pays

Before I discuss some of the failings, let me quickly describe the business model used by the main firms: namely, "issuer pays," where the issuer (a company, a country, a special purpose entity), and not the investor, pays the ratings fees. Since an issuer can't come to the public markets without a rating (as many investors can't or won't buy unrated paper) the agencies have a nice choke-hold on the market: no fee, no rating, no market access.

But perhaps more importantly, this model gives rise to a potential conflict of interest, particularly with regard to structured products, where the agencies have historically acted as consultants to banks, giving advice on how to structure deals so that they attract the highest possible ratings. Not surprisingly, banks have always been interested in deals with top ratings since the resulting bonds can be sold much more readily, and if a particular agency doesn't deliver the proper rating, banks can theoretically go to another one to see if they can get better ratings – a sort of "ratings shopping." As a result of pressures coming from a handful of global banks that have historically dominated the market and the need for agencies to generate repeat business and keep revenues flowing in, the possibility that they will fall victim to some "ratings inflation" has always existed – a point that the agencies have consistently denied. But with a lot of supposed "AAA"-paper confined to the rubbish bin, you can form your own opinion. Paul Krugman's take on the matter: *"they morphed into something quite different: companies that were hired by the people selling debt to give that debt a seal of approval...Issuers of debt – which increasingly meant Wall Street firms selling securities they created by slicing and dicing claims on things like subprime mortgages – could choose among several rating agencies. So they could direct their business to whichever agency was most likely to give a favorable verdict, and threaten to pull business from an agency that tried too hard to do its job."*[2]

Sean Egan, head of Egan-Jones ratings agency (which follows an investor pays model), observed that *"[u]nder the issuer-paid business model, a rating agency which does not come in with the highest rating will, before long, be an underemployed ratings firm. It's that simple and all the explanations and excuses cannot refute the market evidence."*[3] I shall return to Mr Egan in Chapter 7. Unfortunately, this wasn't (or isn't) an academic discussion – but a real one. At least one Moody's executive, Yuri Yoshizawa, noted that *"[t]here was always pressure from banks."*[4] And an internal Moody's e-mail between analysts from April 2006 indicated that *"I am getting serious push back from Goldman on a deal that they want to go to market with today."*[5] A further S&P e-mail from August 2006 said that ratings analysts have *"become so beholden to their top issuers for revenue they have all developed a kind of Stockholm syndrome which they mistakenly tag as Customer Value creation."*[6] Trouble.

Mistakes were made

The three big agencies spent the first part of the decade building up their structured finance ratings business, helping support the rapidly growing global asset-backed bond market and creating significant revenue streams for their shareholders. Their methodologies and structuring advice helped banks (and the housing enterprises) create tens of billions in rated mortgage securities. Of course, the process wasn't terribly new, as the securitization market had existed for years. However it became much more complex and competitive in the millennium, as the banking gurus started cooking up new mortgage structures (including those backed by subprime mortgages, as well as those created with credit derivatives), and as the housing agencies continued to promote home lending. Mistakes were made. Let me illustrate.

Bad assumptions

The agencies entered the middle of the decade with a view of the US housing market that called for reasonable stability. The agency models didn't therefore reflect a collapse in housing prices or a sharp rise in delinquencies and foreclosures – which means that the ratings on many mortgage-related bonds were way too high. So, securities that had been structured to a supposed AAA-standard based on historical data that showed modest house price declines and low delinquencies and foreclosures weren't really AAA at all.

The assumptions went something like this: historical data said that home prices didn't really go down very often and, if they did, they didn't go down by all that much. And they surely didn't go down everywhere, all at the same time. So imagine the surprise of the agencies when home prices fell, and they fell by a whole lot, and they fell everywhere: from Seattle to Boston, San Diego to Palm Beach. And imagine their surprise when the subprime pools – the ones with 100 percent loans, or low/no docs, or negative amortization – showed foreclosure rates that were well in excess of anything ever seen before. If Mr Subprime has little or no equity in the property and the value of the property plunges, why not just walk away? When property prices plunged (everywhere) and delinquency and foreclosure rates soared the assumptions in the agency models fell apart. The AAAs weren't AAA at all...maybe they were BBBs or BBs or CCCs. And if the AAAs were worth 100, you can be sure that the BBBs were worth a whole lot less...red ink.

All of that started becoming evident in 2006 and early 2007 when actual data veered sharply off course. Reality and assumptions were in conflict. In fact, the discrepancies became so large that Moody's had to retrofit its subprime model in April 2007 because, *"the mortgage market has evolved considerably."*[7] S&P had the same problem. And John Bonfiglio, head of Fitch's structured finance, noted at the time that *"yes, there's more risk than we thought."*[8] Not terribly comforting. Fitch's CEO, Stephen Joynt, testified that *"[a]t the early stages of the credit crisis in November 2007, Fitch decided that we needed to conduct a wholesale review of our...methodology.... We subsequently adopted revamped and more conservative criteria...on April 30, 2008."*[9] Of course, by that time it was too late, because bonds had already been issued.

From late 2007 into 2008 the erroneous assumptions took their collective toll, forcing the agencies to downgrade scores of mortgage bonds en masse to reflect the new market realities of lower housing prices and higher foreclosures, especially in subprime; this so-called "express train downgrading", affected thousands of issues, representing billions of outstandings. Krugman observed that *"[o]f AAA-rated subprime-mortgage-backed securities issued in 2006, 93 percent – 93 percent! – have now been downgraded to junk status."*[10] Not a very good showing. You can imagine the lawsuits that started pouring in from aggrieved investors – those who had relied so heavily on the expertise of the agencies.

George Miller, head of American Securitization Forum industry group, observed that *"[e]specially in parts of the residential mortgage market, a favorable economic environment and persistent increase in housing prices masked gaps in credit rating agency models and methodologies that did not sufficiently factor in the risk of nationwide housing price declines."*[11] In what might be regarded as a bit of an understatement, S&P's Bell testified that *"[w]e have all kind of acknowledged – certainly at S&P and I think my colleagues from the other firms would not disagree – that when you look at the ratings of the US sub-prime residential mortgage-backed securities and some of the [collateralized debt obligations] that were backed out of the sub-prime, undoubtedly the assumptions we made about how those would perform in the future turned out not to be correct. There is no doubt about that."*[12]

So what did the agency bosses say about all these bad assumptions? Let me start with Deven Sharma, president of S&P, who noted that *"many of the forecasts we used in our ratings analysis of certain structured finance securities have not been borne out. It is by now clear that a number of the assumptions we used in preparing our ratings on mortgage-backed securities issued between the last quarter of 2005 and the middle of 2007 did not work."*[13] Furthermore, he added, *"[w]hile we endeavored in good faith to assess what we thought would occur in a variety of future economic conditions so that our ratings might withstand the stresses of economic cycles, events have demonstrated that the historical data we used and the assumptions we made significantly underestimated the severity of what has actually occurred."*[14] How truly bizarre: I would've thought that the rating agencies, more than anyone else, would've been very keen to stress, analyze, and question the historical data to the nth degree? To be supremely skeptical? Sharma's predecessor, Kathleen Corbet (who was shown the door in August 2007) noted that *"S&P's assumptions simply did not capture unprecedented phenomena that later occurred with respect to the housing market, borrower behavior and credit correlations."*[15] In other words – all the factors that actually mattered in rating mortgage-backed bonds.

McGraw also waded in: *"As a consequence of these unexpected developments, many of the forecasts and assumptions S&P used in its ratings analysis of certain mortgage-related structured finance securities issued over the past several years have not been borne out."*[16] Then he went on with the usual had-we-but-known argumentation: *"There is no doubt that had we and others anticipated these extraordinary events, we would not have assigned many of the original ratings that we did."*[17] And, finally, to make sure that everyone knew that S&P wasn't the only lemming, McGraw said that *"[w]e take little comfort from the fact that virtually all market participants – financial institutions, ratings firms, homeowners, regulators and investors – did not anticipate the extreme and ongoing declines in the U.S. housing and mortgage markets."*[18]

Still, Sharma defended his organization: *"Providing the public with quality ratings, which is our goal, is both an art and a science. We work hard, very hard to do what we do well and continually to improve the quality and timeliness of our work. But like every human endeavor, S&P continues to learn from its past. Among our disappointments has been the ratings of mortgage-backed securities issued between 2005–2007."*[19] Then, trying to put the error into context, he did a little tap-dancing: *"we have historically had a very good overall track record, and our employees remain devoted to providing their highest quality credit analysis to the markets."*[20] And finally, echoing McGraw: *"S&P is not alone in having been taken by surprise by the extreme decline in the housing and mortgage markets. Virtually no one – be they homeowners, financial institutions, rating agencies, regulators, or investors – anticipated what is occurring."*[21] But, not to worry, as S&P reportedly *"introduced 27 new initiatives, which are a result of both our internal reviews and our dialogue with market participants and global policymakers."*[22] You can breathe easy now.

Over to Moody's. Let me first start with some comments by Moody's CEO Raymond McDaniel from early 2007, when he made very clear the importance of structured finance rating business to the company's bottom line: *"This strong performance was in large part due to the prevalence of new mortgage products, the persistence of low long-term interest rates and an increase in the percentage of mortgages being securitized. As in 2004 and 2005, U.S. structured finance was the largest dollar contributor to Moody's revenue growth."*[23] Little wonder Moody's (and others) were pretty keen to keep the show going as long as possible. Curiously, McDaniel also noted that *"Moody's Structured Finance Group intends to offer best-in-class products to help investors better understand and manage rapidly growing portfolios of securitized instruments worldwide."*[24] I guess that didn't work out too well, as Moody's itself didn't even get it. Then, in a little bit of ill-timed hubris, coming only months before the agency had to revamp its subprime model and the first cracks started appearing in the structured product façade: *"Moody's business stands on the 'right side of history' in terms of the alignment of our role and function with advancements in global capital markets."*[25]

When the full force of the crisis hit, McDaniel had to admit that *"[w]e did not...anticipate the magnitude and speed of the deterioration in mortgage quality or the suddenness of the transition to restrictive lending."*[26] He also pointed out what many were coming to believe – namely, that Moody's *"long-term success depends critically on the confidence of our stakeholders...in Moody's ethics, objectivity and credit judgments. These pillars of stakeholder confidence have come under intense* scrutiny since the reversal of the U.S. housing market and our subsequent rating downgrades of large numbers of mortgage-related debt securities."[27] Furthermore, he observed, "[w]hile examination of the root causes of the situation reveals multiple points of market failure, the speed and extent of rating downgrades clearly contributed to the loss of confidence and undermined the credibility of rating agencies, including Moody's."[28] As expected, McDaniel defended the firm: "Moody's strongly rejects assertions that our work is compromised by any failure of integrity or a lack of independence in our processes.... The question is not whether potential conflicts exist – they always will – but whether they are properly managed."[29] Were they properly managed? When SEC inspectors went in to investigate the conflicts at Moody's (as well as S&P and Fitch) they didn't like what they found. David Gallagher, acting SEC director's view: "The staff examinations... revealed a number of troubling results... the examinations raised serious questions about the [agencies'] management of conflicts of interest, internal audit processes and due diligence activities."[30] So, who's right and who's wrong?

Separately, senior Moody's officer Claire Robinson went on record to say that "Moody's provided early warnings on the weakness in the subprime market, and beginning in 2003 repeatedly published reports in which we pointedly commented on the deterioration in origination standards and rising housing prices."[31] All well and good, of course, but then everyone wonders how come they weren't ahead of the curve in downgrading this stuff? Well, said Robinson, Moody's hadn't "fully anticipated the severity or speed of deterioration in subprime mortgage lending or the rapidity of credit tightening."[32] So all the diligent work in catching the weakness in subprime back in 2003 was for naught?

As 2008 rolled on McDaniel said that "[i]n this financial crisis, lost confidence has greatly extended the scope and extent of financial assets under stress. The loss of confidence corresponds to perceived weaknesses in mechanisms that identify, measure and communicate risk exposures. We will endure, and we will succeed."[33] As the crisis deepened, he noted the harsh realities: "Investor demand will remain subdued absent either continuing government support, restored confidence in rating agencies, or market reforms that leave investors less vulnerable to poor practices."[34]

And then there's the smallest of the three majors, Fitch. CEO Joynt said that "[l]ike all of the major rating agencies, our structured finance ratings have not performed well and have been too volatile. We have downgraded large numbers of structured finance securities, particularly in the subprime mortgage and [collateralized debt obligation] areas, in many cases by multiple rating notches."[35] In a script that could have been taken from Moody's or S&Ps, he said that "[w]hile we were aware of, and accounted for, the many risks posed by subprime mortgages and the rapidly changing underwriting environment... we did not foresee the magnitude or velocity of the decline in the U.S. housing market nor the dramatic shift in borrower behavior *brought on by the changing practices in the market. We also did not foresee and are surprised by the far-reaching impact the subprime crisis has had on markets throughout the world."*[36] I am puzzled by that particular comment – if, the agency was "aware of" the risks, then how could it "not foresee" the particulars of the decline? Joynt also did a little passing-the-buck: *"Nor did we appreciate the extent of shoddy mortgage origination practices and fraud."*[37]

Too complicated?

Lots of what the agencies do is based on ratings models, little black boxes full of complicated math and statistical assumptions about how many people or companies will default, where, how frequently, and so on. The models let the agencies come up with ratings – AAA being great, CCC being brink of disaster. But models are tricky, and those used to determine the probability of default for pools of mortgages are even trickier.

And yet, there was no ex-post admission that maybe, just maybe, all of this stuff was just too complicated even for the ratings experts. Bell: *"we do not believe that these instruments were themselves too complex in their structure to rate…in terms of the structures that we were rating, no, I do not believe that they were inherently too complex."*[38] Robinson noted that *"[w]e aren't loan officers…[o]ur expertise is as statisticians on an aggregate basis. We want to know, of 1,000 individuals, based on historical performance, what percent will pay their loans?"*[39] A similar view came from Yuri Yoshizawa: *"We're structure experts…[w]e're not underlying-asset experts."*[40] Thank heavens for all that statistical and structuring expertise…it worked out really well.

But not everyone agreed. Eric Kolchinsky, one-time head of the unit responsible for rating the most toxic and complex stuff out there, testified that *"I still believe that Moody's is a good company and the vast majority of analysts there are smart, capable and want to do a good job of analyzing financial products. Unfortunately, these ingredients are not sufficient to produce quality ratings or to safeguard the financial system."*[41] He went on to cite conflicts of interest, lack of independence in policy and compliance, and inadequate methodologies as major problem areas. But perhaps most disturbing was his view that *"[m]ethodologies produced by Moody's for rating structured finance securities are inadequate and do not realistically reflect the underlying credits…[r]ating models are put together in a haphazard fashion and are not validated if doing so would jeopardize revenues."*[42] Explaining the problem, Kolchinsky noted that *"[t]hey are masters of their own methodologies. You have to prove their own methodologies are wrong."*[43] He went on to say that *"[collateralized debt obligations] cannot be rated with any certainty and especially not during this volatile period in the capital markets…[t]his toxic product needs to be consigned to the dustbin of bad ideas, but unfortunately, there are still no incentives for rating agencies to say 'No' to a product no matter how poorly thought through.*"[44] Whistleblowers can be a bit inconvenient. Never mind, said Richard Cantor, Moody's chief credit officer, who dismissed Kolchinsky's testimony as being "without merit": *"we have undertaken a number of initiatives to enhance the quality, independence and transparency of our ratings."*[45] Somehow, not terribly comforting. JP Morgan's Dimon summarized it all this way: *"[v]ery complex securities shouldn't have been rated as if they were easy-to-value bonds."*[46]

Unguarded moments

Along with flawed assumptions and the inherent complexities of trying to rate some of the products, the agencies also had to deal with a troubling scene reminiscent of the dot-com bubble (when Wall Street analysts were found to have written all manner of damning e-mails about issuers and clients). In this case, some of the agencies left an electronic trail of embarrassing, if perhaps accurate, communiqués. Let me give you a few choice selections which, as Krugman has said, *"reveal ... a deeply corrupt system."*[47]

One text message by Shannon Mooney at S&P had lots of nuggets, to wit: *"Even if cows were putting this deal together, we would still issue a rating,"*[48] and *"[our rating] model def[initely] does not capture half of the risk."*[49] Colleague Ralu Dilip indicated of a specific deal: *"We should not be rating it."*[50] And, yet, they did. An e-mail from Chris Meyer stated: *"Rating agencies continue to create a bigger monster – the [collateralized debt obligation] market. Let's hope we're all rich and retired when this house of cards collapses : o)."*[51] But it had a cute emoticon, so it's funny, right? Further communiqués were no better: *"Combined, these errors make us look either incompetent at credit analysis, or like we sold our soul to the devil for revenue, or a little bit of both."*[52] Frank Raiter, a former managing director at S&P's mortgage-bond unit said of his firm that *"success bred complacency and an aversion to change."*[53] Why? According to Raiter, management was *"focused on revenue, profit and ultimately share price."*[54] Richard Gugliada, a former S&P official, said that his firm was part of a *"market share war where criteria were relaxed. ...I knew it was wrong at the time. It was either that or skip the business. That wasn't my mandate. My mandate was to find a way. Find the way."*[55] Great.

Over at Moody's Chris Mahoney said in November 2007 that *"[Moody's] has made mistakes in the [collateralized debt obligation] and [mortgage-backed securities] sectors and in particular I think the mezz[anine] and high grade CDO backed by subprime were not rigorous enough."*[56] I think you get the point. No worries, said Michel Madelain, EVP of Moody's: *"these comments would not reflect at all the ethics and the work that are taking place within our organisation."*[57] So, I guess why-let-a-few-bad-apples-spoil-the-whole-damn-bunch applies? I'm not so sure, given the prevalence of the problems. For his part, Fitch's Joynt wanted it made clear that his firm didn't have any smoking gun e-mails: *"Please do not extrapolate those specific claims to Fitch's practices."*[58]

The critics descend

Pretty much everyone has recognized the multiple failures of the agencies – bad models, questionable expertise, slow reaction time, conflicts of interest – and the comments and criticisms have generally been well placed. Let me set the stage with Senator Richard Shelby, ranking minority member on the Banking Committee, who indicated that *"[o]ur current financial crisis, which was caused in part by the credit rating agencies' failure to appreciate the risks associated with complex structured products, demonstrates just how big that systemic risk was."*[59]

Former SEC head Cox concurred: *"The credit rating agencies ... notoriously gave AAA ratings to these structured mortgage-backed securities. But that was not all: the ratings agencies sometimes helped to design these securities so they could qualify for higher ratings. These ratings not only gave false comfort to investors, but also skewed the computer risk models and regulatory capital computations."*[60] From Henry Waxman, California Representative and Chair of the Oversight and Reform Committee: *"The story of the credit rating agencies is a story of colossal failure ... [t]he result is that our entire financial system is now at risk."*[61] Harsh words came also from Bafin's Sanio, who said that the agencies *"grossly underestimated the systemic risk – the collapse of the US housing market as a whole. Their mathematical models worked on the assumption that single risks would be independent; the default of one house buyer was assumed to be independent of the default of another. The recent crisis proved this over-optimistic assumption to be a fallacy."*[62]

Former US Senator Alfonse D'Amato was sharp in his invective, which came in front of a Congressional panel: *"The debacle of the sub-prime mortgage crisis could not have taken place without the total complicity of these credit rating agencies. ... [T]heir failure to detect obvious flaws in the financial products they were evaluating was like not crying fire in a burning theater ... Credit rating agencies have such obvious conflicts of interest and were so derelict in their responsibilities to the investing public in the past few years that their opinions should now be heavily discounted."*[63] And Greenspan weighed in: *"The consequent surge in global demand for U.S. subprime securities by banks, hedge, and pension funds supported by unrealistically positive rating designations by credit agencies was, in my judgment, the core of the problem."*[64]

Then there's the statement put out by the European Commission: *"It is commonly agreed that credit rating agencies contributed significantly to recent market turmoil by underestimating the credit risk of structured credit products."*[65] And, *"when market conditions worsened, the agencies failed to adapt the ratings promptly."*[66] So, the worst of both worlds: getting it wrong in the first instance, and then not reacting quickly enough when the world's falling apart. Bravo! Buiter testified that *"[t]he credit ratings agencies of course and those who used them are culpable. The credit rating agencies got into a line of business that they did not understand. They were reasonable at rating sovereign risk and large corporates but not at rating complex structures, but *they did it anyway, and in addition they were hopelessly conflicted."*[67] Director of the CBI, Lambert, also commented in a rather descriptive way: *"[c]learly credit ratings agencies were part of the process of turning, whatever you call it, stone into gold or whatever the right cliché´ is – alchemy."*[68] Alchemists indeed! Jim Simons, head of hedge fund Renaissance, spoke of a different kind of alchemy: *"As time went on, the quality of the newly created mortgages deteriorated to remarkably low levels, and the rating agencies became increasingly fanciful in their ratings. In my opinion the most culpable, the rating agencies, which failed in their duty and allowed sows' ears to be sold as silk purses."*[69] The Work Foundation's Hutton: *"There was a competitive dynamic going on in the credit ratings agencies and even the sober and better ones found themselves competed into...a more relaxed view of what the risk was."*[70] It sounds like a race to the bottom. New York Congressman Gary Ackerman, for one, grew tired of the fact that the agencies continued to stick to their line that ratings are "opinions" and not "statements of fact" or "professional judgments." To Ackerman, that was akin to saying: *"I'm not a professional, but I play one in the marketplace."*[71] He then added *"If this is just your opinion, why don't we just strip away your government license to operate?"*[72]

Several commented on the inherent conflicts embedded in the rating agency business model. For instance, Arthur Levitt, former head of the SEC, said that the *"credit-rating agencies suffer from a conflict of interest – perceived and apparent – that may have distorted their judgment, especially when it came to complex structured financial products."*[73] SEC Commissioner Kathleen Casey: *"The large rating agencies helped promote the dramatic growth in structured finance over the past decade, and profited immensely by issuing ratings that pleased the investment banks that arranged these pools of securities, but betrayed the trust of investors who were led to believe that investment grade bonds were relatively safe...[a]lthough many of their ratings turned out to be catastrophically misleading, the large rating agencies enjoyed their most profitable years ever during the past decade."*[74] Christopher Wood, CLSA, said that *"[t]heir model was a recipe for massive conflicts of interest."*[75] No, said S&P's Sharma, *"our ratings in the mortgage-backed securities area were not venal."*[76] You decide.

New York University professor Lawrence White described how the inherent conflict of interest influenced the bubble: *"The complexity and opaqueness of the mortgage-related securities that required ratings in the current decade...created new opportunities and apparently irresistible temptations...These three agencies' initially favorable ratings were crucial for the successful sale of the bonds that were securitized from subprime residential mortgages and other debt obligations. The sale of these bonds, in turn, were an important underpinning for the U.S. housing boom of 1998–2006 – with a self-reinforcing price-rise bubble."*[77] Senator Carl Levin, head of the Investigations Committee, characterized the arrangement like this: *"It's like one of the parties in court paying the judges salary."*[78] And Professor John Coffee, of

Columbia University, also put forth an apt analogy: "*They are a watchdog paid by the entities they are expected to watch.*" In addition, he noted, "*[a]s the housing bubble inflated, the ratings agencies slept. Two explanations are possible for their lack of response: (1) the ratings agencies willfully ignored this change, or (2) they managed not to learn about this decline, because issuers did not tell them and they made no independent inquiry.*"[79] Whatever the reason, the damage was enormous.

Blind use of ratings?

Of course, some fault can also be attached to those who used the ratings blindly – which, in reality, is pretty much everyone. So much faith has been assigned to the intellect and prowess of the agencies (periodic stumbling, like Enron and Lehman, notwithstanding) that "outsourcing" of certain risk and investment decisions has been a feature of the financial landscape for years. Senator Shelby put it this way: "*Widespread over reliance on ratings meant that the effects of poor quality or inadequately updated ratings could ripple through the markets.*"[80] Miller, representing the securitization industry, made the point very clearly: "*[M]arket participants became overly reliant on credit ratings, and many failed to perform or to act upon their own assessment of the risks created by certain securitized transaction structures.*"[81] And from the SEC's Schapiro: "*Too many investors and regulators over-relied on credit ratings, especially for complicated financial products.*"[82]

Goldman's Blankfein admits to the false comfort that lulled some into complacency: "*I would say I would be more complacent when I saw something had AAA than if it had a AA or a AA than if it had a single A. So to that extent, I also must have been deferring to a rating agency.*"[83] And to what extent did other big banks rely on the AAA-imprimatur? Many, I think. Rubin and Prince admitted they had lots of AAA-rated mortgage assets on the Citi balance sheet that they didn't even focus on. Sir Tom McKillop, former Chairman of RBS, was candid: "*We never imagined the parts we were holding, a large part of it was triple A...we never imagined...that could end up as 10 cents in the dollar.*"[84] As Greenspan also noted: "*Uncritical acceptance of credit ratings by purchasers of these toxic assets has led to huge losses.*"[85] And, later "*an inordinately large part of investment management was subcontracted to the 'safe harbor' risk designations of the credit rating agencies.*"[86] The same from FDIC's Bair: "*Investors purchased these securities without a proper risk evaluation, as they outsourced their due diligence obligation to the credit rating agencies...[o]nce a rating was accepted, and as long as the securities performed well, few investors found cause to question the accuracy of the rating or to raise questions about rating agencies' opaque proprietary risk-assessment methodologies.*"[87] Regardless of changes that may ultimately come down, I think it will always be caveat emptor with credit ratings...or opinions.

In the aftermath of all the problems, Moody's officials reflected internally on the whole matter (courtesy of a transcript that made its way to the US Congress Oversight Committee). McDaniel noted that *"there are forces around us who have a motivation to find someone to blame."*[88] Senior executive Brian Clarkson also spoke about the blame game: *"If you look at the players in the marketplace, the politicians can't blame the borrower because its their constituents. The investment bankers, well you can't blame the investment bankers. They're big. They're powerful. They know what's going on. And they're regulated. ... you certainly can't blame investors."*[89] So, blame Moody's (and the others). And what of Moody's mistakes? Clarkson: *"At the end of the day we did a pretty good job in identifying the risk, but we didn't do a very good job in measuring the magnitude."*[90] He was very forthright on another point: *"one of the questions everyone asks is why everyone hates us so much. I mean it's clear that they do. It's clear that we're hated in the marketplace."*[91] Maybe because they screwed up and cost investors a few dollars? Ultimately, Moody's Robinson observed that *"[t]his is a business where you're bound to attract criticism. In hindsight, people have 20–20 vision."*[92] Don't worry – everyone hates the bankers, regulators, and politicians, too. Terry McGraw, new CEO of McGraw-Hill agreed that criticism of the agency's methodologies was (and is) fair game, but with limits: *"Well, your assumptions didn't work, so you're complicit or you're incompetent... That's a little over the top."*[93]

And so, as with US and European bankers, and the "housing experts" at Fannie and Freddie, the ratings agencies missed it all – and emerged as big contributors to the crisis.

6
Fuel to the Fire II: Regulators, Politicians, and Lobbyists

Since some outside the financial capitals aided-and-abetted in the grand buildup and collapse, it would be remiss of me not to make some mention of their role. In particular, it pays to understand the behaviors of various "power players," which I take to include all manner of regulators (who, by my count, have missed every single major crisis of the past two decades and have, in fact, helped fuel a few of them), politicians and legislators (who in some cases emerge as rather clueless and hypocritical), and lobbyists (who talk up their particular special interests, regardless of whether the markets are good or bad). Let me illustrate how each one of these groups contributed to the crisis.

Whither the regulators?

Financial regulators are the perennial punching bags of the political class and the private sector. For good reason, too: they are often several steps behind when it comes to the latest crisis, making at least some of us wonder what it is they actually do. To be sure, there are many hard working folks in the regulatory agencies who try and do the best that they can; but they often lack resources, support, direction, or skills, and so are pretty much doomed to reliving the last crisis rather than anticipating the next one. As Wallison has noted, *"The regulators are the least knowledgeable people about what is actually happening in the market."*[1]

In fact, as I rewind the "financial crisis highlights" DVD of the last few decades, I can't point to any single major event where regulators actually helped avoid a major problem; they have either helped create the climate for a crisis, or played a game of reactive catchup. Am I wrong? Consider whether global regulators did anything to anticipate, control, minimize, or otherwise prevent any of the following multibillion dollar fiascoes:

- The LDC crisis in the 1980s, when the moratoria declared by Mexico, Venezuela, Argentina, and dozens of others brought the US money center

banks (and a number of large UK and European banks) to the brink of technical insolvency.
- The US S&L crisis of the late 1980s, when regulators (and politicians) let these unsophisticated banks get involved in all manner of business they didn't understand and actually let insolvent banks create "phantom equity" that artificially inflated their net worth – simply exacerbating and prolonging the crisis.
- The Japanese banking crisis of the 1990s, when a long history of regulatory forbearance let the major city banks, regional banks, and nonbank financial companies pile up loads of bad loans (many of them backed by inflated real estate that ultimately collapsed in value). And then let the banks "restructure" the loans so that that they wouldn't show up as nonperforming.
- The LTCM/Russia crisis of the late 1990s, when banks and securities firms were allowed to leverage up their off-balance sheet activities tremendously and take unsecured credit risk with the hedge fund community (giving the later de-facto infinite leverage).
- And, in the early part of the millennium: the dotcom bubble (with all kinds of research, investment banking, and conflict of interest problems created by securities firms and banks); The accounting scandals and off-balance sheet games of big corporations like Enron, WorldCom, Tyco, Parmalat; The Ponzi schemes of Madoff, Stanford, et al.

You get the point: AWOL – Absent without leave.

Greenspan proffered a view that was very critical, but very accurate: *"Regulators who are required to forecast have had a woeful record of chronic failure. History tells us they cannot identify the timing of a crisis, or anticipate exactly where it will be located or how large the losses and spillovers will be. Regulators cannot successfully use the bully pulpit to manage asset prices, and they cannot calibrate regulation and supervision in response to movements in asset prices. Nor can they fully eliminate the possibility of future crises."*[2] Doesn't sound like they can do much at all. Christopher Caldwell, *Weekly Standard:* "*The profession of banking became more varied, complex and opaque, and as it did, government deregulated and misregulated.*"[3]

And in a bit of "turnaround-is-fair-play" the banking captains weighed in, pointing out multiple problems before and during the latest breakdown. Citi's Pandit described a *"regulatory system that did not keep pace with the ever-increasing sophistication, complexity and interrelatedness of the financial markets."*[4] RBS's Hester noted that *"all regulators around the world, including the FSA, were not concentrating enough on liquidity, it was the most under-developed bit of regulation, people were concentrating on capital, and I think that was the problem."*[5] Morgan Stanley's Roach said that *"[d]isparities in country-specific regulations...led to a regulatory arbitrage that has compounded global imbalances."*[6] Though the never-shy Dimon prefaced comments in 2010 by saying *"we should not and do not blame regulators* for the failures of individual companies, ever – management is solely to blame,"[7] he also pointed out a few of the regulatory stumbles that contributed to the mess: *"Basel capital rules that required too little capital and didn't account for liquidity and relied too much on rating agencies; the Securities and Exchange Commission allowing U.S. investment banks to get too leveraged; and poor regulation of Fannie Mae and Freddie Mac, among many elements of an archaic, siloed regulatory system."*[8] That's quite a laundry list. CLSA's Mayo added: *"I know Jamie Dimon said regulators were not at fault. No, that's not true. Regulators share some blame here, too."*[9] And Angela Knight, CEO of the British Bankers Association (BBA), took a swipe on behalf of the UK banking industry: *"Regulators either did not recognise or capture properly the issues either here or elsewhere."*[10]

AWOL I: The financial regulators

Let me kick off with the regulators of the financial firms that were at the heart of the crisis. Without getting into too much detail on which regulator is responsible for what, it is clear that there were lots of parties that really didn't do anything substantive to warn of, or clamp down on, excessive risks. They seemed to have been as clueless as everyone else, on a global basis. Financial regulators like the Fed, the Office of the Comptroller of the Currency (OCC), the Office of Thrift Supervision, the SEC, the Bank of England, the FSA, Bafin, Bank of Italy, Banque de France, the Swiss National Bank, and a few others blew it – and are thus at least partly culpable.

Ineffective

There seems to be fairly unanimous consent that some financial regulators were simply ineffective in discharging their duties. Paul Volcker, when asked whether his former employer, the Federal Reserve, screwed up, responded by saying: *"[w]ell I think they all did. My problem is the Federal Reserve gets singled out, but I think it wasn't just the Federal Reserve, but the SEC. If anybody dropped the ball in the investment bank area it was the SEC and the OCC and the people in Fannie Mae and Freddie Mac. That was a collective undue relaxation, if I may put it kindly."*[11] He added: *"the Federal Reserve if it's going to remain in the regulatory area...is going to have to be reorganised itself. So that it is less likely to drop the ball in the future."*[12] Larry Summers, former Treasury Secretary and Economic Advisor, noted that the Fed didn't deserve high marks *"when they have been consistently behind the curve"*.[13] Daniel Tarullo, a Fed governor, observed that *"[t]here were shortcomings in supervision at the New York Fed in the years running up to the crisis, and I would say that about every other financial regulator in the US government."*[14]

They seem to have missed the plot over at the OCC as well. The OCC, which regulates US banks (but not bank holding companies) and branches of foreign banks is also meant to provide consumer protections against the predatory lending that was common in the subprime sector. That obviously didn't work out too well. Elizabeth Warren, Harvard professor and head of the Congressional panel overseeing the activities of banks that took government aid noted that *"In every major dispute between customers and banks, the OCC entered the fray on the side of the banks. Clearly, banks – not their customers – were the OCC's primary interest."*[15] Put another way, she said: *"The OCC...has a large consumer division, but its principal responsibility is the profitability of the banks! So, when there have been disputes between banks and consumers...the OCC has gone into court to argue on behalf of the banks – always on behalf of the banks."*[16] And if that wasn't enough, the OCC fell down on examining the financial strength of its charges. According to Warren, *"[t]he banks most at risk were never stress tested. Their ability to withstand a coming storm has never been examined."*[17] German finance minister Steinbrueck apparently agreed: *"We are currently seeing that the stress test in the U.S. is worthless because the central bank exercised influence as well as the Treasury."*[18]

So, the key US regulators weren't necessarily effective. FDIC's Sheila Bair: *"the regulatory system...failed in its responsibilities. There were critical shortcomings in our approach that permitted excessive risks to build in the system. Looking back, it is clear that the regulatory community did not appreciate the magnitude and scope of the potential risks that were building in the financial system."*[19] Darling: *"I think all the evidence we have had, particularly looking at what happened in America where there just simply was not that supervision, is that there are disastrous consequences."*[20]

Of course, similar shortcomings appear in the UK. The House of Common's Treasury Committee, for one, appeared rather unimpressed with the actions and behaviors of the Bank of England and FSA. Labour MP Cousins made note of the fact that on *"September 11 [2008], the Governor of the Bank of England came here and he made a long statement to us. Four days later Lehman Brothers collapsed in a puff of smoke. What the Governor of the Bank of England had said to us did not stand up anymore. Now, if the Governor of the Bank of England cannot read the rumbles, how can some poor woman who is relying on a proper investment of her divorce settlement to see her through the rest of her life, how can she rely on it?"*[21] City law partner Fox noted in his testimony what probably many others felt: *"Is the FSA qualified to make a judgment about excessive risk? Well, I am a bit dubious, quite honestly, because I think that the FSA did not show that they had a better grip on the risk issues than many other organisations."*[22] He was equally critical of the Bank of England, noting that it *"has had a long established supervisory role, but I think that the events of the past year have demonstrated that many, many people did not understand risks and the risks that the financial system was subject to."*[23]

While FSA chief Turner accepted the FSA's failings, he wasn't going down alone: *"failure also existed among many economists, central bankers and finance ministers, who come from a different background...[i]ndeed, I think it is important to realise that up until 2006 and even into 2007 the world was awash with erudite, authoritative arguments put forward not just by bankers who had a self-interest in it but by theoretical economists who thought that they were looking at this in a disinterested fashion, who were arguing that the world, as a result of the development of structured credit and derivatives, had become less risky...So I think there was a very fundamental intellectual failure.*"[24]

MP Fallon was not very happy with the whole scheme: *"But what is the point of a regulator that has cost us, I think it is, £400 million this year, that employs 2,500 people, is given ten big British banks to supervise and allows five of them to collapse?"*[25] And McFall was even more direct, telling Deputy Governor of the Bank of England, Sir John Gieve, that he was *"asleep in the back shop while there was a mugging out front."*[26] Furthermore, *"[t]he answers given to us this morning [say] that you weren't very much alert. It seems to me that you were pretty laid back about it."*[27] He was equally sharp with former FSA CEO Tiner, saying that *"you were not just sleeping, you were comatose."*[28]

Laissez-faire

The governing regulatory philosophy in many financial capitals during the 1990s and 2000s was laissez-faire: basically, hands-off. Deregulation or self-regulation was the order of the day in the US, UK, and other countries. In the US, for instance, Glass-Steagall – which had mandated the separation of commercial and investment banking since the 1930s – was formally laid to rest by the Clinton Administration in 1999. This meant that the big commercial banks (like Citi, B of A, JP) became kids in the candy store, playing with all sorts of risky and tricky products, amplifying leverage through off-balance sheet activities and adopting much more of the proprietary mentality that was characteristic of the likes of the US investment banks.

Another key deregulatory measure in the US: the SEC's decision in April 2004 to allow five big investment banks (Goldman, Morgan Stanley, Bear, Lehman, and Merrill) to use a new formula to compute their capital charges – the net effect of which was to allow them far greater leverage, which they rode full steam into 2007. Abandonment of the previous "gross leverage limit" and implementation of a new risk capital charge based on internal models (à la Basel II) led to miscalculation of the riskiness of assets and widespread use of cross-asset netting – and, ultimately, very significantly greater leverage. No surprise that the investment banks were lobbying the SEC heavily for the rule change.

So, what did the SEC officials supporting this rule think? Roel Campos said: *"I'm very happy to support it...[a]nd I keep my fingers crossed for the future."* Harvey Goldschmid said, rather presciently, *"[w]e've said these are the big guys...but that means if anything goes wrong, it's going to be an awfully big mess."*[29] How bizarre. It doesn't sound like a decision grounded in confidence. Former SEC attorney George Simon noted in the aftermath that *"the leverage became fatal, with small haircuts for particular securities, and with the risk of default inadequately addressed."*[30] Barry Ritholtz of Fusion IQ: *"I'd call it res ipsa loquitur... [i]t's no coincidence that since the SEC created the exemption, all five are now gone."*[31] Lee Pickard, a former SEC official who had a hand in drafting the original rule back in 1975, noted that the SEC *"constructed a mechanism that simply didn't work... [t]he proof is in the pudding – three of the five broker-dealers have blown up."*[32] As I noted in Chapter 2, Goldman and Morgan Stanley are bank holding companies, Merrill a sub of BofA, Lehman bankrupt, and Bear fully absorbed by JP Morgan. Former SEC Commissioner Cox, who inherited the new rule from his predecessor, William Donaldson, defended it in the early stages of the crisis: *"We have a good deal of comfort about the capital cushions at these firms at the moment."*[33] But when Bear hit the wall, the SEC changed its tune, and a proposal to revise the net capital rule was put on the table. All a bit late, of course, because the remaining four horsemen were already fully levered.

The other side of the laissez-faire coin was that meaningful regulatory strengthening of potential hot spots, like over-the-counter derivatives generally and credit derivatives specifically, went nowhere – banks lobbied heavily to keep things "voluntary." Roderick Hills, former head of the SEC, noted that *"[i]t's a fair criticism of the Bush administration that regulators have relied on many voluntary regulatory programs... [t]he problem with such voluntary programs is that, as we've seen throughout history, they often don't work."*[34] Professor James Cox of Duke University observed that *"[w]e foolishly believed that the firms had a strong culture of self-preservation and responsibility and would have the discipline not to be excessively borrowing... [w]e've all learned a terrible lesson."*[35]

In the UK, the concept of "light-touch" and "principles-based" regulation – a sort of loose, self-regulatory approach supported by then-Chancellor of the Exchequer Gordon Brown and promulgated by then-FSA head Tiner – crashed and burned. For a while, though, it was touted as the right way to go. Margaret Cole, head of FSA enforcement, noted in 2005 that *"London's philosophy of 'light touch' regulation has helped it in becoming the world's leading center for mobile capital."*[36] Oops. The crisis revealed that it wasn't the right way at all, with Brown admitting in 2009 that *"[w]e brought in a statutory regulatory system, supervisory system, but of course we couldn't know exactly what was going on in every individual bank."*[37] Well, that's not particularly helpful, is it? Future Prime Minister David Cameron made a little political hay out of the whole thing, reminding the public that his archrival had been the architect of the regulatory regime whilst Chancellor of the Exchequer: *"Just a quick word to the man who says he abolished 'boom and bust' and then saved the world. It was you, Gordon Brown, who designed the system of financial regulation that helped cause the financial crisis."*[38]

Turner explained that *"there was a philosophy of regulation which emerged...which was based upon too extreme a form of confidence in markets and confidence in the ideas that markets were self-correcting, which therefore believed that the fundamental role of the supervision of financial institutions, in particular banks, was to make sure that processes and procedures and systems were in place, while leaving it to the judgment of individual management to make fundamentally sensible decisions."*[39] That obviously wasn't a good idea, as even Turner came to realize: *"I think it is a competent execution of a style of regulation and a philosophy of regulation which was, in retrospect, mistaken."*[40] Darling, commenting on the same issue: *"I suppose the characteristic was light touch...I have said this before, I think there are many lessons to be learned in the way in which institutions are regulated."*[41] Even Volcker couldn't resist a comment: *"that didn't work out too well and I think they should have been more cautious about it in the first place."*[42]

Missed it...

In some cases examiners really didn't do a thorough job of digging into what was going on or taking appropriate actions. For instance, bankruptcy examiner Valukas made note of the SEC's incompetence in the Lehman case: *"The SEC knew that Lehman was reporting sums in its reported liquidity pool that the SEC did not believe were in fact liquid; the SEC knew that Lehman was exceeding its risk control limits; and the SEC should have known that Lehman was manipulating its balance sheet to make its leverage appear better than it was."*[43] Knowing all this, they did nothing? By the way, even as all of these events were [not] taking place, the SEC was also not digging into two mega-Ponzi schemes, Madoff and Stanford. Sounds like a very effective organization.

In other cases regulators simply focused on examining individual institutions without connecting the dots more broadly – a classic "forest for the trees" problem. Lamfalussy noted that *"micro regulators and supervisors have neither been trained to detect those signs nor were they able to do it. The way in which the supervisor, the regulator, was working was basically to look at one single institution and assess the risks attached to what was happening there...there was a global problem around the corner, which you could not have seen if you had looked exclusively at one institution."*[44] That was seconded by Darling: *"I do not think regulators, whilst they were concentrating on what was going on in their own back yard, were as alert as perhaps they should have been to the big pressures that were building up underneath all of them across the globe."*[45] Turner also admitted that *"the most important failures were the failures to see the systemic things."*[46] He also noted that *"in retrospect, the FSA should have been more involved in sectoral analysis, but that was not what was believed at the time."*[47] And, *"[c]learly there should have been more understanding of the dangers...but it is very easy to say that with retrospect. I think the bit which was more clearly an area where regulators and authorities across the world should have focused earlier was...the off balance sheet [vehicles]...I think it is easier to say that was something which ought to have been spotted and things done about their capital adequacy earlier.*"[48] Too late.

Pitt-Watson, senior advisor to fund manager Hermes, provided a rather colorful description: *"[w]hen one thinks about regulation, we need to recognise what we have seen is a systemic crisis...but regulators...tend to be in their own wormhole...If I was to criticise the FSA it would not be for their resources or skills but they needed to look out of their wormhole."*[49] Barclays' Varley said *"all the transparency and all the prudential supervision in the world at the institution specific level would not have prevented the crisis that has occurred. What that tells me in any event is the big issue here, and in a sense the big miss, was the absence to spot the systemic risk that existed."*[50]

Patchwork and gaps

The patchwork nature of global financial regulation was also a problem. Dimon was again candid on the matter: *"it is important to examine how the system could have functioned better. The current regulatory system is poorly organized with overlapping responsibilities, and many regulators did not have the statutory resolution authority needed to address the failure of large, global financial companies."*[51] A similar view was given by Hank Paulson: *"Our regulatory system remains a hopelessly outmoded patchwork quilt for another day and age."*[52] Clearly, if every country is doing its own thing and not communicating properly, then the ability to stop a problem from moving across borders is diminished. Buiter also weighed in on the dysfunctional global regulatory spaghetti: *"I think there are just too many uncoordinated, mutually undercutting regulatory regimes."*[53] From the FDIC's Bair: *"The crisis has clearly revealed that regulatory gaps, or significant differences in regulation across financial services firms, can encourage regulatory arbitrage."*[54] Snow's view was similar: *"It also had become clear that the regulatory system had contributed to the lack of transparency because of a bewildering array of federal and state authorities, with no one regulator having a full view. The regulatory process was proving out of date and in need of modernization."*[55]

The patchwork quilt arose because, as SEC's Schapiro notes, the system operated (and still does) under a *"siloed financial regulatory framework."*[56] Each regulator operated in its own silo, with communication and coordination flying on a wish and a prayer. The Lehman disaster reflects this all too clearly – apparently no one wanted to be the bank's regulator. Valukas testified that *"the [regulatory] agencies were concerned. They gathered information. They monitored. But no agency regulated...[t]he Fed and Treasury took pains to tell us that the SEC was Lehman's regulator...[b]ut former SEC Chairman Cox took equal pains to say, during our interview...that the SEC's statutory jurisdiction was limited to Lehman's broker-dealer subsidiary and that it was not the regulator of Lehman itself."*[57] It sounds rather like a bunch of squabbling children pointing fingers after Mom's vase has been broken. The same sort of problem was also evident in the case of AIG, where Corrigan correctly noted that *"[t]he problem with AIG was the Balkanisation of the American regulatory system and this [derivative] activity existed just in the cracks between these different responsibilities."*[58]

In fact, having things slip between the cracks was not unusual, to wit Turner, referencing his Bank of England colleagues: *"between the FSA and the Bank of England there was so much desire to avoid overlap that there was an underlap."*[59] But Bafin's Sanio put it most colorfully: *"What we had for the last twenty years was 'Swiss cheese regulation': international standards that were sound at their base but otherwise full of holes. Also, there were – and still are – large areas that simply escaped supervision altogether."*[60] All of this adds up to more room for screwups.

Backbone?

Then there's the sometimes spineless nature of some regulators – unwilling to stand firm, to challenge. Buiter's comments are exactly right, and again applicable almost universally: *"During a big asset boom/credit boom there is universal capture of the regulators and the political process by the financial sector. You can see that because who argues with success? People who take home $50 million a year must be doing something right. It is very hard to interrupt that spiral until it is done by brute force through an implosion of the bubble. There is no willingness among the regulators or among the political classes to interfere with an asset boom or a credit boom. I have never seen that."*[61] Neither have I. Eric Sirri head of SEC Traded Markets, commenting on the difficulty of bringing profitable and successful investment banks to heel: *"You would have to have had a view that was contradictory to the view of the entire market."*[62]

Alchemy Partners' Moulton noted in testimony that *"there was a lack of whistleblowing. It was all part of the desire to keep the boom going."* And who in the UK should have been blowing the whistle, but didn't? Moulton: *"Probably the most obvious target would, I am afraid, be the FSA."*[63] Little wonder that UK satirical magazine *Private Eye* dubbed the FSA the "Fundamentally Supine Authority."[64] Ultimately, said King: *"The real problem that any [regulator] would have faced was that if they had said to banks in the City before 2007, 'You are taking big risks', they would have been seen to be arguing against success. The people in the banks would have said, 'Well, who are you to say we are taking too big risks? We have got far brighter and more qualified risk assessors than you have got. We have made massive profits every year for almost ten years. We have paid big bonuses. The City is the most successful part of the UK economy. How dare you tell us that we should stop taking such risks. Can you prove to us that the risks we are taking will necessarily end in tears?' and of course they could not. For an ordinary regulator going about their business, they would have been confronted with this massively difficult task of actually persuading people...that they should have been taking action against institutions that looked very successful and highly profitable."*[65] In fact, it is difficult to remain strong when getting pummeled by bankers.

Don't understand?

Then there's the issue of regulators being led down the garden path by their charges: regulators were often unable to keep up with bankers. LSE's Danielsson pointed out the common smoke-and-mirrors technique used by at least some banks: *"They could make the case to the regulators in a way that the regulators did not understand what they were being told. By making things complicated you look as if you know the answer to the problem and it is very difficult for anybody to argue against it."*[66] That's happened many, many times – the jargon-laced, complex, mathematical, derivative-based products that bankers can spin are intimidating, and difficult for any regulator to try to critique. Indeed, Lamfalussy noted an instance when a bank regulator investigating a troubled bank with toxic assets *"saw it but, believe it or not, they actually congratulated the management"*[67] – because management had created an additional source of profits, never mind that it had become riskier.

Sometimes whole institutions were way too complex for the beleaguered regulators – who could figure out the complex legal, corporate, and business structures of monsters like Citi, AIG, RBS? Moulton characterized it this way: *"Supervision and regulation will only work if it is within the capabilities of the people involved to actually discharge those duties. A large bank with 30 or 40 business lines, huge books of derivatives, is not such an animal."*[68] More broadly: *"[i]n the case of some of these assets the products are simply incapable of being analysed...Northern Rock's last capital issue, an off balance sheet vehicle is on the website, 11 layers of debt, three currencies, interest rate swaps, currency swaps, 415 pages of prospectus, nobody understood it."*[69] Or, as Fox News' Elizabeth MacDonald put it: *"the financial statement disclosures on these trillions of dollars in securities, this drunken daisy chain of paper Kryptonite stretching around the globe, are about as transparent as a bucket of molasses."*[70] And, how about risks coming out of all of those complex financial instruments? FSA's Turner was honest enough to admit: *"I cannot say that I would necessarily have spotted them in advance."*[71]

Bad rules

Of course, some of the problems arose from bad rules, such as the flawed value-at-risk measure I mentioned in Chapter 2. From Turner, a comment that brings back memories of my own angels-on-the-head-of-a-pin conversations with regulators: *"Within institutions we were often led astray in the past by apparently sophisticated mathematical tools like value at risk which purported to suggest that we had a precise fix on how much risk there was on trading books. Both bank management and regulators took far too much assurance from that apparent mathematical precision and failed to realise the inherent uncertainties and pro-cyclicalities of that approach."*[72]

Another example: attempts at standardizing certain rules, like capital to support credit risk business, failed. The much vaunted cross-border rules given to the industry by the Bank for International Settlements via the Basle II Accord did little to ensure that big banks entered the crisis period with enough capital. LSE Professor Goodhart hit the nail on the head: *"Where [Basel II] fell down completely was in looking at the systemic risk, the macro prudential, compared to the micro prudential risk. It is not that Basel II is wrong or bad; it is just totally and completely insufficient in that it did not look appropriately at the systemic issues."*[73] King chimed in: *"The Basel regulation... achieved nothing because it was wildly too complicated."*[74] More generally, he noted: *"when times were unexpected and things went badly wrong the models were useless and yet regulation was based on it."*[75] George Melloan, formerly editor of the *Wall Street Journal*: *"while [Basel II] was a noble effort at international regulatory coordination... it didn't do much to ensure bank safety."*[76] Example? *"Lehman Brothers had close to triple the core capital required by the Basel standards when it crashed."*[77] Not very useful, then. And, from Sanio: *"the standard left some quick escape routes open that banks were able to use to undermine this basic tenet of financial regulation."*[78]

The problems with BIS pro-cyclical capital rules became very apparent during the crisis, as explained by Moulton: *"[f]or the capital structure, Basel II has proved to be quite fatally flawed... The pro-cyclicality is really varied in Basel II in terms of bank capital structures. It looks back, sees what the risk was historically and projects it into the future. The better things are, the less capital you need; the worse things are, the more capital you need. That is exactly the opposite of what we want."*[79]

AWOL II: The other regulators

Of course, regulatory insufficiencies weren't limited to the banking sector, but also the housing agencies, the insurance sector, and the rating agencies.

It is by now clear that the regulation surrounding Fannie and Freddie collapsed completely. Oversight was split between OFHEO (financial matters) and HUD (housing mission matters), which was ultimately a recipe for disaster. Further, OFHEO was rather toothless, certainly compared to other bank regulators like the FDIC and OCC. So how did this split of regulation work? The HUD mandate, per Lockhart: *"HUD was the Enterprises' mission regulator. In particular, HUD had the authority to set affordable housing goals and approve new products. This bifurcation of the safety and soundness and the mission regulators was troublesome. In retrospect, it is easy to see that HUD pushed the housing goals too high."*[80] Some in HUD defended the actions, to wit HUD Spokesman Brian Sullivan's comments on the aggressive entry into subprime: *"Congress and HUD policy folks were trying to do a good thing, and it worked."*[81] Oh yes, it worked: a little too well, and in the wrong direction.

And while OFHEO's mandate was to scrutinize the financial and risk aspects of the twins, it was hamstrung. Per Falcon: *"We accomplished much despite the fact that OFHEO was structurally weak and almost designed to fail. OFHEO lacked the same statutory powers of every other safety and soundness regulator, in key areas such as enforcement powers, capital requirements, funding mechanism, and receivership authority."*[82] How do you regulate two of the largest nonbank financial institutions in the world without being able to set capital and funding? Well, as history has shown – you can't. Who would think it wise to give the politicians, rather than a financial regulator, the power to decide how much capital to set against the Fan/Fred balance sheets based on perceived riskiness? Who allowed that? The politicians.

For all of Fannie's shenanigans, Franklin Raines made one good point: *"While it is primarily the responsibility of the regulated financial institution to manage its own credit risk, it is remarkable that during the period that Fannie Mae substantially increased its exposure to credit risk its regulator made no visible effort to enforce any limits."*[83] Furthermore, *"there remains the question of why regulators did not criticize or restrict the acquisition of such loans by regulated institutions.... In the 2005 to 2007 time period...OFHEO did not seek to restrict the amount of credit risk taken on by the company."*[84] Even Lockhart would admit to failings: *"Although OFHEO warned repeatedly of the systemic risk that Fannie Mae and Freddie Mac presented to the financial markets and took many steps that helped lessen the damage, everybody including OFHEO probably could have done more."*[85] The various legislative fits and starts I summarize later in the chapter yielded nothing tangible in terms of control, leading Dimon to observe that *"[p]erhaps the largest regulatory failure of all time was the inadequate regulation of Fannie Mae and Freddie Mac."*[86]

Sidebar: Returning to Countrywide (Chapter 2) and the political-influence spun via the "Friends of Angelo" preferential mortgage program – the list included a veritable who's who of Washington politics, including those that were responsible in some way for overseeing/regulating Fannie and Freddie (remember, Countrywide sold lots of subprime mortgage to the agencies): Senators Dodd and Conrad on the Financial Services Committee, former HUD Secretary Jackson, former Fannie CEOs Franklin Raines and Jim Johnson, former counsel to the House Financial Services Committee Clinton Jones III, former Clinton Justice official Jamie Gorelick, and a number of staffers involved in oversight of the agencies, or on the staff of the House Financial Services Committee. Forgive me as I channel Captain Renault from Casablanca – *"I'm shocked, shocked to find gambling is going on here!"* Politics and business as usual.

Then there's the insurance sector, where AIG was a classic study in regulatory failure. AIG was (and still is) a sprawling institution with tentacles extending across markets and countries, that has historically written insurance and reinsurance, dealt in a range of financial instruments, structured all manner of guarantees, and operated a few banks. It did so through many legal entities and vehicles, some regulated by state insurers, others by overseas financial authorities, still others by bank regulators; some entities, such as those dealing in financial products, weren't regulated at all. Meaning that AIG, as a complex portfolio of companies, wasn't (and arguably still isn't) regulated properly – there was no single authority that could (or can) understand what AIG was (and is) doing. AIG wasn't doing anything illegal, it was operating within its scope of approved operations, its corporate charter, and what regulators said it was allowed to do. So, I can certainly fault AIG's management for being incompetent, greedy, or imprudent, but not of doing anything that it wasn't allowed to do. What of the regulators? Were they operating as best they could? Certainly they missed the warning signals or failed to monitor big chunks of the business. Perhaps they were equally incompetent or imprudent in their behaviors? In fact, Eric Dinallo, former New York State Insurance superintendent made it clear that there was no strong regulator: *"AIG Financial Products, a federally regulated noninsurance unit with wildly insufficient reserves, caused AIG to stumble and threatened the financial system...AIG's parent company, which had selected the federal Office of Thrift Supervision as its primary regulator was 'largely unregulated'... and not regulated by the states."*[87] Regulatory gaps, regulatory arbitrage, regulatory fingerpointing = recipe for disaster, and that is precisely what happened.

And of course the same lack of robust oversight extended to the rating agencies. First, let me start with the obvious, courtesy of the *Wall Street Journal*: "*the agencies were, and still are, officially anointed in this role by such government agencies as the Federal Reserve and Securities and Exchange Commission.*"[88] So, out of the starting gate the main overseers of the agencies are on the hook for failing to clamp down on all of the problems mentioned in Chapter 5. To be sure years after the Enron fiasco (where the agencies again completely missed the plot), Congress had the SEC look into a tightening-up of the sector. Nothing much happened for awhile, except to make it easier for new rating agencies to be created (with no change in the underlying issuer-pays business model). Senator Shelby was highly critical of the SEC's failures: "*The SEC did little to oversee [rating agencies] once so designated...By encouraging reliance on a small number of big credit rating agencies, bureaucrats at the SEC exposed the economic system to tremendous risk.*"[89] By the time more serious regulations did appear via the Credit Rating Agency Reform Act, in 2006, the cows were out in the pasture with pocketfuls of AAA-rated subprime bonds. Too late.

Rather tellingly the European Commission, in crucifying the rating agencies ex-post, revealed their own shortcomings: "*In 2006 the Commission set out its regulatory approach to credit rating agencies and stated that it would monitor the developments in this area very carefully."*[90] So, before the crisis, 2006, the Commission would be watching the agencies. And what happened? Did they discover ex-ante that the rating agency models were wrong or that conflicts of interest drove bad behavior? Apparently not. Good job, boys! Then, of course: *"[t]he Commission stated that it would consider new proposals if compliance with existing...rules was clearly unsatisfactory or if new circumstances were to arise including serious problems of market failure."*[91] Astounding, but perhaps predictable coming from a mega-bureaucracy: new rules will be considered in case there's a serious market failure, but new rules won't be considered to avoid getting to the point of market failure. It strikes me as rather a fruitless exercise, but perhaps one to be expected from Brussels.

AWOL III: The regulatory policy makers

The regulatory policy makers got it wrong, too – either implementing bad policies or not capturing the essence of what was coming. In Chapter 1, I noted that one of the key catalysts of the crisis was the loose US monetary policy pursued by Greenspan and his successor Bernanke (who took over in 2006, after serving four years as a member of the board of governors). Though Greenspan disputes the role of his low interest rate policy in helping fuel the crisis (as I shall point out in Chapter 8), Professor John Taylor of Stanford, writing in an op-ed, nailed the policy failures on the head: *"Monetary excesses were the main cause of the boom. The Fed held its target interest rate, especially in 2003–2005, well below known monetary guidelines that say what good policy should be based on historical experience. Keeping interest rates on the track that worked well in the past two decades, rather than keeping rates so low, would have prevented the boom and the bust."*[92]

Taylor was not a lone voice, of course. Mayo: *"And what happened in 2001, when Dr Greenspan traded the dot.com bust for the housing boom, he lowered rates down to 1 percent. He made money free, and encouraged all of the lending possible to try to restart the economy after the dot.com bust. I simply think he did a bad job."*[93] Pandit agreed that a key cause of the crisis was *"the Federal Reserve's policy of maintaining historically low interest rates in the post-9/11 period."*[94] And how about one more, this time from former Treasury Secretary Snow: *"This environment of low interest rates underpinned the loose lending practices that led to the housing boom."*[95] You get the point: lots of folks lined up against Alan's denial of loose monetary policy as a cause of the crisis. By any account, this regulatory policy was ill-advised and poorly implemented. Of course the same practice was implemented in various other countries. Morgan Stanley's Roach noted that *"[t]he lack of monetary discipline has become a hallmark of unfettered globalization. Central banks have failed to provide a stable underpinning to world financial markets and to an increasingly asset-dependent global economy."*[96]

Then we have Greenspan's successor, Ben Bernanke. As it happens, Bernanke was as mortal as the rest of us, missing the crisis in the first instance and, once it was playing out, misjudging its severity. In the first quarter of 2007 Bernanke's interpretation of the early warning signals led him to believe that *"[a]t this juncture...the impact on the broader economy and financial markets of the problems in the subprime market seems likely to be contained."*[97] In a speech in May he reiterated the same theme, noting that *"we do not expect significant spillovers from the subprime market to the rest of the economy or to the financial system."*[98] With storm clouds gathering overhead in June, Bernanke still didn't capture the potential magnitude: *"The troubles in the subprime sector seem unlikely to seriously spill over to the broader economy or the financial system."*[99]

Several US Treasury Secretaries missed the whole thing, too. Rewinding to 2005, Snow, commenting on signs of an aggressively priced housing market, noted that *"the idea that we're going to see a collapse in the housing market seems to me improbable."*[100] And in early 2008 Snow was in denial on monetary policy issues: *"Have the Fed and other central banks been asleep at the switch? No."*[101] And then there's Paulson, who told the US House of Representatives in 2007 that *"from the standpoint of the overall economy, my bottom line is we're watching it closely but it appears to be contained."*[102] As the balloon finally went up in August 2007, he noted that *"in an economy as diverse and healthy as this...losses may occur in a number of institutions, but that overall this is contained and we have a healthy economy."*[103] Well, not quite.

So, regulators of all stripes and nationalities missed the crisis – just like the institutions they were meant to be watching. Nassim Taleb was very critical of their performance: *"The center of the problem is that they don't know the center of the problem...[n]obody saw the crisis coming...Bernanke, all these guys, I want them out. They proved incompetent, they crashed the plane."*[104] Former NY Governor Elliott Spitzer agreed, stating that Bernanke and Geithner *"actually built and participated in creating the structure that now has collapsed,"*[105] and calling for their heads. And Ron Paul: *"The Federal Reserve provides the mother's milk for the booms and busts wrongly associated with a mythical 'business cycle.'...If housing prices plummet and millions of Americans find themselves owing more than their homes are worth, the blame lies squarely with Alan Greenspan and Ben Bernanke."*[106]

Clueless: The political wonders

In most countries politicians are supposed to manage aspects of government, to do all the things that ordinary citizens can't do: make laws, collect taxes, spend [wisely] on defense, transportation, entitlements, and the like. At the risk of generalizing a bit, many of them often fail to do what they were elected to do, because the business of legislating and governing and the business of getting elected sometimes run in opposite directions. Sure, there are good and honorable politicians (just as there are actually good and honorable bankers, believe it or not) – but there are also the others: those who didn't (don't) get it.

In the US, it's important to know that Congress not only crafts financial regulation, but has ultimate oversight responsibility over the country's federal agencies, including the financial regulators. The financial oversight is promulgated via the House Financial Services Committee and the Senate Committee on Banking, Housing and Urban Affairs. If the US financial regulators fell down on the job, then obviously the Congressional oversight committees did as well. And yet...not a word from any of the members, except to hold hearings to make regulators, bankers, and rating agencies squirm...

From a legislative perspective, consider that during much of the past decade US politicians either undid existing financial rules (such as Glass-Steagall) or avoided creating new ones to clamp down on certain financial activities (such as derivatives, to wit Caldwell's point that *"Congress opted instead to ban most regulation of derivatives"*[107]). And, of course, they did nothing to keep the housing agencies or subprime lending activities in check. Former banker-turned-financial writer Bethany McLean summarized the situation with considerable accuracy: *"[I]t was Congress that sat by idly as consumer advocates warned that people were getting loans they'd never be able to pay back. It was Congress that refused to regulate derivatives, despite ample evidence dating back to 1994 of the dangers they posed. It was Congress that repealed the Glass-Steagall Act, which separated investment and commercial banking, yet failed to update the fraying regulatory system. It was Congress that spread the politically convenient gospel of home ownership, despite data and testimony showing that much of what was going on had little to do with putting people in homes.... Come to think about it, shouldn't Congress have its turn on the hot seat as well?"*[108] FT's Tett provided a good summary as well: *"Well, Gordon Brown, like every other western leader, was shockingly complacent and negligent in failing to understand what was driving the City. The British government was happy to enjoy the fruits of the boom, but it didn't ask the hard questions. That said, the American government has been worse."*[109] Or, as her colleague, Lionel Barber, so aptly put it, *"[p]olitical leaders were happy to break open the champagne at the credit party; many lingered long after the fizz had gone."*[110]

In the UK Parliament crafts financial laws and carries out its own oversight of the financial regulators via the House of Commons Treasury Committee. Again, it is curious to note that the august body was missing in action as the "light-touch" financial regulation of the British financial system was failing to do a proper job. Some of the system's failures seem to have been the product of political appeasement. Scott Moeller of Cass Business School: *"It's not fair to blame bankers for all the ills, when clearly government policies have encouraged home ownership, encouraged people to take out loans to buy things maybe they can't* afford."[111] Sants: "*You may find that surprising and in hindsight I find it surprising but that is the case. The overall political pressure was to say, 'Why are you looking at these matters? Can't you make it a bit more light touch?'*"[112] And from his former boss, Turner: "*I have to say that I think if we were to roll back and the FSA had come out in 2004 and had started aggressively challenging the mortgage banks to cut back on lending, I suspect that the predominant reaction of many people, including perhaps many people in this House, would have been to be telling us that we should not be holding back the extension of mortgage credit to ordinary people; that we were preventing the democratisation of home ownership. So in hindsight, yes, it would have been better if we did, but I suspect we would have been pushed back politically if we had.*"[113] Sounds a bit like the US. Further, "*it was expressed in speeches on both sides of the House but which suggested that the key priority in regulation was to keep it light rather than to ask ever more searching questions.*"[114]

Germany had its own political problems, mostly those related to the state bank sector. Adam Posten indicated that: "*it is no coincidence that the most spectacular crashes of the recent financial turmoil involved the hybrids on both sides of the Atlantic. In the United States, it was Fannie Mae and Freddie Mac; in Germany, it was Sachsen LB and IKB. In both countries, these neither-fish-nor-fowl institutions were long recognized as financial accidents waiting to happen. But their political utility kept them open: Retired officials and politicians could get high-paying jobs there; government influence could direct credit to purposes with electoral rewards; a section of the electorate that would otherwise be denied credit got some, be it for mortgages (by the US 'agencies') or for Mittelstand financing (by IKB and the German Landesbanken). All very popular, but pointless as public policy.*"[115]

Let me now focus on perhaps the most amazing failure of the political class – the one relating to Fannie and Freddie. I go first to 2003, a time when the Bush Administration was calling for new, and more forceful, oversight of the housing agencies. Snow observed, quite rightly, that "*[t]here is a general recognition that the supervisory system for housing-related government-sponsored enterprises neither has the tools, nor the stature, to deal effectively with the current size, complexity and importance of these enterprises.*"[116] This was seconded by Deputy Treasury Secretary Bodman, who testified in June 2004 that "*[w]e do not have a world-class system of supervision of the housing government sponsored enterprises (GSEs), even though the importance of the housing financial system that the GSEs serve demands the best in supervision to ensure the long-term vitality of that system.*"[117]

The administration wanted to switch oversight from OFHEO, part of HUD, to a new financial regulator under the Department of the Treasury, and to shift the setting of capital levels from Congress to the regulator. Falcon noted at the time that "*I support legislation to strengthen the supervision of Fannie Mae and Freddie Mac. Over the past four years, I have been a consistent advocate of legislation designed to address those shortcomings.*"[118] Most Congressional Republicans supported the legislation as well, including Representative Michael Oxley (then-chairman of the Financial Services Committee): *"There is a broad agreement that the current regulatory structure for the GSEs is not operating as effectively as it should. The Office of Federal Housing Enterprise Oversight is underfunded, understaffed and unable to fully oversee the operations of these sophisticated enterprises."*[119]

Unfortunately the House of Representatives managed to spear the first major piece of reform legislation,[120] largely on a party line vote. Let me point out a few choice bits of the testimony (bearing in mind that was occurring just as Freddie had revealed that it had been falsifying its financial statements for a few years; unbeknownst to the world at large, Fannie was also cooking its books, but wouldn't get caught for another year. So, the two agencies were already out of control).

During the hearings Congressman Barney Frank noted eloquently that *"it is clear that Fannie Mae and Freddie Mac are sufficiently secure so they are in no great danger...I don't think we face a crisis; I don't think that we have an impending disaster."*[121] Furthermore, he said, *"Fannie Mae and Freddie Mac do very good work, and they are not endangering the fiscal health of this country."*[122] By my estimate these statements were wrong on all counts. California colleague Maxine Waters, for her part, sounded quite a rant: *"I have sat through nearly a dozen hearings where, frankly, we were trying to fix something that wasn't broke [sic]... Mr. Chairman, we do not have a crisis at Freddie Mac, and in particular at Fannie Mae, under the outstanding leadership of Mr. Frank Raines...What we need to do today is to focus on the regulator, and this must be done in a manner so as not to impede their affordable housing mission, a mission that has seen innovation flourish from desktop underwriting to 100 percent loans...[t]hese GSEs have more than adequate capital for the business they are in: providing affordable housing. As I mentioned, we should not be making radical or fundamental change...I am absolutely, unequivocally opposed to the transfer to Treasury and the expansion into new activities by either Treasury or HUD."*[123] In fact, Waters got everything wrong: on Franklin Raines (read: cooking the books), on 100% loans (read: subprime), and on sufficient capital (read: insufficient capital). Stunning.

Barney later added: *"I am not entirely sure why we are here, but we killed the afternoon anyway, so we might as well go forward.... I don't see any financial crisis. You can always make things better, but I do think we should dispel the notion that we are here because there is something rotten that has gone on."*[124] As if that wasn't enough: *"I believe there has been more alarm raised about potential unsafety and unsoundness than, in fact, exists. And it has been my experience that when that happens, people start worrying that things are not secure. And the first thing that happens is the poor people get tossed over the side because, after all, they are the least good risk."*[125] In 2004 Frank accused the Bush Administration of ginning up false worries: *"people tend to pay their mortgages. I don't think we are in any remote danger here. This focus on receivership, I think, is intended to create fears that aren't there.*"[126] In the event the legislation didn't pass the House – apparently those voting "no" thought the status quo was okay? Stunning.

So, on to the next proposal a few years later,[127] which was again centered on bring OFHEO and part of HUD under a to-be-created FHFA. That one passed the House but stalled in the Senate, again on a party line vote. According to Barney: *"In the end, lack of reform was the Senate's problem, because the reform bill died in the Senate in part because the White House's failure to make it a priority."*[128] No, actually, it died because the Democrats lined up in opposition. Party line vote, too bad: the Republicans couldn't get five Democrats to cross over and support the package. So what does the record say? Senator Harry Reid: *"while I favor improving oversight by our federal housing regulators to ensure safety and soundness, we cannot pass legislation that could limit Americans from owning homes and potentially harm our economy in the process."*[129] Senator Chris Dodd noted of Fannie/Freddie: *"I just briefly will say…this is one of the great success stories of all time."*[130] Senator Thomas Carper: *"If it ain't broke, don't fix it."*[131] And Senator Chuck Schumer: *"I see an analogy to Social Security…[it] has a problem and there are ideologues who want to undo it. Fannie and Freddie have problems and there are ideologues who want to undo them. But there are ways to fix the problems short of what's been proposed. When the sink is broken, you don't want to tear down the house."*[132] Interesting fact for the record: then-Senator Obama and his colleagues Chris Dodd and John Kerry, the three largest recipients of campaign contributions from Fannie and Freddie, refused to support the legislation. Sidebar: Even as President Obama took to the road to push for financial reform, Wallison reminds us that *"Sen. Obama's conversion as a financial reformer marks a reversal from his actions in previous years, when he did nothing to disturb the status quo."*[133] Don't worry, it's just politics.

Then it was back to the well again: a new round of debates on a reintroduced piece of legislation. Still, the politicos weren't all entirely convinced. There was the "be-cautious crowd," like Senator Bob Bennett (*"So let's not do nothing, and at the same time, let's not overreact."*[134]) and, again, Schumer (*"I think a lot of people are being opportunistic,…throwing out the baby with the bathwater, saying, 'Let's dramatically restructure Fannie and Freddie,' when that is not what's called for as a result of what's happened here."*[135]). Fortunately, there were some with a bit more backbone, like Senator Chuck Hagel: *"what we're dealing with is an astounding failure of management and board responsibility, driven clearly by self-interest and greed. And when we reference this issue in the context of – the best we can say is, 'It's no Enron.' Now, that's a hell of a high standard."*[136]

In the end the Housing and Economic Recovery Act (HERA) of 2008 finally passed, which brought the toothless OFHEO and parts of HUD under the new FHFA, and gave it the oversight responsibilities that OFHEO never had. The real shame: by the time HERA passed it was too late, as just 38 days after it was passed into law, Fannie and Freddie wound up in conservatorship. Good job, boys! Lockhart: *"It is impossible to say whether an earlier passage would have prevented the mortgage crisis and the housing bubble, but it certainly would have lessened the damage...It is very possible to say that the companies' opposition to the legislation for so long was a major mistake and extremely costly to their shareholders."*[137]

So, politics got in the way of attempts to impose more rules on Fannie and Freddie, and helped make Fannie and Freddie riskier, and more leveraged. These political failures caused former President Bill Clinton to note in October 2008 that *"the responsibility the Democrats have may rest more in resisting any efforts by Republicans in the Congress or by me when I was President to put some standards and tighten up a little on Fannie Mae and Freddie Mac."*[138] That, of course, runs counter to Barney's view of the world – in a bit of revisionist history courtesy of an FT op-ed, that *"[r]eality has broken into our economic programming with an important message: the subprime crisis demonstrates the serious negative economic and social consequences that result from too little regulation."*[139] And, later: *"If we had a predatory lending law and had Greenspan acted on authority he was given, we might have avoided the subprime crisis entirely."*[140] Stunning.

If you push aside all of the Congressional posturing, you get to the bottom line, which Lockhart summarized thus: *"The foremost failing by far was the legislative framework...it had to be much stronger. In particular, the capital rules were woefully inadequate for the crisis and compared to other financial institutions. The ability to lever themselves 100 to 1 on what was allowed by law to be partially nonexistent capital was impossible to overcome. The [agency] structure itself was flawed. It allowed the companies to be so politically strong that for many years they resisted the very legislation that might have saved them."*[141] Hayman's Bass has concurred: *"When you talk about what [Fannie/Freddie] did and management and competence or gross incompetence, they were pushed, as you know, by the fair housing authorities. They were pushed by Congress."*[142]

Apart from a small number of folks I'll introduce in the next chapter, there were many in politics that helped fuel the crisis. Most have conveniently forgotten what they said and did. Indeed, some of them also participated in the witch hunts that followed. So much political theater for constituents, so many stupid questions, so much ignorance. In the US, particularly, the Senators and Representatives who sat grilling Wall Streeters and regulators demonstrated time and again how little they knew (know) about the basic workings of finance and banking (one small example: after Senator Carl Levin's attempt to draw and quarter Goldman's Blankfein the *Wall Street Journal* editorial board observed: *"[w]e're note sure which of the politicians...did most to confuse spectators...Senator Levin of Michigan seemed unaware of the difference between a market-maker...and an investment advisor."*[143] The list of similar incidents is long, indeed). Unfortunately the politicians that screwed up the rules in the first place and then conducted these Holy Inquisitions are the very ones that end up writing the new rules and regulations. Melloan's take: *"One of the greater ironies of our times is that the two strongest defenders of the Fannie-Freddie shell game, Chris Dodd and Barney Frank, are now in charge of reforming banking regulation."*[144] I would go a bit further – not an irony, but a tragedy. Save us.

The special interests: Lobbyists and industry groups

I now move to the lobbyists and industry groups: these guys are expected to get things wrong, because their sole interest is in making things look good so that rules are loosened and more money enters the system. If a lobbyist or industry spokesman is negative about the market or sector being represented, that surely won't be appealing to potential customers or investors or politicians. So everything needs to have the right "spin." In the lead-up to this crisis, it was very evident in housing, real estate, and banking, where the lobbyists and representatives always spoke of sunny days, of the great moderation. The interesting question is whether, once the storm clouds were directly overhead, they didn't see them or they didn't want to see them.

Let me begin with those directly or indirectly associated with the US real estate markets: all of them worked hard to put a shiny gloss on the inflating market, using every opportunity to insist that the train would keep on rolling. Here's a small sampling of prognostications, starting with a few from National Association of Realtors chief economist, David Lereah, who predicted in early 2005 that *"in years to come, historians will see the beginning of the 21st century as the 'golden age' of real estate."*[145] If we have just witnessed the "golden age," heaven forbid we should ever encounter the "dark age." Some months later he followed up with another great prediction: *"Real estate is still a great investment opportunity for households. Price appreciation will continue. It may not be at 20%. It may...even go down to 5%."*[146] Note that was "go down to 5%" not "go down by 5%"...or 10% or 40%. Oops. And, to complete the trifecta, in late 2005 he observed that: *"Home sales are coming down from the mountain peak, but they will level out at a high plateau...a plateau that is higher than previous peaks in the housing cycle."*[147] Actually, no.

Then we have Mortgage Bankers Association's (MBA) chief economist, Douglas Duncan, who noted in late 2006 that *"[d]espite sluggish growth, largely due to declining residential investment and auto production in the second half of this year, we are optimistic about a rebound in 2007."*[148] Back in January 2007 Duncan still thought things looked okay: *"Economic growth should accelerate later this year to a trend-like pace as the drag from the housing sector wanes... [e]xisting home price appreciation is expected to slow significantly over the next three years. Median prices should remain relatively flat for both new and existing homes. Price gains for in 2008 and 2009 are expected to limited to about 2 percent... There are some downside risks in forecast... [w]e believe the probability for this scenario to be small."*[149] In fact, not only was price appreciation slow, it turned into a massive depreciation: the "low probability" scenario came true. A month later he presented a charming equation which went something like this: *"The Perfect Calm: Improving property markets + capital availability + innovations in capital markets = strong commercial/multifamily mortgage markets."*[150] Perfect calm? That's about the time HSBC Finance and New Century fired the opening salvoes of the crisis with their big losses. For all of this erroneous forecasting it must be said that the MBA put its money where its mouth was, buying a headquarters building in Washington DC for $79m in 2007, and then selling it three years later for $41m. Welcome to the jungle.

Others were sounding a similar theme. For instance, David Seiders, the chief economist of the National Association of Home Builders, indicated in 2006 that *"we are in the middle innings of the current economic expansion, and the next recession is not yet in sight."*[151] Well, not quite. Something in the water over at the Home Builders Association, no doubt, as the VP of the New Mexico branch noted that *"there is no bubble to burst."*[152] The list goes on and on, but you get the point. So, what's the conclusion? That these folks either had no clue as to what was going on or they were in the tank. Either way the outcome wasn't good.

Of course, lobbyists and industry group do more than just forecast market conditions – they lead the charge in advocacy, which in most cases means trying to persuade legislators and other politicians to keep rules and regulations to a bare minimum. Returning to our friends at MBA, Duncan said in 2007 that *"[t]he mortgage industry has been extremely innovative in developing products and tools that create homeownership opportunities, expand affordability and facilitate greater consumer choice that has helped our country reach a near 70 percent homeownership rate."*[153] Of course, I would logically expect them to come out against any form of regulation, and they didn't disappoint, to wit Duncan's rejoinder: *"MBA is concerned that approaches such as rigid, new underwriting standards and the imposition of suitability requirements will rollback hard fought homeownership and fair lending gains and will stifle innovation and take good financing options out of the hands homeowners, limiting consumer choice. The effect will be to reduce available and affordable credit, undermining our mutual goal of putting Americans in homes and keeping them there."*[154] There you go!

How about expanding the scope of state regulation to bring some of the trickier products (such as adjustable rate mortgages (ARMs)) under greater scrutiny? No way. In early 2007 the MBA was quick to note that such products were the linchpin of homeownership for many, to wit: *"ARMs...are tried and true mortgage financing options that have provided needed credit choices to tens of millions of consumers and helped millions achieve the dream of homeownership...[m]aking these products subject to the Guidance...will only curtail the availability of these options for those who are most in need of credit."*[155] In other words, hands off, because subprime borrowers might get cut off.

Other attempts to rein in subprime mortgages were similarly deflected. John Robbins, MBA's Chairman: *"A recent forecast by an advocacy organization contributed to what MBA believes, based on its own data, is exaggerated concern about the subprime market generally and hybrid ARM products in particular."*[156] Well, maybe that advocacy organization was actually right. Further, *"[a]ny attempt to curb these activities would...unduly limit credit and homeownership opportunities to credit worthy borrowers...[t]he availability of the widest possible range of products to serve consumers' financing needs...[is] of critical importance to MBA."*[157] In 2008 Robbins wanted to make sure that US banks didn't get slapped with larger capital charges, never mind that they might actually need more capital: *"Banks today utilize ever more sophisticated means to measure and manage their risk exposures.... MBA's primary interest...is to ensure that the regulators adopt a capital regime that does not place domestic banks...at a competitive disadvantage relative to their foreign counterparts."*[158]

Not surprisingly, the Fannie/Freddie machine paid handsomely for lobbyists to block any reform deemed to be detrimental. According to Fannie's then-CEO Raines: *"We manage our political risk with the same intensity that we manage our credit and interest rate risks."*[159] I would dare say they managed it with greater intensity, as Fannie clearly didn't manage its credit and interest rate risk much at all. Falcon confirms such pressure, some coming when he ordered up a special look at Fannie's books: *"Fannie's lobbyists were on the Hill spreading misinformation about my motives and asserting that the special exam was unnecessary.... It wasn't long before we realized that Fannie Mae's problems were even worse than Freddie Mac's."*[160] And, *"[i]n 2004, as OFHEO began its special accounting exam of Fannie Mae, the political attacks and obstruction intensified. Fannie was uncooperative with document requests and they engaged their supporters in Congress for assistance."*[161] In fact, during the first decade of the millennium Fannie and Freddie spent hundreds of millions of dollars on lobbyists – money obviously well spent from their perspective, as the pair wasn't brought to heel until it was all way too late. But maybe not so wisely spent from the perspective of the US taxpayer, who got to swallow $200b, $300b, $400b of losses. From Karl Rove: *"The largely unreported story is that to fend off regulation, the GSEs engaged in a lobbying frenzy. They hired high-profile Democrats and Republicans and spent $170 million on lobbying over the past decade. They also constructed an elaborate network of state and local lobbyists to pressure members of Congress."*[162] Indeed,

Snow recalls that *"[t]hroughout this period, we were met with stiff resistance by the housing industry and the mortgage industry."*[163]

Naturally, lobbying and industry group pressures didn't come solely from the real estate and mortgage banking sector: the banks had lots of interests to preserve – before the crisis, when they wanted lots of freedom, but also once the damage was done and the threat of new regulations emerged. Powerful bank lobbyists were at work around the world in the lead-up to the crisis, as observed by Dr Danielsson: *"these complex products were so profitable that the banks lobbied very strenuously against making anything over-the-counter [regulated] and because the products were so complicated the banks had all the cards."*[164]

ABA's Bradley Rock went on the record in 2005 regarding *"the need to reduce or eliminate unnecessary, redundant, or inefficient regulatory burdens that increase costs not only for banks, but also for the customers and businesses that use banks – and that's nearly everyone."*[165] Decrease regulation, Rock said, because *"[e]xcessive regulatory burden is not just a problem for banks – it has a significant impact on bank customers and local economies...[n]ew laws, however well intentioned, have added yet more layers of responsibilities on businesses like ours. While no single regulation by itself is overwhelming to most businesses, the cumulative weight of all the requirements is overwhelming."*[166]

A year later the ABA's Harris Simmons made a push for lower capital constraints, particularly on commercial real estate: *"the advanced capital adequacy framework...is an inappropriately conservative implementation of the international Basel II accord that would place U.S. banks at a competitive disadvantage with banks in other countries and impose a suboptimal use of financial resources.... The regulators risk choking off the flow of credit from banks that are engaging in [property] lending in a safe, sound, and profitable manner."*[167] Further, *"[t]he industry has significantly more capital today than before...and...[b]anks have better risk monitoring systems that catch problems quickly before they escalate."*[168] No and no.

The BBA's Angela Knight, for her part, wanted the brakes put on some of the new rules and regulations, insisting that the existing UK tripartite light-touch system (FSA, Bank of England, Treasury) wasn't as bad as all that: *"[It] is not fundamentally broken but instead needs to operate more efficiently."*[169] There probably aren't a lot of takers on that point. And Mark Brickell, former head of the International Swaps and Derivatives Association, wanted to make sure that things like credit derivatives, which had a role in the crisis, didn't get wrapped up in too much regulatory red-tape: *"A system-wide misjudgment of mortgage risk caused the financial crisis. Understanding how that happened is the essential first step toward policy reforms... [l]egislation that targets over-the-counter derivatives will not further that goal."*[170]

Charlie McCreevy, UK Commissioner for Single Market and Services, was surely up on the whole lobbying game: *"In the case of legislators, I am convinced that over the years there has been too much 'regulatory capture' by the sell side of the financial services market: Their lobbies have been strong and powerful."*[171] Further, he said, *"[w]hat we do not need is to become captive of those with the biggest lobby budgets or the most persuasive lobbyists: We need to remember that it was many of those same lobbyists who in the past managed to convince legislators to insert clauses and provisions that contributed so much to the lax standards and mass excesses that have created the systemic risks. The taxpayer is now forced to pick up the bill."*[172] Volcker was also up on it: *"[n]othing surprises me about the strength of lobbying pressures these days...I think it's certainly more organised, more money involved...these lobbying pressures are in favor of not restricting."*[173] A lot more money: between March 2008 and March 2010 the six largest US banks and the key trade lobbyists spent $600m trying to get things turned their way; they also collectively hired more than 200 former government officials to help in their efforts. Chanos, too, pointed out the power of the bank lobby: *"We have a sorry history of the banking industry driving statutory and regulatory changes...There is a connection between efforts over the past 12 years to reduce regulatory oversight, weaken capital requirements, and silence the financial detectives who uncovered such scandals as Lehman and Enron."*[174]

And, so there is the extra kindling: groups that were perhaps not solely responsible for creating all aspects of this disaster, but which surely had a hand in it.

7
A Handful of Sages

Lest you think that everyone involved in banking, politics, regulation, and lobbying is either a buffoon or involved in something nefarious, I am happy to present in this (unfortunately rather short) chapter, the exceptions that prove the rule: the small cadre of experts who saw the freight train barreling down the tracks, sometimes with unbelievable accuracy. They deserve kudos and many of us probably wish, in retrospect, that we would've heeded their advice, warnings, or counsel – they were dismissed as just so many Cassandras. Perhaps they can serve as "leading indicators" in the future?

So, who's on the select list of sages? In fact, it's a mix of economists, analysts, hedge fund managers, and, yes, even a few political-regulatory types. Not surprisingly, the list doesn't feature any bankers – with rare exception, the banking industry is an industry of lemmings: when one bank has figured out the new "new thing", it gets replicated from Wall Street to Bay Street to the City to Nihon-bashi, so that when it goes wrong, it goes wrong for all of them – just as this crisis demonstrated. To be sure, a small number of banks (and their management teams) didn't play in the deep end – a few Canadians, Australians, and Asians fared reasonably well, suggesting either that their bankers were a bit smarter – or maybe a bit luckier. But the rest of them...forget it.

The economists

Let me start with Nouriel Roubini, New York University professor of economics and head of RGE consultancy, who emerged as one of the sharpest predictors of the crisis – his gloomy, and ultimately prescient, predictions more than a year before events started unfolding even earned him the moniker "Dr Doom." (His reaction? *"Dr. Doom as a nickname was cute and I did like it for a while but what I keep saying now is that I am Dr. Realist."*[1]) Few took him seriously in the face of a seemingly strong global economy, and most just dismissed him as a permanent market bear. But he was clearly on to something.

Let me rewind to August 2006, a year before the first ripples swept through the system: Roubini released an influential report on the US housing report where he indicated, among other things that *"the only debate now is whether housing conditions are the worst in the last 40 years or in the last 53 years. So much for the bullish soft-landing wishful thinking coming out of Wall Street these days.... Every possible indicator of the housing sector that has been coming out in the last few weeks...suggests that the housing market is in free fall."*[2] Then Roubini put a few numbers to it: *"[m]y own estimate...is that, actually, the contraction is more likely to be of the order of 12–15 percent annualized rate in the next several quarters."*[3] And, then, the real warning: *"the simple conclusion from the analysis above is that this is indeed the biggest housing slump in the last four or five decades...[b]y itself this slump is enough to trigger a US recession: its effects on real residential investment, wealth and consumption, and employment will be more severe than the tech bust that triggered the 2001 recession."*[4] Spot on. Roubini also confirmed that this was a global issue: *"the housing bust is not going to be only a US phenomenon...housing bubbles festered in many other economies including many European ones...So, expect the same deadly combinations of three ugly bears (slumping housing, high oil prices, and rising interest rates) to hammer Goldilocks and sharply hurt Europe and other economies in the world."*[5]

A month later he followed up with more warnings: *"there was a speculative bubble. And now that bubble is bursting...that speculative demand is going to disappear now because prices are flattening and falling. Not only is it over, it's going to be a nasty fall."*[6] As to whether the brave bankers would be able to help avert all of this, Roubini was candid: *"Wall Street has been doing well, in part, because we have been living in a bubble, and it is bursting. We're going to have a national recession in early 2007, and Wall Street profits and bonuses will sharply drop."*[7] Prescient, indeed. Of course, Roubini went on to provide a great deal of commentary throughout 2008 and into the aftermath. The main point is that he is now widely, and quite rightly, recognized as one of the guys that got it right.

Let me also mention two other sharp economists, Karl Case (Wellsely) and Robert Shiller (Yale), whose eponymous house pricing index has become a symbol of the US housing market's boom and bust. Case and Shiller, like Roubini, were ahead of the crisis, hinting at a housing collapse as early as 2004: *"our analysis indicates that elements of a speculative bubble in single-family home prices – the strong investment motive, the high expectations of future price increases, and the strong influence of word-of-mouth discussion – exist in some cities."*[8] Later, *"[m]ore declines in real home prices will probably come in cities that have been frothy, notably including some cities on both coasts of the United States, and especially those that have weakening economies. But declines in real estate prices might appear even in cities whose employment holds steady...consequences of such a fall in home prices would be severe for some homeowners."*[9] In fact, that scenario played out as they had predicted, with many markets – frothy and otherwise – getting hit.

By August 2006, the signals were obvious to them: *"The market spoiler was in place some two years ago. At that time, we felt that the spectacular price increases could not be justified. The psychology of that time could not continue indefinitely, and indeed it has not...if housing price changes continue to decline as they have, inflation will turn into deflation, and 12-month price changes might be squarely in negative territory by some time in 2007."*[10] Indeed, that is precisely what happened. Case and Shiller followed with a warning: *"[t]here is the simple psychology of expectations that is part of any speculative boom. These expectations can turn suddenly when alert home buyers get the sense that something might be amiss...Unfortunately, there is significant risk of a very bad period, with slow sales, slim commissions, falling prices, rising default and foreclosures, serious trouble in financial markets, and a possible recession sooner than most of us expected. Deterioration in that intangible housing market psychology is the most uncertain factor in the outlook today. Listen hard and watch out."*[11] Once again, a fair warning – but could the pair have known just how right they would be?

The analysts

Some of the analysts got it right, too: equity and credit analysts and strategists that actually dared to dig into financials, ask probing questions, challenge conventional wisdom – all in an attempt to build alternative, contrarian views. Views, I might add, that were often ridiculed.

Consider the case of Meredith Whitney, then a bank equity analyst at Oppenheimer (and since out on her own as head of Whitney Advisory Group). Whitney was among the first to challenge the big banks on their growing (but as yet unknown) losses during the third quarter of 2007. How did banks manage to lose so much money? According to Whitney, *"[t]ake a bad business and lever it. And, you know, great things come."*[12] Indeed – till the worm turns. Even as the stock market was reaching global highs in October, Whitney was busy skewering Citigroup, noting that the behemoth was severely undercapitalized, would have to slice its dividend and sell core assets. She changed her rating to a "sell equivalent" and the rest is pretty much history: *"In six to 18 months, Citi will look nothing like it does now. Citi's position is precarious, and I don't use that word lightly...[i]t has real capital issues."*[13] A month later: *"They don't have enough capital, pure and simple. They will have to address that, ASAP."*[14] All of her concerns on Citi came to pass – though I wonder if she could have predicted at this point that the US government would take a 1/3 stake in the bank?

Whitney maintained a skeptical view on financials going into 2008, signaling that *"the current credit crisis is far from over...In fact, we believe that what lies ahead will be worse than what is behind us."*[15] You may recall that this view was in contrast to the ones provided by such luminaries as King, Paulson, and Buffett. She also made a timely prediction regarding the impact of monoline insurance companies – firms that lent their "supposed" AAA ratings to issuers of municipal and mortgage bonds, in exchange for a fee – on the likes of Citi, UBS, and Merrill in early 2008: *"The fate of the monoline insurers is of paramount importance to financial stocks, as further downgrades of major monoline insurers by the rating agencies could put another $100 billion in assets held by banks in jeopardy of further write-downs."*[16] In fact, such downgrades did occur, causing the banks to lose extra billions.

In July 2008, even as some hoped the worst was over, Whitney disagreed: *"I keep saying that we're less than 50% of the way done...all the capital that has been raised, hundreds of billions of dollars of capital, has just plugged holes. And the valuations and the assumptions that companies are using and carrying assets, are still unrealistic."*[17] After the run on IndyMac (which led to its closure), banks like Washington Mutual and Wachovia appeared vulnerable: *"what I knew at the time, was that there would be runs on other banks, and those that were heavily weighted towards commercial deposits."*[18] Even as many others failed to pick up on the looming second-leg down, Whitney said *"it was clear that the banks were carrying bad math assumptions."*[19] In fact, she was right. In her view, the math was straightforward: *"it is...clear that the banks still have to play catch-up. The banks, all the big banks anyway, carry their mortgage books with an assumption that home prices would decline peak-to-trough 30%, 31%. Well, we're already there."*[20] Meaning more losses. In retrospect, Whitney provided a good assessment of the whole misadventure: *"I think, we had really dumb risk this time. It wasn't clever risk. It wasn't calculated risk. It was just dumb risk. And that's probably what's so frustrating about it."*[21]

Then there's the interesting case of Christopher Wood, head strategist at CLSA and a long-time top-ranked analyst operating out of the Asian markets. Wood was very early to the party, noting in 2003 that *"[t]he American financial system remains a giant laboratory experiment in securitization which has not yet been properly stress-tested on the downside."*[22] Could he have known just how right he would be? Then, in October 2005 a bold call: *"Investors should sell all exposure to the American mortgage securities market"*[23] – for reasons related to the increasingly worrisome fundamentals of the mortgage market and the overinflated ratings assigned by the three big agencies. Wood observed that *"[t]he US housing market has been like watching a train crash in slow motion. But this is not a housing price bubble, this is a housing finance issue."*[24] In fact, Wood subsequently noted that *"I was actually too early predicting the US sub-prime meltdown"*[25] – which I guess means that he missed a few ticks on the upside, but who cares? Those who heeded his advice avoided the worst of it. In mid-2007, just before the real pain started becoming evident, Wood commented on the key point that would prove damaging to so many banks and institutional investors – the drying up of liquidity, particularly in the most structured mortgage products: *"All the evidence is that the liquidity flow to the market place is ebbing away as investors become less keen to buy exotic mortgage product, not to mention issuers becoming less keen to issue the stuff."*[26] The absence of liquidity that became very pronounced starting in July–August 2007 turned bank risk portfolios into loss-making holes.

Next up is Mike Mayo, bank analyst at CLSA (yes, the same shop as Wood), who was right on a bunch of things, going back to the turn of the millennium. Some of them were of a macro nature, such as the fragile state of the US housing market: *"Many management presentations I went to, they said, 'We want to expand home equity'...[a]nd so, they all had the same goal...and that was certainly a tipoff to me. And that is a tipoff that might not have been gotten by the regulators that early, but analysts who were going to all these meetings would get that."*[27] Furthermore, he said *"[t]he [other] point is simply the leverage. It was as clear as day in the middle part of the last decade...I'm just using regulatory data. In my mind, people just weren't incented to care enough."*[28] Too bad regulators weren't using the same regulatory data to keep an eye on the systemic buildup...

He also made timely calls on individual banks. He was first out of the gate on Citi and Bear, noting in September that both were on the ropes. And, just a month later he was ahead on Merrill's growing troubles, grilling O'Neal for reporting total $8b in red during the third quarter of 2007: *"How did you wind up with such a large concentration in the first place? I guess I am asking about risk management, and what went wrong and what happened in the last three weeks to wind up with $3 billion of additional charges."*[29] Good questions, for which O'Neal had no compelling answers. On Merrill, Mayo commented in November 2007 that *"one-eighth of the company, especially the [collateralized debt obligation] portion, seems much more exposed to additional problems. There could be $5 billion to $10 billion in additional write-downs in the fourth quarter. That could trigger ratings downgrades and possible regulatory involvement."*[30] In the event, Mayo was right about additional mega-losses in 2007 – though even he couldn't have foreseen that less than a year later Merrill would be in the arms of Bank of America. On a more general point Mayo also rightly pointed out that *"[t]he events at Citi and Merrill also raise questions about risk management. It's not enough to say, 'CEO gone. Problem solved.' Risk oversight needs to be addressed at all levels of these firms."*[31] In the end, Mayo gave a unique wrap-up of the crisis: *"The seven deadly sins of banking include greedy loan growth, gluttony of real estate, lust for high yields,* *sloth-like risk management, pride of low capital, envy of exotic fees and anger of regulators."*[32]

Another analyst that got aspects of the crisis right, and also saw through the charade created by the big rating agencies, was Sean Egan, head of Egan-Jones Ratings, a smaller, investor-pays, rating agency. While Egan may have had every desire to torpedo Moody's, S&P, and Fitch, he did so by making clear and compelling arguments as to why the issuer-pays model is fraught with conflict – a point that became all too clear during the crisis: *"The core problem behind the current crisis was a false belief in inflated credit ratings."*[33] Even as Egan-Jones was warning investors off of subprime-backed bonds, believing that they were dangerous, the big agencies continued to view them as AAAs. Furthermore, Egan was well ahead of the pack in calling out the monoline insurance companies (such as MBIA): *"We do not view MBIA companies...as 'AAA' credits and believe they face significant risks over the next couple of years...if MBIA is not rated 'AAA' its business is likely to fall."*[34] In late 2007 Egan said: *"I don't think the downgrades will stop at one notch. If you look at the capitalisation levels of the bond insurers and at the pipeline of expected losses from declining bond valuations, this is likely to go on and on."*[35] In the event, most of the major monoliners ran into trouble during the crisis (e.g., MBIA, FSA, FGIC, Ambac, ACA, and others) losing top ratings and/or requiring significant capital infusions to stay afloat – and those downgrades created further losses for banks holding bonds with monoline guarantees. You get the point – Egan and company were ahead of the game on the monoliners, causing Egan to ask rhetorically in front of a Congressional panel: *"How is it possible that the major rating agencies which have substantially more analysts than at Egan-Jones be six years behind us."*[36]

Egan was critical of the issuer-pays model, noting rather colorfully that *"[y]ou have tainted meat on the inspection line...You have rating firms acting as meat inspectors, and unfortunately the rating firms are being paid by the meat producers. It underscores the severely flawed structure of the industry."*[37] Furthermore: *"With respect to the current wave of credit defalcations, it is clear that the major rating agencies...not just failed to give early warning to investors but their ratings were a major factor in the most extensive and possibly expensive financial calamity in recent America history."*[38] The end result? According to Egan *"Our business is going like mad...better than ever."*[39] Well deserved.

The hedge fund managers

Not all of the divination happened within the community of economists and analysts – some came from the money makers, mostly hedge fund managers like Einhorn, Chanos, Singer, Taleb, and Paulson (John, not Hank). Each one of these gentleman was able to translate bearish views on different parts of the market into a few dollars.

John Paulson, head of hedge fund Paulson & Co, emerged as one of the savviest of the industry's portfolio managers, spotting the misbalance between risk and return on all manner of mortgage instruments before most, profiting handsomely as a result. He also rooted out problems at several big banks– Wachvoia, Washington Mutual, RBS, Lehman, to name a few – and set up positions to take advantage of their deterioration. Paulson's investors did very well as a result of his diligence, and Paulson himself got a 10 figure pay day.

Paulson was in front of the pack on the mortgage bubble, becoming worried about inflating US house prices as early as 2005: *"our firm became very concerned about weak credit underwriting standards, excessive leverage among financial institutions and a fundamental mis-pricing of credit risk."*[40] Further, *"[w]e felt that housing was in a bubble; housing prices had appreciated too much and were likely to come down...[w]e couldn't short a house, so we focused on mortgages."*[41] According to Paulson's analysis subprime mortgage bonds were wildly mispriced, so he positioned his fund to profit from a reversal of the overly optimistic pricing trend – and profited handsomely as everything went south.

Paulson noted in testimony that *"it was so obvious that these securities were completely mispriced and we were living in a casino. I think the other players that were involved in the business they got caught up in the exuberance, they got caught up in the competition to increase their underwriting volumes, caught up in the competition to increase their fees. They were very focused on annual earnings, quarterly earnings and annual bonus pools and with the amount of the liquidity, everyone got caught up in what became a massive credit bubble."*[42] In the event, Paulson *"purchased protection...on debt securities we thought would decline in value due to weak credit underwriting.... As...the value of these securities fell, we realized substantial gains for our investors."*[43] That produced big profits. Some of this was done through a deal arranged by Goldman, which then became the subject of an SEC fraud suit. Of course, no charges were filed against Paulson as he did nothing wrong – he simply capitalized on his view of an overvalued market.

Jim Chanos, head of Kynikos Associates (a well known short-selling fund that correctly targeted fraud-ridden Enron) and Paul Singer of Elliott Associates also made good calls on individual banks as well as the subprime market and structured credit products.

Rewind to April 2007 when Chanos and Singer were sounding warnings on subprime and exotic mortgage securities to those who would listen – but few did. In fact, the pair provided their views at the G7 meeting of world finance ministers where, Chanos recalls, *"Paul got up and proceeded to give a tour de force presentation on the coming crack-up in structured finance, how all these structures* were very unstable and triple A was not going to be triple A...I then segued into my presentation which told the assembled regulators that...the problem would not be hedge funds it would be the regulated banks and brokers who were leveraged 30–1, many of which held glowing, toxic radioactive pieces of securitisation which they could never sell."[44] Unfortunately, none of the finance ministers took much note, as history has since revealed. Chanos observed in Congressional testimony that "[o]ur audience listened politely, but, as events now show, failed to take any meaningful action. The decision by those in charge of regulating our economy to ignore fundamental problems has cost us millions of jobs and lost homes, hundreds of billions in government spending, and trillions of dollars in investment losses."[45]

By July 2007 Chanos was on record saying that all of the exotic mortgage-backed bonds were just so much worthless paper: *"The issue here is passing the hot potato...There's a lot more to come...[w]hat we're seeing already is a spreading of the contagion."*[46] Singer himself noted of the exotica that *"[i]t is still surprising how many investment fads have elaborate spindrifts of ethereal logic which, when stripped away, are really dumb."*[47] In fact, he was worried about the misbalance as early as 2005: *"What we found was an extraordinary level of mispricing of risk... [t]he ratings of the securities were extremely erroneous. Never seen anything like it in 30 years...[f]inancial institutions did not check, and the rating agencies let them down."*[48] He positioned his fund to benefit from the collapse in 2007, profiting handsomely as many others were losing. And probably wondering why all the G7 finance ministers ignored his predictions.

Chanos also went on to drill into Bear and Lehman, becoming one of the more active and vocal short-selling advocates – drawing lots of criticism from the industry and from regulators, who argued that such activity was destabilizing to the individual institutions and the economy at large. Nonsense. Chanos' approach has long been to *"lay the groundwork for people to understand what happened, so when the facts come out, maybe they'll see that the people who were raising the alarms aren't the ones to blame."*[49] With his track record on Enron, Lehman, and others Chanos deserves credit. In his view: *"It sounds kind of crass, but I like being right...It's interesting and fun to find these companies that you see gaming the system and pulling one over on their investors. It's fun to point it out. It's great to say, 'No. These guys are bad guys!'"*[50] He also had scathing remarks for the banking industry as a whole, noting that the toxic securities they cooked up were *"the heart of one of the greatest heists of all time,"*[51] and that *"[t]here's no doubt in my mind that this is fraud."*[52] Furthermore, according to Chanos: *"we are going to find out when we go through the accounting that in fact these things were never that profitable."*[53] Meaning that bankers got handsomely paid for something that was ultimately worthless.

Nassim Taleb may not want to be classified as a hedge fund manager – he's a mix of ex-trader, academic/intellectual, and author, but he does run a "black swan" hedge fund, Universa, so I include him here, with apologies. Taleb has been consistent in warning against the "black swan" – the improbable, devastating event that actually occurs more frequently than the tidy bell curve underpinning lots of risk models would otherwise imply. As I mentioned in Chapter 2, he has long been a vocal critic of the rather simplistic models used by major banks and widely supported by regulators – the very models that fail to take account of the "black swans." Back in 2006 he noted that *"you are relying on something with false confidence and running larger positions than you would have otherwise. You're worse off relying on misleading information than on not having any information at all. If you give a pilot an altimeter that is sometimes defective he will crash the plane."*[54] Furthermore: *"Thirteen years ago, I warned that 'VaR encourages misdirected people to take risks with shareholders', and ultimately taxpayers' money.' I have since been begging for the suspension of these measurements of tail risks. But this came a bit late…. April 28, 2004 was a very sad day, when the SEC, at the instigation of the investment banks, initiated the abandonment of hard (i.e. robust) risk measures like leverage, in favor of more model-based probabilistic, and fragile, ones."*[55] Banks did, in fact, build big risk positions atop such weak foundations in the lead-up to the crisis. The rest is painful financial history. In short, Taleb has said, *"[t]he general public needs to know that a lot of bogus claims have been made by the financial economics establishment, based on metrics that we know don't work, and a lot of portfolios are based on these underestimations of wild uncertainty."*[56]

Taleb was also correct on Fannie (and Freddie), noting well before the blow-up that there was trouble brewing. As early as 2003 he observed that *"Fannie Mae's models (for calibrating to the risks of rare events) are pseudoscience."*[57] In addition, he pointed out in 2007 – more than a year before conservatorship – that *"Fannie Mae, when I look at its risks, seems to be sitting on a barrel of dynamite, vulnerable to the slightest hiccup. But not to worry: their large staff of scientists deemed these events 'unlikely'."*[58] Regarding the crisis in general, Taleb indicated that *"very few people saw it coming, I guarantee. Nobody saw the real cost. And let me tell you the problem. The system used to analyze risk is completely defective, and actually could not keep up with the complexity of the financial products that are involved."*[59]

On to David Einhorn, head of hedge fund Greenlight Capital, who was right on Lehman and the bank's increasingly precarious state prior to September 2008. Of course, he applied similar analysis to a whole basket of banks that he believed were overexposed to some of the more complex bits of the mortgage market and shorted them (in other words, *"[a] big macro call. One percent of this, one percent of that. No large positions. We were looking for the firms that we thought had the most exposure."*[60]). But he really made his mark on Lehman. Einhorn noted in the Spring of 2008 that *"Lehman's exposures are worse than Bear's on an apples-to-apples basis"*[61] and became particularly critical of Lehman's CFO

Callan, noting during investor calls that *"[w]e had our questions, we were organized, but she was evasive, dishonest. Their explanations didn't make any sense."*[62] In mid-April Einhorn grew increasingly skeptical about what he saw: *"I believe the outlook for Lehman's stock is dim."*[63] And, then: *"The world just broke apart. On the one side, you had Goldman, which obviously had it right, and Lehman, which said they were like Goldman...[i]t just didn't make any sense."*[64] In the end Einhorn was right – Lehman was a disaster.

More broadly, Einhorn's observation that *"[t]he investment banks outmaneuvered the watchdogs"*[65] is absolutely correct – though arguably, it extends also to many other classes of banks and nonfinancial institutions, who played the same game and reaped the same results. Further: *"With no one watching, the managements of the investment banks did exactly what they were incentivized to do: maximize employee compensation. Investment banks pay out 50 percent of revenues as compensation. So more leverage means more revenues which means more compensation."*[66]

Political-regulatory types

It's not often that those traveling in the political or regulatory sphere buck the trend of conventional wisdom and sound warnings. But I have a few examples to talk about. While these folks may not have seen the whole thing coming, they did go out on a limb, warning about some of the things that were starting to appear a bit out of whack.

Let me start with former Treasury Secretary Snow. He wasn't perfect: I mentioned in the previous chapter that he missed the early warnings signs of the housing bubble and he later went on to defend some of the Greenspan monetary policy actions. Still, he got a critical part of the equation right – he was an early advocate of greater control and scrutiny of the housing agencies, noting that *"we began to see potential problems with over-leverage and attendant systemic risks. These potential problems – which were most visible in the context of Fannie Mae and Freddie Mac – intensified over time."*[67] As I noted in Chapter 6, Snow pushed for regulatory reform *"[o]ut of concern that the existing regulatory structure over all housing [agencies]...was inadequate, I came before Congress...to urge enactment of legislation to protect taxpayers and the integrity of the housing finance market."*[68] While he didn't see an imminent problem, he advised that if a problem were to arise, the position of the housing agencies *"could cause systemic risk to the whole financial system."*[69] More precisely, if *"[t]he risks undertaken by the [agencies], if not properly managed, may pose a threat to their solvency, the stability of other financial institutions and the strength of the economy."*[70] Despite repeated attempts, he was rebuffed: *"Unfortunately, we were unable to persuade Congress to pass any version of the legislative options we put forward."*[71] In hindsight even Snow had to admit that the total scope of the problem escaped him: *"[w]hat eluded us, however, was a clear picture of the full extent of the risks to the financial system because of insufficient transparency."*[72]

Then there's the case of Congressman James Leach, Representative from Iowa, who was quite vocal in his concerns about Fannie and Freddie, even when others like Barney Frank and Maxine Waters were looking the other way. Leach noted in mid-2005 that *"[l]ike all artificially created bubbles, the boom in housing prices cannot last forever. When housing prices fall, homeowners will experience difficulty as their equity is wiped out. Furthermore, the holders of the mortgage debt will also have a loss. These losses will be greater than they would have been had government policy not actively encouraged over-investment in housing."*[73] He urged his colleagues not to support legislation that didn't limit, in some way, the implicit guarantee provided to Fannie and Freddie, noting: *"this legislation creates new government programs that will further artificially increase the demand for housing [and] increases the economic damage that will occur when the housing bubble bursts."*[74] And, again, very, very presciently, *"I hope my colleagues join me in protecting taxpayers from having to bail out Fannie Mae and Freddie Mac when the housing bubble bursts."*[75] Note the repeated use of the word "when" and not "if." And, finally, *"[t]he failure of either institution could potentially make the savings and loan crisis of a generation ago look somewhat minor...they disproportionately become on the hook if very extraordinary things happen in the economy, something that is not beyond thinking."*[76] As I mentioned in Chapter 4 the Fannie/Freddie losses alone did greatly outweigh those generated by the S&L crisis. So Leach was right, and he was three years ahead of his time. Bravo. Too bad more of his Congressional colleagues didn't listen.

Ron Paul was also on the money. As I noted earlier in the book, Paul has long been an outspoken critic of the Fed, its policies, and its lack of transparency (having written an entire manifesto on the subject). He hounded Greenspan (and later Bernanke) regularly, criticizing the Fed's monetary policy, the continued growth of debt at all levels in the system, and the steady devaluation of the dollar. In 2002, after the implosion of the stock market, he told Greenspan: *"[where] you have come up short is in failing to explain why we have financial bubbles. I think when you have fiat money and excessive credit you create financial bubbles and you also undermine the value of the dollar and now we are facing that consequence."*[77]

Of course, even as Paul was grilling Greenspan about the last bubble, the next bubble – housing – was already inflating. In 2004 Paul commented *"Never mind, says Mr. Greenspan. Mortgage refinancing, made wildly popular by artificially low interest rates established by the Fed, will be the saving grace of American households. They can simply borrow against their homes to finance living beyond their means, a practice encouraged by Fed policies. But what happens when home prices stop going up? What happens when families reach a point where they cannot make payments on two, three, or even more mortgages? How can the Fed chairman equate mortgage credit with real economic growth?"*[78] Indeed, that is precisely what US households were doing.

Paul was also on top of the Fannie/Freddie powder keg. He testified back in September 2003 that *"the government's policy of diverting capital to other uses creates a short-term boom in housing... [l]ike all artificially created bubbles, the boom in housing prices cannot last forever. When housing prices fall, homeowners will experience difficulty as their equity is wiped out. Furthermore, the holders of the mortgage debt will also have a loss. These losses will be greater than they would have otherwise been had government policy not actively encouraged over-investment in housing."*[79] He was highly critical of the weak regulatory structure and the implicit guarantees (you know, the ones that Barney Frank was sure didn't exist): *"Ironically, by transferring the risk of widespread mortgage defaults to the taxpayers through government subsidies and convincing investors that all is well because a 'world-class' regulator is ensuring the GSEs' soundness, the government increases the likelihood of a painful crash in the housing market."*[80]

More generally he said that *"the Federal Reserve can stave off the day of reckoning by purchasing [housing agency] debt and pumping liquidity into the housing market, but this cannot hold off the inevitable drop in the housing market forever... postponing the necessary, but painful market corrections will only deepen the inevitable fall."*[81] How right he was. He tried, at that time, to introduce the Free Housing Market Enhancement Act to remove the government line of credit extended to Fannie and Freddie. Why? *"This implicit promise by the government to bail out the GSEs in times of economic difficulty helps the GSEs attract investors who are willing to settle for lower yields than they would demand in the absence of the subsidy. Thus, the line of credit distorts the allocation of capital. More importantly, the line of credit is a promise on behalf of the government to engage in a massive unconstitutional and immoral income transfer from working Americans to holders of GSE debt."*[82] It comes as no surprise that the bill went nowhere. In retrospect, he observed: *"[e]ven as early as 7 years ago, I introduced legislation that would have removed the line of credit to the Treasury, which was encouraging the moral hazard and the malinvestment."*[83]

On to Peter Wallison, fellow at the American Enterprise Institute and former Treasury and White House official, who was one of the most vocal critics of Fannie and Freddie. Consider, for instance, that back in May 2005 he indicated that *"If Congress can bring itself to overcome the furious political opposition of the GSEs and their supporters, it will direct the new GSE regulator to reduce the size of Fannie's and Freddie's portfolios... This will solve, finally, the problem of two entities using their implicit government backing to control the residential mortgage market, which creates massive risks for the taxpayers and the economy in general. If Congress cannot take this essential step, however, no amount of additional authority – given* to a purported 'world-class regulator' – will significantly change the course of events. Fannie and Freddie will continue to grow, and one day...there will be a massive default with huge losses to the taxpayers and systemic effects on the economy."[84] Commenting on the regulatory reforms on the table at the time, Wallison said, "[i]t is a classic case of socializing the risk while privatizing the profit. The Democrats and the few Republicans who oppose portfolio limitations could not possibly do so if their constituents understood what they were doing."[85] And, yet, oppose they did...The power of Fannie and Freddie was all quite clear to Wallison: "They have over the years been able to put themselves in a position where there was a real question whether Congress was in charge of them or they were in charge of Congress."[86] I think the answer to that one is quite clear.

After conservatorship, Wallison testified that "I say this as a person who has spent ten years studying, writing about, and warning that Fannie Mae and Freddie Mac would have a disastrous impact on the financial world, and that ultimately the taxpayers of this country would be required to bail them out. This wasn't a wild guess on my part. Because they were seen as backed by the government, Fannie and Freddie were relieved of market discipline and able to take risks that other companies could not take....Utimately, however, the risks they took in exploiting their subsidy caused their collapse and will cause enormous losses for U.S. taxpayers."[87]

And then there's Alan Greenspan. I've already noted that he was part of the cadre of regulators who got it wrong on interest rates and the inflating housing bubble. So, how can he be on the sage list? Well, he's still a smart guy and he deserves some credit for being correct about the fact that Fannie and Freddie were getting way too big and starting to pose something of a risk to the system. Let me go back to a speech he gave in October 2005, when he told the audience, "[w]e at the Federal Reserve remain concerned about the growth and magnitude of the mortgage portfolios of the [agencies], which concentrate...risk...and make our financial system dependent on their ability to manage these risks,"[88] adding that "the strong belief of investors in the implicit government backing of the agencies...create[s] systemic risks for the U.S. financial system as the [agencies] become very large."[89] And getting large, they were: "[T]he government guarantee for [agency] debt inferred by investors enables Fannie and Freddie to profitably expand their portfolios of assets essentially without limit"[90] – from about $100b in 1990 to more than $1.2t in 2005, and several trillion by the time things blew up.

Alan went on: "When these institutions were small, the potential for such risk, if any, was small. Regrettably, that is no longer the case."[91] So, he was homing in on the real problem and wanted some action from legislators on this: "Without changes in legislation, Fannie and Freddie will, at some point, again feel free to multiply profitability through the issuance of subsidized debt,"[92] and "if we fail to strengthen GSE regulation, we increase the possibility of insolvency and crisis. We at the Federal Reserve believe this dilemma would be resolved by placing limits on the *[agencies'] portfolios of assets."*[93] Ultimately, noted Greenspan: *"[w]ithout restrictions on the size of [agency] balance sheets, we put at risk our ability to preserve safe and sound financial markets in the United States, a key ingredient of support for homeownership."*[94] In fact, limits didn't appear till much later in the game, when Fannie and Freddie were already massive and close to the edge. And once they went over the edge, the limits were again suspended.

Largely unnoticed was another prescient comment that Greenspan made, which must have seemed like a throwaway at the time: *"Congress will need to clarify the circumstances under which a[n agency] can become insolvent ... [t]his process must be unambiguous before it is needed. Current law, which contemplates conservatorship and not receivership for a troubled [agency], requires the federal government to maintain [agencies] as ongoing enterprises."* Guess, what? Not resolved, so Fannie and Freddie exist on life support in the Intensive Conservatorship Unit.

Then there were a few politicians in Europe. German Chancellor Angela Merkel and her compatriot, Finance Minister Peer Steinbrueck, were a bit ahead of the curve. In early 2007 Merkel said: *"We want to minimise the structural risks in the international capital markets through greater transparency"*[95] and offered up some new regulations to that effect. Steinbrueck noted ruefully afterwards that the proposals *"elicited mockery at best or were seen as a typical example of the German penchant for overregulation."*[96] In fact, it's a bit of a shame that Merkel and Steinbrueck weren't also trying to get the German house in order at the time ... you know, the one with Sachsen LB, IKB, Hypo Real Estate, WestLB ...

And then there's the case of Liberal MP Vincent Cable – the gentleman who famously said of the Bank of England's second bank rescue package for RBS, Lloyds TSB-HBOS, et al: *"it now looks like someone giving the kiss of life to a corpse."*[97] Cable didn't view himself as one who called the whole US housing market crisis: *"one of the problems of being a British MP is that you do tend to get rather parochial and I haven't been to the States for years ... so I wouldn't claim to have any feel for what's been going on there."*[98] But he did focus on fundamental issues in the UK housing sector as early as 2003: *"On the housing market, is not the brutal truth that with investment, exports and manufacturing output stagnating or falling, the growth of the British economy is sustained by consumer spending pinned against record levels of personal debt, which is secured, if at all, against house prices that the Bank of England describes as well above equilibrium level? ... [W]hat action will the Chancellor take?"*[99] He later noted of his 2003 comments that *"I don't think my statement was a prediction so much as a warning about bad policy."*[100] And it did, indeed, prove accurate, as the likes of HBOS, Northern Rock, Bradford & Bingley, and others with a heavy mortgage footprint, eventually discovered. He also expressed irritation in mid-2009 regarding the slow pace of regulatory reform: *"I think there's far too much attention at the moment being paid to bureaucratic reorganisation rather than getting on with the job – there's this silly argument* between the Bank of England and the FSA, which is really just a turf dispute, what I call a quango war, and we don't need it, and it is taking up a lot of time and energy which should be spent on the British economy."[101] And, again somewhat presciently, he warned in 2009 of an impending *"repossession time bomb – repossessions are being stored up, because at the moment banks are showing forbearance, which is a good thing, the government schemes are only temporary, and there is a possibility of interest rates rising next year – all these things will lead to a big upsurge."*[102]

Media?

How about the media space? Surely in this world of 24/7 business coverage, some within the press must've been able to see this one coming? There were a few, but not many. Lots of the financial press continued to promote the rising markets in real estate and stocks through 2006 and into 2007, sounding no real warning signals. A survey of US financial media indicated that more than 2/3 thought they had dropped the ball. Dan Abrams, who conducted the survey said *"there's a lot of self-examination going on within the financial media about what happened and why."*[103] Charlie Gasparino, financial author and business commentator on Fox Business was perhaps the most honest and forthright about the matter, taking the financial media to task: *"What's interesting about this, this bubble, is that a lot of people on the inside didn't think anything was wrong…We all failed."*[104] How refreshing! The same seems to have happened in the UK, where pre-crisis warnings weren't, in the main, properly sounded. Financial journalist turned professor Marie Kinsey: *"[J]ournalists can or should hold their hands up and say, 'perhaps we didn't sound the alarm bells as early as we might have done,'…There is a sense that they too almost swallowed the line that the bankers put across [about] these wonderful financial instruments, [about] words people hadn't used before, derivatives and all the rest of it, what was happening to risk."*[105] FT editor Lionel Barber: *"The financial media are accused of missing the global financial crisis. Asleep at the wheel. Head in the clouds. No cliché has been left unturned as reporters, commentators – yes, even editors – have been castigated for failing to warn an unsuspecting public of impending disaster."*[106] Why? Barber went on to explain that financial journalists, by and large, failed to prove the danger of over-the-counter derivatives and off-balance sheet activities, the implicit guarantees of Fan/Fred and the growing web of systemic risks. Not that it's any excuse, but *MarketWatch*'s Jon Friedman put it this way: *"Wall Street reporters have a difficult job. The public relations machines at various Street firms are as tough to crack as the Kremlin's."*[107]

But one who got an early read on the situation was the FT's Gillian Tett, who started writing in 2006 and early 2007 about the growing problems in complex credit structures. Not that many were paying attention. Per Tett: *"You could see everyone's eyes glazing over…But my team, not just me, we very much warned* of the dangers. Though I don't think we expected the full scale of the disaster that's unfolded."[108] Furthermore, she said, "[w]hat made the credit bubble different this time around was that we've had this incredible wave of innovation in recent years that made the system very opaque. So nobody saw just how bad the loans were, and nobody saw just how big the credit bubble had become until it was far too late."[109]

In fact, she was denounced in the lead-up to the crisis for her sometimes critical writings on the topics of complexity, leverage, and the refusal for people to see that things could unwind in a messy fashion; she was also ahead of the game on some specific problems, like Northern Rock. *"We had enormous kickback from the bankers in the City saying, 'Why are you being so critical of the industry? Why are you being so negative?' All that kind of stuff."*[110] Wall Street and the City didn't necessarily appreciate her critiques, such as those coming in 2007: *"the financial sector has spent much of this decade operating with a short-term view that was focused on the future, not the past. Indeed, as recently as this spring, it was rare to find any financial trader who spent much time pondering events more than a decade old – or beyond the data points typically found on a trading terminal."*[111] When it finally hit, *"it came out of the blue for many people – investors, policymakers, bankers, our readers were suddenly completely at sea, at a loss to make sense of it."*[112]

At the beginning of 2007 Tett noted that complex products had *"created a challenge for policy makers because it makes it much harder for regulators, let alone ordinary investors, to see where the risks in the financial system lie and to see where trends or problems could be building up...whether that's creating new dangers for financial stability and, if so, how exactly regulators can respond."*[113] And of course it is now clear that the wave of products did create financial instability and regulators were unable to respond. Tett also added some months later what many in the industry knew, but what many regulators and politicians seem now to be shocked about: *"there is concern...that some investors are using derivatives to embrace increasingly risky and potentially dangerous strategies because credit conditions have appeared to be so safe in recent years. There is certainly little evidence investors wish to use the flexibility derivatives offer to reduce risk, preferring instead to increase the benefits of taking the same risks."*[114] Tett was also right in pointing out that bank risk managers (and regulators) had been guilty of focusing on the source of the last big problem, the last big losses, rather than looking forward to the next problem areas. So, in the millennium, everyone was focused on the problems caused by large hedge funds that run aground – not just LTCM, but more recent problems, like Amaranth, Archeus, Mother Rock. She rightly observed that *"while risk managers have been obsessively watching hedge funds, another problem has been brewing, unnoticed – conduits and structured investment vehicles."*[115] In fact, I am quite sure that few, if any, risk managers were paying too much attention to these vehicles, which bought in mortgage bonds and financed the purchases by issuing commercial paper. And when the crisis hit and commercial paper could no longer be rolled over, all those vehicles had to liquidate their mortgage bond portfolios – in illiquid markets, at deep discounts, meaning lots of red ink.

Once a sage, always a sage?

There were certainly other sages that got it right – consider this as a representative sample. Folks like Ken Rogoff (economist and professor), Peter Schiff (money manager and one-time advisor to Ron Paul), Bill Ackmann (fund manager), Steve Eisman (hedge fund manager), Marc Faber (investment advisor), Jim Rogers (investor), and some others all have a record showing that they saw aspects of this disaster coming one, two, or three years in advance. That said, the absolute number of sages is certainly far, far smaller than the number of those that got it wrong. And, unfortunately, most of what they said was ignored, in some cases ridiculed. Conventional wisdom trumped all – who, after all, wanted to be the spoiler at the never-ending party?

So, what makes a sage? Why did these (and a small number of other) people get aspects of this right, while so many others got it wrong? It is difficult to say, without making it all seems so "ex-post obvious," but I suppose the essential items are keen intellect and analytical skills, ability to detect something important that others can't (won't) see, and the courage to stand by one's convictions. Bucking conventional wisdom is very difficult to do, especially when the majority of the "experts" are making pots of money by following the conventional path. And one can't be a perpetual contrarian: at some point "the boy who cried wolf" syndrome sets in, and the market will surely ignore the next cautionary call. So the contrarianism must be well grounded, and it must be revealed at an opportune moment.

It's important to keep in mind that no one gets it right all of the time. The people that I've mentioned above, as good as they were in predicting what was to come, may be as fallible as everyone else – they can't, and don't, get it right all the time, though I certainly wish them luck in keeping their "winning streaks" going. In fact, financial history has lots of "fallen sages," – those who made brilliant calls, and then followed up with equally bad ones. So I can't assume that a small group of folks will always get it right. What we really need to do is look for some of the thoughtful contrarian messages that emerge during the next period of pre-crisis euphoria. Perhaps that will yield the next crop of sages – ones that we might want to heed before it's too late.

8
The Blame Game: Fingerpointing and Apologies

It is interesting in the aftermath of the crisis to correlate red ink and failed performance with apologies and admissions of culpability from those in a position of power, influence, and responsibility. In other words, it's interesting to see who does and doesn't feel accountable for the annihilation of so much wealth. In the past chapters I've mentioned all the different groups that contributed to the screwup – the question is, how many have actually owned up to it? Based on my admittedly unscientific review, there seems to be an entire spectrum that ranges from "genuine mea culpa" to "mistakes were made" to "not my fault." But before I get into the specifics, let me set the stage by first looking at how of some of the global political leaders reacted to the crisis.

The global leaders speak...

So, who did the world's leaders think was responsible for this crisis? Not surprisingly, there's a pretty strong consensus that the US was (is) solely to blame; only in a few cases did some of the world's leaders also acknowledge their own national mistakes.

First up is Gordon Brown, who said in October 2008 that *"[t]his problem started in America. They have got to sort it out."*[1] Furthermore: *"People were taking risks that were excessive – and that was mainly in my view in America and we are paying a price for what has come out of America."*[2] And then again: *"Well it is pretty clear to me that this problem started in America, it started with irresponsible actions and lending by individual institutions. Some of it was hidden from the regulators, some of it was never reported in companies' balance sheets, in some cases nobody actually knew in the board of the company what irresponsible lending was done."*[3] Damn Yankees...

Still, let's not forget that the City of London (or as Vince Cable has said, *"Iceland-on-the-Thames"*[4]), has been at the forefront of toxic financial engineering for many years. And that the big UK banks – RBS, HSBC, Barclays, HBOS – created as much of the toxic stuff as the US banks. And that the UK had its own real estate bubble built atop many poor lending practices. And that London enjoyed the benefits of light-touch regulation for many years. And that Northern Rock's collapse was unrelated to anything going in the US. You get the point.

In the end Brown was forced to admit that even the UK bankers kind of screwed up, too – but still always managed to bring it back to the US: *"These [British] guys have taken irresponsible risks; that is completely unacceptable. The problem is they didn't know what they were buying from America."*[5] Really? It wasn't widows and orphans buying supposedly AAA-rated mortgage securities, it was sophisticated institutional players. Why did they not do their analysis and due diligence? And again: *"Now where there have been regulatory issues, such as on Northern Rock, the FSA have said that they could have done certain things better. But the problem essentially arises, starting out of the United States of America where we had this highly leveraged lending, it ran into trouble because people were not sure and taking huge risks about the products that they were involved in, it has become a problem for the whole banking system and we have got to deal with it."*[6] Damn Yankees...

David Cameron was a bit of an enigma on this issue. In October 2008 he said *"we will not allow what happened in America to happen here"*[7] – never mind that what had happened in America had already happened in the UK. And then, *"[m]any bankers in the City were quite simply irresponsible. They paid themselves vast rewards when it was all going well and the minute it went wrong, they came running to us to bail them out."* True enough. Yet one month before that he had said *"[w]hat you won't get from me this week is the sort of easy cheap lines beating up on the market system, bashing financiers. It might get you some easy headlines but it's not going to pay a single mortgage, it's not going to save a single job."*[8] So, I'm not really sure...

In Germany things were very clear to an irate finance minister Steinbrueck, who said: *"The United States, and let me emphasize, the United States is solely to be blamed for the financial crisis. They are the cause for the crisis and it is not Europe and it is not the Federal Republic of Germany... [it was] the Anglo-Saxon drive for double-digit profits and massive bonuses for bankers and company executives that were responsible for the financial crisis."*[9] So, I guess a bunch of salespeople from Goldman and JP and Merrill went over to IKB and Sachsen LB and the other "yield chasers" and forced them to buy AAA subprime mortgage bonds? I don't think so. [N.B. Steinbrueck: check out Deutsche's or Commerz/Dresdner's US operations – they've been quite significant for the past decade, they've been every bit as involved in the same financial alchemy, and they've been paying the same bonuses as the other American big boys.] Furthermore, Steinbrueck said, *"The world will never be the same as it was before the crisis. The US will lose its status as the superpower of the global financial system.*"[10] And, from Steinbrueck's boss, Chancellor Angela Merkel, a bit more: *"I'm criticizing the self-image of the financial markets – which have unfortunately resisted voluntary rules for too long with the support of Great Britain and the United States."*[11] Whilst I am in Germany, let me also mention Bafin's Sanio (a Springsteen fan?), who observed: *"How could this scam go on operating successfully for several years? The answer is easy: the 'originators' of the underlying mortgages in the USA were insufficiently regulated. This financial crisis was definitely 'born in the USA'. The absence of US-wide regulatory lending standards enforced by effective financial supervision led to reckless lending on a scale that the world had never seen before."*[12] Not so fast, said Reinhard Buetikofer, head of the opposition Green Party: *"For a while, a large segment of the public considered all this as innocent German banks caught in an American mess. ... Only recently has the public started to understand how much we are involved, and how much of this has been our doing, too."*[13]

Elsewhere, Johannes Laitenberger said on behalf of the EU Commission that *"[t]he United States must take its responsibility in this situation, must show statesmanship for the sake of their own country, and for the sake of the world."*[14] China's Premier Wen Jiabao blamed the US by implication (being polite enough not to mention the US by name), noting that *"[i]nappropriate macroeconomic policies of some economies and their unsustainable model of development characterised by prolonged low savings and high consumption"*[15] were at the heart of the problem. Furthermore, there was the problem of *"an excessive expansion of financial institutions in blind pursuit of profit, lack of self discipline among financial institutions and ratings agencies."*[16] Spain's Minister for Industry, Miguel Sebastian, said *"It's evident that the crisis started in the United States."*[17] Indeed. Unfortunately Spain saw its own homegrown housing bubble burst in 2008–9, which forced a local economic slowdown and a spike in unemployment above 20 percent – and its own big banks to stumble in 2010. Nothing to do with the US.

And perhaps savoring just a little dollop of schadenfreude, Russian President Medvedev observed that *"[c]onfidence in the United States as the leader of the free world and the free market, the trust in Wall Street as the center of this confidence, has been undermined – for good, I think."*[18] Prime Minister Putin, for his part, said: *"Although the crisis was simply hanging in the air, the majority strove to get their share of the pie, be it one dollar or one billion, and did not want to notice the rising wave ... I just want to remind you that just a year ago, American delegates speaking from this rostrum emphasised the US economy's fundamental stability and its cloudless prospects."*[19] Putin added that *"investment banks, the pride of Wall Street, have virtually ceased to exist. In just 12 months they have posted losses exceeding the profits they made in the last 25 years. This example alone reflects the real situation better than any criticism the existing financial system has failed. Sub-standard regulation has contributed to the crisis, failing to duly heed tremendous risks."*[20] Hard to disagree.

French President Sarkozy, while critical of the US, realized that his countrymen were also to be held to account: *"What were they doing screwing around in the United States?"*[21] Further: *"Who is responsible for this disaster? That those responsible will be held accountable and punished and that we government leaders will assume our responsibilities."*[22] And, leaving no stone unturned, let me introduce a most bizarre comment courtesy of Brazilian President Lula DaSilva, who observed that: *"This is a crisis that was caused by people, white with blue eyes. And before the crisis they looked as if they knew everything about economics...[s]ince I am not acquainted with any black bankers, I can only say that this part of humanity that is the major victim of the world crisis, these people should pay for the crisis? I cannot accept that."*[23] [N.B. to Lula: Stan O'Neal (ex-Merrill), Franklin Raines (ex-Fannie)....]

To be sure, the problems started in Vegas. Unfortunately, they were exacerbated by the same driving forces of greed, arrogance, incompetence – which certainly didn't seem to have much regard for national boundaries.

Apologies?

Let me now move to those who had a hand in the crisis. As I said, there seems to be an entire spectrum here, so I'll start with those who actually apologized and move down from there. Before diving in, though, let me also say that even amongst those admitting mistakes and assuming responsibility, there was often an element of puffery in their public communiqués. Looking at the printed record it's easy to see the degree to which the big money losers imparted Janus-like messages during and after the crisis. On the one hand every bank was forced to declare, for obvious reasons, how many billions were lost when the **** hit the fan – those ugly facts couldn't be swept under the carpet. But with a surprisingly deft and confident tone, some also attempted to convince the market that they did so many things "right" that they actually managed to avoid losing extra billions. So, it went something like this: as investors in Bank ABC we should be grateful that our institution only lost $20b during the crisis; because of the hard work of our risk management team and the insight and dedication of executive management, we avoided losing $40b (like our competitors did). In other words, "my disaster site wasn't as toxic as your disaster site." Does that make anyone feel better?

We are responsible, we are sorry

First there's JP Morgan's Dimon, who was perhaps the most vocal about the screwups: *"Yes, we made mistakes...[w]e accept complete responsibility for any and all mistakes we made or may have made."*[24] He also indicated that *"I blame the management teams 100 percent, and no – no one else."*[25] Further, *"While we were* able to withstand the crisis and I believe emerge as a stronger institution, we, like many others, made mistakes."[26] One more: "if you do everything right in business, you are going to make mistakes. And you really have to look at the continuum of how many, how big. Even if you were right, you'll make some. Hopefully, they'll be smaller and won't be threatening to our your institution or anybody else."[27] The bank did a good job spelling out all of the ways in which it screwed up: "We underestimated the size of the housing bubble and the rapid rate of depreciation...we misjudged the impact of more aggressive underwriting standards...we would have been better off if we had placed tighter controls on the outside mortgage business...we should have been more diligent in structuring and negotiating commitment letters."[28] And so on.

Meanwhile, over at Citibank, Chuck Prince was amongst the first of the big executives to fall on the sword: "It is my judgment that given the size of the recent losses in our mortgage-backed securities business, the only honorable course for me to take as chief executive officer is to step down...[t]his is what I advised the board."[29] In testimony he would eventually express contrition: "I can only say that I am deeply sorry that our management – starting with me – was not more prescient and that we did not foresee what lay before us."[30] Interestingly, John Reed, once co-CEO with Sandy Weill (chief architect of the financial supermarket concept), came out of the woodwork, too: "I'm sorry...[t]hese are people I love and care about. You could imagine emotionally it's not easy to see what's happened."[31] Pandit, who inherited the mess and wasn't really accountable, tried to atone for the sins of the industry and his illustrious predecessors: "I can completely understand how people on Main Street, people who are not close to this industry would be furious at what's happened and furious at kind of where we've gotten to....[i]f you start throwing everybody under the bus, we're going to need a very large bus."[32] Then he put himself on the hook for any future debacle: "I do consider the role of the CEO as that of a risk manager. I'll take that. That is my role, very clear about that."[33] Let us all hope that risk management at Citi doesn't fail again.

Over to John Mack and Morgan Stanley: "We are sorry for it. I am especially sorry for what's happened to shareholders and more broadly, to all Americans...[c]learly, as an industry, we have accountability and we're taking responsibility.... I'll take responsibility for my firm."[34] Furthermore, he said "I think from Morgan Stanley's point of view, if you could play the clock over again, we'd definitely do things differently."[35] And then he focused on the banking industry 's failures: "We recognize that our industry has much to do and to regain the trust of taxpayers, investors and public officials."[36] And, finally: "[i]n retrospect, many firms were too highly leveraged, took on too much risk and did not have sufficient resources to manage those risks effectively in a rapidly changing environment."[37]

There weren't many apologies emanating from the executive suites over at the toxic twins. About the only one who stepped up was Fannie's Mudd, who said: "I was the CEO of the company and I accept responsibility for everything that *happened on my watch.*"[38] The others? Not a word. Maybe they were too busy counting their money.

Contrition appears to have extended across the Atlantic. At Barclays CEO Varley explained that *"I've said in public many times during the past three years there is much to be sorry about.... [a]s a chief executive of a big bank, I acknowledge that and am grateful that governments, through the injection of taxpayers' money, rescued the global banking system."*[39] Furthermore, *"I would say we must acknowledge our contribution to the problem, we must apologise, but we must not lose our appetite to take risks because the members of the public, whether they are businesses or households, need banks which are prepared to take risks, and we are."*[40] More generally, *"[b]anks and bankers must show humility and acknowledge what's happened."*[41] Former RBS CEO Goodwin: *"I apologised in full, and am happy to do so again...there is a profound and unqualified apology for all of the distress that has been caused and I would not wish there to be any doubt about that whatsoever."*[42] Former HBOS Chairman Lord Stevenson joined the chorus: *"we are profoundly and, I think I would say, unreservedly sorry at the turn of events. Our shareholders, all of us, have lost a great deal of money, including of course a great number of our colleagues, and we are very sorry for that. There has been huge anxiety and uncertainty caused in particular for our colleagues but also for periods of time for our customers...we said it publicly at the EGM and we have felt it throughout."*[43] Furthermore: *"I would also say we are sorry at the effect it has had on the communities we serve."*[44] A similar message came from former CEO McKillop: *"In November of last year I made a full apology, unreserved apology, both personally and on behalf of the Board, and I am very happy to repeat that."*[45]

Some at UBS also stepped up, which makes sense given the quantity of Swiss francs the bank sucked up from its citizens. Marcel Ospel, in resigning as Chairman in April 2008, said that *"I'm the chairman of this firm and ultimately responsible for what has happened."*[46] Further, *"I have always stated that I ultimately take responsibility for the bank's situation."*[47] Ex-CEO Rohner admitted *"[w]e made some mistakes."*[48] Yes, rather a lot of them. In addition, he said, *"it is clear that we have undermined our reputation,"*[49] and *"[e]very bank would like to manage its situation on its own, but if you need to take a drastic step to protect the bank, then that is what has to be done."*[50]

The banking lobbyists also stepped up. Angela Knight, as CEO of the BBA, came forth with a sort of "blanket apology" for the entire British banking industry: *"it is clear that one of the causes was the failure by some significant elements of the banking industry to measure risk effectively. The industry must take its share of responsibility for this and it does. Not all banks have been appropriately vigilant in managing risk – for that omission, and for the expectations of the industry's customers and clients and other stakeholders which have been disappointed, the industry expresses regret and apologises."*[51]

And the regulators? Some of the European regulators and policy makers also spoke up, such as Darling who said *"I have said to you that I accept responsibility for everything that I am responsible for"*[52] and *"I think all of us have to accept responsibility for the regulatory regime we have."*[53] FSA's Turner had several admissions: *"Let us be absolutely clear: the FSA has accepted entirely and has, I think, been more open than any other institution at apologising for the fact that it made specific failures in the supervision of Northern Rock. That is absolutely clear."*[54] Furthermore, *"I think, to be honest, it is an admission that at the level of the whole world there was a failure to see enormous risks developing in our financial system."*[55] And then there's King: *"I think the Bank of England has accepted responsibility for those things for which it was responsible. I do not think we can be responsible for actions taken by others."*[56] In addition, *"I am sure we got things wrong, and obviously so."*[57] Bafin's Sanio was also very clear: *"There is no shortage of blame to go around for the fiasco that exposed the glaring shortcomings of the financial system which now need urgent correction. That's just the normal blame game that follows any accident of a serious magnitude and is rarely ever fair. If I point the finger of blame at others it is not to deflect blame from myself as a regulator. We regulators should be forthright enough to shoulder part of the blame and not pretend to be innocent."*[58] It is unfortunately difficult to find much in the way of apologies from the US regulators.

What of the politicians? Not many stepped up (certainly not in the US), though George Bush managed to say: *"I'm sorry it's happening, of course...I don't like the idea of people losing jobs, or being worried about their 401(k)s. On the other hand, the American people got to know that we will safeguard the system. I mean, we're in. And if we need to be in more, we will."*[59] And in the UK? MP John Mann did, making a collective statement: *"Clearly people can blame politicians, Parliament, governments, for not highlighting these questions more succinctly and as a higher priority previously, so we should not be ducking our responsibilities."*[60] Sidebar: MP Fallon wanted to know why Brown didn't come clean: *"[o]n Gordon Brown we have not had a full apology from him for the failures of banking supervision which he set up. Why is that?...[I]t was the then Chancellor who was in overall charge of the financial system and it was the then Chancellor who has ended up leaving us all this debt."*[61] George Osborne, Darling's successor at the Exchequer, said: *"When the Chancellor and the Prime Minister are openly divided over the causes of recession and their responsibility for the mess the British economy is in, what confidence can anyone have that they can lead us into a recovery? Gordon Brown is deeply implicated in the mistakes of the past – and even if he won't apologise for them he can't escape them."*[62] And Brown's response? This was about as close as he came, just before losing reelection in May 2010: *"In the 1990s, the banks all came to us and said: 'Look, we don't want to be regulated, we want to be free of regulation.' And everybody in the City was saying you know and all the complaints I was getting from people was, 'look, you're regulating them too much.' And actually the truth is that, globally and nationally, we should have been regulating them more. So I've learnt from that."*[63] Who cares?

Of course, not everyone was sure about all of these apologies. Were they really heartfelt? MP McFall wasn't convinced: *"They did give an apology and it seemed fulsome, but, as the session went on, I think they were drawing back from that and saying 'Well, look, there were events outside our control'. If you ask me my opinion – yes, they were advised to do it (apologise). Was there a hint of arrogance still there? Absolutely."*[64] BBC's Robert Preston saw it this way: *"the problem with the sorries uttered by the former bosses of Royal Bank of Scotland and HBOS is that they lacked a detailed account of why they did what they did. Mistakes were admitted – but motivation was glossed over."*[65] In the States, Representative Michael Capuano was even more skeptical, telling a bunch of US bankers: *"basically, you come to us today on your bicycles after buying Girl Scout cookies and helping out Mother Teresa, telling us, 'We're sorry; we didn't mean it; we won't do it again; trust us.' Well, I have some people in my constituency that actually robbed some of your banks, and they say the same thing. They're sorry. They didn't mean it. They won't do it again. Just let them out."*[66]

Mistakes were made

Then there's the group that confessed to all manner of mistakes – but didn't necessarily issue an apology or step up to take responsibility. Maybe that's splitting hairs, but maybe not.

Blankfein certainly admitted the failures of his Goldman team. Though he defended many of the firm's practices, he also confessed that *"[w]e got caught up in and participated in and therefore contributed to elements of froth in the market."*[67] He extended that thought: *"Knowing now what happened, whatever we did, whatever the standards of the time were, it didn't work out well. Of course, I'd go back and wished we had done whatever it took not to be in the position that we find ourselves."*[68] Blankfein also noted that *"[r]ationalizations... were made to justify that the downward pricing of risk was justified.... [w]e rationalized because a firm's interest in preserving and growing its market share, as a competitor, is sometimes blinding – especially when exuberance is at its peak."*[69] Like Mack, Blankfein criticized the industry at large: *"I know we all rationalized the way a lot of people have rationalized.... And I think we talked... [ourselves]... into a place of complacency, which we should not have gotten ourselves into."*[70] He also observed: *"it was a failure of competence rather than incentives."*[71] While much of the postmortem focus has centered on bonuses and greed as the driving factors in some of the stupid actions, there is some possibility that many people got it wrong because they didn't see it, or get it, or didn't understand the way the dominos would topple. In the end Blankfein said that *"[a]nyone who says I wouldn't change a thing, I think, is crazy."*[72]

Bank of America's past and present CEOs talked mostly about mistakes. First there's longtime CEO Ken Lewis, who stepped down under pressure. He indicated that *"this journey has been a rocky one, and not for the faint of heart...and I am disappointed in how we managed credit risk."*[73] That was about it. His replacement, Brian Moynihan, said *"I want...the American people to know that I fully understand and appreciate the gravity of the crisis that we are now just coming through,"*[74] and *"[b]efore and during the recent crisis, many of our collective business judgments missed the mark."*[75] Furthermore, he said: *"[t]hat is not to say we at Bank of America made no mistakes. As borrowers sought to monetize the equity in their homes, we expanded our position to become a leading provider of prime second mortgages. We as bankers have learned some hard lessons from the recent financial crisis. First and foremost is humility: at its core, our job is to manage risk,"*[76] and, *"the mistakes we made and the most losses we've taken have actually been in credit cards and mortgages."*[77] So, mistakes and lessons.

Sifting through the ashes at Bear Stearns, Jimmy Cayne said that *"I walk around with a horrible, horrible heavy heart each day...[i]t's a severity of pain that cannot be measured, because you can't measure the pain of 14,000 families."*[78] Or $900 m of personal losses. He also said *"[y]ou got a bad grade on your test. That's it. No appeal. I felt sad for me and sad for my Bear Stearns family."*[79] Even though he assigned some blame to the short sellers and rumormongers that tightened the liquidity noose and helped drive down the stock price, he admitted failings: *"It was not knowing what to do. It's not being able to make a definitive decision one way or the other, because I just couldn't tell you what was going to happen."* It was quite a confession: *"I didn't stop it. I didn't rein in the leverage."*[80] Again, mistakes, feeling bad...but sorry? In fact, when Cayne and co testified in front of the Financial Crisis Inquiry Commission in 2010, they were raked over the coals when they claimed events were out of their control – something which Angelides described as the *"immaculate calamity"*[81] and Commissioner Byron Georgiou called a *"pathetic mythology."*[82]

Then there's Dick Fuld and his fallen Lehman. In testimony just weeks after the bank's implosion, Fuld talked mostly about pain: *"I feel horrible about what happened"*[83] and *"I will try my best to be helpful...so that what happened to Lehman Brothers does not happen to other companies; so that their shareholders, creditors, clients and employees do not have to feel the enormous pain that our shareholders, creditors, clients and employees are feeling right now."*[84] That was about it, as he went on to remind everyone that Lehman wasn't the only one that screwed up: *"[a]s incredibly painful as this is for all those connected to or affected by Lehman Brothers – this financial tsunami is much bigger than any one firm or industry."*[85] In a second round of Congressional testimony he still stopped short of an apology: *"I would say bad judgments were made regarding the markets, yes...I'm very much aware that one day we had a firm, the next day we did not. A lot of people got hurt, and I have to live with that."*[86] And, of course, he went after the short sellers for bringing down the house: *"[n]aked short selling...is an invitation to market *manipulation...[t]he naked shorts and rumormongers succeeded in bringing down Bear Stearns. And I believe that unsubstantiated rumors in the marketplace caused significant harm to Lehman Brothers...History has already shown how wrong and ill-advised it is to allow naked short selling.*"[87] But of course, that's a bit like shooting the messenger: naked shorts or regular shorts, they were short because Lehman was a bad shop.

Then there's a grab-bag of comments from various folks who also admitted that they, or the industry, got it wrong, but didn't necessarily offer up any apologies. HSBC's Stephen Green confessed the sins of the banking sector: *"The industry has done many things wrong...we must also remember that there have been too many that have profoundly damaged the industry's reputation. Inappropriate products were sold inappropriately by many.*"[88] Deutsche's Ackermann: *"We all made mistakes, which we openly admit."*[89] And, by the way (in case you were wondering): *"I've lost a lot of money myself."*[90] And of the industry itself? Ackermann indicated that *"[w]ithout question, structural weaknesses existed. Mistakes were made. Rewards grew out of proportion to the risks that were being taken. Some financial instruments were so complex that the risks they posed were not properly understood. We underestimated the interconnectedness of the banking system."*[91]

On the politico-regulatory front ex-Treasury Secretary Snow, commenting on the Fannie/Freddie problems, admitted the strategy was wrong: *"We...strove to achieve the right balance between regulatory oversight and expanded opportunity. In retrospect, the bipartisan consensus to promote housing went too far. There was a push for too much of a good thing. Those excesses eventually came home to roost."*[92]

Not really my (our) fault?

And then there's the group that either rejected any responsibility, feigned ignorance/cluelessness, or had the temerity to actually point fingers at others.

One of the most curious cases involved Robert Rubin, the executive board member and "special advisor" to Citigroup I mentioned in Chapter 2, who noted in a late 2007 interview that he bore no responsibility for any of Citi's mounting losses: *"The answer is very simple...it didn't go on under my nose. I am not senior management. I have this side role."*[93] Okay. Or, later: *"I don't feel responsible, in light of the facts as I knew them in my role."*[94] Somehow, in my obviously naïve, Bearle-and-Means view of corporate governance, I was under the impression that board directors, particularly executive (e.g., internally appointed) board directors, had some modicum of responsibility to protect shareholder interests. I guess I am mistaken. But wait, a year later he was suddenly in the mix: *"It's a funny way to think about it. I think I've been a very constructive part of the Citigroup environment. That has become particularly manifest since August '07.*

I have been very involved."⁹⁵ Involved, side-role, responsible, not responsible? Who knows? In the event, he finally left Citi in January 2009, expressing some bit of remorse in his resignation letter: "*My great regret is that I and so many of us who have been involved in this industry for so long did not recognize the serious possibility of the extreme circumstances that the financial system faces today.*"⁹⁶ Then, when hauled in front of the Angelides Committee he managed to say that "*[w]e all bear responsibility for not recognizing this, and I deeply regret that.*"⁹⁷ Angelides was as confused as I seem to be: "*You were not a garden-variety board member...I think to most people chairman of the executive committee of the board of directors implies leadership. Certainly $15 million a year guaranteed implies leadership and responsibility.*"⁹⁸ Ouch. Still, ex-CEO Prince defended Rubin to the end: "*It is absolutely incorrect to suggest that Mr. Rubin had central responsibility, or any central responsibility for what happened to Citigroup.*"⁹⁹ What a sweet job that must've been. In fact, Bill Thomas, sitting on the Angelides Commission, was having none of it, criticizing both Prince and Rubin heavily: "*What do you get paid for if it isn't having some intuition, understanding, knowledge? Or do you just do what everybody else is doing because everybody else is doing it, and if you don't do it then you won't make money – because I do think it's all about money. And it was big money on the way up, but never at any point is it on the way back down.*"¹⁰⁰

Over at AIG it was a mixed bag. Interim CEO Ed Liddy was pretty forthright: "*While I can offer little comfort to those of you who suffered severe losses as AIG shareholders, I can assure you that everyone at AIG is working hard to preserve as much value as possible.*"¹⁰¹ Heartfelt, probably, as Liddy was doing this for the good of the system, but cold comfort to the losers. He added: "*Mistakes were made at AIG on a scale few could have ever imagined possible...[t]his was typified by the creation of what grew to become an internal hedge fund.*"¹⁰² Then there's one-time board member-turned-CEO Willumstad, who said that "*I regret the pain that events in the market have caused to AIG's employees and its shareholders.*"¹⁰³ But then added, "*[l]ooking back on my time as CEO, I don't believe AIG could have done anything differently. The market seizure was an unprecedented global catastrophe. We took every step we could to protect AIG's balance sheet and its liquidity.*"¹⁰⁴ And, "*[f]undamentally, AIG was affected by an unexpected and unprecedented market-wide crisis of confidence and the resulting seizure of the credit markets.*"¹⁰⁵ So, that's kind of strange – like "I'm sorry, but it's not really my fault, it was the market's fault and I wouldn't have done anything differently." Actually, no, it was AIG's fault – and that includes the board of directors, of which Willumstad was a member. They loaded the books with risk – and can't really blame the market for that.

Before that there's ex-CEO Sullivan, who oversaw big increases in risk between 2005 and 2007: "*I have spent my entire adult life in service to AIG, and I am heartbroken at what has happened. I hope to see the company, and indeed the entire global* economy, emerge from this crisis."[106] But Sullivan wanted to make clear that the nasty stuff that sunk the company was originally started up by Hank Greenberg, pointing out that *"I encountered...unintended [accounting] effects through the credit default swap portfolio of AIG-Financial Products, a business that my predecessor had established and funded many years earlier."*[107] Of course, Greenberg was having none of it, making it clear that the breakdown took place after he left in 2005: *"When I was AIG's CEO, AIG management closely monitored AIGFP and its risk portfolio. AIGFP was subject to numerous internal risk controls...Our model worked."*[108] So, how did all of this blow up? Greenberg explained: *"the volume of this [derivative] business exploded after I left the company in March 2005. AIGFP reportedly wrote as many credit default swaps...in the nine months following my departure as it had written in the entire previous seven years combined."*[109] Further: *"reports indicate that the risk controls my team and I put in place were weakened or eliminated after my retirement."*[110] So, just a bunch of fingerpointing and, on the whole, none of this is very satisfying.

The rating agency bosses, for their part, made some admissions about their screwups on ratings, but didn't ever seem to apologize. S&P's Sharma: *"Let me begin by acknowledging – as S&P has been saying for quite some time – that S&P is profoundly disappointed with the performance of many of its ratings on the aforementioned mortgage-backed instruments.... Their performance has not matched our historical track record."*[111] And Fitch's Joynt: *"I have also previously acknowledged that too many of our rating opinions – particularly in some of the most impacted structured finance asset classes – did not perform as expected, with too many downgrades of too many notches."*[112] Further: *"Understandably, the rating agencies have lost some confidence of the market for which I am very disappointed. I think it will be a long and difficult road to win back market confidence."*[113] And Moody's McDaniel: *"We have learned important lessons from these fast-changing market conditions."*[114] So, from the agencies some lessons and disappointment. That's about it.

And then there's the maestro himself, Alan Greenspan. To be sure, Greenspan admitted to general mistakes over his career, which is a noble thing: *"I was right 70 percent of the time, but I was wrong 30 percent of the time. And there were an awful lot of mistakes in 21 years."*[115] Perfectly fine, we all make lots of mistakes. But on the key point of the crisis he wanted all and sundry to know that the policies he implemented whilst head of the US Fed had nothing to do with the housing bubble. So he tried to set the record straight in March 2009 with an op-ed (intended partly to contradict the views of John Taylor, who I mentioned earlier in the book). Greenspan indicated, in part, that *"[t]here are at least two broad and competing explanations of the origins of this crisis. The first is that the 'easy money' policies of the Federal Reserve produced the U.S. housing bubble that is at the core of today's financial mess...The second, and far more credible, explanation agrees that it was indeed lower interest rates that spawned the speculative euphoria.*

However, the interest rate that mattered was not the federal-funds rate, but the rate on long-term, fixed-rate mortgages."[116] And, of course, the Fed can't directly control long-term mortgage rates, therefore it ain't his fault. As a result of the disconnect between short- and long-term rates, Alan says, *"accelerating the path of monetary tightening that the Fed pursued in 2004–2005 could not have 'prevented' the housing bubble."*[117]

So what, then, caused the crisis? According to Greenspan *"[t]he rate of global housing appreciation was accelerated beginning in late 2003 by the heavy securitization of American subprime and Alt-A mortgages, bonds that found willing buyers at home and abroad, many encouraged by grossly inflated credit ratings."*[118] Furthermore: *"The evidence strongly suggests that without the excess demand from securitizers, subprime mortgage originations (undeniably the original source of crisis) would have been far smaller and defaults accordingly far fewer."*[119] That, and not a low interest rate policy, was the main cause of the crisis.

As if all the protestations weren't enough, Alan patted himself on the back a little, via economist Friedman: *"All things considered, I personally prefer Milton Friedman's performance appraisal of the Federal Reserve. In evaluating the period of 1987 to 2005, he wrote on this page in early 2006: '[t]here is no other period of comparable length in which the Federal Reserve System has performed so well.'"*[120] So, was Alan a goat or a god? Well, if polls are to be believed, the maestro appeared repeatedly among the top 3 of those most responsible for the crisis. You decide.

Then there's Greenspan acolyte Bernanke, who also refused to admit that loose money had anything to do with the crisis: *"When historical relationships are taken into account, it is difficult to ascribe the house price bubble either to monetary policy or to the broader macroeconomic environment."*[121] That's a tough swallow for most of us, and it rightly drew jeers, scorn, and disbelief from lots of industry watchers, economists, bankers, and other regulators. In fact, according to Bernanke *"[s]tronger regulation and supervision aimed at problems with underwriting practices and lenders' risk management would have been a more effective and surgical approach to constraining the housing bubble than a general increase in interest rates."*[122] And there you have it. Perhaps most worrisome is this: if the last two bosses of the Federal Reserve don't think that the extended period of low rates had anything to do with inflating the bubble, what happens next time we are in the bubble phase? Head buried in the sand = lots of trouble.

Naturally, some chose not to take any blame at all, at least not publicly. It's difficult to find any signs of contrition from some of the biggest offenders, such as Merrill's O'Neal or Countrywide's Mozilo. And there were certainly no mea culpas emanating from the US politicians. In their own minds, they did nothing wrong. AEI's Wallison noted of the Washington political elite: *"Most people were very proud of the fact, especially here in this building and elsewhere in Washington, were very proud of the fact that subprime loans were being made. Now, when it turns out that these mortgages failed and caused, I believe – at least there are indications that they caused the financial crisis – everyone is running away from it and trying to point fingers at who made these loans."*[123] Expect no contrition from any politician involved with Fannie/Freddie, deregulation or misregulation.

In the end said Peter Solomon, head of Solomon advisory: *"It's just management. It's how you set the standards, how you set the risk and how you manage the risk, and your own hubris at managing the risk. You see, a lot of this is just pure management failure even in the best of institutions. You heard Mr. Dimon, Mr. Blankfein – all of them – Mr. Mack – say that 'we failed.' They're right."*[124] And I think the same thoughts extend to all the others who were part of the disaster – regulators, rating agencies, and, yes, even the common person.

Enough already!

Even after some of the guilty parties stepped up to take responsibility (verbally, monetarily, professionally) the drumbeat for further reparations sounded steadily for some time. And little wonder: the disaster caused by the collective failures of so many created a destructive global recession that left many millions unemployed or underemployed, investment and retirement accounts in tatters, and some without homes. The rage was palpable and understandable.

At some point, of course, the rage has the potential of becoming counterproductive. As much as the population at large hates banking, banks, and bankers, the function and industry remain essential to economic progress. If banking becomes inefficient and dysfunctional we will all collectively pay the price in terms of poorer service, higher fees, constrained access to credit, and so forth. So, as 2010 came along, those that had been maligned called for a time-out...enough already! The BBA's Knight came out thus: *"The financial services industry is much more than the banks but banking forms an integral part of any modern economy. If we continue to demonise our own banking industry, there is no shortage of other jurisdictions which will leap at the chance of taking the business if we chose to discard it in this way as we have done with many of our great industries in the past."*[125] Jeff Immelt, CEO of GE, said that *"damning Wall Street isn't good for the American economy. People need to tone down the rhetoric around financial services and stop the populism and act like adults...The world doesn't need the US in a food fight right now."*[126]

Naturally, the bank bosses weighed in. Deutsche's Ackermann sounded a stern warning: *"We should stop the blame game and we should start looking forward. If you don't have a strong financial sector to support this recovery...you are making a huge mistake and you will regret that later on."*[127] And Dimon, never shy about speaking his mind, echoed a similar view: "*The premise that all banks would have failed had it not been for the government's actions is incorrect...We should acknowledge that the worst offenders among financial companies no longer are in existence. And while it is true that some of the surviving banks would not, or might not, have survived, not all banks would have failed.*"[128] Accordingly, he said, *"[w]e have to stop slipping into a cacophony of fingerpointing and blame. And while bad actors always should be punished, we also should note that not all who got into trouble were irresponsible. The crisis of the past couple of years has had far-reaching consequences, among them the declining public image of banks and bankers."*[129] Importantly, when banks suffer, so do average investors, who hold bank shares in their own portfolios: *"Very often, when the public or politicians take punitive efforts against banks like ours, they think they are punishing only the senior management team, when, in fact, they are punishing ordinary shareholders as well. Contrary to popular perception, Main Street owns our biggest banks and corporations through savings and retirement funds."*[130] Varley said: *"If the global economy is going to grow, then that has to be facilitated by banks doing their job well. If banks are successful, they invest in business; they lend; they employ a lot of people; they pay dividends; they pay tax. Society benefits as a result. I don't expect these things to be much recognised in this environment. But in time they will be recognised again."*[131]

So, now that rage has been vented, perhaps it is in everyone's interest to move on. At some point the recriminations will cease, the apologies will be done, and the wounds will start to heal...only to reopen next time around.

9
Closing the Barn Door

Every crisis brings with it the promise of change, including new rules and new discipline so that the lapses and losses won't be replayed in the future. In other words, a bit of "barn-door closing." And so it has been with this crisis – though, it must be said, with a bit more zeal, because this one has had some extra zeros in the red ink column. Not surprisingly, there is a populist element to the exercise: politicians and regulators need to be seen to be doing the "right thing" for their constituents so that they can get reelected or otherwise keep their jobs – though by now I'm sure that they don't know exactly what the right thing is.

Still, something has to be done, right? Rules and regulations have to be fixed so that bankers and other perpetrators of the crisis can be brought to heel. Perhaps. But maybe Wallison is right: *"Calling for more regulation is in fact a simple-minded solution – a band-aid – done more to solve Congress's problem [the need to show the public that it is taking action] than a clear-eyed response to what is really the issue."*[1] Never mind. Brown and Sarkozy jointly declared that *"[p]eople rightly want a post-crisis banking system which puts their needs first. To achieve that, nothing less than a global change is required."*[2] Sounds ambitious. Indeed, if the politicians and regulators can't get it together, then the bankers and other risk-takers will continue to run wild. As Darling noted, *"I do not think there is a country in the world where you can point to a regulatory regime...and say it was perfect, there were not lessons to be learned. The important thing is that we do learn those lessons and we implement them."*[3] Further: *"banks everywhere need to change the way they operate. Society needs banks as much as banks need society, and banks need to recognise that sense of mutual duty."*[4] Sounds idealistic. And Cable: *"We're not going back to business as normal...[T]he banking sector is going to have to accept disciplines on the way it operates, regulatory disciplines, and there is going to be a restructuring."*[5] Sounds optimistic.

Of course, the captains of the banking industry have also had to demonstrate that they are cleaning up their own shops: waking up their directors, refining their business strategies, overhauling risk management, and paying lip service to at least some of the new regulatory barn-door closing measures. If they can't do that in a very splashy and public way, then it'll be that much more difficult to justify the multimillion dollar (pound, euro) pay packages that have already resumed.

All of this activity is well and good, but if history is any guide some of these efforts will almost certainly go by the wayside over the next few years, once the sun is shining again...

More rules and regulations

In the aftermath of the blowup, politicians and regulators everywhere convened blue ribbon commissions, panels, and inquiries to find out what had gone wrong and, perhaps more importantly, how things could be changed. Soon thereafter, virtually every regulator rushed forward to point out that, whilst not everything was decided or fixed, big changes were underway. Former FSA CEO Sants: *"The supervisory changes that are required to deliver effective supervision to the earlier point are two thirds to 80% done and in the core areas are currently delivering."*[6] Same from his boss, Turner: *"We are in the process of putting in place a whole load of changes."*[7] Further, the FSA *"is going to be fit for purpose, given the changes that we are going to make and we are making...these are not minor changes; these are a revolution in approach."*[8] Sidebar: FSA was shut down in 2010, with its operations transferred to the Bank of England. Good job, boys! And NY Fed President William Dudley said of his overhauls: *"We're basically halfway done...[b]ut there is still a lot to do to make our financial system more resilient and robust, and we are working urgently on all these fronts."*[9] Similar pronouncements came from the FDIC, the SEC, the...but does it really matter? Really? Much of the discussion has been based on politico-regulatory groupthink: managing to the last crisis, not the next one. I'm pretty sure that the next crisis won't be caused by subprime mortgages and securitization, or excessive risk in leveraged loans or other illiquid assets, or because banks are too big or bank bonuses too large. But a new pile of rules and regulations will appear to guard against these factors, even as we are dealing with a Greek debt crisis (oh yes, that's already underway), or inflating a big bubble in Chinese real estate, or building up excess risks in middle-market loans, or property derivatives, or credit card debt, or some super off-balance sheet leveraged juiced-up turbo deal, or, or, or....

So, what are the key elements of the latest round of barn-door closings? Basically a load of new regulations. Some of these are external, to be developed by legislators and imposed by regulators, like reshaping compensation, slimming down the banks, creating skilled, systemic "super" regulators, separating proprietary trading from bank activities, re-routing all derivatives onto public exchanges, doing something (meaningful?) with the rating agencies, enhancing consumer protections, increasing "transparency" by beefing up disclosures, doing away with the old Fannie and Freddie private/public model, making banks keep pieces of risk that they sell to others and boosting capital levels. Others are internal to banks and other risk-takers, like improving the skills of board directors and shoring up risk management.

So, this crisis has generated lots of new ideas for improvements. And, yet, curiously, we still have bigger and more frequent crises. So, what are we actually accomplishing? I'm not sure – but let me describe a few of these ideas anyway.

Reshaping compensation

It's not surprising that one of the main "fixes" has centered on compensation. Why? Because there is widespread belief that all of those rich bonus packages caused bankers to behave badly, gambling with bank capital in hopes of a generating a big personal payoff. Basically banker's compensation is just a free option: if the bankers get it right they get an extra zero in the paycheck, if they get it wrong, they don't. And if they are dissatisfied in any way, there's generally a bid at another bank (while that's especially true for the really good bankers, it also applies to mediocre ones). There's just not much downside.

Stiglitz has stated that compensation was absolutely an issue in the crisis: *"management was rewarded for higher returns, whether those returns were produced merely by increasing risk or by truly outperforming the market...[a]nyone can do the former; the latter is almost impossible. Again, no wonder that all the financial wizards took the easier route – and it was this excessive risk taking that helped bring capitalism to the brink. These problems in incentive pay have long been recognized. Unless appropriate care is paid to the quality of what is produced, those who are paid on the basis of the quantity produced will put more effort into quantity than quality."*[10] And, in case you had any doubt as to his position: *"[t]he financial sector has been particularly creative in finding accounting frameworks that increase apparent profits in the short run – with losses revealed only later...They had an incentive to engage in excessive risk-taking, they had an incentive to engage in deceptive accounting, and they had an incentive to use – and seemingly believe – models that allowed them to undertake excessive risk. They had an incentive not to enquire too deeply into the assumptions used in those models. And they had an incentive not to think too deeply about how their incentive structures distorted, and continue to distort, behavior."*[11] Meaning lots of incentives to behave badly.

Various politicians took a similar view, such as Sarkozy: *"There is indecent behavior that will no longer be tolerated by public opinion in any country of the world...*

[t]hat those who create jobs and wealth may earn a lot of money is not shocking. But that those who contribute to destroying jobs and wealth also earn a lot of money is morally indefensible."[12] Brown weighed in: *"we are insisting now in any dealings with individual banks that we will have to be satisfied, on behalf of the taxpayer, that when we make these investments, executive remuneration is on the agenda so that excessive risk is not being rewarded, as it has been in the past."*[13] And, whilst stumping on financial reform in 2010 [multimillionaire] President Obama reminded his friendly handpicked audience just how awful the "fat cat" bankers were (are), noting that *"I do think at a certain point you've made enough money."*[14] How much would that be, Mr. President? $1m, $5m, $10m, $100m? Is this reserved only for the greedy bankers, or do the Gates, Buffetts and Jobs of the world fall within the net also?

And several regulators agreed that money was, indeed, the root of all evil. Darling, for one: *"I have been clear that the authors of this crisis should not be rewarded for their failures. It is wrong to reward people whose excessive risk-taking brought down the banks causing misery to millions of their customers. Success should be rewarded, failure should not."*[15] Furthermore, *"[t]here is no doubt, and there was no doubt then, that some of the incentives were geared to making people take unacceptable risk"*[16] and *"[i]n terms of excessive behaviour, as I have said before, there needs to be a culture change."*[17] And, from the FDIC's Bair: *"[M]ost financial-institution compensation systems were not properly linked to risk management. Formula-driven compensation allows high short-term profits to be translated into generous bonus payments, without regard to any longer-term risks.... These short-term incentives magnified risk-taking."*[18] The SEC's Schapiro agreed, speaking of *"[p]erverse incentives and asymmetric compensation arrangements that encouraged significant risk-taking."*[19] McCreevy, UK Commissioner for Single Market and Services: *"Incentive structures have been overwhelmingly aligned to short term performance rather than performance through the cycle. In most of those firms where this was most pronounced there has been complete destruction or massive dilution of shareholder value."*[20]

A similar refrain came from Bank of England's King, who also threw in a few barbs on the failure of governance: *"the real debate is how on earth was it that at the time shareholders, boards, the financial press, all thought it was a great idea to reward people in this way. These bonuses were absolutely astronomic. Gamblers if they won the gamble but there was no loss if you lost it. It is obvious that if you do that you will give incentives to people to gamble."*[21] From MP McFall: *"The issue of bonuses...is that there is a recklessness about the situation, because they are dealing in the short term, dealing with other people's money but, irrespective of success or failure, they are rewarded."*[22] IMF's Strauss Kahn said: *"compensation [reform] has more political momentum. So for politicians it may be the right way to get at the problem, because they have some political support for doing that."*[23] Draghi: *"Compensation* is now fully in the realm of supervisors...[i]t used to be they were told it was a private contract. It's now quite clear that when compensation is not aligned with risk- taking incentives, regulators have the right to have their say."[24]

Some of the banking captains admitted the same. For instance, HSBC's Green said: "*Compensation practices ran out of control and perverse incentives led to dangerous outcomes.*"[25] And RBS's Hester: "*I regard this as inevitably a no-win subject...I think that there have been significant instances of pay that is hard to justify in parts of the banking industry, and I completely understand the public interest in that and the political interest in that...until the banking industry can demonstrate that in times of crisis it does not need public support in the level that has been given, the banking industry I think has invited on itself this kind of scrutiny and intervention.*"[26] And Barclays' Varley: "*I say it again – I think the compensation structure in the banks contributed to the fuelling of that pursuit of yield.*"[27] Furthermore, he said, "*it is clear that the banks have contributed to that failure and it is clear that part of that problem has been the issue of compensation...[i]t is very clear to me that, not all, but some, aspects of it in the past have not served either the industry or society well.*"[28]

Others didn't see compensation as the driving issue. Hester's predecessor at RBS, Goodwin, noted that "*I find it hard, looking at the specifics of the case, to point to remuneration as being a cause of what happened on the ground.*"[29] Of course, Goodwin got raked over the coals for the size of his exit pension. Others suggested that most bankers believed their bets were justified, they operated within the rules they were given, they made or lost money for their banks and they did or didn't get paid – most preserving a medium-term view of their financial prospects with their employers. City law partner Fox: "*It seems to me that there are a great many people who took risks, and substantial risks, who were not in receipt of bonuses. They took risks because they thought it was the right thing to do, not because of the way they were remunerated. I think the people who did receive large bonuses, often did so because they were perceived as having performed very well in what they did.*"[30]

CLSA's Mayo gave arguably a dispassionate view about the cause of the crisis: "*one word's going to come up as being a key cause. And that one word is incentives. People do what they're incented to do. And if you look at the banking industry compensation, what the industry pays out is pretty constant as a percentage of revenues.*"[31] Charles Cronin, Head of the Chartered Financial Analysts Institute, said "*I think there ought to be a more measured way of delivering remuneration that matches the risk and the duration of the asset as opposed to just bagging the fees and running.*"[32]

The public's ire has made reform a focus. Treasury Secretary Geithner: "*we're committed to strong reforms of compensation practices.*"[33] The key: how to lower overall pay for bankers (which virtually the entire population outside of the banking world believes is unjustified and unwarranted), and how to tie pay to some long-term performance metric (e.g., stock price) so as to reduce the temptation to pile on too much risk. So, are measures like capping pay, linking bonuses to long-term performance of a bank's stock and clawing back bonuses in case something blows up in the future likely to be effective? Will they make bankers behave better?

Capping pay may be a nonstarter. In the aftermath of the crisis, various government officials raised a big fuss and managed to keep compensation in check – primarily for those that took, or were forced to take, government capital. The US assigned a special "pay czar" to review the compensation packages of all senior execs at all institutions that took government funds – which, by the time he got to the files, was limited to seven (some of which weren't even banks, e.g., Chrysler and GM). In France, Lagarde emerged as a big proponent of pay caps: "*We have this good bad cop, this gendarme, who is a very senior gentleman, former head of the IMF, in his 70s, highly respected, who is checking all the compensation plans and saying 'ok there, fine, it's in line with the rules, there excessive, please redraft'.*"[34] The UK decided to run with a pseudo-cap by way of a bonus tax – a sort of punishment for City workers.

What was the end result of this activity? Actually, nothing, except to provide some nice sound bites for the TV cameras: the politicians, channeling populist outrage, looked strong and were seen to be taking firm action (of course, none of the politicians or regulators involved in fomenting some of this disaster volunteered to cap their own pay packages – indeed, some US financial regulators got extra bonuses in 2006 and 2007 for their excellent work in overseeing financial institutions. Good job, boys!) In fact, many of the US banks that had taken government capital under "pressure" from the US Treasury (e.g., Goldman, JP Morgan, Morgan Stanley, and a few others) paid their funds back really quickly (with interest), so that they could escape the clutches of the pay czar and resume their previous practices. In the UK, a number of foreign banks spread the bonus hit around the rest of their employees in other countries, so that the UK bankers didn't feel any pain. And the lack of uniform treatment across borders meant room for arbitrage – Germany, for instance, didn't cap or tax compensation, meaning an instant competitive advantage. To be sure, some banks have or will put the issue of maximum compensation packages up for review and vote by their shareholders ("say on pay") but you probably know the record of shareholders when it comes to showing up or voting on issues – not a lot of enthusiasm, particularly as the hot embers of the crisis start to die out.

The idea of tying compensation to long-term performance of a bank's stock is hardly novel – that's how execs on Wall Street and the City have been getting paid for the past few decades. At Merrill, for instance, we got a good chunk of our bonuses paid in restricted stock and options, which vested over a few years, so we were all quite interested in seeing the stock price go up over the medium-term. And, happily, it did. That process continued after I left, but obviously it didn't stop O'Neal and co. from running the bank into the ground – I'm sure all of the Merrill folks with stock were furious when they saw Merrill's price plummet, but what could they do? Executive management and risk management blew it, even though they also suffered financially. There was no misalignment of interests. Same at Bear, same at Lehman, same at RBS. FSA's Turner: *"Just be careful of not over-stating what we will achieve by that. The head of Lehman Brothers owned a hell of a lot of the stock of Lehman's so when people are convinced by irrational exuberance, the fact that they own a lot of the stock of the company, they are still taken in with their own rhetoric."*[35] Hester echoed that view: *"[I]f you look at the evidence of the crisis, the two investment banks with the highest percentage of employee ownership, Lehman Brothers and Bear Stearns, went bust. Investment banks with the lowest proportion of employee ownership, like Credit Suisse…had a good crisis as these things go, so there simply was no correlation that you could draw between the extent to which the employees felt their personal wealth was at risk and what happened to the institution."*[36]

Some plans also call for a claw-back period, where the company can take back stock granted if things go really bad over some multiyear period. Fine. But that's not going to fundamentally change anyone's behavior. Bonuses are based on revenues, revenues are based largely on risk-taking – that's what banks do. Whether you monkey with longer vesting periods or stock/cash mix or claw-backs it is just shuffling the deck chairs: the drivers are the same, the motivations are the same, and the behaviors are the same. According to HSBC's Green: *"I don't think there's any question of going back to the status quo ante…. I think this was a sufficiently searing experience that the after-effects will be around for some time."*[37] Maybe. But unless a zero is dropped from the pay packs, behavior won't change. And zeros will not be dropped, even if Obama thinks bankers make too much.

Proprietary trading: The Volcker Rule and its narrow banking cousins

Let me now turn to the "Volcker Rule" – coined for its creator, Paul Volcker, who I've mentioned earlier in the book. In early 2010 Volcker introduced a version of "Glass-Steagall lite," in this case a new rule focused on separating bank proprietary trading from client activities – never mind that it's really hard to figure out accurately the scope of proprietary trading, as HSBC CFO Douglas Flint observed: *"I think there is a considerable difficulty in defining what we mean by proprietary trading. Everything we do is as principal. There is no concept of agency anymore."*[38] So, just how do you identify what is, and what is not, prop trading? Volcker's response: *"It's like pornography. You know it when you see it."* Not very helpful (except maybe over at the SEC, where dozens of senior executives were caught trolling the Internet for pornography on company time). It would be easy for me to argue that virtually any risky trading position on a bank's book is in some way tied to client activities (whether or not it actually is), and it would be really hard for any regulator to prove otherwise. Pointless and useless.

The idea behind this proposal was to make sure that banks that lend money to individuals and companies don't ever get into a situation where their risky trading activities create such big losses that their ability to accept deposits and make loans is threatened. The corollary: institutions deemed to be "too big to fail" should also keep such activities in check so that they don't let risk-trading create a systemic problem. So, if banks can't trade for their own accounts, they can't lose money and can therefore keep lending. Yes, maybe. Unless their lending standards are so bad that they lose money from lending rather than prop trading – kind of like what happened during this crisis, where the biggest black holes came from bad loans to individuals (e.g., mortgages, credit cards, auto loans) and companies (e.g., leveraged loans, commercial real estate loans). Kind of what happened in the S&L crisis. Kind of what happened in the LDC debt crisis. Kind of what happened in the Japanese bank crisis. None of those disasters had anything to do with proprietary trading activities, and nothing in the Volcker rule deals with such risks. Rob Nichols, head of Financial Services Forum: *"Trading – proprietary or otherwise – didn't lead to the recent crisis."*[39] King also put it quite nicely when he said that *"there are plenty of imprudent and risky decisions that banks make which are not of the kind that require a degree in higher mathematics. Indeed, as someone said not so long ago, it is amazing that banks go to such trouble to find new ways of losing money when the old ones seem to be doing perfectly well, thank you."*[40] Note that a parallel notion of "narrow banking" also generated some discussion in the European sphere, with concept papers drawn up on how best to divide true retail banking from wholesale banking (in whatever manner one might define wholesale, including proprietary activities).

The Obama Administration made a splashy announcement regarding this great new idea, the President himself announcing it with Volcker at his side. Volcker's own view? *"Makes good sense so it ought to be enacted...I think it's important obviously."*[41] Further: *"the implication for Goldman Sachs or any other institution is do you want to be a bank? You want to come within the safety net, follow the banking rules. If you don't want to follow those rules, you want to go out and do a lot of proprietary stuff, fine, but don't do it with a banking license."*[42] For those opting to move over to give in to the dark side, Volcker had an easy answer: *"We'll give you a nice coffin and an easy cushion...but you're not going to be saved."*[43]

Not surprisingly, not many bankers lined up in support (except Citi's Pandit: *"I believe banks should be bank servicing clients. I believe banks should not speculate with their capital."*[44] Does this mean that whatever happens, Citi will pull out of prop trading? Forever? Really?)

And the practical impact of the Volcker Rule? It would push lots of risk-taking elsewhere – wherever that might be, probably hedge funds, securities firms, other nonbank financials. That surely wouldn't help transparency and it still has the possibility of creating some serious systemic risk. So, that's a good fix? Doesn't sound like it. HSBC's Douglas: *"I think that the very narrow banking model...is, in my view, flawed, in the sense that the platform that the banking system provides for the bringing together of all risk in an economy...and if it was not in the banking system it would be somewhere else."*[45] Goldman's Corrigan said: *"[f]or me to take a position which does not conform in all of its details to the position [Volcker] is advocating is a wrenching human experience. I do not like to be in that position at all, but it is my best call and I have to call it as I see it. That is how I see it. Because I do not think it will work. That is the short answer."*[46] More importantly: *"we have to be careful...if the structural reform effectively chases all of the risk out of the core of the financial system are we any better off or not; or have we simply hidden the risk, pushed it further out to the near bank or non-bank sector such that systemic risk actually is going up rather than down?"*[47]

Never mind – soon after the announcement, five former US Treasury secretaries jumped in with a collective endorsement: *"Banks benefiting from public support by means of access to the Federal Reserve and FDIC insurance should not engage in essentially speculative activity unrelated to essential bank services....[the rule] is...a key element in protecting our financial system and will assure that banks will give priority to their essential lending and depository responsibilities."*[48] And what is an essential banking service? A bad mortgage loan?

But legislators, the rest of the industry, and a bunch of regulators were rather less certain. One time SEC Chairman Arthur Levitt noted that *"[f]ar from ending the problem of 'too big to fail', the Volcker rule practically institutionalizes it."*[49] Princeton economist and Former Fed vice chairman Alan Blinder said *"the firms that take the biggest proprietary risks are not banks at all...[y]et some of these non-banks are too big to fail, whether we like it or not."*[50] And, of course, Volcker conceded that *"[t]here was a lot of problem in non-banks. That's not directly addressed by these proposals."*[51] Lamfalussy also had some doubts: *"The difficulty is, and we have already referred to the Volcker process, how to define the specificity and how to cover the risk. His basic approach is to try to separate out the genuinely risky, bring it under specific supervision, and let others muddle through. This separation, to my mind, is extraordinarily difficult to achieve in any complex system.... I would love to see it happen but for that reason I do not think there is a chance of being able to make a proper definition."*[52] Thurston, head of HSBC's UK operations, noted that such an approach doesn't solve the problem: "*I am not convinced that [a narrow bank solution] does because if you look at some of the banks that got into considerable difficulty you might say they were narrow banks. They were either retail and commercial banks or stand-alone investment banks.*"[53]

And Bair wasn't sure about all of the splits, particularly those involving a separation of derivative activities, because such would move risk into institutions "*beyond the reach of federal regulation*"[54] – in other words, off the radar screen. King explained the unintended consequences of splitting up bank activities: "*Instinctively, I find the narrow bank idea very attractive but the argument that is put against it, which I have reluctantly over the years come to accept has some real validity, is that if you try to restrict deposit protection and regulation to the narrow banks and say to people that if you put your money into a narrow bank it is safe whereas if you put your money into a wider bank, you take your own pot luck, the problem is that the wider banks, precisely because they are not regulated, will be able for most of the period to offer higher returns, and many depositors will not be strong enough to [resist].*"[55] According to King, there are benefits to multiple lines of business: "*[t]he problem that faced Northern Rock was that it didn't have any other real kind of banking activity and although the risks it took were not dissimilar in nature from the risks that other bigger banks took, they were much more serious for Northern Rock because essentially it was just a mortgage bank.*"[56]

Hester tried to focus on the lack of a strict link between scope of business and past financial troubles: "*there is no evidence deriving from the financial crisis to support a renewed Glass-Steagall. When you look at the banks that have failed, the preponderance of banks that have failed were simple banks...either narrow investment banks like Lehman Brothers or Bear Stearns, or narrow mortgage banks like Bradford & Bingley and Northern Rock, or narrow commercial banks like in the US Wachovia and Washington Mutual...[m]y own view is that there is an enormous public policy/economic management/bank regulatory issue around how to allow banks to fail but I do not think that is the same as prescribing what business activities they should undertake.*"[57] And, from Varley: "*Nor do I think that combinations of activity, by definition, create risk – they very often diversify risk. At the heart of our ability to generate profits for our shareholders is the diversity of our business portfolio, which creates advantages for customers and shareholders alike.*"[58]

Turner made some good points, but also hedged his bets a little. First, "*I do not want [banks] to be involved in proprietary trading unrelated to customer service. The issue is: how do you do that?*"[59] More, precisely "*I told [Volcker] that I entirely agreed with the objective but I asked how exactly we would do it...The issue...is: how do you distinguish between positions which are required and occur day by day in support of market-making for customer service and proprietary trading?*"[60] Don't ask Volcker – he only knows it when he sees it. Furthermore, "*I think there are very major issues about how we make sure that proprietary trading activity does not contaminate the*

172 *See No Evil*

ability of banks to perform their fundamental functions in commercial and retail banking, and clearly there have been instances where that has occurred."[61] However, he noted, there are *"inherently global banks which have done better than most at avoiding some of the problems, they are deeply involved in this process of lubricating a global economy... which, in order to do that, cannot be entirely away from things that happen in trading rooms, markets that need to be made, derivative products that are legitimately offered."*[62] Ultimately, he said, *"[t]here are benefits in diversification."*[63] Straddling the fence?

Then there was a bit of middle ground, where folks like Mayo advocated some degree of split: *"there should be some separation, and I am shocked and amazed because banks are still allowed to do all the activities they were doing before the crisis. But I'm not sure it has to go that far where you automatically separate everything off."*[64] In the event, a form of the Volcker Rule was inserted in the new US financial regulations of mid 2010 – many other national systems failed to follow suit, so expect some new cross-border arbitrage.

Slimming down

One of the other rules on the table centered on slimming down the banks – if they don't get "too big" then they can't be "too big to fail" right? So, some in the US, the UK and other countries have explored the issue of limiting how big any single bank (or nonbank, for that matter) can become – meaning no more Citigroups, AIGs, RBSs. Geithner's view: *"we're going to make sure that we don't have a system in the future where banks get to the point where they are so large that they threaten the stability of the system."*[65] Furthermore, he said: *"Regulators must be empowered with explicit authority to force major financial firms to reduce their size or restrict the scope of their activities when necessary to limit risk to the system."*[66] Greenspan: *"If they're too big to fail, they're too big.... In 1911 we broke up Standard Oil – so what happened? The individual parts became more valuable than the whole. Maybe that's what we need to do."*[67]

In fact, the response to this charming idea wasn't very enthusiastic, certainly not amongst the biggest of the big. RBS's Hester: *"I do think that RBS became too big but the issue was not size; it was in a sense relationships; it was how big the balance sheet was relative to the capital resources; it was how unstable the funding was; it was how many disparate things that RBS was in that were not good; it was how good the management culture was. There are other banks, like HSBC, that were bigger than RBS that came through very well. So again, I think size is a red herring."*[68] Even more to the point, according to Hester: *"you can go bust in all shapes and sizes."*[69] And Dimon: *"If you consider the institutions that have failed during the crisis, many have been small."*[70] Meaning, *"[t]he solution is not to cap the size of financial firms."*[71] Dimon also indicated that *"[t]he arguments that 'big is bad' and that 'too consolidated is bad' are refuted by many examples of countries with large, consolidated banking systems that did not have problems... [c]apping the size of America's largest banks won't change the needs of big business. Instead, it will force these companies to turn to foreign banks that won't face the same restrictions."*[72] B of A's Moynihan made the point that it *"starts with recognizing that 'interconnectedness' and not 'bigness' is what led to the need for taxpayer bailouts."*[73] Varley said that *"big banks are not aggregators, but diversifiers of risk. The system would not be sound by making big banks smaller. The system would be sound by making big banks safer."*[74] Furthermore: *"I don't think that the size of a bank is a good indicator of its riskiness."*[75] His colleague, Bob Diamond, had a similar view: *"I've seen no evidence that shrinking banks and making banks...more narrow is the answer."*[76]

Of course, all of these bankers have a vested interest in keeping their banks big, so their comments are hardly surprising. But it's worth remembering that lots of small banks going south at the same time can also pose a massive risk – don't forget the damage caused by lots of little US S&Ls in the 1980s, lots of little Japanese nonbank financials in the 1990s. Even Darling observed that *"the large-small thing doesn't run. Northern Rock was very small in global terms but systemically it was quite important when it got into trouble."*[77] So, I'm not sure that putting banks on an asset diet does much.

Financial author Roger Lowenstein had a different take: *"Although Congress is focusing on the size of banks, big banks aren't more unstable than small ones. But highly leveraged ones are...[s]o it's appropriate for the government to offset the risks that it has helped to create by imposing costs on riskier firms."*[78] Which is basically another way of saying "tax scheme." In fact, when it became increasingly clear that the asset diet wasn't going to work, regulators returned to an earlier proposal for a "bank tax" – a special charge levied on the big, systemically important, banks that would go into a special fund – or taxes that would be applied to various financial transactions. CBI's Lambert: *"You may or may not be in favour of a Tobin-style tax on financial transactions – for the record, I am definitely not. But as Adair Turner himself acknowledges, you'd have to be mad to impose such a levy unilaterally without it being imposed at the same time in the rest of the world."*[79] And we know how good regulators are at coordinating with one another.

Lots more (anticyclical) capital...lots more

One thing that is usually evident in a financial crisis is the degree to which banks and other risk-takers look undercapitalized as losses mount. The same, of course, happened during this crisis. King observed that *"[o]ne of the lessons from this is that the amounts of capital that banks were required to hold were simply too low."*[80] So, the argument is that in order to avoid intensifying systemic pressures in the future, banks must be prepared to hold lots more capital. Geithner: *"Regulators must be able to impose tougher requirements – most crucially, stronger capital rules...[t]his would provide strong incentive for these firms* to shrink, simplify, and reduce their leverage."[81] The same thought came from Lagarde: "It's going to be different. To take the example of the banks, they know for sure that they are not going to make the same amount of money, they're not going to generate the same amount of profits because they're going to have to put in more capital."[82] Turner said in relation to prop trading capital that "we've got to raise it by five or 10 times because we just had the weights on trading books completely and utterly wrong."[83]

And what of the brilliant Basel II regime that was meant to get the capital charges right? Turner votes for "[s]ignificant adjustment but not ripping up."[84] Yes – really significant adjustments, please. In fact, there has been much talk about anticyclicality and the need to encourage building up of capital reserves in good times, for protection during bad times – precisely the reverse of the Basel II regime. Seems sensible, according to Lamfalussy: "I think one set of proposals the Stability Forum is making is about pro-cyclicality. I find that is a very, very important issue. This is what helped, in a positive sense, the Spanish banks because they acted anti-cyclically and that turned out to be very helpful, especially in the present situation when the real economy is in trouble but the banks are not."[85] Lockhart: "we need to create a countercyclical capital regime. Capital requirements should increase when housing prices get too far above trendlines."[86] Perhaps this might work? Perhaps – but of course it won't in the absence of some "loophole closing," an explicit cap on leverage, and a reevaluation of the riskiness of all manner of assets (and not just the ones that have been crushed in the most recent crisis, but ones that will get crushed in the future). In case you're wondering: discussions on version 3.0 of Basel were fast-tracked and approved during the first part of 2010, to try and seal up some of the cracks in version 2.0.

Skin in the game

Another barn-door measure: have banks keep on their books a slice of all the nastiness they plan to serve up to clients as a way of making sure they do their best to make sure it's not all that nasty. The theory goes that if the banks have some skin in the game, they will be more vigilant – thus keeping moral hazard in check. Greenspan's view: "As much as I would prefer it otherwise, in this financial environment I see no choice but to require that all securitizers retain a meaningful part of the securities they issue."[87]

In fact, European regulators were first out of the blocks, stipulating that banks will now have to hold 5 percent of any securitized bonds they create. McCreevy: "Originators or managers of these securitizations will be required to retain a meaningful stake in each tranche of the securitization issue. I was pilloried from the rooftops about this proposal when I originally put it forward."[88] The US then followed suit through its new regulatory overhaul of 2010. But some have wondered whether the rule will just kill a business that, when properly managed, is actually useful. Ian Linnell of Fitch: *"In some cases, the option under the retention rule that best achieves the stated objective of aligning originator and investor incentives may also remove the economic incentive to securitise; undermining broader regulatory and policy efforts to restore effective securitisation markets."*[89] Plus, this has the makings of another bank dumping ground once the market for securitized bonds gets back into full gear: it's not hard to imagine banks starting once again to accumulate things they can't sell. Look out...

Permission to euthanize

One of the big problems of the crisis was that certain regulators lacked the power to seize hobbled institutions and effectively euthanize them – through whatever means deemed best, including selling or transferring portions to a third party, liquidating the assets, or putting them on government life support. To be sure, this "resolution authority" already exists in certain regimes (like the US national and regional banks sector, where various regulators can work in concert to pull the plug). But it has long been missing for nonbanks (securities firms, insurers) and is entirely missing in certain countries (various European nations).

Geithner, for his part, said that *"the federal government must have the ability to resolve failing major financial institutions in an orderly manner, with losses absorbed not by taxpayers but by equity holders, unsecured creditors and, if necessary, other large financial institutions."*[90] By this I can only presume he means major non-bank financial institutions, since authority to resolve major financial institutions has existed for some time! Draghi's view: *"We want to be in a position where we are free to let fail any institution without paying the exorbitant price we are paying ... [t]he most important point is to have a mechanism that gives power, ability and funding to allow whichever public authority steps in to continue preserving the core functioning of the failed institution."*[91] And the German perspective, courtesy of Jochen Sanio: *"Personally, I am in favour of introducing a resolution regime making it possible to liquidate banks that are in trouble without creating contagious effects."*[92] But he also captured another reality: *"as most systemic financial institutions operate globally what we really need is an international agreement on a truly global resolution regime. I know this is only a pipe dream."*[93]

Dimon weighed in this way: *"we at JP Morgan Chase have argued for an enhanced resolution authority that would let regulators wind down failing firms in a controlled way that minimizes damage to the economy and will never cost the taxpayer anything...Just giving regulators this authority...would reduce the likelihood of failure as managements and boards would recognize there is no safety net."*[94] Support also came from the US bankers' lobby, with Yinling confirming that the *"ABA also strongly supports creating a mechanism for the orderly resolution of systemically*

176   *See No Evil*

important non-bank firms. Our regulatory authorities should never again be in the position of making up a solution on the fly to a Bear Stearns or an AIG, or of not being able to resolve a Lehman Brothers."[95]

Some outfits were very nervous about the special resolution authorities – to wit the BBA's Knight: "*We are extremely concerned about the aggressive legislative timetable the Government is proposing to follow, particularly on the complex Special Resolution Regime and bank-specific insolvency arrangements.*"[96] Why? Because "*there remain highly significant questions over the operation of the proposed SRR.... Our concerns centre principally on the sweeping powers that the authorities would have to vary, suspend or restrict creditor rights in the case of partial transfers of the business of an failed bank or, more precisely, the potential adverse consequences that those powers could have on the cost and availability of funding.*"[97]

So, resolution authority (aka living wills/going-gone concern) became a front-and-center issue. Mind you, this will do nothing to help stop an institution from getting into trouble – it just makes it easier to dispose of it when the end is nigh. But the solutions are political and not easy, as Corrigan observed: "*Are we going to be able to take prompt corrective action from a slogan to a policy? Are we going to be able to make enhanced resolution authority work? My answer is neither of those things is going to be easy. They are going to be very, very difficult.*"[98]

A few things for the rating agencies

Then came the ideas for the rating agencies, major players in the disaster: getting them to improve their black box rating models, manage conflicts of interest (only doing ratings, not providing any consulting/advisory services), increase their transparency, and tighten up on cross-border loopholes. Happily, the European Commission was right on top of the situation: "*Self-regulation based on voluntary compliance...code does not appear to offer an adequate, reliable solution to the structural deficiencies of the business.*"[99] Yes, too bad we had to run the gauntlet to discover this...

Of course, the agencies generally jumped to attention after their failures, apparently trying to look a bit better before suffering from a real regulatory clampdown, to wit Fitch's Joynt observation that "*we are moving forward, we are not waiting for someone to establish a new set of regulations for us to follow, we are responsive today to adjusting our process and our thinking to what we would anticipate in the main are reasonable proposals.*"[100] And, further, "*we want to strengthen in terms of identifying, and the management of, conflicts of interest in how we go about assigning ratings...and the transparency with which we present not just our rating but our analysis and our conclusion.*"[101] Indeed. Sounds pretty fundamental to the ratings process, so why didn't all of that happen before the crisis? Moody's

Madelain: "*The key to us is that we believe that the current model is the best model but it needs to be managed effectively and as we mentioned before we can do our share to give credibility to that model.*"[102] I do wonder about that – why would the agencies, who have been discredited, be able to do their "share" to "give credibility"? And why is the model that got us into trouble the "best" model?

SEC's Schapiro spelled out some of the new rules that came into effect in the lead-up to the crisis: "*amended rules require [rating agencies] to make additional public disclosures about their methodologies ... to publicly disclose the histories of their ratings, and to make additional internal records and furnish additional information to the [SEC] in order to assist staff examinations ... The amendments also prohibit [agencies] and their analysts from engaging in certain activities that could impair their objectivity, such as recommending how to obtain a desired rating and then rating the resulting security.*"[103] But no change to the "issuer-pays" model?

Additional ideas were put forth post-crisis, including increasing even further the degree of oversight and increasing the liability of the agencies should something go badly wrong. The US Senate proposed the creation of a "credit rating board" (comprised of investors, a rating agency and a bank), which would analyze the accuracy of ratings on an annual basis, and perhaps punish those that screw up too frequently. In addition, though the agencies would set issuer fees, the SEC would have the right to ensure the fees remain reasonable. Needless, to say, this didn't sit well with the big three. Chris Atkins, S&P, observed that "*[c]redit-rating firms would have less incentive to compete with one another, pursue innovation and improve their models ... [t]his could lead to a more homogenized rating opinion and, ultimately, deprive investors of valuable, differentiated opinions on credit risk.*"[104]

Whilst S&P's Sharma agreed that reforms were necessary, he also wanted to defend the perimeter, saying that "*some of the recent proposals to increase oversight of [agencies] are problematic and, in our view, would bring unintended harm to the markets. These proposals include amendments to the federal securities laws that would treat [agencies] far more harshly ... and other measures that would interfere with [agencies'] analytical independence .... This would add greater hazards, systemic risks and inefficiencies to the market, and would cause confusion among market participants.*"[105] Probably difficult for him to get much of a hearing.

Sean Egan, who I mentioned in the last chapter, cast a different light on proposed changes: "*These proposals are well-intentioned and may move the process in a better direction, but like many of the reforms suggested to date they share a common problem: they proceed from the erroneous premise that the major rating agencies are in the business of providing timely and accurate ratings for the benefit of investors and now taxpayers when, in fact, these companies have, for the last 35 years, been in the business of facilitating the issuance of securities for the benefit of issuers and underwriters.*"[106]

Fundamentally, according to Egan, *"[t]he only real reform for the ratings industry is to return the industry to the business of representing those who invest in securities, not those who issue them."*[107]

Coordinated, systemic super-regulators

One of the obvious problems of the crisis was the degree to which different regulators did their own things. Sure, there were attempts at harmonization of rules through Basel II, but lots of other activities followed separate, generally divergent, national paths. Accordingly, another reform idea has centered on creating some greater amount of global uniformity and coordination on regulations, so that the main national systems would be seen to be marching in the same direction. Gordon Brown said that *"[t]he ability of banks in Britain to operate as we wish depends not only their management at home but on getting regulation right internationally. Our banking systems have been shown to be totally interdependent and interconnected."*[108] Barclays' Varley agreed: *"What I think we need is convergence on regulation activity, rather than independent regulation activity."*[109] Chancellor Merkel echoed a similar view: *"The current crisis shows us you can do some things on the national level, but the overwhelming majority must be agreed to on the international level. We must push for clearer regulations so that a crisis like the current one cannot be repeated."*[110] Similar views came from her countryman, Sanio: *"These days it is more important than ever for the supervisors of different countries to cooperate closely. Supervision today stands or falls by cross-border cooperation."*[111] Furthermore, he said: *"The days when each regulator could plough his own national furrow are long gone. Regulators can no longer achieve very much by playing a lone hand nationally. These days national borders don't mean much for risk any longer...National financial crises could rapidly grow into international financial crises. We therefore need common European and internationally recognised standards."*[112] Geithner agreed that no country can go it alone – new rules can't apply only to the US, for example, *"'Cause if we just do it here, then the risk will just go somewhere else."*[113] All of this seems terribly sensible, but I still can't help but wonder whether it will ever really occur? National politics can be very powerful, and unless the political interests of, say, the US, UK, German, Italy, France, Japan, Switzerland, and a few others really line up, it's not hard to imagine such efforts falling apart.

I've also mentioned in Chapter 6 that one of the consistent themes raised by regulators and bankers was the extent to which systemic risk wasn't captured. Not surprisingly, various proposals were put forth to try and corral this risk – as if it didn't somehow exist before 2007. What about systemic risk in the late 1980s when sovereign moratoria almost brought banks in the UK, US, France, Germany, and other countries to their knees? What about systemic risk in the LTCM/Russia crisis a decade later, when the hedge fund's excessive leverage almost torpedoed lots of financial heavyweights, and which demanded eleventh-hour intervention by a government/private consortium? Where were the politicians and regulators on those occasions? So here we are again, a decade later, now with a proposal to deal with systemic risk – this time by creating something at a supranational level, under the auspices of a body like the Bank for International Settlements, or maybe at the national level, with greater communication and cooperation amongst countries.

Dimon: "[t]here was no systemic regulator trying to look around the corner and say, 'Well, if a money market fund has a problem, that's going to cause a problem for X.' It's not a mystery. It's not a surprise. And we know we have crises every five or 10 years."[114] The question is whether a super regulator will change anything? Dimon voiced support: "we will need a systemic regulator charged with effectively monitoring the spread and level of risk across the financial system in its entirety. Think of it as a 'super risk' regulator. Such a regulator would not eliminate all future problems, but it would be able to mitigate them."[115] Varley indicated that "one of the learning points for me as I think about this is that we need to create the wherewithal and the structures in regulatory supervision going forward that ensure that it is the explicit obligation of a member of the regulatory body to be looking out for the big systemic risks because I think it is a failure of systemic risk that characterises the history of the last two years."[116] Hermes' Pitt-Watson: "We need to have someone who is overseeing the whole chain of regulation because right now it does not fit together."[117] Fuld, from his vantage point as an ex-Wall Streeter: "The idea of a 'super regulator' that monitors the financial markets for systemic risk, I believe, is a good one."[118] And Stanley's Mack also came out in support: "[w]e do need a regulator who has more resources...I would like to see some consolidation. I would like to see a kind of a head regulator, not just here in the U.S. but tied to other regulators across the world in a global economy."[119] Further, "we need fundamentally improved systemic regulation. Our fragmented regulatory structure simply hasn't kept pace with increasingly complex and global markets. I agree...with your proposal to create a systemic risk regulator."[120] Bair went on the record this way: "the FDIC supports the creation of a Systemic Risk Council to oversee systemic risk issues, develop needed prudential policies and mitigate developing systemic risks."[121]

But Wallison had his doubts: "is it realistic to believe that any agency can set capital ratios for companies as diverse as banks, hedge funds, insurance companies, securities firms, private equity firms, and finance companies? All these firms operate in different ways and compete with one another...[i]t is highly doubtful that any systemic regulator will be able to do these things effectively."[122] And Roach also had a different take: "Rather than attempt to create a new systemic risk regulator, I would argue that it is more important to take a careful look at the central banking function, itself – namely, considering the possibility of making explicit changes to policy mandates that would force central banks to make systemic risk control an integral part of their mission."[123]

In addition, there have also been proposals for more, and better, regulators. A bigger army, with soldiers that won't be outgunned and who can stand firm in the face of enemy fire. Draghi confirmed that *"[t]here is a clear need for supervisors, regulators and other authorities to raise their own game, nationally and internationally. At both levels, authorities need to become more responsive to and more nimble and effective in mitigating emerging risks."*[124] And King: *"I think that means very talented, very experienced people who are willing to speak out and that is not easy.... it is quality and the willingness to sit back and most of all take an independent view."*[125] Darling proposed a little more regulatory probing: *"I think the supervisory system does need to ask more questions and it does need to be more intrusive."*[126] This only happens when you've got regulators with skill and confidence – can they be attracted from the Goldmans, Morgans and Barclays of the world? It won't be easy. In the aftermath of the crisis Schapiro was concerned that *"the SEC has been unable to maintain stable, sufficient long-term funding necessary to conduct long-term planning and lacks the flexibility to apply resources rapidly to developing areas of concern."*[127] Good luck.

Better controls: Risk management and directors

Not surprisingly, most of the US and European bankers that missed the crisis figured they needed to sharpen up on their risk management processes and strengthen their board directors – in short, to improve the quality of their controls, independent of any new regulatory rules, so as to minimize the damage from the next crisis. In fact, this is a fairly regularly exercise, appearing in the aftermath of every crisis once the requisite postmortems are complete. It's happened in some form after each and every crisis – though arguably to limited effect, as the crises seem to be bigger than ever before.

In the event, most of the major banks made declarations of their risk control improvements (actual or prospective), perhaps to calm the ire of politicians, regulators, and investors. For instance, B of A's Moynihan said that *"[w]e also have adopted an improved approach to risk management...[w]e've clarified risk management roles and responsibilities. We're putting in place management routines that will foster more open debate on risk-related issues, and we're taking action based on those debates."*[128] A few improvements from Citi's Pandit as well: *"[i]n risk management, for instance, the leadership team was thoroughly overhauled with an impressive array of veteran talent from outside, as well as inside."*[129] And at Goldman, where Blankfein indicated that although *"the past two years have validated our conservative approach to liquidity and to managing our risk, they have also prompted significant change within our organization. Specifically, we have embraced new realities pertaining to regulation and ensuring that our financial strength remains in line with our commitment to the long-term stability of our franchise and the overall markets."*[130] Lots of other banks made similar moves.

And what of the risk models – the ones that banks and regulators relied on so heavily? Taleb: *"we need to examine the toxicity of models; financial regulators should have the same test as the Food and Drug Administration does. The promoter of the probability model must be able to show that no one will be harmed even if the event is rare.... [b]ut we cannot afford to wait 200 years to find out that the medicine is far worse than the disease. We cannot afford to wait even months."*[131] Schapiro: *"Going forward, risk managers and regulators must recognize the inherent limitations of these (and any) models and assumptions – and regularly challenge models and their underlying assumptions to consider more fully low probability, extreme events."*[132] The models will always be of limited use – perhaps it's time to rely a little bit more on experience and judgment and a little less on model output?

How about directors? Ever since the global corporate scandals at the turn of the millennium, the push has been on in many countries to strengthen governance practices generally and the role of board directors specifically – focusing particularly on those who are meant to be looking after the interests of the shareholders. There's little doubt that the directors (both executive and nonexecutive) of banks and other companies that blew up during this crisis were asleep at the wheel. HSBC's Flint: *"you need to have...proper supervision of management and governance over management, which is the board structure and the regulatory framework."*[133] Sorely lacking, pretty much everywhere.

Professor Hahn of John Cass University noted quite rightly that *"[o]ne of the things that has been exposed, I think, internationally is the lack of understanding of the modern banking sector and its risks by the boards."*[134] Pitt-Watson seconded that view, indicating that *"[t]here has been a failure in corporate governance. I believe that if 18 months ago we had all scratched our heads people would have looked at a lot of the things we are looking at now and recognised there was a problem and perhaps something ought to be done about it."*[135] Commenting on the role of the audit committees of board directors, Hayward, CEO of Independent Audit observed that: *"[t]he other part of the responsibility is around the oversight of the risk management in these organisations and self evidently that has not been so successful."*[136] Rather. MP John Thurso observed that *"that a board of part-timers will never actually be able to deal with things that are as complex."*[137] His colleague, MP Cousins, echoed a sentiment that perhaps many board directors have felt in recent years: *"If I was a member of an audit committee [of the board] of one of these major banks I think I would be tempted to do what the Danish politician suggested he would do if he was attacked by the Russians which is simply send a telegram saying 'I surrender.'"*[138]

What to do? Chambers, CEO of Legal and General's investment arm, noted that: *"[a] lot of the banks still have balance sheets in excess of £1 trillion. They are very substantial bodies with which to get to grips. My view and that of my firm is that non-executive directors should be more involved and devote considerably more* time to each non-executive position they hold...[they] should be able to do a much deeper dive into companies, speak to people and review businesses further down to get a more all-round view."[139] Turner: "Can I say, I think it is important to make sure that we have appropriate non-execs...[i]t is appropriate to make sure that they have adequate time and visibility of the issues."[140] Indeed, some banks moved to shore up their boards. For instance, over at Citibank Pandit announced that: "[a]t the Board of Directors level, there also have been impressive additions of talent important to our positioning for the future."[141] Will it work? I'm not sure, but obviously some attempt has to be made: perhaps by insisting that directors have some minimum qualifications regarding the business they're supposed to be overseeing – some super directors that can help decipher the alphabet soup of financial engineering that is still a fixture of modern finance. And insisting that they devote enough time to the matter, meaning no more multiple directorships. And where to find these folks? Probably the only way is to raid the hen house. And will they be willing to sign up? If the D&O insurance policies provide really good indemnity cover – else, why bother?

Still, it's important to be realistic about what directors will ultimately be able to do. Turner recognized the limitations: "if I had to identify what will decrease the likelihood that our equivalents are here in 10 years' time...[i]t will be a better system of capital adequacy, a counter-cyclical system of capital adequacy, more robust and effective policies on liquidity. It is those, I think, which are most likely to decrease the likelihood of overall systemic problems...more likely to do it than operating through the competence of the executives or the nonexecutives of specific institutions."[142] King was equally skeptical about the possibilities: "I find it very hard to believe that a particular process of corporate governance is going to guarantee people behaving prudently.... [I]n the end what we have to have is a culture in which people on boards are willing to stand up."[143]

And in the final analysis...

Lots of the rules and regulations put on the table elicited strong responses from those in favor and those opposed. Many in the political and regulatory class wanted to flex their muscles and bring the bankers to heel. The public wanted change, both at banks and within the regulatory community. A few wanted to focus on the human element of the disaster. HSBC's Green put it very cogently: "no amount of rules and regulations will be sufficient if the culture does not encourage people to do the right thing."[144] Roach echoed a similar thought: "we can't delude ourselves into thinking that the lessons of this crisis rest solely in new rules and regulations. They are a necessary – but not sufficient – condition for a more robust post-crisis architecture. Our problems also have a very important human dimension – namely, they are an outgrowth of the poor judgment that was endemic in this reckless era of self-regulation."[145]

While there was no shortage of officials calling for more rules and regulations (to wit Geithner's pledge that *"[w]e're not going to adopt an approach that does stuff at the margin and delays any changes to help preserve market practices that helped make this crisis much more dangerous"*[146]), there were others from government/regulation and industry that urged a bit of restraint – not avoidance, but not a mad rush toward an over-the-top regime of new rules, either. For instance, though Canadian Prime Minister Stephen Harper wanted some reform, he also noted that *"Canada will not go down the path of excessive arbitrary or punitive regulation of its financial sector."*[147] Bair was conscious of the need to do something intelligent, not just pile on more rules and regulations: *"if the thrust of reform is to simply layer more regulation upon insured banks, we will simply provide more incentives for financial activity to be conducted in less-regulated venues and exacerbate the regulatory arbitrage that fed this crisis."*[148] Takafumi Sato, head of Japan's FSA said that *"[w]hile the work to extinguish the burning fire as soon as possible is of course necessary, it is also essential to put in place a framework to prevent the recurrence of the same kind of crisis. On the one hand, if the policies lean too much toward crisis management, it could cause moral hazard or distort the system in the longer run. On the other hand, hasty implementation of medium-term measures could rather exacerbate the situation and make crisis management even more difficult."*[149] Ron Paul also issued a warning: *"The ... problem is the trust that people blindly put in regulations, and the moral hazard this creates. Too many people trust government regulators so completely that they abdicate their own common sense to these government bureaucrats. They trust that if something violates no law, it must be safe."*[150]

Not surprisingly, similar views came from the big banks and banking lobbies in the US and UK. Goldman's Blankfein: *"We should resist a response ... that is solely designed around protecting us from the 100-year storm. Taking risk completely out of the system will be at the cost of economic growth. We know from economic history that innovation – and the new industries and new jobs that result from it – require risk taking."*[151] Dimon: *"We should avoid the temptation to have multiple regulators just for the sake of having them ... [t]hree or four different regulators all looking at (and fighting over) the same issue is not a wise use of taxpayer money ... [c]reating duplicative and overlapping functions could increase costs and reduce credit opportunities for the consumers we are trying to protect."*[152] The end result? *"When profits fall too sharply then capital will move somewhere else, where there is more money to be earned, for example non-regulated markets ... [T]he question is, is that what regulators want?"*[153] Rick Waugh, CEO of Bank of Nova Scotia, held a similar view: *"There are some warning signs that regulators could go too far and have implications on growth ... [o]verregulation can be as detrimental to growth, to jobs, to economies as not having enough."*[154] Deutsche's Ackermann also worried that the new regulations would *"undermine the global recovery ... [t]he banking sector will be given tighter boundaries and the profitability of the financial industry as a whole will be lower."*[155]

No surprise how the lobbyists viewed things. ABA's Rock: *"Legislation should create as little disruption as possible for the marketplace. Extreme care needs to be taken not to saddle banks – which generally had nothing to do with the current problems – with more burdens which inevitably impede all types of lending....[w]ith any legislation, the potential for unintended consequences exists."*[156] And, from the BBA's Knight: *"Now, as we look to the future, there is a real need to ensure that pragmatic, sensible and practical measures underpin what changes need to be made. We must ensure that banks can continue to take managed risks and are not so restrained by the regulatory consequences of this crisis that risk-taking stops. A banking system that removes all risk is a system that fails to serve society...if we over-regulate or if we take steps that are not necessarily required in the heat of the moment, either here or in Brussels, then we will jeopardise our future."*[157] Back to Dimon, who provided an important warning: *"When we reduce the debate over responsibility and regulation to simplistic and inaccurate notions, such as Main Street vs. Wall Street, big business vs. small business or big banks vs. small banks, we are indiscriminately blaming the good and the bad – this is simply another form of ignorance and prejudice."*[158]

Nonsense, said Lagarde: *"insufficient regulation is a much more serious problem than too much."*[159] Draghi agreed, saying that it was *"premature for banks to be worried about excessive rules."*[160] So did McCreevy: *"[f]inancial institutions – and their trade bodies – who have been so vigorously opposed to meaningful reform are doing themselves no favours at all."*[161] And the same from Will Hutton of the Works Foundation: *"do not allow anyone from the financial community to tell you that any more regulation is going to stifle innovation and somehow damage the City of London."*[162]

Still others remained completely skeptical about the whole barn-door closing exercise. Even as the US passed a big piece of legislation with bits and pieces of the things described earlier in the chapter, there were doubters. Senator Russ Feingold: *"The test for this legislation is a simple one – whether it will prevent another financial crisis...[a]s the bill stands, it fails that test."*[163] Harvey Pitt, former SEC Chairman, said of the panoply of US reforms: *"[t]he bills address last year's crisis...they assure we will experience anew the law of unintended consequences."*[164] James Grant: *"Congress and the regulators dream up yet more ways to try to outsmart the people who have made it their business in life not to be outsmarted. And so it is again in today's debate over financial reform. From the administration and from both sides of the congressional aisle come proposals to micromanage the business of lending, borrowing and market-making: new accounting rules (foolproof this time, they say), higher capital standards, more onerous taxes. If piling on new federal rules was the answer, we'd long ago have been in the promised land."*[165] Taleb said that lots of these measures are just setting us up for the next crisis – same actors, same script: *"A lot of people are telling us what to do now. I just want to make sure it's not the same people who were flying the plane and crashing who are going to fly the plane again."*[166] Guess what? It's the same people. In keeping with transportation metaphors, he said *"[p]eople who were driving a school bus blindfolded (and crashed it) should never be given a new bus. The economics establishment (universities, regulators, central bankers, government officials, various organizations staffed with economists) lost its legitimacy with the failure of the system. It is irresponsible and foolish to put our trust in the ability of such experts to get us out of this mess. Instead, find the smart people whose hands are clean."*[167] In fact, he has counseled a different, rather more extreme, approach: shift all risk-taking from banks to hedge funds, so that banks themselves are simply pass-throughs providing services to clients, and the real risks are borne by hedge funds backed by investor capital – with no safety net. In other words: *"ban banks from risk-taking because society is going to pay the price. This is not the first time ... [b]anks are going to become a utility.... and the risks taken will be borne by individuals like myself who have capital, and who know the risks, with their own money. Otherwise you're going to keep having a cycle that's deeper every time."*[168] The question, of course, is whether such private pools of capital become so big and interconnected that they generate their own level of systemic risk?

Ultimately, I suppose the real issue is whether some useful reforms can be crafted? Some changes have been adopted, some rejected, and still others are under debate and discussion – a process that could take years to finish. If all of these rules are eventually passed, will we have really closed the barn doors for good? Are we really sure that the risky beasts will remain in the barn, no longer free to run through the pasture wreaking all manner of financial damage? I doubt it.

10
Get Ready for the Next One...

In this book I've summarized what happened during the fateful crisis period that came to the forefront in August 2007 – but which had been percolating for at least several years before that. I've mentioned some of the people that got it wrong (along with a very few that got it right), and examined who fell on the sword and who ran for the hills. In the last chapter I've also described some of the "fixes" that have either been put in place or proposed as a way of making sure this never happens again.

So, where does all of this leave us? What's next? Are their new rules going to help us out? Have the bankers and regulators been sufficiently chastened that behaviors will change? Will politicians be more constructive in the future? Have we seen the worst that will ever happen to the global financial system and the world's economies, and is it all sunshine and blue skies from now on? Or will we have another episode – when our luck runs... out?

While it's difficult to read what lies ahead, on this issue I am convinced that, despite all of the financial and emotional pain we've just been through, we will experience a similar event at some point in the (not-too-distant) future. We should get ready for the next one, because there will be a next one. Unfortunately, I'm not the only one with this view. IMF's Strauss-Kahn has said that *"[c]rises never end. You are always dealing with the consequences of the previous crisis until you reach the next crisis."*[1] CLSA's Mayo observed that *"these once-in-a-lifetime events happen every couple of years."*[2] And, from King: *"I am rather doubtful if the need for future inquiries will ever disappear because banking does run these risks that every now and then there is a crisis."*[3] More generally, Peter Solomon supplied an intriguing analogy: *"Groundhog. We wake up every day and it's the same thing...[t]his is like recurring non-recurring losses."*[4] Roubini was of the same mind: *"Current efforts to reform financial regulation are 'cosmetic' and won't prevent another crisis...The way I think about this crisis is not in terms of black swans (a sudden, rare event), but white swan events. Crises are much more common than we think."*[5] MIT's Andrew Lo put it a bit more formally: *"Financial crises may be an unavoidable aspect of modern capitalism, a consequence of the interactions between hardwired human behavior and the unfettered ability to innovate, compete, and evolve."*[6]

Turner agreed that another problem will invariably arise, though his timeline is longer than mine: *"We are very susceptible to those intellectual fashions and assumptions that the world has changed. The best we can do is structure intellectual challenges into the system that try to guard against it. I think that is a risk in 15 years' time rather than the next five years. I am pretty confident that we shall be very much on our guard against that sort of conventional wisdom for at least five or 10 years."*[7] I hope he's right, but I think he's being optimistic. Japan FSA's Sato gave his unique home country view: *"Given the seriousness of the impact it has had on the global economy, it is not without reason that the current financial crisis has been labeled as 'once-in-a-century.' As you all know, however, it was not so long ago that Japan experienced the last serious crisis. Remembering my own experience in the financial regulatory authority ten or so years ago, my feeling is rather that the current financial stress is the 'second-in-a-decade' in my country."*[8] So, once every five years! Former Fed official Alan Blinder noted that *"[w]e shouldn't delude ourselves into thinking we are going to build a panic-proof system...[b]ut there are choices between less and more panics, more virulent ones, less virulent ones, and that is the way we want to push the system."*[9] Certainly – but can we? Finally, from Bafin's Sanio, a very honest comment: *"The bold assumption that crises can be prevented once and for all would betray an exaggerated opinion of our own capabilities."*[10]

So, there is little doubt in my mind – and apparently in the minds of others – that we will continue to have big financial crises. The obvious questions? Why and when, and in what form.

Why?

Even a casual review of financial history shows that dislocations aren't actually that unusual, even the nasty variety we've just been through. If you're not a fan of financial history, it's kind of boring listing all the episodes, dates, and causes, so I won't go through that exercise.[11] But if I was to rewind to, say, the seventeenth century, I could list literally hundreds of events, including dozens that might be classified as very severe. Some of these occurred because speculative bubbles burst, or because bank runs caused the man and woman on the street to lose confidence in the banks. Others happened because the financial system was mismanaged, or because of regulatory malfeasance, political stumbling, or failed risk management. Whatever the specific drivers, the historical record is clear: financial crises happen more frequently than we think. So why should things change in the future? In fact, I can think of eight reasons why they won't change – why we'll have a variation on this conversation in due course (and where "due course" is three or five years, not 10 or 15 years).

1: Risk will always exist. Bankers have been crucified because of their risk mismanagement (right) and have since been told that the risk they can take in the future will be limited (wrong). Our politicians want to make it seem as though imposing various constraints on big banks will reduce systemic risk – like all that extra risk will be absorbed by some black hole and just go away. Quite wrong. It will simply morph into another form and make its way into the financial system in another way – maybe not through the big banks (this time), but through hedge funds, nonbank financial companies, off-balance sheet vehicles, private equity funds, Bermuda reinsurers, trusts, ... whatever. Or maybe through some new mechanism that the clever bankers haven't even invented yet (and they're always inventing something ...). Let's remember that different kinds of institutions have been at the center of different crises in the past: nonbank financial institutions (UK Secondary banking crisis, Japan banking crisis), hedge funds (LTCM/Russia crisis), savings & loans (US S&L crisis of the 1980s), big international banks (LDC crisis), and so on. And let's also remember that different risky products have served as transmission mechanisms: so, this time it was credit default swaps and structured mortgage products, meaning everyone is focused on those. But don't forget LIBOR-based loans (LDC crisis), foreign currencies (Asian/Mexican crises), exchange-traded derivatives (Barings crisis), local emerging market bonds (Russian crisis), high-flying Internet stocks (dot-com crisis). The point is, it doesn't matter which institutions are involved, or which products are used – risk exists, it will always exist and it cannot be regulated out of existence. Sorry. Goldman's Blankfein has it right: *"We must never forget that risk is just that – risk, with all its consequences."*[12] Equally, as Sanio reminds us: *"[b]anking is risk-taking"*.[13] And if risk exists, then the chance of a risk-induced crisis exists.

2: The next bubble in already inflating. Though at least some central bankers want to deny that their loose money policies had anything at all to do with this (or any previous) crisis, I think we all know better. There is always another bubble inflating, whether it's in dot-com stocks, emerging market bonds, mortgages and real estate, or commodities. And when these bubbles inflate to some particular size, they burst and cause financial pain – and may even create some amount of "contagion." Granted, some bubbles are bigger than others, but that's a secondary consideration: in an age when everything is very connected, even a small bubble can have big consequences. Greenspan's view: *"Unless there is a societal choice to abandon dynamic markets and leverage* *for some form of central planning, I fear that preventing bubbles will in the end turn out to be infeasible. Assuaging their aftermath seems the best we can hope for.*"[14] A similar thought came from Ron Paul: "*Unless and until we get the Federal Reserve out of the business of creating money at will and setting interest rates, we will remain vulnerable to market bubbles and painful corrections.*"[15] And Banque de France Governor Noyer: "*Bubbles are, however, complex phenomena: hard to detect, hard to prevent, hard to fight.*"[16] Keep an eye on your local central bankers, because they're probably inflating something as you read this.

3: Bankers will always get paid. This should be obvious. Those who have decided to become bankers have done so, in part, to get a big paycheck. Whether it's fair in the eyes of society is irrelevant. Of course it is easy to argue that a banker (or trader or risk manager) shouldn't get paid in seven figures and it's difficult for any banker to mount a compelling defense. But in some ways, it doesn't matter: Wall Street and the City have a long tradition of paying, and that will continue. It doesn't matter what a "pay czar" says, or what the politicians say, or even what the shareholders say. Sure, more compensation may be given in the form of restricted stock and may be subject to some claw-backs, but seven figures will still be seven figures (and, frankly, if you are working at Citibank while its trading at $3.50/share, you will be really, really, really happy to get paid in stock). This means bankers will have every incentive to generate as much revenue as possible, and some of that revenue will invariably come from risky business – though hopefully wise, rather than dumb, risky business. Risky business will multiply (especially during the bubble phase of the next market cycle) and the stage will be set for the next blowup. Some CEOs and bankers will get clawed back when the balloon goes up, but by then the damage will have been done. MP Thurso might want to stuff the genie back in the bottle, maybe returning to the Dickensian merchant banking days of old: "*The problem is that the City thought of itself as the masters rather than the servants of commerce, and that we have actually moved from the old-fashioned, traditional British banking model...to taking in a great deal of the American model, that greed is good and short-termism, and above all we need a return to a culture which is more of the old and traditional and less of the new.*"[17] Ain't gonna happen.

4: Lobbyists will always be powerful. Lobbyists serve a very specific purpose: they use their access to try and convince legislators or other political powers that certain things should or shouldn't be done on behalf of some constituency – whatever constituency. They get paid handsomely to pull the right levers, and they tend to be effective in shaping the political agenda of whatever party happens to be in power. Attempts to limit or curtail the influence of lobbyists have regularly failed, certainly in the US, meaning they have become an entrenched part of the political power scene. Where money is at stake, there will be lobbyists, and where lobbyists are involved, there will be a push for power. This is certainly the case when it comes to bank lobbyists – we may expect them to be front and center in any issues that will impact their bank clients: too much regulation, too many restrictions on their activities, attempts to rein in compensation, and the like, will all be countered by teams of highly paid, highly skilled representatives – who will always retain their power, and may indeed be able to "persuade" pliable politicians on the "correct" way to cast their votes. And even though new regulatory barriers will be erected to deal with the fallout from this crisis, you may be sure that the lobbyists will be battling to undo some or all once the ink is dry.

5: Politicians will always be political. We must accept the fact that politicians are a necessary evil. They are almost certainly less popular than bankers among the public at large, which is no mean feat. As much as we might not want to have our representatives, senators, members, or executive leaders in a position of power, we are stuck with them. And that means we can expect all manner of ignorance and nonsense in the years to come, including statements, actions, legislation, and even executive orders that run contrary to common sense, or place us all on a dangerous path. The record of failed oversight and legislative screwups impacting the global banking system dates back many, many years, well before the current crisis (e.g., deregulating the savings and loan industry and secondary bank industry, eliminating Glass-Steagall, permitting lower capital to be held against risky products, etc.), and there is nothing to suggest that this will change in the future: politicians will be playing up to their constituents or trading votes and cutting backroom deals in order to promote or block law and regulation. And that means we can expect more disasters from the political wing.

6: Regulators will never be totally up to the task. Regulators – can't live with 'em, can't live without 'em. They mean well, but most just don't get it, and unfortunately never will. Who works at regulatory agencies? Often it's those that can't work at the very institutions they are regulating. I know that sounds harsh and perhaps a bit unkind, but it is the unfortunate truth. As a general rule, the rank and file don't have the same level of skills one might find in a bank, meaning they will always be a step or two behind. And that means they won't be able to keep up with the sharper bankers and will be forever regulating to yesterday's problem rather than tomorrow's. Ron Paul: *"Immediately after a problem in the banking industry comes to light, the media and Congress inevitably blame it on regulators who were 'asleep at the switch.' Yet most politicians continue to believe that giving more power to the very regulators whose incompetence (or worse) either caused or contributed to the problem somehow will prevent future crises!"*[18] And so it has been with this crisis. Sanio was equally realistic about the whole matter: *"Sherlock Holmes' successful business model of knowing what others do not is beyond the means of financial supervisors."*[19]

7: Everyone will always want a good deal. Fundamentally, we all want to feel like we're getting a good deal – whatever that deal might be: investors want better returns, homeowners want cheaper mortgages, companies want lower financing costs, retirees want richer annuities. Greed, or self-interest, is compelling and prevalent – pretty much everyone (except some small handful of do-gooders) wants to cash in. Bankers are in charge of cooking up these good deals, always thinking about the next big thing – usually something that creates risk that has to be managed or transferred. If people were satisfied with not having the next good deal the system would have a lot less risk... and would be in better shape to keep things safer. But that's not the way it is.

8: No one really pays attention to the very rich pickings of history. In fact, it's a shame that more of us don't learn from these lessons, because everything we've seen in the latest crisis is just some variation on past disasters. Every crisis is an expensive and wrenching exercise, for everyone: so why not try to analyze, dissect, and overlay, so that the next one isn't as severe? It seems obvious, but it won't happen. Most of us will ignore these past lessons for the reasons mentioned immediately above: the collective forces of 1 to 7 far outweigh any wisdom that can be drawn from history. Think about it: how many bankers, regulators, lobbyists, politicians, rating analysts fundamentally recalibrated themselves after the Japanese bank, LDC, S&L, Russia, dot-com, etc., crises? I'm not talking about cosmetic changes that make it appear changes have been implemented, I'm talking about really fundamental, structural changes. Obviously not very many, because almost everyone suffered from, or contributed to, the latest disaster – a disaster measured with a "t" in the loss column. In 2004, recalling the US S&L disaster of the late 1980s, Greenspan told an audience that *"[t]he managers of these surviving organizations had deeply impressed upon them anew the need to manage risks, to control costs, to build capital and reserves, and generally to focus on the lessons of banking history."*[20] They obviously did none of those things, since a decade after the end of the S&L crisis they had started building up excesses and ignoring controls. He also noted that *"as time passes, more and more bank managers will not have the first-hand memories of times of banking stress."*[21] No particular fear of that happening, if we experience a fresh round of financial dislocations every few years! In fact, memories are very short, especially when the markets are marching toward new highs, economies are rebounding, employment is on the rise, home prices are strengthening, pensions are being replenished...

I suppose all of this sounds a bit cynical – though I would prefer to consider it "realistic." If we dissect any of the past crises we see some, usually all, of these forces at work. So why should we believe that anything will be different in the future, when we are so heavily dependent on some unpredictable intangibles, like human behavior, self-interest, politics, and assumptions? Buiter observed that *"[f]or three years [those hurt] will withdraw. That is the half-life of memory in the financial markets."*[22] I can argue about whether its two, three, or five years, but the point is correct.

When?

Trying to answer "when" is, of course, an attempt to answer the multibillion, or perhaps multitrillion, dollar question. If any of us knew, then we would start preparing. Or, if we were smart enough, we would actually try to profit from it, like some of folks I mentioned earlier. The one thing to remember is what Taleb has made clear – there are more black swans out in the lake than we might like to believe. The tails of the distribution are fatter, the unthinkable happens more often. Which means the next disaster will happen sooner than we think (and it'll be bigger than we think), regardless of all the so-called "fixes" that our politicians and regulators have, or may, put in place.

Unfortunately, it's impossible to say precisely when the next disaster will occur. It may not happen next year or the year after, and maybe not even in five years. But it certainly won't be decades or generations from now. Those days are over. It's quite possible – perhaps even certain – that we are already in the process of building toward the next disaster. The global low interest rate environment that often features in the aftermath of a crisis provides the kindling for the next crisis. And despite declarations by central bankers that they will be "super vigilant" in the future so as to avoid a repeat, we know that they don't (always, usually, ever) get it right.

One thing is sure: when the next crisis appears, it will impact multiple countries and markets very quickly. We live in a world where everything is connected and information is distributed instantaneously – the transmission of a crisis from market A to market B is so much easier now than during the Panic of 1907 or the Great Depression. Darling: *"in the past if an American bank started getting deeper and deeper into the sub-prime mire, that might have been a problem for an American state of the United States, it is now a problem for us within weeks."*[23] That is the "new normal." Fasten your seatbelts – for whenever the next one hits.

What will it look like?

So, what will the next one will look like? Surely it won't be bad mortgages in Las Vegas – right? We've already seen that one, so it can't happen again. Right? Don't be so sure – remember rule 8. But it will probably take a few years for bad mortgage lending practices to vanish from memory, so it's not going to be the next thing that hits us. But something else will.

We've seen lots of different crises in the past, coming from all manner of forces and catalysts. As I mentioned earlier, in the past few years alone the trigger events have been as varied as floating rate loans to the emerging markets, energy sector loans, commercial real estate loans, blue chip stocks/portfolio insurance, junk bonds, the Mexican peso, the Thai baht, Russian rouble government bonds, highly leveraged hedge funds, dot-com stocks, subprime mortgages, leveraged loans. Pretty much any asset class or any market sector is fair game, and of course it's hard to know exactly which one's going to hit next.

Of course what we need to remember is the dominos. It almost doesn't matter which asset or sector serves as the catalyst – the dominos can topple in any (seemingly random) way, with a reach that will unfortunately still startle us. So, if the first domino to go is the Latvian government bond market, it may very quickly wind its way into Scandinavian bonds and equities, then Eurozone bonds, then emerging market stocks, and then US stocks, dragging down bank shares again. Or, if the first domino is US credit card debt, it is easy to imagine a whole stack off dominos toppling in response – which ones, and in what sequence, has to be examined. Or, heaven forbid, if the first domino is the almost inevitable downgrade of US Treasury Bonds to AA, hang on…lots and lots of dominos will fall. The lesson from this, and virtually every other, crisis centers on correlation: pretty much everything can head in the same direction at the same time during a period of stress, which makes the domino-toppling broader and deeper. Every asset class or sector is, theoretically, vulnerable. To figure out what the catalyst might be, look for the clues: look for leverage, look for excesses, look for the "crowded trade," look for the "me-too" business strategy, look for euphoria, look for a misbalance between risk and return, look for the man and woman on Main Street or High Street piling in to the next "sure thing."

So, what to do?

If the scenario I've described above is correct, what then should we do about it? Actually, the question isn't "should" but "can" – what *can* we do about it? Given that question, then the answer is – nothing. Let me preface my comments by noting that in the first instance we should try to do whatever we can do to make things less painful. But in the end we also need to be realistic – some, many, or most will get hurt, regardless of what we do.

Lipstick on the pig?

Treasury Secretary Geithner said in 2010 that *"the biggest challenge is to make sure we change the rules of the game so this doesn't happen again. That's the biggest challenge. That's the hardest challenge."*[24] In fact, that particular challenge comes on multiple fronts: figuring out what the right rule changes ought to be (substance, not form), getting everyone to agree to those rule changes, ensuring that they aren't so burdensome that the financial process becomes inefficient and expensive, making sure that there aren't too many loopholes that clever folks can slither through, and ensuring that there's sufficient firepower to enforce the rules.

Can all this be resolved successfully "so this doesn't happen again"? I don't think so, and I don't think we can prevent this from happening again. In fact, Geithner himself had to backtrack a bit, and admit that it's not possible to guarantee that it won't "happen again": *"we can't do that. But what we have an obligation to do is to make sure that we put in place rules here and around the world to make that much less likely.... Make the system much more stable. That's the obligation of governments."*[25] It's a noble goal, to be sure.

Again, it doesn't mean we can't try to change some things – but we should be realistic about our expectations and we shouldn't create false comfort. So, we can try to put in a few new regulations, like anticyclical capital, hard leverage limits for all risk-takers, minimum time and experience requirements for board members (and regulators!), regulatory audits of the rating agencies. But we should avoid piling on rules for the sake of trying to impress constituents. Even though Greenspan may have been wrong about the interest rate bubble, he's right about new rules: *"the appropriate policy response is not to bridle financial intermediation with heavy regulation...[t]he solutions for the financial-market failures revealed by the crisis are higher capital requirements and a wider prosecution of fraud – not increased micromanagement by government entities."*[26] And King: *"I find it very hard to think that we will solve the regulatory challenges by creating more committees, processes, etc. Committees are useful and they have their place and they are important, I am not saying we should not have them, but they are not the answer to fundamental challenges to regulation."*[27] In other words: *"[t]he conclusion I draw from that is there is a lot to be said for trying to build in very simple, very robust mechanisms to put some sand in the wheels of the expansion of the financial sector. Keep it simple."*[28] And a further cautionary note from Mayo: *"If you overdo the regulation, overdo the safeguards, money will leave and go elsewhere."*[29]

Sanio, for his part, said that *"even though supervisors have nerves of steel, one thing is clear: we do not want to face this kind of crisis again."*[30] Surely not, but of course we will. Here I note wise words from Corrigan: *"In one case you are hoping that the regulators are going to do a better job in the future than they did in the past. In the other case you are hoping that this radical or at least fundamental restructuring of the financial system is going to work. Either way you are hoping."*[31]

And Turner: *"I believe regulators, academics, governments and management were all seduced by a long boom and theories about 'the great moderation' and this self-equilibrating system. We know at the very least that it is not true and so we are looking for things, but we will not be perfect at finding them....We can increase the likelihood that we guard against that but we will never make it perfect."*[32] He expanded a bit more: *"I think we can do a better job than we did before the last crisis but we cannot do it perfectly.... because the probable distribution of future potential risks it is inherently uncertain."*[33] A similar view came from King: *"I think it is difficult to say there is one simple answer which means, if implemented, we can go away and forget about the problem. That will never be the case. Do we really think that we are going to come up with the answer that will prevent hundreds of years of banking crises, suddenly come to a halt? No, we are not going to be able to that. We can try to make it less likely, we can try to diminish the damage, we can try to get into a position where we can deal with the consequences more easily, but these are really fundamental questions about the nature of risk-taking in a market economy."*[34]

And we should try to get the central bankers to pay a bit more attention to how much cheap money is flowing into the system and how quickly the asset bubbles are inflating. Morgan Stanley's Roach believes central banks *"need to break their one-dimensional fixation on CPI-based inflation and also give careful consideration to the extremes of asset values."*[35] Further, *"[t]he current financial crisis is a wake-up call for modern-day central banking. The world can't afford to lurch from one bubble to another. The cost of neglect is an ever-mounting systemic risk that could pose a grave threat to an increasingly integrated global economy. The art and science of central banking is in desperate need of a major overhaul – before it's too late."*[36] Hedge fund manager George Soros had a similar view: *"it's generally accepted that the Fed tries to control core inflation, but not asset prices. I think that control of asset prices has to be an objective in order to prevent asset bubbles because they are so frequent."*[37] Correct – and yet there has been no evidence of this being seriously discussed, so don't expect much.

Of course, we can try to reduce the influence of lobbyists and we can ask the politicians to be constructive (or at least not destructive). And maybe we should introduce what I call the "hubris indicator" – a decidedly unscientific and informal way of measuring where we are in the next bubble phase. It works like this: by searching bank annual reports, media interviews, regulatory speeches, and other discussion documents in the public domain for certain key words, we can gain some idea of whether we are near a new bursting of the bubble and toppling of the dominos. Which key words? How about "leading edge," "intellectual capacity," "solid control foundation," "undoubted," "best-in-class," "maximizing returns," "optimized risk profile," "transparency," "transformational," and so on. When these appear with increasing frequency, the hubris indicator should be pointing toward the danger zone and protective action should be undertaken.

All of these fixes might, theoretically, take a little sharpness off the edge of the blade. But in the end we shouldn't fool ourselves into believing that such changes are really anything more than lipstick on the pig: they won't really prevent a crisis from happening. Why? For the eight reasons I've outlined above. Those are powerful forces that are almost certain to overwhelm any attempt to halt the onset of the next disaster. King is absolutely right: *"I asked the question rhetorically. I said, 'Are we really so much wiser than the financiers of the past?' The answer is we are not."*[38] Indeed we are probably not smarter than the Rothschilds, Barings, and Morgans of yesteryear – and yet the hubris surrounding all those that directly or tangentially touch the financial industry makes it sometimes seem as though we are.

I think the analogy to natural disasters is appropriate here. A hurricane, to take one example, is a devastating force of nature that is governed by its own properties, which forms and moves based on the physical environment around it – sea surface temperatures, wind speed, currents, location. There is nothing ex-ante we can do to stop the next hurricane from forming in the Atlantic and making its way toward land. It will strike at a location, and with an intensity, over which we have no control. We can, of course, set up some rules related to building codes and building materials so that structures can withstand hurricane force winds – though of course not every location has such codes. Given this, we know Miami (with codes) will fare a bit better than Kingston or Havana (without codes). We can also take out insurance policies to spread the risk of destruction amongst a broader population. These are all good, prudent measures – but they will never stop the hurricane from forming and slamming into the coastline. When it hits Miami or Kingston or Havana, some damage will occur, guaranteed. It may be bad or it may be really bad, and either way it'll be a painful experience for those involved. Same thing for the financial disaster: we can collectively take some preventative measures, but we will never stop the next financial hurricane from forming and slamming into the national or global economy.

Let 'em fail

Far more powerful than any of the remedial measures noted above is, I think, the specter of bankruptcy. That is perhaps the only way we can get risk-takers (who we need) to take wise, rather than dumb, risk. In fact, the only discipline the free market respects is the prospect of failure. If you can't succeed, you fail. Those operating in a free market capitalist system that is governed by the rule of law, private property, bankruptcy, and creditor rights must accept that there can be no bailouts. If we don't follow this edict, moral hazard will win out and future crises will invariably be larger rather than smaller. Every time there's a bailout of a major institution or sector it just builds up pressure for the next one – nothing is resolved! Think LTCM, think Japanese bad banks.

This means we must let the strong ones survive and let the weak ones perish. In fact, this isn't a particularly unique view, and actually happens every day, especially with small firms – both financial and nonfinancial. The sticky situation comes when it's no longer the small firms, but the big, systemically important, ones, and here we find mixed views. There are those who think bailouts of the big guys are justifiable if they can reduce the systemic knock-on effect – moral hazard be damned. Bailing out RBS, Bear, Fannie, Freddie, Citi, Northern Rock, IKB, AIG, Fortis, and others was necessary, because collapse of any one of them would have been catastrophic for everyone. Didn't Lehman prove that? Can you imagine the heartache that would've been averted if the FSA had let Barclays scoop up Lehman on September 15, instead of a few days later, post-filing?

And then there's the other camp – the one that says all of those firms should have gone down, and all those in a similar state in the future should go down. This group says that the concept of bankruptcy has to be reintroduced into our vocabulary, as it has been missing for at least 36 months. Soros' view: *"Each time, it's the authorities that bail out the market, or organize companies to do so. So the regulators have precedents they should be aware of."*[39] And yet, the bailouts seem to continue. Analyst Mayo: *"The B is for bankruptcy. We should allow firms to fail. The prudent should not have to subsidize the imprudent."*[40] JP Morgan's Dimon: *"[b]ut let me be clear: No institution, including our own, should be too big to fail."*[41] And Ron Paul: *"systemic fraud should not be tolerated. Some banks on Wall Street should fail. Fannie and Freddie should fail. They are perpetrating fraud against the people."*[42] Geithner agreed that *"any individual firm that puts itself in a position where it cannot survive without special assistance from the government must face the consequences of failure."*[43] And as Volcker has noted *"we want to make it credible that [banks] can fail."*[44] And how about nonbanks? *"Non-banks in my view by and large are not regulated as tightly as banks, but they're going to be subject to this resolution procedure. If they got in trouble, the theory is they will not be rescued, but they will have an orderly demise where I think of [it] as euthanasia rather than life support... [w]e have to kind of embed this in consciousness."*[45] This was echoed by five US Treasury Secretaries in a collective statement: *"[non-bank] firms and funds are and should also be free to compete and to innovate. They should, like other private businesses, also be free to fail without explicit or implicit taxpayer support."*[46] FDIC's Bair concurred: *"[w]e must impose market discipline by ending too big to fail."*[47] From Stiglitz: *"The result of the flawed incentives, perhaps even worse in the *aftermath of the crisis, can be called ersatz capitalism, with losses socialized and profits privatized; it is an economic system that is neither fair nor efficient."*[48] MP John McFall: *"I will tell you the politics, it is dead easy. You have got organisations which are too big to fail and the taxpayer helps them out, so until we get to the stage where there are not going to be any bank bailouts and the taxpayer is going to be off the hook then politics and banking have to go hand-in-hand."*[49]

Perhaps the most colorful version came from Kyle Bass, testifying before the Angelides Committee: *"if they fail, they need to be able to fail. In my testimony, I say, you know, capitalism without bankruptcy is like Christianity without hell. Right. There have to be consequences of excessive risk taking."*[50] James Grant's view was similar: *"capitalism without financial failure is not capitalism at all, but a kind of socialism for the rich."*[51] Then, to put it into terms that bankers can understand, he said: *"Let the senior financiers keep their salaries and bonuses, and let them do with their banks what they will. If, however, their bank fails, let the bankers themselves fail. Let the value of their houses, cars, yachts, paintings, etc. be assigned to the firm's creditors."*[52] In other words, move back to the partnership model of unlimited liability. From Bernanke: *"It is unacceptable that large firms that the government is now compelled to support to preserve financial stability were among the greatest risk-takers during the boom period."*[53] So, Ben, let 'em fail. Risk-taking is fine and should be encouraged by those with (at least ostensibly) the skills and resources – but if they get it wrong, then they need to go under. This view needs to be agreed upon and implemented, because until then we have twisted incentives. The only way to try and inject some discipline is to remove the bailout net – perhaps that is the most effective rule that can be implemented in advance of the next disaster.

And there you have it. This crisis – a crisis born of bad behavior and bad decisions enacted by a number of players – has been a wrenching experience. It has touched people in all walks of life directly and indirectly, and it has revealed the very dark side of banking...and regulation, politics, and personal responsibility. It should serve as a significant cautionary note for us all and I live in hope that we won't ignore its powerful lessons. But I'm also realistic enough to realize that this is part of the pattern of who we are and how we live and work. The battle rages on...so get ready for the next one.

Notes

Prologue: Crisis redux

1. Banks, E. (2004). *The Failure of Wall Street*. London: Palgrave Macmillan, p.280.

1 A quick recap

1. http://www.federalreserve.gov/BOARDDOCS/Speeches/2004/20041005/default.htm
2. *Wall Street Journal*, February 9, 2009.
3. http://www.lewrockwell.com/paul/paul166.html
4. http://www.lewrockwell.com/paul/paul526.html
5. http://motherjones.com/mojo/2010/01/work-begins-pecora-pt-ii?utm_source=feedburner&utm_medium=feed&utm_campaign=Feed%3A+Motherjones%2Fmojoblog+%28MotherJones.com+%7C+MoJoBlog%29
6. Treasury Select Committee, EV366.
7. http://money.cnn.com/galleries/2007/fortune/0708/gallery.crisiscounsel.fortune/9.html
8. http://motherjones.com/mojo/2010/01/work-begins-pecora-pt-ii?utm_source=feedburner&utm_medium=feed&utm_campaign=Feed%3A+Motherjones%2Fmojoblog+%28MotherJones.com+%7C+MoJoBlog%29
9. http://thefinanser.co.uk/fsclub/2009/09/quotes-of-the-crisis.html
10. http://www.mbaa.org/NewsandMedia/PressCenter/51336.htm
11. http://www.aba.com/NR/rdonlyres/222CE044-577A-11D5-AB84-00508B95258D/49940/BradRockStatementFINAL.pdf
12. http://www.fcic.gov/hearings/pdfs/2010-0113-Transcript.pdf, p.65.
13. http://www.sajaforum.org/2008/11/business-vikram-pandit-on-charlie-rose.html
14. http://www.fcic.gov/hearings/pdfs/2010-0113-Transcript.pdf, p.32.
15. Treasury Select Committee, EV112.
16. http://www.lewrockwell.com/paul/paul376.html
17. http://www.npr.org/templates/story/story.php?storyId=101751604
18. http://banking.senate.gov/public/index.cfm?FuseAction=Hearings.Testimony&Hearing_ID=3699770d-9c39-4aab-9b6a-7aec8941fe9b&Witness_ID=e58834e0-6d91-4bfb-8a45-7a93bcbcd073
19. Treasury Select Committee, EV241.
20. http://oversight.house.gov/images/stories/Hearings/110th_Congress/Fannie_Freddie/Testimony_Raines.pdf
21. http://commdocs.house.gov/committees/bank/hba92628.000/hba92628_0f.htm, p.157.
22. *Wall Street Journal*, February 9, 2009.
23. http://www.publications.parliament.uk/pa/cm200910/cmselect/cmtreasy/uc261-vii/uc26102.htm. Contents reflect the uncorrected version, not yet formally approved.
24. http://www.imf.org/External/Pubs/FT/GFSR/2006/01/pdf/chp2.pdf

25. http://www.imf.org/External/Pubs/FT/GFSR/2006/01/pdf/chp2.pdf
26. http://www.ustreas.gov/press/releases/hp350.htm
27. http://www.fcic.gov/hearings/pdfs/2010-0409-Lockhart.pdf
28. http://www.fcic.gov/hearings/pdfs/2010-0113-Transcript.pdf, p.60.
29. http://oversight.house.gov/images/stories/documents/20081023100525.pdf
30. *Wall Street Journal*, "A Churchillian Defense of the Markets," February 13, 2010.
31. Treasury Select Committee, EV241.
32. http://business.timesonline.co.uk/tol/business/columnists/article2358402.ece
33. http://www.independent.co.uk/news/uk/politics/this-is-the-worst-recession-for-over-100-years-1605367.html
34. http://www.bafin.de/cln_179/nn_992932/SharedDocs/Downloads/EN/Service/Jahresberichte/2008/annualreport__08__vorwuinh,templateId=raw,property=publicationFile.pdf/annualreport_08_vorwuinh.pdf
35. http://www.fsa.gov.uk/pubs/other/turner_review.pdf
36. http://news.bbc.co.uk/2/hi/asia-pacific/7628495.stm
37. http://www.nytimes.com/2008/09/20/business/worldbusiness/20yen.html
38. http://www.nytimes.com/2008/09/20/business/worldbusiness/20yen.html
39. http://business.timesonline.co.uk/tol/business/industry_sectors/banking_and_finance/article2441754.ece
40. http://business.timesonline.co.uk/tol/business/industry_sectors/banking_and_finance/article2817746.ece
41. http://www.qfinance.com/quotes/boom-and-bust
42. http://forums.hannity.com/showthread.php?t=901301
43. ibid.
44. Ibid.
45. http://uk.reuters.com/article/idUKL2561340920080526
46. *New York Times*, September 25, 2008.
47. http://www.number10.gov.uk/Page17114
48. http://www.allbusiness.com/finance/408959-1.html
49. http://www.house.gov/apps/list/hearing/financialsvcs_dem/stiglitz.pdf
50. http://news.bbc.co.uk/2/hi/business/7658277.stm
51. http://www.number10.gov.uk/Page17114
52. http://www.swissinfo.ch/eng/Swiss_bank_bailout_plan_announced.html?cid=5326
53. http://www.spiegel.de/international/germany/0,1518,627935,00.html
54. http://www.telegraph.co.uk/finance/financetopics/financialcrisis/3190311/Banking-bail-out-France-unveils-360bn-package.html
55. Ibid.
56. http://www.publications.parliament.uk/pa/cm200910/cmselect/cmtreasy/uc261-iv/uc26102.htm. Contents reflect the uncorrected version, not yet formally approved.
57. http://motherjones.com/politics/2010/01/financial-crisis-wall-street-anger
58. *Wall Street Journal*, "Blasting the Bailout Blues," May 13, 2010.
59. http://banking.senate.gov/public/index.cfm?FuseAction=Hearings.Testimony&Hearing_ID=8e6b5806-3d70-447b-a823-bc4f3335a13f&Witness_ID=845ef046-9190-4996-8214-949f47a096bd
60. http://www.house.gov/apps/list/hearing/financialsvcs_dem/stiglitz.pdf
61. http://www.bis.org/review/r090603a.pdf
62. http://www.newsweek.com/id/216214?from=rss
63. http://www.europarl.europa.eu/document/activities/cont/201002/20100226ATT69696/20100226ATT69696EN.pdf

64. http://www.sbs.com.au/dateline/story/transcript/id/600336/n/Interview-with-Christine-Lagarde
65. http://www.guardian.co.uk/politics/audio/2008/oct/27/vince-cable-liberal-democrats
66. http://www.telegraph.co.uk/news/newstopics/theroyalfamily/3386353/The-Queen-asks-why-no-one-saw-the-credit-crunch-coming.html
67. http://www.dailyfinance.com/story/british-economists-to-the-queen-sorry-mlady-for-that-financia/19111698/
68. http://uk.reuters.com/article/idUKL2561340920080526
69. http://www.bloomberg.com/apps/news?pid=newsarchive&sid=arBvX8ylcQdM
70. http:// www.fcic.gov/hearings/pdfs/2010–0113-Blankfein.pdf
71. http://www.standardandpoors.com/servlet/Testimony of Deven Sharma.
72. http://www.fcic.gov/hearings/pdfs/2010–0407-Greenspan.pdf
73. http://banking.senate.gov/public/index.cfm?FuseAction=Hearings.Statement&Statement_ID=6c0d898a-4432–403e-95b1-bb6f51f3d34d
74. http://www.nybooks.com/articles/archives/2008/may/15/the-financial-crisis-an-interview-with-george-soro/
75. http://www.cato.org/pub_display.php?pub_id=9696
76. http://www.usagold.com/amk/usagoldmarketupdate082707.html
77. http://www.lewrockwell.com/paul/paul376.html
78. Treasury Select Committee, EV91.
79. http://www.independent.co.uk/news/uk/politics/this-is-the-worst-recession-for-over-100-years-1605367.html
80. Treasury Select Committee, EV311.
81. Treasury Select Committee, EV312.
82. http://www.bis.org/review/r090615a.pdf
83. http://money.cnn.com/2010/01/13/news/economy/Bank_CEO/
84. Krugman, Paul (2009). *The Return of Depression Economics and the Crisis of 2008*. W.W. Norton Company Limited. ISBN 978–0–393–07101–6.
85. http://www.europarl.europa.eu/document/activities/cont/201002/20100226ATT69696/20100226ATT69696EN.pdf
86. http://www.roubini.com/roubini-monitor/255627/the_worst_economic_and_financial_crisis...
87. http://abcnews.go.com/GMA/timothy-geithner-economy-diane-sawyer-interview-treasury-secretary/story?id=8569713&page=4
88. http://www.ny.frb.org/newsevents/speeches/2006/gei060914.html
89. Treasury Select Committee, EV366.
90. Treasury Select Committee, EV310.
91. http://commentsfromleftfield.com/2008/09/larry-kudlow-blames-liberals-in-congress-for-mortgage-crisis
92. Congressional Testimony, Report on The Risks of Financial Modeling, VaR and the Economic Breakdown, September 2009.
93. http://www.fcic.gov/hearings/pdfs/2010–0407-Greenspan.pdf
94. Ibid.
95. U.S. Department of Housing and Urban Development, The National Homeownership Strategy: Partners in the American Dream, May 1995, section 4, pp. 4, 5, 10.
96. http://www.fcic.gov/hearings/pdfs/2010–0113-Blankfein.pdf
97. *Wall Street Journal*, "What About Fan and Fred Reform?", May 4, 2010.
98. *Wall Street Journal*, "Fannie and Freddie Amnesia", April 20, 2010.
99. Treasury Select Committee, EV91.

100. http://www.fcic.gov/hearings/pdfs/2010-0113-Transcript.pdf, p.114.
101. http://www.fcic.gov/hearings/pdfs/2010-0114-Bair.pdf
102. http://www.fcic.gov/hearings/pdfs/2010-0114-Bair.pdf
103. http://www.aba.com/NR/rdonlyres/222CE044-577A-11D5-AB84-00508-B95258D/49940/BradRockStatementFINAL.pdf
104. http://www.fcic.gov/hearings/pdfs/2010-0113-Transcript.pdf, p.65.
105. http://www.publications.parliament.uk/pa/cm200910/cmselect/cmtreasy/uc261-vi/uc26102.htm Contents reflect the uncorrected version, not yet formally approved.
106. http://www.fcic.gov/hearings/pdfs/2010-0113-Moynihan.pdf
107. http://motherjones.com/mojo/2010/01/work-begins-pecora-pt-ii?utm_source=feedburner&utm_medium=feed&utm_campaign=Feed%3A+Motherjones%2Fmojoblog+%28MotherJones.com+%7C+MoJoBlog%29
108. http://freddiemac.com/investors/ar/2007/03.htm
109. Shiller, Robert J. (2008). *The Subprime Solution*. Princeton, NJ: Princeton University Press, p.6.
110. http://commentsfromleftfield.com/2008/09/larry-kudlow-blames-liberals-in-congress-for-mortgage-crisis
111. Treasury Select Committee, EV41.
112. Treasury Select Committee, EV294.
113. http://oversight.house.gov/images/stories/documents/20081023100438.pdf
114. http://oversight.house.gov/images/stories/documents/20081023100505.pdf
115. http://oversight.house.gov/images/stories/documents/20081023100505.pdf
116. http://www.bis.org/review/r090710a.pdf
117. http://www.publications.parliament.uk/pa/cm200910/cmselect/cmtreasy/uc261-vii/uc26102.htm. Contents reflect the uncorrected version, not yet formally approved.
118. http://www.bafin.de/nn_992932/SharedDocs/Downloads/EN/Service/Jahresberichte/2007/annualreport__07__vorwuinh,templateId=raw,property=publicationFile.pdf/annualreport_07_vorwuinh.pdf
119. http://www.fcic.gov/hearings/pdfs/2010-0113-Transcript.pdf, p.116.
120. Treasury Select Committee, EV14.
121. http://www.dw-world.de/dw/article/0,,3669958,00.html
122. http://online.wsj.com/article/SB10001424052748704608104575218071029226354.html
123. Ibid.
124. Treasury Select Committee, EV269.
125. Treasury Select Committee, EV271.
126. http://www.washingtonpost.com/wp-dyn/content/article/2010/04/22/AR2010042204208.html
127. http://www.publications.parliament.uk/pa/cm200910/cmselect/cmtreasy/uc261-iv/uc26102.htm. Contents reflect the uncorrected version, not yet formally approved.
128. http://www.reuters.com/article/idUSL795389120090416
129. http://www.wrap20.com/files/At_Davos_Bankers_Face_Global_Ire_-_WSJ.pdf
130. Treasury Select Committee, EV240.

2 The US banks got it wrong...

1. http://www.guardian.co.uk/business/2010/jan/13/financial-crisis-inquiry-mistakes

2. Treasury Select Committee, EV99.
3. http://www.bloomberg.com/apps/news?pid=20601087&sid=aDgzfxGflUMg&pos=2
4. Ibid.
5. http://www.bafin.de/nn_992932/SharedDocs/Downloads/EN/Service/Jahresberichte/2007/annualreport__07__vorwuinh,templateId=raw,property=publicationFile.pdf/annualreport_07_vorwuinh.pdf
6. http://www.time.com/time/business/article/0,8599,1853531,00.html
7. Banks, E. (2004). *The Failure of Wall Street*. London: Palgrave Macmillan, p.167.
8. http://www.ny.frb.org/newsevents/speeches/2006/gei060914.html
9. http://oversight.house.gov/images/stories/documents/20081023100438.pdf
10. http://www.fcic.gov/hearings/pdfs/2010-0407-Greenspan.pdf
11. Congressional Testimony, Report on The Risks of Financial Modeling, VaR and the Economic Breakdown, September 2009.
12. http://www.rte.ie/news/2009/0209/mccreevyc.html
13. Congressional Testimony, Report on The Risks of Financial Modeling, VaR and the Economic Breakdown, September 2009.
14. http://www.fsa.gov.uk/pubs/other/turner_review.pdf
15. Congressional Testimony, Report on The Risks of Financial Modeling, VaR and the Economic Breakdown, September 2009.
16. http://online.wsj.com/article/SB123785319919419659.html
17. http://oversight.house.gov/images/stories/documents/20081113120556.pdf
18. Testimony, House Committee on Financial Services, January 22, 2010.
19. http://www.ml.com/media/50152.pdf
20. http://www.ml.com/annualmeetingmaterials/2006/ar/letter2.asp
21. http://www.ml.com/annualmeetingmaterials/2006/ar/pdfs/annual_report_2006_complete.pdf, p.18.
22. http://www.ml.com/annualmeetingmaterials/2006/ar/letter4.asp
23. http://www.ml.com/media/73056.pdf
24. http://seekingalpha.com/article/53642-great-conference-call-moments-mike-mayo-deutsche-bank
25. Ibid.
26. http://www.msnbc.msn.com/id/21450003/
27. http://money.cnn.com/magazines/fortune/fortune_archive/2007/11/26/101234162/index.htm
28. http://www.bloomberg.com/apps/news?pid=20601087&sid=aap3.z0pzEIc&refer=home
29. http://www.npr.org/templates/story/story.php?storyId=15768986
30. http://www.bloomberg.com/apps/news?pid=20601087&sid=aap3.z0pzEIc&refer=home
31. http://findarticles.com/p/articles/mi_m0EIN/is_2007_Oct_30/ai_n27425894?tag=content;col1
32. http://money.cnn.com/2007/10/30/news/companies/merrill_oneal/index.htm?postversion=2007103116
33. http://www.ml.com/media/14050.pdf
34. http://www.ml.com/annualmeetingmaterials/2007/ar/pdfs/annual_report_2007_complete.pdf
35. http://www.generationaldynamics.com/cgi-bin/D.PL?xct=gd.e080731
36. *Wall Street Journal*, January 18, 2008, p.C1.
37. *Wall Street Journal*, January 18, 2008, p.C1.
38. Ibid., p.2.
39. Bloomberg, April 24, 2008.

40. http://www.ml.com/annualmeetingmaterials/2007/ar/letter3.asp
41. Gasparino, C. (2009). *The Sellout*. New York: Harper, p.417.
42. Ibid.
43. http://online.wsj.com/article/SB124080394182958429.html
44. http://blogs.reuters.com/summits/2009/11/18/thain-says-put-shareholders-first/?utm_source=feedburner&utm_medium=feed&utm_campaign=Feed%3A+reuters%2Fblogs%2Freuters-dealzone+%28Blogs+%2F+US+%2F+Reuters+Dealzone%29
45. http://media.corporate-ir.net/media_files/irol/71/71595/reports/2006_AR.pdf
46. http://groc.edgeboss.net/download/groc/transfer/testimony.of.mr.kenneth.d.lewis.pdf
47. http://oversight.house.gov/images/stories/documents/20090715180923.pdf
48. http://www.federalreserve.gov/newsevents/testimony/bernanke20090625a.htm
49. http://oversight.house.gov/images/stories/Hearings/Committee_on_Oversight/121109_Boa-ML/TESTIMONY-Bair.pdf
50. http://oversight.house.gov/images/stories/documents/20090616185204.pdf
51. http://oversight.house.gov/images/stories/documents/20090616185111.pdf
52. http://oversight.house.gov/images/stories/Hearings/Committee_on_Oversight/121109_Boa-ML/Kucinich_Opening_statement_Final_.pdf
53. http://www.bloomberg.com/apps/news?pid=20601087&sid=arKmiVGd8ucU&pos=5
54. http://www.fcic.gov/hearings/pdfs/2010-0113-Transcript.pdf, p.62.
55. http://www.fcic.gov/hearings/pdfs/2010-0113-Moynihan.pdf
56. http://www.bloomberg.com/apps/news?pid=newsarchive&sid=aQ4gD_50jmjA
57. http://media.www.sternopportunity.com/media/storage/paper697/news/2004/10/26/Features/An.Interview.With.Citigroup.Ceo.Chuck.Prince-782954-page2.shtml
58. http://www.citigroup.com/citi/fin/data/ar06c_en.pdf,p.4.
59. Ibid., p.5.
60. http://dealbook.blogs.nytimes.com/2007/07/10/citi-chief-on-buyout-loans-were-still-dancing/
61. http://www.icis.com/blogs/chemicals-and-the-economy/2007/08/interesting-quotes.html
62. http://www.fcic.gov/hearings/pdfs/2010-0407-Bowen.pdf
63. Ibid.
64. http://paul.kedrosky.com/archives/2007/10/16/mike_mayo_heart.html
65. http://money.cnn.com/2007/11/08/news/companies/citigroup_alwaleed.fortune/index.htm
66. Ibid.
67. Ibid.
68. Ibid.
69. http://www.fcic.gov/hearings/pdfs/2010-0408-Prince.pdf
70. http://www.fcic.gov/hearings/pdfs/2010-0408-Prince.pdf
71. http://www.pbs.org/nbr/site/onair/transcripts/ex_citigroup_ceo_apologizes_100408/
72. http://www.nytimes.com/2010/04/09/business/09panel.html?ref=business
73. http://www.fcic.gov/hearings/pdfs/2010-0408-Rubin.pdf
74. http://www.fcic.gov/hearings/pdfs/2010-0407-Bushnell.pdf
75. http://www.citigroup.com/citi/fin/data/ar07c_en.pdf
76. http://www.citigroup.com/citi/fin/data/ar08c_en.pdf
77. http://www.sajaforum.org/2008/11/business-vikram-pandit-on-charlie-rose.html
78. http://cop.senate.gov/documents/testimony-030410-pandit.pdf
79. http://www.sajaforum.org/2008/11/business-vikram-pandit-on-charlie-rose.html

80. Treasury Select Committee, EV321.
81. Morgan Stanley 2005 Annual Report, p.4.
82. Morgan Stanley 2005 Annual Report, p.8.
83. Morgan Stanley 2006 Annual Report, p.5.
84. http://www.fcic.gov/hearings/pdfs/2010-0113-Mack.pdf
85. http://www.fcic.gov/hearings/pdfs/2010-0113-Mack.pdf
86. http://www.fcic.gov/hearings/pdfs/2010-0113-Transcript.pdf, p.69.
87. http://www.fcic.gov/hearings/pdfs/2010-0113-Transcript.pdf, p.52.
88. http://www.guardian.co.uk/business/2010/jan/13/financial-crisis-inquiry-mistakes
89. http://www.fcic.gov/hearings/pdfs/2010-0505-Cayne.pdf
90. http://www.fcic.gov/hearings/pdfs/2010-0505-Spector.pdf
91. http://www.fcic.gov/hearings/pdfs/2010-0505-Schwartz.pdf
92. http://online.wsj.com/article/SB119387369474078336.html
93. http://www.nytimes.com/2008/05/07/business/07bear.html?pagewanted=2&_r=1
94. Gasparino, p.337.
95. http://www.cnbc.com/id/23590249
96. http://www.fcic.gov/hearings/pdfs/2010-0505-Cayne.pdf
97. http://www.businessinsider.com/2008/9/chanos-what-bear-stearns-ceo-alan-schwartz-didn-t-tell-you-48-hours-before-firm-croaked
98. Ibid.
99. http://www.fcic.gov/hearings/pdfs/2010-0505-Molinaro.pdf
100. http://www.fcic.gov/hearings/pdfs/2010-0505-Molinaro.pdf
101. http://www.fcic.gov/hearings/pdfs/2010-0505-Schwartz.pdf
102. http://blogs.ft.com/gapperblog/2010/05/live-blog-jimmy-cayne-ex-bear-stearns-at-fcic/
103. http://files.shareholder.com/downloads/ONE/565875514x0x283417/92060ed3-3393-43a5-a3c1-178390c6eac5/2008_AR_Letter_to_shareholders.pdf, p.9.
104. Ibid.
105. http://blogs.ft.com/gapperblog/2010/05/live-blog-jimmy-cayne-ex-bear-stearns-at-fcic/
106. Wessel, D. (2009). *In Fed We Trust*. New York: Crown, p.194.
107. http://www.publications.parliament.uk/pa/cm200910/cmselect/cmtreasy/uc261-iv/uc26102.htm. Contents reflect the uncorrected version, not yet formally approved.
108. http://www2.goldmansachs.com/our_firm/investor_relations/financial_reports/annual_reports/2006/pdf/MDandA.pdf, p.31.
109. http://www2.goldmansachs.com/our-firm/investors/financials/archived/annual-reports/2007-annual-report.html
110. Ibid.
111. http://www.fcic.gov/hearings/pdfs/2010-0113-Transcript.pdf, p.35.
112. http://www2.goldmansachs.com/our-firm/investors/financials/current/annual-reports/2009-complete-annual.pdf
113. *Wall Street Journal*, "Investigators Interview Tourre," April 26, 2010.
114. *Wall Street Journal*, "Senate Readies Goldman Assault," April 27, 2010.
115. Ibid.
116. http://www2.goldmansachs.com/our-firm/investors/financials/current/annual-reports/2008-annual-report.html#/letter6
117. http://www.publications.parliament.uk/pa/cm200910/cmselect/cmtreasy/uc261-iv/uc26102.htm. Contents reflect the uncorrected version, not yet formally approved.

118. http://www.ft.com/cms/s/0/780d9d64-175d-11df-87f6-00144feab49a.html
119. http://www.businessinsider.com/lloyd-blankfein-says-he-is-doing-gods-work-2009-11
120. http://files.shareholder.com/downloads/ONE/565875514x0x86633/919253b5-8fda-4509-98a9-f601b21264fa/Letter_to_shareholders.pdf, p.3.
121. Ibid., p.5.
122. Ibid., p.10.
123. http://files.shareholder.com/downloads/ONE/565875514x0x184757/b3a93ea7-677a-4116-b7ba-69af38eed533/2007AR_LettertoShareholders.pdf, p.10.
124. Ibid.
125. Ibid., p.11.
126. *Wall Street Journal*, "Ex-WaMu Chief Blames the 'Club'," April 14, 2010.
127. http://money.cnn.com/2010/01/13/news/economy/Bank_CEO/
128. http://files.shareholder.com/downloads/ONE/565875514x0x283417/92060ed3-3393-43a5-a3c1-178390c6eac5/2008_AR_Letter_to_shareholders.pdf, p.14.
129. http://findarticles.com/p/news-articles/ceo-wire/mi_8092/is_20070823/countrywide-financial-ceo-interview/ai_n50674874/
130. http://vdare.com/Sailer/090622_mozilo.htm
131. *National Mortgage News*, "Mozilo: End Downpayment Requirement," February 17, 2003.
132. Ibid.
133. Ibid.
134. http://www.cnbc.com/id/20411403
135. Ibid.
136. Gasparino, p.322.
137. http://us.ft.com/ftgateway/superpage.ft?news_id=fto061320081427074808
138. *Wall Street Journal*, May 17, 2008.
139. Valukas Report 2, p.205.
140. http://oversight.house.gov/images/stories/Hearings/110th_Congress/Fuld_Statement.pdf
141. Valukas Report, p.7.
142. http://www.guardian.co.uk/business/2010/apr/21/lehman-brothers-dick-fuld-admits-mistakes
143. http://www.house.gov/apps/list/hearing/financialsvcs_dem/lee__4.20.10.pdf
144. http://www.house.gov/apps/list/hearing/financialsvcs_dem/fuld_4.20.10.pdf
145. http://www.house.gov/apps/list/hearing/financialsvcs_dem/fuld_4.20.10.pdf
146. http://www.house.gov/apps/list/hearing/financialsvcs_dem/valuks_4.20.10.pdf
147. Ibid.
148. Ibid.
149. Valukas Report, p.167.
150. Valukas Report, p.46.
151. http://nymag.com/daily/intel/2010/04/richard_fuld_still_insisting_t.htm
152. McDonald, L. and Robinson, P. (2009). *A Colossal Failure of Common Sense*. New York: Crown, p.307.
153. http://www.house.gov/apps/list/hearing/financialsvcs_dem/valuks_4.20.10.pdf
154. Wessel, *In Fed We Trust*, p.14.
155. Ibid., p.21.
156. http://money.cnn.com/2009/09/08/news/economy/geithner_lehman_bankruptcy.fortune/index.htm
157. Ibid., p.19.

158. Paulson, H. (2010). *On the Brink*. New York: Business Plus, p.210.
159. Ibid.
160. http://oversight.house.gov/images/stories/Hearings/110th_Congress/Fuld_Statement.pdf
161. http://inform.com/politics/french-minister-paulson-mistake-lehman-474793a
162. http://www.washingtonpost.com/wp-dyn/content/article/2008/10/09/AR2008100902842.html
163. http://www.nytimes.com/2008/10/01/business/worldbusiness/01global.html
164. http://money.cnn.com/2009/09/08/news/economy/geithner_lehman_bankruptcy.fortune/index.htm
165. http://money.cnn.com/2009/09/08/news/economy/geithner_lehman_bankruptcy.fortune/index.htm
166. Gasparino, p.317.
167. http://oversight.house.gov/images/stories/Hearings/110th_Congress/Fuld_Statement.pdf
168. http://oversight.house.gov/images/stories/Hearings/110th_Congress/Fuld_Statement.pdf
169. http://www.iimagazine.com/article.aspx?articleID=2356113
170. http://www.ezonlinedocuments.com/aig/2006/annual/HTML2/aig_ar2005_0004.htm, p.2.
171. Ibid., p.3.
172. Ibid., p.39.
173. Ibid.,p.39.
174. Gretchen Morgenson. (2008). "Behind Insurer's Crisis, Blind Eye to a Web of Risk." *New York Times*, September 28.
175. http://www.ezonlinedocuments.com/aig/2007/annual/HTML2/aig_ar2006_0036.htm, p.34.
176. http://oversight.house.gov/images/stories/documents/20081007101007.pdf
177. http://oversight.house.gov/images/stories/documents/20081007101007.pdf
178. AIG, 2007 Annual Report, 10-K.
179. http://www.ezodproxy.com/AIG/2008/AR2007/HTML2/aig_ar2007_0007.htm, p.5.
180. Ibid., p.10.
181. http://oversight.house.gov/images/stories/documents/20081007101054.pdf
182. Ibid.
183. http://oversight.house.gov/images/stories/documents/20081007101054.pdf
184. http://www.businessweek.com/news/2010-03-13/aig-was-unprepared-for-financial-crisis-former-top-lawyer-says.html
185. Ibid.
186. Ibid.
187. Wessel, *In Fed We Trust*, p.194.
188. Ibid.
189. http://www.nypost.com/p/news/business/what_congress_missed_at_aig_geithner_H1rhDxyH4vrcOMONwmkjxO
190. http://www.publications.parliament.uk/pa/cm200910/cmselect/cmtreasy/uc261-iv/uc26102.htm. Contents reflect the uncorrected version, not yet formally approved.
191. http://www.house.gov/apps/list/hearing/financialsvcs_dem/111-20.pdf
192. http://www.house.gov/apps/list/hearing/financialsvcs_dem/111-20.pdf
193. http://phx.corporate-ir.net/External.File?item=UGFyZW50SUQ9MTQ4OHxDaGlsZElEPS0xfFR5cGU9Mw==&t=1, p.1.

194. http://phx.corporate-ir.net/External.File?item=UGFyZW50SUQ9MTQ4OHxDaGls ZElEPS0xfFR5cGU9Mw==&t=1, p.4.
195. http://www.fcic.gov/hearings/pdfs/2010-0113-Transcript.pdf, p.100.

3 ... And so did the European banks

1. http://www.fcic.gov/hearings/pdfs/2010-0407-Greenspan.pdf
2. http://www.investis.com/reports/hsbc_ar_2006_en/report.php?type=1&zoom=1&submit.x=20&submit.y=9&page=8
3. Ibid.
4. Ibid.
5. http://www.investis.com/reports/hsbc_ar_2007_en/report.php?type=1&zoom=1&page=2ee0f764cf5dd3165539085710fb3324
6. Ibid.
7. http://www.investis.com/reports/hsbc_ar_2009_en/report.php?type=1&zoom=1&page=11
8. Ibid.
9. http://www.publications.parliament.uk/pa/cm200910/cmselect/cmtreasy/uc261-iv/uc26102.htm. Contents reflect the uncorrected version, not yet formally approved.
10. http://business.timesonline.co.uk/tol/business/industry_sectors/banking_and_finance/article1356470.ece
11. http://files.shareholder.com/downloads/RBS/838643498x0x306867/541f0576-e3c1-4926-819b-a44d4ec5cec2/FYR06.pdf, p.3.
12. Ibid., p.4.
13. http://files.shareholder.com/downloads/RBS/838643498x0x306838/976ea577-2bb7-4ff5-80b5-c9a74795a4d5/FYR07.pdf, p.7.
14. Ibid., p.5.
15. http://files.shareholder.com/downloads/RBS/838643498x0x306821/519951c0-9c5a-4437-82c2-41533bddd62a/interim2008.pdf, p.8.
16. http://www.telegraph.co.uk/finance/newsbysector/banksandfinance/3270367/Im-not-done-yet-says-Sir-Fred-Goodwin.html
17. Treasury Select Committee, EV247.
18. Treasury Select Committee, EV225.
19. http://www.fsa.gov.uk/pubs/other/turner_review.pdf
20. Treasury Select Committee, EV234.
21. Treasury Select Committee, EV223.
22. Treasury Select Committee, EV241.
23. Treasury Select Committee, EV223.
24. Treasury Select Committee, EV249.
25. Treasury Select Committee, EV259.
26. http://www.independent.co.uk/news/uk/politics/hint-of-arrogance-as-bankers-apologise-1605670.html
27. http://www.guardian.co.uk/business/2009/feb/10/bankers-apologise-to-mps
28. http://www.timesonline.co.uk/tol/news/politics/article5549514.ece
29. Treasury Select Committee, EV266.
30. Treasury Select Committee, EV259.
31. http://files.shareholder.com/downloads/RBS/838643498x0x306193/aed2c307-d2cb-43f3-9b16-6b5707a8ecc8/final_announcement_190109_us.pdf

32. http://www.publications.parliament.uk/pa/cm200910/cmselect/cmtreasy/uc259-i/uc25902.htm. Contents reflect the uncorrected version, not yet formally approved.
33. Treasury Select Committee, EV275.
34. http://www.investor.barclays.co.uk/results/2006/annualreport/annualreview2006/downloads/pdf2/group_chief_exec_review.pdf
35. Ibid., p.7.3
36. http://www.barclaysannualreport.com/downloads/full_annual_report.pdf
37. Ibid.
38. http://www.barclaysannualreport.com/ar2008/files/pdf/Annual_Report_2008.pdf
39. Ibid.
40. http://www.iimagazine.com/article.aspx?articleID=2356113
41. http://www.lloydsbankinggroup.com/media/pdfs/investors/2006/2006_HBOS_Review.pdf
42. http://www.lloydsbankinggroup.com/media/pdfs/investors/2006/2006_HBOS_Review.pdf
43. http://www.lloydsbankinggroup.com/media/pdfs/investors/2007/2007_HBOS_Review.pdf
44. http://www.lloydsbankinggroup.com/media/pdfs/investors/2008/2008_HBOS_R&A.pdf
45. http://www.lloydsbankinggroup.com/media/pdfs/investors/2008/2008_HBOS_R&A.pdf
46. Ibid., Treasury Select Committee, EV244.
47. Ibid., Treasury Select Committee, EV244.
48. Treasury Select Committee, EV227.
49. Ibid., Treasury Select Committee, EV237.
50. Ibid., Treasury Select Committee, EV235.
51. http://www.independent.co.uk/news/business/news/dismissed-executive-warned-hbos-of-risk-1606036.html
52. http://www.independent.co.uk/news/business/news/dismissed-executive-warned-hbos-of-risk-1606036.html
53. http://www.publications.parliament.uk/pa/cm200910/cmselect/cmtreasy/uc259-i/uc25902.htm. Contents reflect the uncorrected version, not yet formally approved.
54. Treasury Select Committee, EV376.
55. http://www.ubs.com/1/e/investors/annualreporting/archive.html, 2006 Annual Report.
56. Ibid.
57. http://www.nytimes.com/2008/04/06/business/06ubs.html
58. Treasury Select Committee, EV291.
59. http://www.nytimes.com/2008/04/06/business/06ubs.html
60. Ibid.
61. http://www.bloomberg.com/apps/news?pid=20601087&sid=aRivOg8LNsIc&dlbk
62. Ibid.
63. http://www.google.com/search?q=interview+with+UBS+rohner&hl=en&sa=2
64. http://www.swissinfo.ch/eng/Swiss_bank_bailout_plan_announced.html?cid=5326
65. http://www.euromoney.com/Article/2098544/Category/17/ChannelPage/0/Why-Rohner-left-UBShis-last-interview-as-UBS-CEO.html?p=1
66. http://business.timesonline.co.uk/tol/business/industry_sectors/banking_and_finance/article3658290.ece
67. http://www.ubs.com/1/e/investors/annualreporting/2008.html.
68. Ibid.

210 *Notes*

69. http://www.nytimes.com/2008/04/06/business/06ubs.html
70. http://annualreport.deutsche-bank.com/en/2006/ar/letterfromthechairmanofthemanagementboard.html
71. http://annualreport.deutsche-bank.com/en/2006/ar/stakeholders/clients/corporateandinvestmentbank/globalmarkets.html
72. http://annualreport.deutsche-bank.com/en/2006/ar/letterfromthechairmanofthemanagementboard.html
73. Ibid.
74. http://annualreport.deutsche-bank.com/en/2007/ar/letterfromthechairmanofthemanagementboard.html
75. Ibid.
76. Ibid.
77. http://annualreport.deutsche-bank.com/en/2008/ar/letterfromthechairmanofthemanagementboard.html
78. Ibid.
79. Ibid.
80. Ibid.
81. http://www.reports.fortis.com/2007/en/annualreview/messagefromtheboardofdirectors.html
82. http://www.reports.fortis.com/2007/en/annualreview/messagefromtheboardofdirectors.html
83. http://forums.anandtech.com/archive/index.php/t-192126.html
84. http://afp.google.com/article/ALeqM5iTlbxqsJZJ0_oYfCcQMDM-9LeDOA
85. http://afp.google.com/article/ALeqM5iTlbxqsJZJ0_oYfCcQMDM-9LeDOA
86. http://www.ft.com/cms/s/0/5ed92aae-e8c2–11dd-a4d0–0000779fd2ac.html
87. http://www.ft.com/cms/s/0/5ed92aae-e8c2–11dd-a4d0–0000779fd2ac.html
88. http://www.managementtoday.co.uk/search/article/463769/the-mt-interview-adam-applegarth/
89. http://business.timesonline.co.uk/tol/business/industry_sectors/banking_and_finance/article2451723.ece
90. http://companyinfo.northernrockassetmanagement.co.uk/downloads/results/res2006PR_AnnualReportAndAccounts.pdf, p.2.
91. Ibid., p.8.
92. Ibid., p.8.
93. http://business.timesonline.co.uk/tol/business/industry_sectors/banking_and_finance/article2441754.ece
94. http://www.house.gov/apps/list/hearing/financialsvcs_dem/yingling_-_aba.pdf
95. http://business.timesonline.co.uk/tol/business/industry_sectors/banking_and_finance/article2817746.ece
96. http://business.timesonline.co.uk/tol/business/industry_sectors/banking_and_finance/article2817746.ece
97. http://www.telegraph.co.uk/news/newstopics/politics/1570366/Northern-Rock-fiasco-could-have-been-avoided.html
98. http://www.telegraph.co.uk/finance/markets/2816256/Chris-Wood-the-man-who-predicted-the-subprime-crisis.html
99. http://www.telegraph.co.uk/finance/economics/2815968/Housing-market-crisis-for-UK-suggests-Christopher-Wood.html
100. http://www.telegraph.co.uk/finance/markets/2820093/How-sub-prime-foreclosed-an-American-dream.html

101. http://news.bbc.co.uk/2/hi/business/7036446.stm
102. http://www.telegraph.co.uk/finance/newsbysector/banksandfinance/2787050/FSA-chief-admits-to-Northern-Rock-errors.html
103. http://news.bbc.co.uk/2/hi/business/7036446.stm
104. Ibid.
105. http://www.telegraph.co.uk/finance/newsbysector/banksandfinance/2787050/FSA-chief-admits-to-Northern-Rock-errors.html
106. http://www.timesonline.co.uk/tol/comment/columnists/guest_contributors/article5548797.ece
107. http://www.dailymail.co.uk/news/article-517850/Financial-watchdog-boss-tried-gag-MP-warned-Northern-Rock-heading-disaster.html
108. http://companyinfo.northernrockassetmanagement.co.uk/downloads/2007_annual_report.pdf, p.3.
109. Treasury Select Committee, EV54
110. Ibid.
111. Ibid.
112. http://www.investis.com/reports/bbg_ar_2006_en/report.php?type=1&zoom=1&page=d8d17214e73196daa121f103e6906038
113. Ibid.
114. http://corporate.bbg.co.uk/~/media/Files/B/Bradford-And-Bingley-Corporate/pdf/results-and-publications/year-2007/ar2007.pdf, p.4.
115. Ibid., p.5.
116. Ibid.
117. http://corporate.bbg.co.uk/~/media/Files/B/Bradford-And-Bingley-Corporate/pdf/results-and-publications/year-2008/ar2008_03_04_09.pdf
118. Ibid.
119. Treasury Select Committee, EV41
120. Ibid., Treasury Select Committee, EV48
121. http://www.telegraph.co.uk/finance/newsbysector/banksandfinance/3378851/WestLB-becomes-latest-bank-to-tap-German-states-bail-out-fund.html
122. http://www.impactlab.com/2008/03/28/german-state-owned-banks-on-verge-of-collapse/
123. http://business.timesonline.co.uk/tol/business/industry_sectors/banking_and_finance/article2378952.ece
124. http://www.theatlantic.com/business/archive/2010/04/goldmans-victim-in-sec-case-was-a-yield-chaser/39464/
125. *Wall Street Journal*, April 22, 2010.
126. http://www.bloomberg.com/apps/news?pid=20601087&sid=aTdYazq1ex_c&refer=home
127. http://business.timesonline.co.uk/tol/business/industry_sectors/banking_and_finance/article2378952.ece
128. http://www.bloomberg.com/apps/news?pid=20601087&sid=aTdYazq1ex_c&refer=home
129. http://www.westlb.de/cms/sitecontent/westlb/westlb_de/en/wlb/ir/finanzinformationen/geschaeftsberichte/archiv/gb2006_1.-bin.acq/qual-SingleAttachment.Single.AttachmentAttachmentFile/WLBI2006e.pdf
130. http://www.bloomberg.com/apps/news?pid=20601087&sid=aTdYazq1ex_c&refer=home
131. http://www.reuters.com/article/idUSL1212000720071112

132. http://www.westlb.de/cms/sitecontent/westlb/westlb_de/en/wlb/ir/finanzinformationen/geschaeftsberichte/archiv/gb2007.-bin.acq/qual-SingleAttachment.Single.AttachmentAttachmentFile/GBWestLBK07e.pdf
133. http://www.telegraph.co.uk/finance/markets/2784104/German-bank-WestLB-to-slash-jobs.html
134. http://www.westlb.de/cms/sitecontent/westlb/westlb_de/en/wlb/ir/finanzinformationen/geschaeftsberichte/archiv/gb2007.-bin.acq/qual-SingleAttachment.Single.AttachmentAttachmentFile/GBWestLBK07e.pdf
135. http://www.politicalfriendster.com/showConnection.php?id1=7230&id2=7637
136. http://www.telegraph.co.uk/finance/markets/2784104/German-bank-WestLB-to-slash-jobs.html
137. http://business.timesonline.co.uk/tol/business/industry_sectors/banking_and_finance/article2378952.ece
138. http://www.iie.com/publications/opeds/oped.cfm?ResearchID=988
139. http://www.newsweek.com/id/201749
140. http://www.acus.org/new_atlanticist/financial-crisis-view-europe
141. *Wall Street Journal*, "Report on Iceland's Banking Collapse Blasts Ex-Officials," April 13, 2010.
142. Ibid.
143. Treasury Select Committee, EV14.
144. Treasury Select Committee, EV14.
145. Treasury Select Committee, EV271.

4 The Fannie and Freddie sinkhole

1. http://www.lewrockwell.com/paul/paul282.html
2. http://banking.senate.gov/public/index.cfm?FuseAction=Hearings.Testimony&Hearing_ID=0a0b4f0d-55bc-49ed-bb8b-18ba417fc3bf&Witness_ID=88d31047-c665-4405-bc57-701ac33882d4
3. http://www.fcic.gov/hearings/pdfs/2010-0409-Lockhart.pdf
4. http://www.nytimes.com/2008/08/05/business/05freddie.html
5. http://www.fcic.gov/hearings/pdfs/2010-0409-Mudd.pdf
6. Ibid.
7. http://georgewbush-whitehouse.archives.gov/news/releases/2008/10/20081009-10.html
8. http://commdocs.house.gov/committees/bank/hba92628.000/hba92628_0f.htm, p.111.
9. http://www.aei.org/outlook/22514
10. http://www.fcic.gov/hearings/pdfs/2010-0113-Transcript.pdf, p.96.
11. http://newsgroups.derkeiler.com/Archive/Alt/alt.politics.bush/2008-10/msg00290.html
12. http://online.wsj.com/article/SB122290574391296381.html
13. http://www.fcic.gov/hearings/pdfs/2010-0409-Falcon.pdf
14. http://www.fcic.gov/hearings/pdfs/2010-0114-Bair.pdf
15. http://www.fcic.gov/hearings/pdfs/2010-0409-Lockhart.pdf
16. *Wall Street Journal*, February 8, 2010.
17. http://www.washingtonpost.com/wp-dyn/content/article/2008/06/09/AR2008060902626_3.html
18. Morse, Neil (2004). "Looking for New Customers," *Mortgage Banking*, December 1, 2004.

19. Ibid.
20. *Weekly Standard*, "American Oligarchy," May 10, 2010.
21. http://www.washingtonpost.com/wp-dyn/content/article/2008/06/09/AR2008060902626_2.html
22. http://www.washingtonpost.com/wp-dyn/content/article/2008/06/09/AR2008060902626_3.html
23. http://www.fcic.gov/hearings/pdfs/2010-0409-Lockhart.pdf
24. http://www.fanniemae.com/media/speeches/printthispage.jhtml?repID=/media/speeches/2007/speech_267.xml
25. http://banking.senate.gov/public/index.cfm?FuseAction=Hearings.Testimony&Hearing_ID=0a0b4f0d-55bc-49ed-bb8b-18ba417fc3bf&Witness_ID=ba0448f8-6396-4e57-8534-f3cff3a8e771
26. http://banking.senate.gov/public/index.cfm?FuseAction=Hearings.Testimony&Hearing_ID=0a0b4f0d-55bc-49ed-bb8b-18ba417fc3bf&Witness_ID=88d31047-c665-4405-bc57-701ac33882d4
27. http://www.nytimes.com/2008/08/05/business/05freddie.html?_r=1&adxnnl=1&adxnnlx=1267549361-omdDFom6eqP5JbrwjakjJw
28. "The Role of Government Affordable Housing Policy in Creating the Global Financial Crisis of 2008," Staff Report, July 7, 2009.
29. Ibid.
30. http://voices.washingtonpost.com/washbizblog/2008/04/regulator_to_dismiss_charges_a.html
31. http://www.lewrockwell.com/paul/paul486.html
32. http://www.thestreet.com/story/10287502/feds-fine-arrogant-and-unethical-fannie-mae.html
33. http://commdocs.house.gov/committees/bank/hba92628.000/hba92628_0f.htm, p.75.
34. http://goliath.ecnext.com/coms2/gi_0199-4049325/Freddie-Mac-Releases-Board-Counsel.html
35. http://commdocs.house.gov/committees/bank/hba92628.000/hba92628_0f.htm, p.69
36. http://www.govtrack.us/congress/record.xpd
37. Ibid.
38. http://newsgroups.derkeiler.com/Archive/Alt/alt.politics.bush/2008-10/msg00290.html
39. http://online.wsj.com/article/SB123137220550562585.html
40. http://www.fcic.gov/hearings/pdfs/2010-0409-Falcon.pdf
41. Ibid.
42. http://www.fcic.gov/hearings/pdfs/2010-0409-Lockhart.pdf
43. Ibid.
44. http://www.fanniemae.com/ir/pdf/annualreport/2006/ceo_shareholder_letter.pdf;jsessionid=UM0YBDKSATUKTJ2FQSISFGI, p.2.
45. http://www.fcic.gov/hearings/pdfs/2010-0409-Lockhart.pdf
46. http://www.fcic.gov/hearings/pdfs/2010-0409-Falcon.pdf
47. Ibid., p.4.
48. Ibid., p.5.
49. http://www.fanniemae.com/ir/pdf/annualreport/2007/ceo_shareholder_letter.pdf, p.3.
50. Ibid., p.9.
51. Ibid., p,5.
52. Ibid., p.5.

214 Notes

53. http://www.fcic.gov/hearings/pdfs/2010-0409-Mudd.pdf
54. http://freddiemac.com/investors/ar/pdf/2005annualrpt.pdf
55. Ibid., p.11.
56. http://www.fcic.gov/hearings/pdfs/2010-0409-Lockhart.pdf
57. http://freddiemac.com/investors/ar/2006/03_01.htm
58. Ibid.
59. http://freddiemac.com/investors/ar/2007/03.htm
60. Ibid.
61. Ibid.
62. http://www.fanniemae.com/ir/pdf/earnings/2008/form10k_022609.pdf
63. http://freddiemac.com/news/archives/investors/2009/2008er-4q08.html
64. http://www.treas.gov/press/releases/reports/fhfa_statement_090708hp1128.pdf
65. Ibid.
66. http://freddiemac.com/news/archives/investors/2009/2009er-3q09.html
67. http://www.fcic.gov/hearings/pdfs/2010-0113-Transcript.pdf, p.120.
68. *Wall Street Journal*, February 9, 2010, p.16.
69. Ibid.
70. *Wall Street Journal*, March 1, 2010.
71. http://www.goodreads.com/quotes/show_tag?name=bailout
72. http://banking.senate.gov/public/index.cfm?FuseAction=Hearings.Statement&Statement_ID=71738f59-df84-4784-bf1f-55d3f1ee2968
73. http://oversight.house.gov/images/stories/Hearings/110th_Congress/Fannie_Freddie/Testimony_Raines.pdf
74. Ibid.
75. Ibid.
76. Ibid.
77. http://economiccrisis.us/2010/04/greed-caused-fannie-freddie-fail/
78. http://www.nytimes.com/2008/08/05/business/05freddie.html
79. Ibid.
80. http://www.fcic.gov/hearings/pdfs/2010-0113-Transcript.pdf, p.158.
81. http://banking.senate.gov/public/index.cfm?FuseAction=Hearings.Testimony&Hearing_ID=0a0b4f0d-55bc-49ed-bb8b-18ba417fc3bf&Witness_ID=88d31047-c665-4405-bc57-701ac33882d4
82. http://banking.senate.gov/public/index.cfm?FuseAction=Hearings.Testimony&Hearing_ID=0a0b4f0d-55bc-49ed-bb8b-18ba417fc3bf&Witness_ID=08f51963-df8c-419b-8952-e863ed083b37
83. *Wall Street Journal*, "A Fannie Mae Political Reckoning," May 6, 2010.
84. *Wall Street Journal*, "Fannie Needs Billions More," May 11, 2010.
85. http://www.fcic.gov/hearings/pdfs/2010-0113-Transcript.pdf, p.115.
86. Ibid., p.147.
87. http://banking.senate.gov/public/index.cfm?FuseAction=Hearings.Testimony&Hearing_ID=0a0b4f0d-55bc-49ed-bb8b-18ba417fc3bf&Witness_ID=88d31047-c665-4405-bc57-701ac33882d4
88. *Wall Street Journal*, "View Conflict on Fannie Meltdown," March 10, 2010.
89. Ibid.
90. http://banking.senate.gov/public/index.cfm?FuseAction=Hearings.Statement&Statement_ID=fad3fe2d-2aae-48b9-80f7-d05d5e57a97a
91. http://www.pbs.org/newshour/bb/business/jan-june10/banks_01-21.html
92. *Wall Street Journal*, "A Fannie Mae Political Reckoning," May 6, 2010.
93. http://www.bloomberg.com/apps/news?pid=20601103&sid=adlpm8xxYeRQ

94. *Wall Street Journal*, "What About Fan and Fred Reform," May 4, 2010.
95. *Wall Street Journal*, "Republicans and Obama's New Deal" May 21, 2010.

5 Fuel to the fire I: The rating agencies

1. http://www.house.gov/apps/list/hearing/financialsvcs_dem/egan_jones.pdf
2. http://www.nytimes.com/2010/04/26/opinion/26krugman.html
3. Ibid.
4. *Wall Street Journal*, "Paulson Role Not Made Clear," April 24, 2010.
5. *Wall Street Journal*, "Credit Raters' Emails Show Concerns," April 23, 2010.
6. Ibid.
7. http://query.nytimes.com/gst/fullpage.html?res=9900EFDE143DF934A15757C0A96E9C8B63&sec=&spon=&pagewanted=7
8. http://w4.stern.nyu.edu/news/news.cfm?doc_id=7630%20
9. http://www.house.gov/apps/list/hearing/financialsvcs_dem/joynt.pdf
10. http://www.nytimes.com/2010/04/26/opinion/26krugman.html
11. http://banking.senate.gov/public/index.cfm?FuseAction=Hearings.Testimony&Hearing_ID=3699770d-9c39-4aab-9b6a-7aec8941fe9b&Witness_ID=f0e952a8-a502-4703-8740-8b8b240b386b
12. Treasury Select Committee, EV164.
13. http://oversight.house.gov/images/stories/Hearings/Committee_on_Oversight/Deven_Sharma_Written_Statement_10_22_08.pdf
14. Ibid.
15. *Wall Street Journal*, "Paulson Role Not Made Clear," April 24, 2010.
16. McGraw-Hill Companies, Annual Report, 2008.
17. Ibid.
18. Ibid.
19. http://www.standardandpoors.com/servlet/Testimony of Deven Sharma.
20. Ibid.
21. http://oversight.house.gov/images/stories/Hearings/Committee_on_Oversight/Deven_Sharma_Written_Statement_10_22_08.pdf
22. Ibid.
23. http://files.shareholder.com/downloads/MOOD/881137230x0x165513/23AA9DCF-DD23-4199-976A-632DFE13B19C/annualreport2006.pdf
24. Ibid.
25. Ibid.
26. http://www.bloomberg.com/apps/news?pid=20601087&sid=ac8Bkp_7F4Rc
27. http://files.shareholder.com/downloads/MOOD/881137230x0x181773/F099885F-F1B2-4861-A5A0-4BA8FCF109BB/2007_Annual_Report.pdf
28. Ibid.
29. Ibid.
30. http://www.house.gov/apps/list/hearing/financialsvcs_dem/sec_gallagher.pdf
31. http://banking.senate.gov/public/index.cfm?FuseAction=Hearings.Testimony&Hearing_ID=709b68d2-6e2b-4048-bf86-19fdc01ecec3&Witness_ID=00fd87c5-4517-496c-9dca-1772ddc2de44
32. Ibid.
33. http://files.shareholder.com/downloads/MOOD/881137230x0x284658/FFA8DD07-E843-456F-BCB7-0ECDFFF32937/MCO_08AR-10K_040109.pdf
34. http://files.shareholder.com/downloads/MOOD/881137230x0x357694/7E564B28-2436-4C87-AA6E-FA853E1262AC/Moody_s_2009_Annual_Report.pdf

35. http://banking.senate.gov/public/index.cfm?FuseAction=Hearings.Testimony& Hearing_ID=709b68d2-6e2b-4048-bf86-19fdc01ecec3&Witness_ID=c55c4283-79bc-4b7a-98fd-3334236184b5
36. Ibid.
37. http://www.bloomberg.com/apps/news?pid=20601087&sid=ac8Bkp_7F4Rc
38. Ibid.
39. http://query.nytimes.com/gst/fullpage.html?res=9900EFDE143DF934A15757C0A96E9C8B63&sec=&spon=&pagewanted=7
40. Ibid.
41. http://oversight.house.gov/images/stories/documents/20090930083904.pdf
42. Ibid.
43. http://www.newsweek.com/id/216486
44. http://oversight.house.gov/images/stories/documents/20090930083904.pdf
45. http://oversight.house.gov/images/stories/documents/20090930084204.pdf
46. http://query.nytimes.com/gst/fullpage.html?res=9900EFDE143DF934A15757C0A96E9C8B63&sec=&spon=&pagewanted=7
47. http://www.nytimes.com/2010/04/26/opinion/26krugman.html
48. http://oversight.house.gov/images/stories/Hearings/Committee_on_Oversight/Instant_Message_Conversation_between_Shannon_Mooney_and_Ralul_Dilip_Shah_April_5_2007.pdf
49. Ibid.
50. Ibid.
51. http://oversight.house.gov/images/stories/Hearings/Committee_on_Oversight/E-mail from Belinda Ghetti, December 16, 2006.
52. Ibid.
53. *Wall Street Journal*, "Paulson Role Not Made Clear," April 24, 2010.
54. Ibid.
55. http://money.cnn.com/2009/04/16/news/companies/cohan_mcgraw.fortune/index2.htm
56. http://oversight.house.gov/images/stories/Hearings/Committee_on_Oversight/E-mail_from_Christopher_Mahoney_to_Mark_Almeida_et_al._November_16_2007.pdf
57. Ibid.
58. http://www.house.gov/apps/list/hearing/financialsvcs_dem/joynt.pdf
59. http://banking.senate.gov/public/index.cfm?FuseAction=Hearings.Statement&Statement_ID=6c0d898a-4432-403e-95b1-bb6f51f3d34d
60. http://oversight.house.gov/images/stories/documents/20081023100525.pdf
61. http://www.speaker.gov/blog/?p=1557
62. http://www.europarl.europa.eu/document/activities/cont/201002/20100226ATT69696/20100226ATT69696EN.pdf
63. http://oversight.house.gov/images/stories/documents/20090930100906.pdf
64. http://oversight.house.gov/images/stories/documents/20081023100438.pdf
65. http://ec.europa.eu/internal_market/securities/docs/agencies/proposal_en.pdf, p.2.
66. Ibid.
67. Treasury Select Committee, EV93.
68. Treasury Select Committee, EV100.
69. http://oversight.house.gov/images/stories/documents/20081113120509.pdf
70. Ibid.
71. http://www.huffingtonpost.com/2009/05/19/credit-rating-agency-head_n_205555.html

72. Ibid.
73. http://www.nytimes.com/2008/04/27/magazine/27Credit-t.html
74. http://www.sec.gov/news/speech/2009/spch020609klc.htm
75. http://www.telegraph.co.uk/finance/economics/2815968/Housing-market-crisis-for-UK-suggests-Christopher-Wood.html
76. http://www.house.gov/apps/list/hearing/financialsvcs_dem/sharma_final.pdf
77. http://oversight.house.gov/images/stories/documents/20090930084433.pdf
78. *Wall Street Journal*, "Paulson Role Not Made Clear," April 24, 2010.
79. http://banking.senate.gov/public/index.cfm?FuseAction=Hearings.Testimony&Hearing_ID=89e91cf4-71e2-406d-a416-0e391f4f52b0&Witness_ID=27638a5b-0bba-46e6-b167-d4f2c0ad0188
80. http://banking.senate.gov/public/index.cfm?FuseAction=Hearings.Statement&Statement_ID=6c0d898a-4432-403e-95b1-bb6f51f3d34d
81. http://banking.senate.gov/public/index.cfm?FuseAction=Hearings.Testimony&Hearing_ID=3699770d-9c39-4aab-9b6a-7aec8941fe9b&Witness_ID=f0e952a8-a502-4703-8740-8b8b240b386b
82. http://www.fcic.gov/hearings/pdfs/2010-0114-Schapiro.pdf
83. http://www.fcic.gov/hearings/pdfs/2010-0113-Transcript.pdf, p.65.
84. Treasury Select Committee, EV243.
85. http://oversight.house.gov/images/stories/documents/20081023100438.pdf
86. http://www.fcic.gov/hearings/pdfs/2010-0407-Greenspan.pdf
87. http://www.fcic.gov/hearings/pdfs/2010-0114-Bair.pdf
88. http://oversight.house.gov/images/stories/Hearings/Committee_on_Oversight/Moodys_Town_Hall_Transcript_September_2007.pdf
89. Ibid.
90. Ibid.
91. Ibid.
92. Ibid.
93. http://money.cnn.com/2009/04/16/news/companies/cohan_mcgraw.fortune/index2.htm

6 Fuel to the fire II: Regulators, politicians, and lobbyists

1. http://www.bloomberg.com/apps/news?pid=20601103&sid=aePB9cb.K2nU
2. http://www.fcic.gov/hearings/pdfs/2010-0407-Greenspan.pdf
3. *Weekly Standard*, "American Oligarchy," May 10, 2010.
4. http://cop.senate.gov/documents/testimony-030410-pandit.pdf
5. Ibid., Treasury Select Committee, EV273.
6. http://www.theglobalist.com/StoryId.aspx?StoryId=7880
7. http://media.ft.com/cms/1d11280c-3d20-11df-b81b-00144feabdc0.pdf
8. Ibid.
9. http://www.fcic.gov/hearings/pdfs/2010-0113-Transcript.pdf, p.115.
10. http://www.bba.org.uk/bba/jsp/polopoly.jsp?d=613&a=14748
11. http://www.ft.com/cms/s/0/780d9d64-175d-11df-87f6-00144feab49a.html
12. Ibid.
13. http://business.timesonline.co.uk/tol/business/markets/article3239801.ece
14. *Wall Street Journal*, "For NY Fed Chief, A New Fix-It Job," May 15, 2010.
15. http://www.huffingtonpost.com/2010/04/29/elizabeth-warren-gop-refo_n_556362.html

16. http://www.thefreelibrary.com/Leveling+the+playing+field:+Dr.+Elizabeth+Warren – head+of+Congress's...-a0224313392
17. *Wall Street Journal*, February 11, 2010, p.C4.
18. http://www.smartbrief.com/news/cfa/storyDetails.jsp?issueid=B48D8F3D-90A1-416C-B286-47991C49F1CF&copyid=470CBDF0-6667-43E2-B545-8B3FFE464D9C
19. http://www.fcic.gov/hearings/pdfs/2010-0114-Bair.pdf
20. Treasury Select Committee, EV385.
21. http://www.publications.parliament.uk/pa/cm200809/cmselect/cmtreasy/144/144i.pdf, EV26.
22. Ibid., Treasury Select Committee, EV74.
23. EV74.
24. Treasury Select Committee, EV277.
25. Treasury Select Committee, EV278.
26. http://www.telegraph.co.uk/finance/economics/2821239/The-rise-of-John-McFall-credit-crisis-key-figure.html
27. http://business.timesonline.co.uk/tol/business/industry_sectors/banking_and_finance/article2500761.ece
28. http://www.telegraph.co.uk/finance/economics/2821239/The-rise-of-John-McFall-credit-crisis-key-figure.html
29. http://www.nytimes.com/2008/10/03/business/03sec.html
30. http://www.realclearmarkets.com/articles/2009/02/the_sec_killed_wall_street_on.html
31. Ibid.
32. http://www.nysun.com/business/ex-sec-official-blames-agency-for-blow-up/86130/
33. http://www.nytimes.com/2008/10/03/business/03sec.html
34. http://www.nytimes.com/2008/10/03/business/03sec.html?_r=1&pagewanted=2
35. Ibid.
36. *Wall Street Journal*, "Reports of FSAs Demise Are Proving Premature," May 17, 2010.
37. http://iaindale.blogspot.com/2009/02/quote-of-day-gordon-brown.html
38. http://www.independent.co.uk/news/uk/politics/camerons-big-speech-the-key-quotes-1799661.html
39. Treasury Select Committee, EV280.
40. Treasury Select Committee, EV278.
41. Treasury Select Committee, EV366.
42. http://www.ft.com/cms/s/0/780d9d64-175d-11df-87f6-00144feab49a.html
43. Ibid.
44. http://www.publications.parliament.uk/pa/cm200910/cmselect/cmtreasy/uc261-vii/uc26102.htm
45. Treasury Select Committee, EV367.
46. Treasury Select Committee, EV278.
47. Treasury Select Committee, EV281.
48. http://www.publications.parliament.uk/pa/cm200809/cmselect/cmtreasy/144/144i.pdf, EV12.
49. Treasury Select Committee, EV143.
50. Treasury Select Committee, EV272.
51. http://www.fcic.gov/hearings/pdfs/2010-0113-Dimon.pdf
52. Paulson, H. (2010). *Back from the Brink*. New York: Business Plus, p.439.
53. Treasury Select Committee, EV89.
54. http://www.fcic.gov/hearings/pdfs/2010-0114-Bair.pdf
55. http://oversight.house.gov/images/stories/documents/20081023100505.pdf

56. http://www.fcic.gov/hearings/pdfs/2010-0114-Schapiro.pdf
57. http://www.house.gov/apps/list/hearing/financialsvcs_dem/valuks_4.20.10.pdf
58. http://www.publications.parliament.uk/pa/cm200910/cmselect/cmtreasy/uc261-vi/uc26102.htm Contents reflect the uncorrected version, not yet formally approved.
59. Treasury Select Committee, EV281.
60. http://www.europarl.europa.eu/document/activities/cont/201002/20100226ATT69696/20100226ATT69696EN.pdf
61. Ibid.
62. Ibid.
63. Treasury Select Committee, EV100.
64. *Wall Street Journal*, "Reports of FSA's Demise Are Proving Premature," May 17, 2010.
65. Treasury Select Committee, EV310.
66. Treasury Select Committee, EV92.
67. http://www.publications.parliament.uk/pa/cm200910/cmselect/cmtreasy/uc261-vii/uc26102.htm
68. Treasury Select Committee, EV99.
69. Treasury Select Committee, EV100.
70. http://www.cbsnews.com/stories/2008/09/16/business/marketwatch/main4452181.shtml
71. http://www.publications.parliament.uk/pa/cm200910/cmselect/cmtreasy/uc261-vi/uc26102.htm. Contents reflect the uncorrected version, not yet formally approved.
72. http://www.publications.parliament.uk/pa/cm200910/cmselect/cmtreasy/uc261-vi/uc26102.htm. Contents reflect the uncorrected version, not yet formally approved.
73. Treasury Select Committee, EV88.
74. Treasury Select Committee, EV311.
75. Treasury Select Committee, EV313.
76. *Wall Street Journal*, "The Lesson of Basel's Bean Counters," April 24, 2010.
77. Ibid.
78. http://www.europarl.europa.eu/document/activities/cont/201002/20100226ATT69696/20100226ATT69696EN.pdf
79. Treasury Select Committee, EV101.
80. http://www.fcic.gov/hearings/pdfs/2010-0409-Lockhart.pdf
81. http://www.washingtonpost.com/wp-dyn/content/article/2008/06/09/AR2008060902626.html
82. http://www.fcic.gov/hearings/pdfs/2010-0409-Falcon.pdf
83. http://oversight.house.gov/images/stories/Hearings/110th_Congress/Fannie_Freddie/Testimony_Raines.pdf
84. Ibid.
85. http://www.fcic.gov/hearings/pdfs/2010-0409-Lockhart.pdf
86. http://files.shareholder.com/downloads/ONE/565875514x0x283417/92060ed3-3393-43a5-a3c1-178390c6eac5/2008_AR_Letter_to_shareholders.pdf, p.17.
87. Eric Dinallo (2010). "What I Learned at the AIG Meltdown," *Wall Street Journal*, February 3, 2010.
88. *Wall Street Journal*, "The Credit Raters Brawl," May 14, 2010.
89. http://banking.senate.gov/public/index.cfm?FuseAction=Hearings.Statement&Statement_ID=6c0d898a-4432-403e-95b1-bb6f51f3d34d
90. http://ec.europa.eu/internal_market/securities/docs/agencies/proposal_en.pdf, p.2.
91. Ibid.
92. *Wall Street Journal*, February 9, 2009.
93. http://www.fcic.gov/hearings/pdfs/2010-0113-Transcript.pdf, p.154.

220 Notes

94. http://cop.senate.gov/documents/testimony-030410-pandit.pdf
95. http://oversight.house.gov/images/stories/documents/20081023100505.pdf
96. http://money.cnn.com/galleries/2007/fortune/0708/gallery.crisiscounsel.fortune/9.html
97. http://www.slate.com/id/2171739/
98. http://www.federalreserve.gov/newsevents/speech/Bernanke20070517a.htm
99. http://www.federalreserve.gov/newsevents/speech/Bernanke20070605a.htm
100. http://www.anonymoushints.com/2008/09/28/credit-crisis-quotes-from-the-experts-then-and-now/
101. http://business.timesonline.co.uk/tol/business/markets/article3239801.ece
102. http://www.slate.com/id/2171739/
103. http://www.treasury.gov/press/releases/hp525.htm
104. http://www.thebigmoney.com/articles/judgments/2009/03/26/mr-taleb-goes-washington
105. http://www.democracynow.org/2009/12/4/eliot_spitzer_geithner_bernanke_complicit_in
106. http://www.lewrockwell.com/paul/paul376.html
107. *Weekly Standard*, "American Oligarchy," May 10, 2010.
108. http://www.nytimes.com/2010/04/27/opinion/27mclean.html
109. http://www.guardian.co.uk/business/2008/oct/31/creditcrunch-gillian-tett-financial-times
110. http://www.ft.com/cms/s/0/95c4cf3e-2ea7-11de-b7d3-00144feabdc0.html
111. http://www.reuters.com/article/idUSL795389120090416
112. http://www.independent.co.uk/news/business/news/fsa-boss-pledges-revolution-as-he-rejects-lighttouch-policy-1632541.html
113. Treasury Select Committee, EV281.
114. Treasury Select Committee, EV280.
115. http://www.iie.com/publications/opeds/oped.cfm?ResearchID=988
116. http://www.nytimes.com/2003/09/11/business/new-agency-proposed-to-oversee-freddie-mac-and-fannie-mae.html
117. http://whitehouse.gov/news/releases/2009/09.
118. Ibid., p.20.
119. http://commdocs.house.gov/committees/bank/hba92628.000/hba92628_0f.htm, p.2.
120. HR2575.
121. Ibid., p.4.
122. Ibid., p.5.
123. Ibid., p.14.
124. Ibid., p.110.
125. Ibid., p.156.
126. Frank, Barney. (2004). "GSE Failure A Phony Issue," *American Banker*, April 21, 2004.
127. HR1461.
128. http://www.usnews.com/blogs/sam-dealey/2008/09/23/barney-frank-fesses-up-on-financial-crisis.htm
129. http://rightamerican.wordpress.com/gse-meltdown-time-line/
130. http://online.wsj.com/article/SB122290574391296381.html
131. http://online.wsj.com/article/SB123137220550562585.html
132. http://investment-blog.net/did-you-not-hear-barney-franks-testimony-regarding-freddie-mac-and-fannie-mae-just-before-they-imploded/
133. http://online.wsj.com/article/SB122212948811465427.html

134. http://online.wsj.com/article/SB122290574391296381.html
135. Ibid.
136. Ibid.
137. http://news.alibaba.com/article/detail/markets/100275008-1-wrapup-1-ex-fannie-ceo-apologizes%252C-faults.html
138. http://www.digitaljournal.com/article/260301
139. http://www.barneyfrank.net/quotes
140. http://www.usnews.com/blogs/sam-dealey/2008/09/23/barney-frank-fesses-up-on-financial-crisis.htm
141. http://www.fcic.gov/hearings/pdfs/2010-0409-Lockhart.pdf
142. http://www.fcic.gov/hearings/pdfs/2010-0113-Transcript.pdf, p.158.
143. *Wall Street Journal*, "Senators vs. Goldman," April 28, 2010.
144. *Wall Street Journal*, "The Lesson of Basel's Bean Counters," April 24, 2010.
145. http://thefinanser.co.uk/fsclub/2009/09/quotes-of-the-crisis.html
146. Ibid.
147. Ibid
148. Ibid.
149. http://www.mortgagebankers.org/NewsandMedia/PressCenter/47628.htm
150. http://www.mortgagebankers.org/files/Conferences/2007/CREFFebruary/Dough Duncan.pdf
151. Ibid.
152. Ibid.
153. http://www.mortgagebankers.org/NewsandMedia/PressCenter/48292.htm
154. Ibid.
155. http://www.mbaa.org/files/Advocacy/TestimonyandCommentLetters/Joint CommentLetter,1-29-2007,NCNontraditionalMortgageProducts.pdf
156. http://www.mbaa.org/files/Advocacy/TestimonyandCommentLetters/MBA CommentLetter,5-7-2008,ProposedStatementonSubprimeMortgageLending.pdf
157. Ibid.
158. http://www.mbaa.org/files/Advocacy/TestimonyandCommentLetters/MBAComment Letter3-21-2008Risk-BasedCapitalStandards-AdvancedCapitalAdequacyFrame work(BaselII).pdf
159. http://www.investors.com/NewsAndAnalysis/Article.aspx?id=460396
160. http://www.fcic.gov/hearings/pdfs/2010-0409-Falcon.pdf
161. Ibid.
162. http://online.wsj.com/article/SB123137220550562585.html
163. http://oversight.house.gov/images/stories/documents/20081023100505.pdf
164. Treasury Select Committee, EV92.
165. http://www.aba.com/NR/rdonlyres/222CE044-577A-11D5-AB84-00508B95258D/44046/BRockTestimony05192005.pdf
166. Ibid.
167. Ibid.
168. Ibid.
169. http://www.bba.org.uk/content/1/c6/01/45/18/15th_Sept_letter_to_Chancellor.pdf
170. *Wall Street Journal*, "In Defense of Over-the-counter Derivatives," May 14, 2010.
171. http://www.rte.ie/news/2009/0209/mccreevyc.html
172. Ibid.
173. http://www.ft.com/cms/s/0/780d9d64-175d-11df-87f6-00144feab49a.html
174. http://online.wsj.com/article/SB123785319919419659.html

7 A handful of sages

1. http://www.ft.com/cms/s/2/2cb543cc-595b-11df-99ba-00144feab49a.html
2. http://www.roubini.com/roubini-monitor/142759/the_biggest_slump_in_us_housing_in_the_last_40_yearsor_53_years
3. Ibid.
4. Ibid.
5. Ibid.
6. http://nymag.com/realestate/features/21675/
7. Ibid.
8. http://www.econ.yale.edu/~shiller/pubs/p1089.pdf, p.341.
9. Ibid., p.344.
10. http://online.wsj.com/article/SB115688653772648766.html
11. Ibid.
12. http://www.forbes.com/2009/04/05/meredith-whitney-transcript-intelligent-investing-credit.html
13. http://www.businessweek.com/bwdaily/dnflash/content/nov2007/db20071126_178760.htm
14. http://www.businessweek.com/bwdaily/dnflash/content/nov2007/db2007111_029434.htm
15. Ibid.
16. http://www.marketwatch.com/story/merrill-lynch-downgraded-on-exposure-to-bond-insurers-subprime
17. http://www.generationaldynamics.com/cgi-bin/D.PL?xct=gd.e080731
18. http://www.forbes.com/2009/04/05/meredith-whitney-transcript-intelligent-investing-credit.html
19. Ibid.
20. Ibid.
21. Ibid.
22. http://stressonomics.wordpress.com/2007/08/29/the-man-who-saw-it-coming-sounding-the-subprime-alarm-in-2005/
23. http://www.telegraph.co.uk/finance/markets/2816256/Chris-Wood-the-man-who-predicted-the-subprime-crisis.html
24. Ibid.
25. http://www.telegraph.co.uk/finance/markets/2816256/Chris-Wood-the-man-who-predicted-the-subprime-crisis.html
26. http://ftalphaville.ft.com/blog/2007/07/27/6190/greed-fear-goes-into-the-us-subprime-mire/
27. http://www.fcic.gov/hearings/pdfs/2010-0113-Transcript.pdf, p.156
28. Ibid.
29. http://seekingalpha.com/article/53642-great-conference-call-moments-mike-mayo-deutsche-bank
30. http://money.cnn.com/magazines/fortune/fortune_archive/2007/11/26/101234162/index.htm
31. Ibid.
32. http://www.housingwire.com/2009/04/06/analyst-speaks-of-seven-deadly-banking-sins-bank-shares-dive/
33. http://money.cnn.com/galleries/2008/fortune/0809/gallery.kimes_prophets.fortune/
34. http://www.house.gov/apps/list/hearing/financialsvcs_dem/egan_jones.pdf

35. http://business.timesonline.co.uk/tol/business/markets/united_states/article3007121.ece
36. http://www.house.gov/apps/list/hearing/financialsvcs_dem/egan_jones.pdf
37. http://www.bloomberg.com/news/marketsmag/mm_0108_story3.html
38. http://oversight.house.gov/images/stories/Hearings/Committee_on_Oversight/Egan_Statement.pdf
39. Spiegel Online, May 6, 2009.
40. http://online.wsj.com/public/resources/documents/johnpaulson.pdf
41. http://www.portfolio.com/executives/features/2009/01/07/John-Paulson-Profits-in-Downturn/index3.html
42. http://www.distressedvolatility.com/2009/12/john-paulson-stiglitz-speak-at.html
43. http://online.wsj.com/public/resources/documents/johnpaulson.pdf
44. http://waugh.standard.co.uk/2009/08/brown-ignored-warnings-re-toxic-loans-and-financial-crisis.html
45. http://www.house.gov/apps/list/hearing/financialsvcs_dem/testimony_-_chanos,_cpic.pdf
46. http://www.bloomberg.com/apps/news?pid=20601103&sid=aCG3RgrgPmNo&refer=news
47. Ibid.
48. Ibid.
49. http://nymag.com/news/business/52754/index3.html#ixzz0iFPJPJ77
50. Ibid.
51. http://www.forbes.com/2009/05/07/bank-earnings-chanos-markets-equity-wall-street.html
52. Ibid.
53. http://advisoranalyst.com/glablog/2009/02/04/jim-chanos-ftcom-interview/#ixzz0iFOGAC8X
54. http://www.derivativesstrategy.com/magazine/archive/1997/1296qa.asp
55. Congressional Testimony, Report on The Risks of Financial Modeling, VaR and the Economic Breakdown, September 2009.
56. http://www.time.com/time/business/article/0,8599,1853531,00.html
57. Congressional Testimony, Report on The Risks of Financial Modeling, VaR and the Economic Breakdown, September 2009.
58. http://www.fooledbyrandomness.com/imbeciles.htm
59. http://www.time.com/time/business/article/0,8599,1853531,00.html
60. http://nymag.com/news/businessfinance/47844/
61. Ibid.
62. Ibid.
63. Ibid.
64. Ibid.
65. http://www.docstoc.com/docs/20990516/Grants-Spring-Investment-Conference-David-Einhorn-Private-Profit
66. Ibid.
67. http://oversight.house.gov/images/stories/documents/20081023100505.pdf
68. Ibid.
69. Ibid.
70. bid.
71. Ibid.
72. Ibid.
73. http://www.govtrack.us/congress/record.xpd

74. Ibid.
75. Ibid.
76. Ibid.
77. http://www.lewrockwell.com/paul/paul46.html
78. http://www.lewrockwell.com/paul/paul159.html
79. http://www.lewrockwell.com/paul/paul128.html
80. http://www.lewrockwell.com/paul/paul282.html
81. Ibid.
82. http://www.lewrockwell.com/paul/paul282.html
83. http://www.lewrockwell.com/paul/paul526.html
84. http://www.aei.org/outlook/22514
85. Ibid.
86. http://www.npr.org/templates/story/story.php?storyId=92529364
87. http://www.house.gov/apps/list/hearing/financialsvcs_dem/wallison031709.pdf
88. http://www.federalreserve.gov/boarddocs/testimony/2005/20050406/default.htm
89. Ibid.
90. Ibid.
91. Ibid.
92. Ibid.
93. Ibid.
94. http://www.federalreserve.gov/boarddocs/testimony/2005/20050406/default.htm
95. http://business.timesonline.co.uk/tol/business/economics/article4925797.ece
96. Ibid.
97. http://www.timesonline.co.uk/tol/comment/columnists/guest_contributors/article5548797.ece
98. http://www.timesonline.co.uk/tol/news/politics/article5949844.ece
99. http://hansard.millbanksystems.com/commons/2003/nov/13/interest-rates
100. http://www.timesonline.co.uk/tol/news/politics/article5949844.ece
101. http://www.myfinances.co.uk/investments/features-guides/investment-advice/vince-cable-in-conversation-$1310988.htm
102. Ibid.
103. http://www.huffingtonpost.com/2009/01/08/abrams-research-survey-fi_n_156369.html
104. http://www.huffingtonpost.com/2009/11/30/charlie-gasparino-dont-bl_n_373629.html
105. http://www.rferl.org/content/Media_Under_Scrutiny_For_Talking_Up_Financial_Crisis_/1492272.html
106. http://www.ft.com/cms/s/0/95c4cf3e-2ea7-11de-b7d3-00144feabdc0.html
107. http://www.cbsnews.com/stories/2008/09/16/business/marketwatch/main4452181.shtml
108. http://www.guardian.co.uk/business/2008/oct/31/creditcrunch-gillian-tett-financial-times
109. http://www.npr.org/templates/story/story.php?storyId=101751604
110. Ibid.
111. http://us.ft.com/ftgateway/superpage.ft?news_id=fto082620071455490540
112. http://www.guardian.co.uk/business/2008/oct/31/creditcrunch-gillian-tett-financial-times
113. http://www.ft.com/cms/s/2/6fb8a930-ad41-11db-8709-0000779e2340.html
114. http://www.ft.com/cms/s/0/6b42ed8c-0e4b-11dc-8219-000b5df10621.html
115. http://www.ft.com/cms/s/0/9ffb0bea-5cac-11dc-9cc9-0000779fd2ac.html

8 The blame game: Fingerpointing and apologies

1. http://abcnews.go.com/International/story?id=5987055&page=1
2. http://www.spiegel.de/international/germany/0,1518,579707,00.html
3. http://www.number10.gov.uk/Page17114
4. http://www.timesonline.co.uk/tol/comment/columnists/guest_contributors/article5548797.ece
5. http://abcnews.go.com/International/story?id=5987055&page=1
6. http://www.number10.gov.uk/Page17114
7. http://www.timesonline.co.uk/tol/news/politics/article4862103.ece
8. http://www.dailymail.co.uk/news/article-1063595/David-Cameron-refuses-blame-bankers-global-financial-crisis.html
9. http://blogs.abcnews.com/worldview/2008/09/german-leaders.html
10. http://www.spiegel.de/international/germany/0,1518,580709,00.html
11. http://www.spiegel.de/international/germany/0,1518,579707,00.html
12. http://www.europarl.europa.eu/document/activities/cont/201002/20100226ATT69696/20100226ATT69696EN.pdf
13. http://abcnews.go.com/International/story?id=5987055&page=1
14. http://www.msnbc.msn.com/id/26962762
15. http://www.guardian.co.uk/business/2009/jan/28/china-blames-america-for-credit-crisis
16. Ibid.
17. http://latimesblogs.latimes.com/presidentbush/2008/10/white-house-con.html
18. Ibid.
19. http://business.timesonline.co.uk/tol/business/economics/wef/article5610252.ece?token=null&offset=12&page=2
20. Ibid.
21. Ibid.
22. http://afp.google.com/article/ALeqM5iQvXaV8mO0SRtfD9FEWqf4Vyrzrg
23. http://www.independent.co.uk/news/world/politics/financial-crisis-caused-by-white-men-with-blue-eyes-1655354.html
24. http://media.ft.com/cms/1d11280c-3d20-11df-b81b-00144feabdc0.pdf
25. http://www.fcic.gov/hearings/pdfs/2010-0113-Transcript.pdf, p.78.
26. http://www.fcic.gov/hearings/pdfs/2010-0113-Dimon.pdf
27. http://www.fcic.gov/hearings/pdfs/2010-0113-Transcript.pdf, p.59.
28. http://files.shareholder.com/downloads/ONE/565875514x0x184757/b3a93ea7-677-a-4116-b7ba-69af38eed533/2007AR_LettertoShareholders.pdf
29. http://money.cnn.com/2007/11/04/news/companies/citigroup_prince/index.htm
30. http://www.fcic.gov/hearings/pdfs/2010-0408-Prince.pdf
31. http://www.bloomberg.com/apps/news?pid=20601087&sid=a.z4KpD77s80&pos=6
32. http://www.sajaforum.org/2008/11/business-vikram-pandit-on-charlie-rose.html
33. Ibid.
34. http://voices.washingtonpost.com/economy-watch/2009/02/kanjorski_to_bankers_pay_us_ba.html
35. http://www.pbs.org/newshour/bb/business/jan-june10/economy_01-13.html
36. Ibid.
37. http://uk.reuters.com/article/idUKN1315021320100113
38. http://news.alibaba.com/article/detail/markets/100275008-1-wrapup-1-ex-fannie-ceo-apologizes%252C-faults.html
39. http://www.newstatesman.com/business/2010/01/chief-executive-bank-pay
40. Treasury Select Committee, EV276.

41. http://www.newstatesman.com/business/2010/01/chief-executive-bank-pay
42. Treasury Select Committee, EV221.
43. Ibid.
44. http://www.independent.co.uk/news/uk/politics/hint-of-arrogance-as-bankers-apologise-1605670.html
45. Ibid.
46. http://www.nytimes.com/2008/04/06/business/06ubs.html
47. http://business.timesonline.co.uk/tol/business/industry_sectors/banking_and_finance/article3658290.ece
48. http://www.nytimes.com/2008/04/06/business/06ubs.html?pagewanted=4&_r=1
49. http://www.euromoney.com/Article/2098544/Category/17/ChannelPage/0/Why-Rohner-left-UBShis-last-interview-as-UBS-CEO.html?p=1
50. Ibid.
51. http://www.bba.org.uk/bba/jsp/polopoly.jsp?d=613&a=14748
52. Treasury Select Committee, EV3.
53. http://www.publications.parliament.uk/pa/cm200809/cmselect/cmtreasy/144/144i.pdf, Treasury Select Committee, EV3.
54. Treasury Select Committee, EV278.
55. Treasury Select Committee, EV2.
56. Treasury Select Committee, EV306.
57. Treasury Select Committee, EV309.
58. http://www.europarl.europa.eu/document/activities/cont/201002/20100226ATT69696/20100226ATT69696EN.pdf
59. http://www.mixxbosses.com/home/bush-apologizes-for-the-economic-crisis/
60. Treasury Select Committee, EV310.
61. Treasury Select Committee, EV367.
62. http://www.independent.co.uk/news/uk/politics/pm-i-wont-apologise-for-economic-crisis-1636837.html
63. http://www.telegraph.co.uk/news/election-2010/7587497/General-Election-2010-Gordon-Brown-admits-his-mistakes-added-to-financial-crisis.html
64. http://www.independent.co.uk/news/uk/politics/hint-of-arrogance-as-bankers-apologise-1605670.html
65. http://www.bbc.co.uk/blogs/thereporters/robertpeston/2009/02/not_quite_the_full_sorry.html
66. http://www.nytimes.com/2009/03/26/business/26quotes.html
67. Ibid., p.25.
68. Ibid., p.33.
69. http://www.fcic.gov/hearings/pdfs/2010–0113-Blankfein.pdf
70. Ibid., p.64.
71. http://www.fcic.gov/hearings/pdfs/2010–0113-Transcript.pdf, p.72.
72. http://money.cnn.com/2010/01/13/news/economy/Bank_CEO/
73. http://blogs.wsj.com/deals/2009/09/30/ken-lewis-farewell-letter-this-was-my-decision-and-mine-alone/tab/article/
74. http://www.pbs.org/newshour/bb/business/jan-june10/economy_01–13.html
75. http://media.corporate-ir.net/media_files/irol/71/71595/reports/2009_AR.pdf
76. http://www.fcic.gov/hearings/pdfs/2010–0113-Moynihan.pdf
77. http://www.fcic.gov/hearings/pdfs/2010–0113-Transcript.pdf, p.61
78. http://www.nytimes.com/2008/05/07/business/07bear.html?pagewanted=2&_r=1
79. Ibid

80. http://money.cnn.com/2008/07/31/magazines/fortune/rise_and_fall_Cayne_cohan.fortune/index3.htm
81. http://www.latimes.com/business/la-fi-bear-stearns-20100506,0,7580265.story
82. Ibid.
83. http://oversight.house.gov/images/stories/Hearings/110th_Congress/Fuld_Statement.pdf
84. Ibid.
85. Ibid.
86. http://www.guardian.co.uk/business/2010/apr/21/lehman-brothers-dick-fuld-admits-mistakes
87. http://oversight.house.gov/images/stories/Hearings/110th_Congress/Fuld_Statement.pdf
88. http://www.investis.com/reports/hsbc_ar_2009_en/report.php?type=1&zoom=1&page=8b02c7a1c5767a6c0a37604bf90fffb8
89. http://www.thelocal.de/money/20081230-16443.html
90. Ibid.
91. http://dealbreaker.com/2010/04/deutsche%e2%80%99s-ackermann-%e2%80%9cmistakes-were-made%e2%80%9d/?utm_source=feedburner&utm_medium=feed&utm_campaign=Feed%3A+dealbreaker+%28Dealbreaker%29
92. http://oversight.house.gov/images/stories/documents/20081023100505.pdf
93. http://money.cnn.com/2007/11/09/news/newsmakers/merrill_rubin.fortune/index.htm?postversion=2007111119
94. http://thestrangedeathofliberalamerica.com/the-tragedy-of-robert-rubin-the-fall-of-citigroup-and-the-financial-crisis-continued.html
95. *Wall Street Journal*, November 29, 2008.
96. http://www.citibank.com/citi/press/2009/090109d.htm
97. http://www.fcic.gov/hearings/pdfs/2010-0408-Rubin.pdf
98. http://www.nytimes.com/2010/04/09/business/09panel.html?ref=business
99. Ibid.
100. http://industry.bnet.com/financial-services/10008353/citigroups-charles-prince-robert-rubin-innocent-as-sin/
101. http://phx.corporate-ir.net/External.File?item=UGFyZW50SUQ9MTQ4OHxDaGlsZElEPS0xfFR5cGU9Mw==&t=1, p.1.
102. http://www.house.gov/apps/list/hearing/financialsvcs_dem/fsc_testimony_of_mr_edward_liddy.pdf
103. http://oversight.house.gov/images/stories/documents/20081007101054.pdf
104. Ibid.
105. Ibid.
106. Ibid.
107. http://oversight.house.gov/images/stories/documents/20081007101236.pdf
108. http://oversight.house.gov/images/stories/documents/20081007101332.pdf
109. Ibid.
110. Ibid.
111. http://www.standardandpoors.com/servlet/Testimony of Deven Sharma
112. http://www.house.gov/apps/list/hearing/financialsvcs_dem/joynt.pdf
113. http://banking.senate.gov/public/index.cfm?FuseAction=Hearings.Testimony&Hearing_ID=709b68d2-6e2b-4048-bf86-19fdc01ecec3&Witness_ID=c55c4283-79bc-4b7a-98fd-3334236184b5
114. http://www.bloomberg.com/apps/news?pid=20601087&sid=ac8Bkp_7F4Rc

228 Notes

115. http://dealbook.blogs.nytimes.com/2010/04/09/for-crisis-panel-dark-humor-during-questioning/
116. *Wall Street Journal*, March 10, 2009.
117. Ibid.
118. http://www.fcic.gov/hearings/pdfs/2010-0407-Greenspan.pdf
119. http://oversight.house.gov/images/stories/documents/20081023100438.pdf
120. Ibid.
121. http://www.nytimes.com/2010/01/04/business/economy/04fed.html
122. Ibid.
123. http://edition.cnn.com/TRANSCRIPTS/1004/08/cnr.04.html
124. http://www.fcic.gov/hearings/pdfs/2010-0113-Transcript.pdf, p.148.
125. http://www.bba.org.uk/bba/jsp/polopoly.jsp?d=613&a=16598
126. http://www.ft.com/cms/s/0/d3d9726c-597f-11df-99ba-00144feab49a,dwp_uuid=3ee7fd72-e9dd-11dc-b3c9-0000779fd2ac.html
127. http://www.wrap20.com/files/At_Davos_Bankers_Face_Global_Ire_-_WSJ.pdf
128. http://media.ft.com/cms/1d11280c-3d20-11df-b81b-00144feabdc0.pdf
129. Ibid.
130. Ibid.
131. http://www.newstatesman.com/business/2010/01/chief-executive-bank-pay

9 Closing the barn door

1. http://www.house.gov/apps/list/hearing/financialsvcs_dem/wallison031709.pdf
2. http://news.bbc.co.uk/2/hi/8405125.stm
3. Treasury Select Committee, EV366.
4. http://www.independent.co.uk/opinion/commentators/alistair-darling-the-banks-are-to-blame-for-this-crisis-1605389.html
5. http://www.ft.com/cms/s/0/9a707cdc-5fd8-11df-a670-00144feab49a.html
6. Treasury Select Committee, EV295.
7. Ibid., Treasury Select Committee, EV296.
8. Treasury Select Committee, EV278.
9. *Wall Street Journal*, "For NY Fed Chief a New Fix-it Job," May 15, 2010.
10. Testimony, House Committee on Financial Services, January 22, 2010
11. Ibid.
12. http://www.wrap20.com/files/At_Davos_Bankers_Face_Global_Ire_-_WSJ.pdf
13. http://www.number10.gov.uk/Page17114
14. http://theweek.com/article/index/202479/Obama_Youve_made_enough_money
15. http://www.independent.co.uk/opinion/commentators/alistair-darling-the-banks-are-to-blame-for-this-crisis-1605389.html
16. Treasury Select Committee, EV370.
17. Treasury Select Committee, EV385.
18. http://www.fcic.gov/hearings/pdfs/2010-0114-Bair.pdf
19. http://www.fcic.gov/hearings/pdfs/2010-0114-Schapiro.pdf
20. http://www.rte.ie/news/2009/0209/mccreevyc.html
21. Treasury Select Committee, EV314.
22. Treasury Select Committee, EV322.
23. http://www.newsweek.com/id/216214?from=rss
24. http://www.bloomberg.com/apps/news?pid=newsarchive&sid=aZw2ko5oVZLU
25. http://www.investis.com/reports/hsbc_ar_2009_en/report.php?type=1&zoom=1&page=8b02c7a1c5767a6c0a37604bf90fffb8

26. http://www.publications.parliament.uk/pa/cm200910/cmselect/cmtreasy/uc259-i/uc25902.htm Contents reflect the uncorrected version, not yet formally approved.
27. Treasury Select Committee, EV269.
28. Treasury Select Committee, EV252.
29. Treasury Select Committee, EV223.
30. Treasury Select Committee, EV64.
31. http://www.fcic.gov/hearings/pdfs/2010-0113-Transcript.pdf, p.115.
32. Treasury Select Committee, EV25.
33. http://abcnews.go.com/GMA/timothy-geithner-economy-diane-sawyer-interview-treasury-secretary/story?id=8569713
34. http://www.sbs.com.au/dateline/story/transcript/id/600336/n/Interview-with-Christine-Lagarde
35. Treasury Select Committee, EV291.
36. http://www.publications.parliament.uk/pa/cm200910/cmselect/cmtreasy/uc259-i/uc25902.htm Contents reflect the uncorrected version, not yet formally approved.
37. *Wall Street Journal*, February 13, 2010, p.A11.
38. http://www.publications.parliament.uk/pa/cm200910/cmselect/cmtreasy/uc261-iv/uc26102.htm Contents reflect the uncorrected version, not yet formally approved.
39. *Wall Street Journal*, "New Life for the Volcker Rule," May 1, 2010.
40. Treasury Select Committee, EV321.
41. http://www.ft.com/cms/s/0/780d9d64-175d-11df-87f6-00144feab49a.html
42. Ibid.
43. Wall Street Journal, "New Life for the Volcker Rule," May 1, 2010.
44. Ibid.
45. http://www.publications.parliament.uk/pa/cm200910/cmselect/cmtreasy/uc261-iv/uc26102.htm. Contents reflect the uncorrected version, not yet formally approved.
46. Ibid.
47. Ibid.
48. http://www.cnbc.com/id/35516716
49. *Wall Street Journal*, February 22, 2010, p.A19.
50. *Wall Street Journal*, February 16, 2010, p. A19.
51. Ibid.
52. http://www.publications.parliament.uk/pa/cm200910/cmselect/cmtreasy/uc261-vii/uc26102.htm. Contents reflect the uncorrected version, not yet formally approved.
53. Treasury Select Committee, EV275.
54. *Wall Street Journal*, "Regulator Warns Against New Cubs on Banks' Trading", May 3, 2010.
55. Treasury Select Committee, EV320.
56. http://business.timesonline.co.uk/tol/business/industry_sectors/banking_and_finance/article2817746.ece
57. http://www.publications.parliament.uk/pa/cm200910/cmselect/cmtreasy/uc259-i/uc25902.htm Contents reflect the uncorrected version, not yet formally approved.
58. http://www.newstatesman.com/business/2010/01/chief-executive-bank-pay
59. http://www.publications.parliament.uk/pa/cm200910/cmselect/cmtreasy/uc261-vi/uc26102.htm. Contents reflect the uncorrected version, not yet formally approved.
60. Ibid.
61. Treasury Select Committee, EV291.
62. Ibid.
63. Treasury Select Committee, EV299
64. http://www.fcic.gov/hearings/pdfs/2010-0113-Transcript.pdf, p.153.

230 *Notes*

65. http://www.pbs.org/newshour/bb/business/jan-june10/banks_01-21.html
66. http://www.house.gov/apps/list/hearing/financialsvcs_dem/geithner_-_treasury.pdf
67. http://dealbook.blogs.nytimes.com/2009/10/15/greenspan-break-up-banks-too-big-to-fail/#more-129317
68. http://www.publications.parliament.uk/pa/cm200910/cmselect/cmtreasy/uc259-i/uc25902.htm Contents reflect the uncorrected version, not yet formally approved.
69. Ibid.
70. http://www.fcic.gov/hearings/pdfs/2010-0113-Dimon.pdf
71. Ibid.
72. http://media.ft.com/cms/1d11280c-3d20-11df-b81b-00144feabdc0.pdf
73. http://www.fcic.gov/hearings/pdfs/2010-0113-Moynihan.pdf
74. *Wall Street Journal*, February 10, 2010, p.C2.
75. http://www.newstatesman.com/business/2010/01/chief-executive-bank-pay
76. http://www.wrap20.com/files/At_Davos_Bankers_Face_Global_Ire_-_WSJ.pdf
77. *Sunday Times*, January 24, 2010.
78. http://www.bloomberg.com/apps/news?pid=20601039&sid=ajUo9TLRyePI
79. http://www.cbi.org.uk/pdf/20090309-cbi-richard-lambert-north-east-annual-dinner.pdf
80. Treasury Select Committee, EV308.
81. http://www.house.gov/apps/list/hearing/financialsvcs_dem/geithner_-_treasury.pdf
82. http://www.sbs.com.au/dateline/story/transcript/id/600336/n/Interview-with-Christine-Lagarde
83. *Wall Street Journal*, February 16, 2010, p.C4.
84. Treasury Select Committee, EV304.
85. http://www.publications.parliament.uk/pa/cm200910/cmselect/cmtreasy/uc261-vii/uc26102.htm. Contents reflect the uncorrected version, not yet formally approved.
86. http://www.fcic.gov/hearings/pdfs/2010-0409-Lockhart.pdf
87. http://oversight.house.gov/images/stories/documents/20081023100438.pdf
88. http://www.rte.ie/news/2009/0209/mccreevyc.html
89. http://www.fitchratings.com/creditdesk/public/teleconference_detail.cfm?pr_id=548785&resdet=teleconf_det
90. http://www.house.gov/apps/list/hearing/financialsvcs_dem/geithner_-_treasury.pdf
91. http://www.bloomberg.com/apps/news?pid=newsarchive&sid=an0cge3sLqSE
92. http://www.europarl.europa.eu/document/activities/cont/201002/20100226ATT69696/20100226ATT69696EN.pdf
93. Ibid.
94. http://media.ft.com/cms/1d11280c-3d20-11df-b81b-00144feabdc0.pdf
95. http://www.house.gov/apps/list/hearing/financialsvcs_dem/yingling_-_aba.pdf
96. http://www.bba.org.uk/bba/jsp/polopoly.jsp?d=1569&a=13443&artpage=2
97. http://www.bba.org.uk/content/1/c6/01/45/18/15th_Sept_letter_to_Chancellor.pdf
98. http://www.publications.parliament.uk/pa/cm200910/cmselect/cmtreasy/uc261-iv/uc26102.htm Contents reflect the uncorrected version, not yet formally approved.
99. http://ec.europa.eu/internal_market/securities/docs/agencies/proposal_en.pdf, p.3.
100. Treasury Select Committee, EV170.
101. Ibid.

102. Treasury Select Committee, EV171.
103. http://www.fcic.gov/hearings/pdfs/2010-0114-Schapiro.pdf
104. http://www.bloomberg.com/apps/news?pid=20601087&sid=acBdsg7ybEGw&pos=1
105. http://www.standardandpoors.com/servlet/Testimony of Deven Sharma.
106. http://www.house.gov/apps/list/hearing/financialsvcs_dem/egan_jones.pdf
107. Ibid.
108. http://www.guardian.co.uk/politics/2009/jan/26/gordon-brown-economic-policy
109. *Wall Street Journal*, February 10, 2010, p.C2.
110. http://blogs.abcnews.com/worldview/2008/09/german-leaders.html
111. http://www.cmb.gov.tr/filesys/twinning/konferans_I/sunumlar/JochenSanio_en.pdf
112. Ibid.
113. http://abcnews.go.com/GMA/timothy-geithner-economy-diane-sawyer-interview-treasury-secretary/story?id=8569713
114. http://www.fcic.gov/hearings/pdfs/2010-0113-Transcript.pdf, p.78.
115. http://media.ft.com/cms/1d11280c-3d20-11df-b81b-00144feabdc0.pdf
116. Treasury Select Committee, EV272.
117. Treasury Select Committee, EV143.
118. http://www.house.gov/apps/list/hearing/financialsvcs_dem/fuld_4.20.10.pdf
119. http://www.fcic.gov/hearings/pdfs/2010-0113-Transcript.pdf, p.77.
120. http://www.house.gov/apps/list/hearing/financialsvcs_dem/john_j._mack_-_morgan_stanley.pdf
121. http://www.fcic.gov/hearings/pdfs/2010-0114-Bair.pdf
122. http://www.house.gov/apps/list/hearing/financialsvcs_dem/wallison031709.pdf
123. http://www.theglobalist.com/StoryId.aspx?StoryId=7880
124. http://www.bis.org/review/r090615a.pdf
125. Treasury Select Committee, EV312.
126. Treasury Select Committee, EV381.
127. http://www.house.gov/apps/list/hearing/financialsvcs_dem/schapiro_4.20.10.pdf
128. http://media.corporate-ir.net/media_files/irol/71/71595/reports/2009_AR.pdf
129. http://www.citigroup.com/citi/fin/data/ar09c_en.pdf
130. http://www2.goldmansachs.com/our-firm/investors/financials/current/annual-reports/2009-complete-annual.pdf
131. Congressional Testimony, Report on The Risks of Financial Modeling, VaR and the Economic Breakdown, September 2009.
132. http://www.house.gov/apps/list/hearing/financialsvcs_dem/schapiro_4.20.10.pdf
133. http://www.publications.parliament.uk/pa/cm200910/cmselect/cmtreasy/uc261-iv/uc26102.htm. Contents reflect the uncorrected version, not yet formally approved.
134. Treasury Select Committee, EV72.
135. Treasury Select Committee, EV146.
136. Treasury Select Committee, EV163.
137. Treasury Select Committee, EV238.
138. Treasury Select Committee, EV162.
139. Treasury Select Committee, EV146.
140. Treasury Select Committee, EV14.
141. http://www.citigroup.com/citi/fin/data/ar09c_en.pdf
142. Ibid., Treasury Select Committee, EV14.
143. Treasury Select Committee, EV319.
144. http://www.investis.com/reports/hsbc_ar_2009_en/report.php?type=1&zoom=1&page=12

232   *Notes*

145. http://www.theglobalist.com/StoryId.aspx?StoryId=7880
146. http://www.bloomberg.com/apps/news?pid=newsarchive&sid=arBvX8ylcQdM
147. http://www.iimagazine.com/worldeconomicforum/rss/Articles/2382633/Prime-Minister-Stephen-Harper-of-Canada-Presses-for-Financial-Regulation.html
148. http://www.fcic.gov/hearings/pdfs/2010-0114-Bair.pdf
149. http://www.fsa.go.jp/en/announce/state/20090130.html
150. http://www.lewrockwell.com/paul/paul488.html
151. http://www.fcic.gov/hearings/pdfs/2010-0113-Blankfein.pdf
152. http://dealbook.blogs.nytimes.com/2009/06/29/jpmorgans-dimon-warns-against-too-many-regulators/
153. http://www.cnbc.com//id/36627658
154. http://www.financialpost.com/story.html?id=2067815
155. http://www.bloomberg.com/apps/news?pid=newsarchive&sid=aUwpL15FmZtI
156. http://www.aba.com/NR/rdonlyres/222CE044-577A-11D5-AB84-00508-B95258D/49940/BradRockStatementFINAL.pdf
157. http://www.bba.org.uk/bba/jsp/polopoly.jsp?d=613&a=14748
158. http://media.ft.com/cms/1d11280c-3d20-11df-b81b-00144feabdc0.pdf
159. http://www.bloomberg.com/apps/news?pid=newsarchive&sid=arBvX8ylcQdM
160. Ibid.
161. http://www.rte.ie/news/2009/0209/mccreevyc.html
162. Treasury Select Committee, EV106.
163. http://www.nytimes.com/2010/05/24/business/24strategy.html?ref=politics
164. *Wall Street Journal*, "Learning from History on Financial Reform," May 16, 2010.
165. Ibid.
166. http://www.time.com/time/business/article/0,8599,1853531,00.html
167. Congressional Testimony, Report on The Risks of Financial Modeling, VaR and the Economic Breakdown, September 2009.
168. http://www.time.com/time/business/article/0,8599,1853531,00.html

10   Get ready for the next one...

1. http://www.newsweek.com/id/216214?from=rss
2. http://www.fcic.gov/hearings/pdfs/2010-0113-Transcript.pdf, p.129
3. Treasury Select Committee, EV14.
4. http://www.fcic.gov/hearings/pdfs/2010-0113-Transcript.pdf, p.176.
5. http://www.marketobservation.com/blogs/index.php/2010/05/19/current-efforts-to-reform-financial-regulation-are-cosmetic-and-won-t-prevent-another-crisis-nouriel-roubini?blog=3
6. http://oversight.house.gov/images/stories/documents/20081113101922.pdf
7. http://www.publications.parliament.uk/pa/cm200910/cmselect/cmtreasy/uc261-vi/uc26102.htm Contents reflect the uncorrected version, not yet formally approved.
8. http://www.fsa.go.jp/en/announce/state/20090130.html
9. http://www.bloomberg.com/apps/news?pid=20601087&sid=adZFGmw7A6zw&refer=home
10. http://www.europarl.europa.eu/document/activities/cont/201002/20100226ATT69696/20100226ATT69696EN.pdf
11. Those seeking some degree of boredom may indeed refer to one of several books I've written on topics related to financial crises, including *The Rise and Fall of the*

Merchant Banks (1999), *The Failure of Wall Street* (2004), and *Risk and Financial Catastrophe* (2009).
12. http://www2.goldmansachs.com/our-firm/investors/financials/archived/annual-reports/2007-annual-report.html
13. http://online.wsj.com/article/BT-CO-20100114-712485.html
14. *New York Times*, "Fed Misjudged Bubble, Greenspan Says," March 19, 2010.
15. http://www.lewrockwell.com/paul/paul376.html
16. http://www.bis.org/review/r090710a.pdf
17. Treasury Select Committee, EV320.
18. http://www.lewrockwell.com/paul/paul249.html
19. http://www.bafin.de/nn_992932/SharedDocs/Downloads/EN/Service/Jahresberichte/2007/annualreport__07__vorwuinh,templateId=raw,property=publicationFile.pdf/annualreport_07_vorwuinh.pdf
20. http://www.federalreserve.gov/BOARDDOCS/Speeches/2004/20041005/default.htm
21. Ibid.
22. Treasury Select Committee, EV90.
23. http://www.number10.gov.uk/Page17114
24. http://abcnews.go.com/GMA/timothy-geithner-economy-diane-sawyer-interview-treasury-secretary/story?id=8569713
25. Ibid.
26. *Wall Street Journal*, March 10, 2009.
27. Treasury Select Committee, EV311.
28. Ibid.
29. http://www.fcic.gov/hearings/pdfs/2010-0113-Transcript.pdf, p.162
30. http://www.bafin.de/nn_992932/SharedDocs/Downloads/EN/Service/Jahresberichte/2007/annualreport__07__vorwuinh,templateId=raw,property=publicationFile.pdf/annualreport_07_vorwuinh.pdf
31. http://www.publications.parliament.uk/pa/cm200910/cmselect/cmtreasy/uc261-iv/uc26102.htm. Contents reflect the uncorrected version, not yet formally approved.
32. http://www.publications.parliament.uk/pa/cm200910/cmselect/cmtreasy/uc261-vi/uc26102.htm Contents reflect the uncorrected version, not yet formally approved.
33. http://www.publications.parliament.uk/pa/cm200910/cmselect/cmtreasy/uc261-vi/uc26102.htm Contents reflect the uncorrected version, not yet formally approved.
34. Treasury Select Committee, EV321.
35. http://money.cnn.com/galleries/2007/fortune/0708/gallery.crisiscounsel.fortune/9.html
36. Ibid.
37. http://www.nybooks.com/articles/archives/2008/may/15/the-financial-crisis-an-interview-with-george-soro/
38. Treasury Select Committee, EV313.
39. http://www.nybooks.com/articles/archives/2008/may/15/the-financial-crisis-an-interview-with-george-soro/
40. http://www.fcic.gov/hearings/pdfs/2010-0113-Transcript.pdf, p.116.
41. http://uk.reuters.com/article/idUKN1315021320100113
42. http://www.lewrockwell.com/paul/paul486.html
43. http;//www.house.gov/apps/list/hearing/financialsvcs_dem/geithner.pdf
44. http://www.ft.com/cms/s/0/780d9d64-175d-11df-87f6-00144feab49a.html
45. Ibid.
46. http://www.dailymarkets.com/economy/2010/02/23/volcker-rule-gets-support-of-former-us-treasury-secretaries/

47. http://www.fcic.gov/hearings/pdfs/2010-0114-Bair.pdf
48. http://www.house.gov/apps/list/hearing/financialsvcs_dem/stiglitz.pdf
49. http://www.publications.parliament.uk/pa/cm200910/cmselect/cmtreasy/uc261-iv/uc26102.htm Contents reflect the uncorrected version, not yet formally approved.
50. http://www.fcic.gov/hearings/pdfs/2010-0113-Transcript.pdf, p.135.
51. *New York Times*, Op-Ed, August 26, 2007
52. http://www.washingtonpost.com/wp-dyn/content/article/2010/04/22/AR2010042204208.html
53. http://www.federalreserve.gov/newsevents/speech/bernanke20090113a.htm

Index

Abrams, Dan, 144
Ackerman, Gary, 102
Ackermann, Josef, 67–8, 156, 183
Adamson, Simon, 76
AIG, 17, 54, 113, 116–17, 157
Allison, Herb, 88
Alwaleed, Prince, 42
American Bankers Association (ABA), 8
Andrukonis, David, 82–3
Angelides, Phil, 8, 43, 157
Apgar, William, 82
Applegarth, Adam, 70–1
Aso, Taro, 16
Atkins, Chris, 177

Bailouts, 18–19
Bair, Sheila, 27, 81, 103, 108, 112, 171, 179
Balls, Ed, 16, 23
Bank of America, 39–41, 154–5
Bank of England, 16, 108, 113
Bank of Italy, 17
Bankers, 7–8
Banque de France, 30
Barber, Lionel, 120, 144
Barclays, 63, 152
Basel II, 115
Basel III, 174
Bass, Kyle, 89–90, 124, 198
Bear Stearns, 16, 45–7, 155, 168
Bell, Ian, 96, 99
Bennett, Bob, 123
Bernanke, Ben, 6, 40, 56, 119, 159, 198
Black Swan, 34, 138
Blankfein, Lloyd, 6, 22, 26, 32, 47–8, 103, 154, 180, 183, 188
Blinder, Alan, 170, 187
Board directors, 181–2
Bodman, Samuel, 121
Bonfiglio, John, 95
Bookstaber, Richard, 35
Bowen, Richard, 41–2
Bradford and Bingley, 73–4
Brickell, Mark, 128
British Bankers Association (BBA), 107

Brown, Gordon, 17–18, 62, 110, 147–8, 153, 164
Buetikofer, Reinhard, 149
Buffett, Warren, 17, 20, 56
Buiter, Willem, 23, 26, 41, 101, 113, 192
Bush, George W., 17, 153
Bushnell, David, 43

Cable, Vince, 72, 143–4, 147, 162
Caldwell, Chris, 82, 106, 120
Cameron, David, 110, 148
Campos, Roel, 109
Cantor, Richard, 100
Capital adequacy, 173–4
Capuano, Michael, 154
Carper, Thomas, 123
Case, Karl, 131–2
Casey, Kathleen, 102
Cassano, Joe, 55
Cayne, Jimmy, 45–7, 155
Chanos, Jim, 35, 46, 129, 136–7
Cisneros, Henry, 26
Citigroup, 41–4, 132, 151
Clarkson, Brian, 104
Clinton, Bill, 124
Coffee, John, 102–3
Cole, Margaret, 110
Community Reinvestment Act, 81
Compensation, 164–8
Congress, 120
Corbet, Kathleen, 96
Corrigan, Gerald, 19, 31, 47–8, 56, 170, 176, 194
Countrywide, 49, 116
Cousins, Jim, 108, 181
Cox, Christopher, 14, 101, 110
Cox, James, 110
Credit Suisse, 168
Crisis
  Blame and apology, 147–61
  Next, 192–8
  Recap, 5–31
Cronin, Charles, 166
Cuomo, Andrew, 81

236 Index

D'amato, Alfonse, 101
Dallara, Charles, 21
Daniels, Eric, 65
Danielsson, Jon, 114, 128
Darling, Alistair, 6, 18, 53, 65, 71, 111, 153, 162, 165, 173, 192
DeMarco, Edward, 91
Deregulation, 109–10
Deutsche Bank, 67–8
Diamond, Bob, 54, 63, 173
Dierckx, Filip, 69–70
Dilip, Ralu, 100
Dimassimo, Vince, 52
Dimon, Jamie, 6, 14, 23, 28, 46, 48–9, 80, 106–7, 112, 116, 150–1, 172–3, 175, 179, 184, 197
Dinallo, Eric, 117
Dodd, Chris, 89, 123
Donaldson, William, 110
Draghi, Mario, 17, 23, 165–6, 175, 179, 184
Dudley, William, 163
Dugan, John, 19–20
Duncan, Douglas, 125–6

Edwards, John, 37
Egan, Sean, 94, 135, 177–8
Einhorn, David, 51, 138–9
European banks, 57–77

Falcon, Armando, 85–6, 90–1, 109, 116, 121, 127
Fallon, Michael, 62, 72, 153
Fannie Mae, 17, 78–92, 121, 138–9, 140–3, 151
Federal Deposit Insurance Corporation (FDIC), 27, 40
Federal Reserve, 108, 141
Feingold, Russ, 184
Financial Services Authority (FSA), 16, 108, 110–11, 113, 121
Fischer, Thomas, 75
Fitch, 93, 158
Flint, Douglas, 60, 168–9
Fortis, 68–70
Fostek, Sandra, 82
Fox, Ronnie, 108, 166
Frank, Barney, 11, 80, 84, 91, 121–4, 139, 140–3
Freddie Mac, 17, 78–92, 151

Friedman, Jon, 144
Friends of Angelo, 116
Fuld, Dick, 51–4, 155–6, 179

Gallagher, David, 98
Gasparino, Charlie, 144
Geithner, Timothy, 24, 34, 53, 56, 91, 166, 172–3, 175, 178, 183, 193–4, 197
Glitnir, 77
Goldman Sachs, 33, 47–8, 154
Goldschmid, Harvey, 109
Goodhart, Charles, 115
Goodwin, Fred, 60–2, 152, 166
Gould, George, 84
Grant, James, 31, 184, 198
Green, Stephen, 15, 59–60, 156, 166, 168, 182
Greenberg, Alan, 45, 58
Greenberg, Hank, 158
Greenspan, Alan, 5, 6, 8, 26, 29, 35, 106, 118, 140–3, 158–9, 174, 188–9, 191, 194
Griffin, Ken, 36

Hagel, Chuck, 123
Hahn, Peter, 181
Haldeman, Charles, 88–9
Harper, Stephen, 183
HBOS, 63–5
Hein, Dieter, 76
Hensarling, Jeb, 84
Hester, Stephen, 62, 106, 166, 171–2
Hills, Roderick, 110
Hornby, Andy, 64
Housing and Urban Development (HUD), Department of, 115
HSBC, 59–60

IKB, 74
International Monetary Fund (IMF), 12–13
Irving, William, 10

Joynt, Stephen, 95, 98–9, 100, 158, 176
JP Morgan, 46, 48, 150–1

Kaupthing Bank, 77
Kelly, Martin, 51
Kent, Rod, 73
Killinger, Kerry, 49

King, Mervyn, 16, 17, 44, 71–2, 113, 153, 165, 169, 171, 173, 182, 186, 194–6
Kinsey, Marie, 144
Knight, Angela, 107, 128, 152, 176
Kolchinsky, Eric, 99
Krugman, Paul, 23, 94, 96
Kucinich, Dennis, 40
Kudlow, Larry, 25–6

Lagarde, Christine, 20, 53, 167, 184
Lambert, Richard, 33, 102
Lamfalussy, Alexandre, 12, 30, 111, 114, 170, 174
Landesbanken, 74, 121
Landsbanki Islands, 77
Leach, James, 140
Lee, Matthew, 51–2
Lehman Brothers, 17–18, 50–4, 138–9, 155–6, 168
Lenihan, Brian, 53
Lereah, David, 125
Levin, Carl, 102, 124
Levitt, Arthur, 102, 170
Lewis, Ken, 39–40, 154–5
Liddy, Ed, 57, 157
Linnell, Ian, 174
Lippens, Maurice, 68
Lloyds TSB, 65
Lo, Andrew, 187
Lobbyists, 125–9, 189–90
Lockhart, James, 13, 79, 81–3, 85, 87–8, 115–16, 124
Lowenstein, Roger, 173

MacDonald, Elizabeth, 114
Mack, John, 44–5, 151
Madelain, Michel, 100, 177
Mahoney, Chris, 100
Mann, John, 153
Main Street, 27–8
Marchionne, Sergio, 67
Mayo, Mike, 27, 30, 37, 91, 107, 118, 134–5, 166, 172, 186, 194, 197
McCreevy, Charles, 35, 128–9, 165, 174, 184
McDaniel, Raymond, 97–8, 104
McFall, John, 62, 72, 77, 109, 154, 165, 198
McGraw, III, Harold, 93, 96–7
McGraw, Terry, 104

McHale, Sharon, 82
McKillop, Tom, 10, 15, 61, 103, 152
McLean, Bethany, 120
Medvedev, Dmitry, 149
Melloan, George, 115
Merkel, Angela, 19, 143, 149, 178
Merrill Lynch, 36–9
Meyer, Chris, 100
Miller, George, 96, 103
Moeller, Scott, 120
Moffett, David, 88
Molinaro, Sam, 46
Moody's, 93
Mooney, Shannon, 100
Moore, Paul, 65
Morgan Stanley, 44–5, 151
Mortgage Bankers Association (MBA), 125–7
Moulton, Jon, 113, 115
Moynihan, Brian, 28, 40–1, 155, 173, 180
Mozilo, Angelo, 49–50
Mudd, Daniel, 26, 79, 82, 85–6, 151–2
Munger, Charlie, 30

New rules, 162–85
Nichols, Rob, 169
Norberg, Johan, 22
Northern Rock, 70–3
Noyer, Christian, 30, 189

O'Neal, Stan, 34, 36–8, 134
Oakeshott, Matthew, 72
Obama, Barack, 165
Office of Federal Housing Enterprise Oversight (OFHEO), 115–16
Office of the Comptroller of the Currency (OCC), 108
Osborne, George, 153
Ospel, Marcel, 66–7, 152
Oxley, Michael, 122

Pandit, Vikram, 8, 43–4, 106, 118, 151, 170, 180, 182
Parliament, 120–1
Paul, Ron, 6, 9, 22, 79, 83, 119, 140–1, 183, 189, 190, 197
Paulson, Hank, 17, 40, 53, 56, 119
Paulson, John, 136
Pickard, Lee, 110
Pitt Watson, David, 112, 179

Politicians, 25–7, 119–25, 190
Posten, Adam, 76, 121
Preston, Robert, 154
Prince, Chuck, 41–3, 151, 157
Proprietary trading, 168–72
Putin, Vladimir, 149
Pym, Richard, 29, 73–4

Raines, Franklin, 11, 18, 80, 82–3, 89–90, 116, 122, 127
Raiter, Frank, 100
Rating agencies, 21–2, 93–104, 117, 135, 176
Reed, John, 151
Reese, Ann, 38
Regulators
    Financial, 107–15, 190
    Non-financial, 115–18
    Policymakers, 118–19
Regulators, politicians and lobbyists, 105–46
Regulatory coordination, 178–80
Reid, Harry, 123
Resolution authority, 175
Ridley, Matt, 70
Risk management, 32–6, 180–2
Ritholtz, Barry, 110
Roach, Stephen, 22, 106, 118, 182, 195
Robbins, John, 8, 127
Robinson, Claire, 98–9
Rock, Bradley, 27, 128, 184
Rohner, Marcel, 66–7, 152
Rosen, Kenneth, 90–1
Roubini, Nouriel, 23, 130–1, 186–7
Rove, Karl, 85, 127
Royal Bank of Scotland (RBS), 60–2, 152
Rubin, Robert, 41, 43, 156

Sachsen Landesbank, 74
Sandler, Ron, 72–3
Sands, Peter, 31
Sanio, Jochen, 23, 30, 33, 101, 113, 115, 149, 153, 175, 187, 189, 190, 194
Sants, Hector, 121, 163
Sarkozy, Nicolas, 16, 19, 150, 164
Sato, Takafumi, 183, 187
Schapiro, Mary, 112, 165, 177, 180
Schumer, Chuck, 84–5, 123
Schwartz, Alan, 45–7
Sebastian, Miguel, 149

Securities and Exchange Commission (SEC), 111
Securitization, 10, 11
Seiders, David, 126
Shadow banking system, 12
Sharma, Deven, 21, 96–7, 158, 177
Shear, William, 90
Shelby, Richard, 22, 91, 101, 117
Sherman, Brad, 19
Shiller, Robert, 28–9, 131–2
Sigurdardottir, Johanna, 77
Simmons, Harris, 128
Simon, George, 110
Simons, Jim, 102
Singer, Paul, 136–7
SIrri, Eric, 113
Smith, Win, 37
Snow, John, 29–30, 118–19, 121, 127–8, 139, 156
Solomon, Peter, 186
Soros, George, 195, 197
Sowell, Thomas, 89
Sptizer, Elliott, 119
Standard and Poor's (S&P), 93, 158
Steinbrueck, Peer, 30, 74–5, 108, 143, 148–9
Stevenson, Dennis, 64
Stiglitz, Joseph, 18, 20, 164, 197–8
Strauss-Kahn, Dominique, 20, 165, 186
Stuhlmann, Alex, 75–6
Subprime, 7–9, 28–9, 57, 81, 133, 136
Sullivan, Brian, 115–16
Sullivan, Martin, 54, 157–8
Summers, Larry, 107
Syron, Richard, 28, 79, 87, 90

Taleb, Nassim, 34, 35, 119, 137–8, 181, 184–5
Tarullo, Daniel, 107
Taylor, John, 6, 11, 118, 158
Tett, Gillian, 10, 120, 144–6
Thain, John, 39
Thomas, Bill, 157
Thurso, John, 31, 62, 181
Thurston, Paul, 77, 171
Touree, Fabrice, 33
Turner, Adair, 16, 28, 29, 35, 61, 66, 108–9, 111, 113–15, 121, 163, 168, 182, 187, 194–5
Turner, Lynn, 55
Tutton, Peter, 8

UBS, 65–7, 152
US banks and securities firms, 36–56
US bank disasters, 50–7

Valukas, Anton, 52, 111–12
Varley, John, 31, 63, 152, 166, 178–9
Verheugen, Gunter, 76
Veron, Nicolas, 74
Volcker, Paul, 48, 107, 111, 129, 168–9, 170, 197

Wachter, Susan, 82
Wallison, Peter, 26, 79, 80, 82, 83, 90–2, 105, 123, 141–2, 159–60, 162, 179
Warren, Elizabeth, 108
Watanabe, Akio, 16

Waters, Maxine, 122
Waugh, Rick, 183
Waxman, Henry, 101
Wen, Jiabao, 149
Westdeutsche Landesbank, 75
Whalen, Chris, 26, 35
White, Lawrence, 102
Whitney, Meredith, 132–3
Williams, Mike, 89
Willumstad, Robert, 55–6, 157
Wilmers, Robert, 26, 92
Wolf, Robert, 66
Wood, Chris, 72, 102, 133–4

Yingling, Ed, 71, 175
Yoshizawa, Yuri, 94, 99

GPSR Compliance

The European Union's (EU) General Product Safety Regulation (GPSR) is a set of rules that requires consumer products to be safe and our obligations to ensure this.

If you have any concerns about our products, you can contact us on

ProductSafety@springernature.com

In case Publisher is established outside the EU, the EU authorized representative is:

Springer Nature Customer Service Center GmbH
Europaplatz 3
69115 Heidelberg, Germany

www.ingramcontent.com/pod-product-compliance
Ingram Content Group UK Ltd.
Pitfield, Milton Keynes, MK11 3LW, UK
UKHW021021050925
462611UK00012B/1347